Standard Catalogue of British Coins

COINS OF ENGLAND

AND

THE UNITED KINGDOM

27th Editio

KU-525-727

Edited by

Stephen Mitchell and Brian Reeds

adapted, with additional material, from catalogues originally

compiled by H. A. and P. J. Seaby

Seaby

London

A Catalogue of the Coins of Great Britain
and Ireland
first published 1929

Standard Catalogue of British Coins
Coins of England and the United Kingdom

27th edition, 1991

© B.A. Seaby Ltd.
7 Davies Street
London W1Y 1LL

Typeset & printed by Latimer Trend & Co Limited, Plymouth
and bound by Biddles of Guildford and Kings Lynn

ISBN 1 85264 072 3

CONTENTS

PREFACE

Over twenty years ago we prepared the text for the first issue of *Coins of England and the United Kingdom* as the first volume of Seaby's 'Standard Catalogue of British Coins', which itself had been an adaptation and improvement upon our *Standard Catalogue of the Coins of Great Britain and Ireland*, first published in 1945. Over the years the text has been subject to considerable change, the most important being in 1978 when the first of the current series of revised editions was published in a format consistent with our other catalogues on Greek, Roman and Byzantine coins.

For the collector the principal improvements may be seen in the steady increase of detailed information; in values being stated in more than one grade of preservation; in the constant improvement and revision of the text to take into account new coins found each year, and to keep abreast of current numismatic research.

We do not try to lead the market or consciously to anticipate demand for any particular series of coins; we try to reflect the market, taking note of fixed and auction prices during the year. As only a very few of the coins herein actually turn up in any one year, our aim, as far as possible, is to present to the collector our opinion of what he may reasonably expect to pay for a particular coin.

The catalogue, then, is primarily intended for the collector, but it will also be found to be a compact general handbook for the archaeologist, museum curator and amateur coin finder and, for that matter, any person who has a coin to identify and who wishes to know its approximate value.

We would like to acknowledge the help we have received from a number of collectors and specialists in certain series – especially David Fletcher – and we have particularly valued the comments and suggestions of those who have used previous editions of the catalogue.

THIS CATALOGUE

Arrangement

The arrangement of this catalogue is not completely uniform, but generally it is divided into metals (gold, silver, copper, etc) under each reign, then into coinages, denominations and varieties. In the Celtic section the uninscribed coins are listed before the dynastic coins; under Charles II all the hammered coins precede the milled coinage; the reign of George III is divided into coins issued up to 1816 and the new coinage from 1816 to the end of the reign; and under Elizabeth II the decimal issues are separated from the £.s.d. coinages.

Every major coin type is listed though not every variety. We have endeavoured to give rather more coverage to the varieties of relatively common coins, such as the pence of Edward I, II and III, than to the very much rarer coins of, for instance, King Offa of Mercia.

Values

The values given represent the range of retail prices at which coins are being offered for sale at the time of going to press and **not** the price which a dealer will pay for those coins. These prices are based on our knowledge of the numismatic market, the current demand for particular coins, recent auction sale prices and, in those cases where certain coins have not appeared for sale for some years, our estimation of what they would be likely to sell at today, bearing in mind their rarity and appeal in relation to somewhat similar coins where a current value *is* known. Values are given for two grades of preservation from the end of the 10th century and for three grades of preservation for most coins of the 19th and early 20th centuries (except for Ancient British where the price is for the condition in which the coin usually appears).

Seaby's endeavour to be reasonably conservative in grading the state of preservation of coins, as our clients well know. Collectors normally require coins in the best condition they can afford and, except in the case of a really rare coin, a piece that is considerably worn is not wanted and has little value. The values given in the catalogue are for the exact state of preservation stated at the head of each column; and bearing in mind that a score of identical coins in varying states of wear could be lined up in descending order from mint condition (FDC, *fleur de coin*), through *very fine* (VF) to *poor* state, it will be realized that only in certain instances will the values given apply to particular coins. A 'fine' (F) coin may be worth anything between one quarter and a half of the price quoted for a 'very fine' (VF), on the other hand a piece in really mint condition will be valued substantially higher than the price quoted for 'extremely fine' (EF). The designation BV has been adopted for coins whose value on the market has yet to exceed its bullion value.

We emphasize again that the purpose of this catalogue is to give a general value for a particular class of coin in a specified state of preservation, and also to give the collector an idea of the range and value of coins in the English series. The value of any particular piece depends on three things:

Its exact design, legend, mintmark or date.
Its exact state of preservation; this is of prime importance.
The demand for it in the market at any given time.

Some minor varieties are much scarcer than others, and, as the number of coins issued varies considerably from year to year, coins of certain dates and mintmarks are rarer and of more value than other pieces of similar type. The prices given for any type are for the commonest variety, mintmark or date of that type.

Ordering coins from this catalogue

This is not a catalogue of coins held for sale. It is a guide to the current values of all the coins of the realm.

A BEGINNER'S GUIDE TO COIN COLLECTING

The Scope

Coin collecting is a fascinating recreation. It requires little physical exertion and only as much mental effort as one wishes to give at any time. Numismatics has vast scope and boundless ramifications and byways. It encompasses not only things historical and geographical, but also touches on economics, metallurgy, heraldry, literature, the fine arts, politics, military history and many other disciplines. This catalogue is solely concerned with British coinage, but from the start the beginner should appreciate that the coinage of our own nation may be seen as a small but important part of the whole gamut of world currency.

The first coins, made of electrum, a natural alloy of gold and silver, were issued in western Asia Minor about the middle of the seventh century B.C. Over the next century or so coinage of gold and silver spread across the Aegean to mainland Greece, southwards to the eastern Mediterranean lands and eventually westward to the Adriatic cities and the Greek colonies in southern Italy, Sicily and beyond. The coins of the Greeks are noted for their beautiful, sometimes exquisite craftsmanship, with many of the coin types depicting the patron deities of their cities. Coins of Philip II of Macedon (359–336 B.C.), father of Alexander the Great, circulated amongst the Celtic peoples of the Danubian basin and were widely copied through central Europe and by the Gauls in France. Gold Gaulish staters were reaching Britain around the beginning of the first century B.C. and the earliest gold to be struck in the island must have been produced shortly afterwards.

The coins of the Romans cover some seven centuries and comprise an enormous number of different types current throughout a major part of the civilized world from Spain to further Syria and from the Rhine in the north to the Sudan in the south. The Roman province of Britain was part of this vast empire for four hundred years and innumerable Roman coins have been recovered from sites in this country, most being made of brass or bronze and many being quite inexpensive.

Following the revival of commerce after the Dark Ages, coinage in Western Europe was virtually restricted to silver until the thirteenth century, though gold was still being minted at Byzantium and in the Islamic world. In the Middle Ages many European cities had their own distinctive coinage, and money was issued not only by the kings but also by many lesser nobles, bishops and abbots. From the time of the later Crusades gold returned to the west; and the artistic developments of the Renaissance brought improved portraiture and new minting techniques.

Large silver crown-size thalers were first minted at Joachimsthal in Bohemia early in the sixteenth century. With substantial shipments of silver coming to Europe from the mines of Spanish America over the next couple of centuries a fine series of larger coins was issued by the European states and cities.

Both Germany and Italy became unified nation states during the nineteenth century but balancing the reduction in European minting authorities were the new coins of the indpendent states of South and Central America. Over the past quarter century many new nations have established their independence and their coinage provides a large field for the collector of modern coins.

It can be seen that the scope for the collector is truly vast, but besides the general run of official coinage there is also the large series of token coins—small change unofficially produced to supplement the inadequate supply of authorized currency. These tokens were issued by merchants, innkeepers and manufacturers in many towns and villages in the 17th, 18th and 19th centuries and many collectors specialize in their local issues.

Some coins have designs of a commemorative nature; an example being the recent Royal Wedding crown, but there are also large numbers of commemorative medals which, though never intended for use as coinage, are sometimes confused with coins, being metal objects of a similar shape and sometimes a similar size to coins. This is another interesting field for collectors as these medals may have excellent portraits of famous men or women, or they may commemorate important events or scientific discoveries. Other metallic objects of coin-like appearance may be reckoning counters, advertising tickets, various other tickets and passes, and items such as brass coin weights.

Minting processes

From the time of the earliest Greek coins to about the middle of the 16th century coins were made by hand.

The method of manufacture was simple. The obverse and reverse designs were engraved or punched into the prepared ends of two bars of iron, shaped or tapered to the diameter of the required coin. The obverse die, known as the *pile*, was usually spiked to facilitate its being anchored firmly into a block of wood or metal. The reverse die, the *trussel*, was held by hand or grasped by tongs.

The coin was struck by placing a metal blank between the two dies and striking the trussel with a hammer. Thus, all coinage struck by this method is known as 'hammered' money. Some dies are known to have been hinged to ensure exact register between the upper and lower die. Usually a 'pair of dies' consisted of one obverse die (normally the more difficult to make) and two reverse dies. This was because the shaft of iron bearing the reverse design eventually split under the constant hammering; two reverse dies usually being needed to last out the life of the obverse die.

Some time toward the middle of the 16th century, experiments, first in Germany and later in France, resulted in the manufacture of coins by machinery.

The term 'milled' which is applied to all machine-made coins comes from the type of machinery used, the mill and screw press. With this machinery the obverse die was fixed and the reverse die brought into contact with the blank by heavy vertical pressure applied by a screw or worm-drive connected to a cross bar with heavy weights at each end. These weights usually had long leather thongs attached which allowed a more powerful force to be applied by the operators who revolved the arms of the press. New blanks were placed on the lower die and struck coins were removed by hand. The screw press brought more pressure to bear on the blanks and this pressure was evenly applied.

Various attempts were made during the reigns of Elizabeth I and Charles I to introduce this type of machinery with its vastly superior products. Unfortunately problems associated with the manufacture of blanks to a uniform weight greatly reduced the rate of striking and the hand manufacture of coins continued until the Restoration, when Charles II brought to London from Holland the Roettiers brothers and their improved screw press.

The first English coins made for circulation by this new method were the silver crowns of 1662, which bore an inscription on the edge, DECVS ET TVTAMEN, 'an ornament and a safeguard', a reference to the fact that the new coins could not be clipped, a crime made easier by the thin and often badly struck hammered coins.

The mill and screw press was used until new steam powered machinery made by Boulton and Watt was installed in the new mint on Tower Hill. This machinery had been used most successfully by Boulton to strike the 'cartwheel' two- and one-penny pieces of 1797 and many other coins, including 'overstriking' Spanish eight real pieces into Bank of England 'dollars', the old Mint presses not being able to exert sufficient power to do this. This new machinery was first used at the Mint to strike the 'new coinage' halfcrowns of 1816, and it operated at a far greater speed than the old type of mill and screw presses and achieved a greater sharpness of design.

The modern coining presses by Horden, Mason and Edwards, now operating at the new mint at Llantrisant, are capable of striking at a rate of up to 300 coins a minute.

Condition

One of the more difficult problems for the beginner is accurately to assess the condition of a coin. A common fault among collectors is to overgrade and, consequently, overvalue their coins.

Most dealers will gladly spare a few minutes to help new collectors. Dealers, such as ourselves, who issue price lists with illustrations, enable collectors to see exactly what the coins look like and how they have been graded.

Coins cannot always be graded according to precise rules. Hammered coins often look weak or worn on the high parts of the portrait and the tops of the letters; this can be due to weak striking or worn dies and is not always attributable to wear through long use in circulation. Milled coins usually leave the mint sharply struck so that genuine wear is easier to detect. However a ×8 or ×16 magnifying glass is essential, especially when grading coins of Edward VII and George V where the relief is very low on the portraits and some skill is required to distinguish between an uncirculated coin and one in EF condition.

The condition or grade of preservation of a coin is usually of greater importance than its rarity. By this we mean that a common coin in superb condition is often more desirable and more highly priced than a rarity in poor condition. Few coins that have been pierced or mounted as a piece of jewellery have an interest to collectors.

One must also be on the lookout for coins that have been 'plugged', i.e. that have been pierced at some time and have had the hole filled in, sometimes with the missing design or letters re-engraved.

Badly cleaned coins will often display a complexity of fine interlaced lines and such coins have a greatly reduced value. It is also known for coins to be tooled or re-engraved on the high parts of the hair, in order to 'increase' the grade of coin and its value. In general it is better to have a slightly more worn coin than a better example with the aforementioned damage.

Cleaning coins

Speaking generally, *don't* clean coins. More coins are ruined by injudicious cleaning than through any other cause, and a badly cleaned coin loses much of its value. A nicely toned piece is usually considered desirable. Really dirty gold and silver can, however, be carefully washed in soap and water. Copper coins should never be cleaned or washed, they may be lightly brushed with a brush that is not too harsh.

Buying and selling coins

Swopping coins at school or with other collectors, searching around the antique shops, telling your relatives and friends that you are interested in coins, or even trying to find your own with a metal detector, are all ways of adding to your collection. However, the time will come for the serious collector when he wants to acquire specific coins or requires advice on the authenticity or value of a coin.

At this point an expert is needed, and generally the services of a reputable coin dealer will be sought. There are now a large number of coin dealers in the U.K., many of whom belong to the B.N.T.A. or the I.A.P.N. (the national and international trade associations) and a glance through the 'yellow pages' under 'coin dealer' or 'numismatist' will often provide local information.

We at Seaby's have been publishing the Standard Catalogue of Coins of England and the UK since 1929. It serves as a price guide for all coin collectors. We also publish books on many aspects of English, Greek, Roman and Byzantine coins and on British tokens. These books serve as a valuable source of information for coin collectors. Our books are available from our premises at 7 Davies Street or your local bookseller. W H Smith stock the Seaby Standard Catalogue.

Useful suggestions

Security and insurance.   The careful collector should not keep valuable coins at home unless they are insured and have adequate protection. Local police and insurance companies will give advice on what precautions may be necessary.

Most insurance companies will accept a valuation based on the Standard Catalogue. It is usually possible to have the amount added to a householder's contents policy. A 'Fire, Burglary and Theft' policy will cover loss only from the assured's address, but an 'All Risks' policy will usually cover accidental damage and loss anywhere within the U.K. We can recommend a Lloyd's broker, if requested.

Coins deposited with a bank or placed in a safe-deposit box will usually attract a lower insurance premium.

Keeping a record.   All collectors are advised to have an up-to-date record of their collection, and, if possible, photographs of the more important and more easily identifiable coins. This should be kept in a separate place from the collection, so that a list and photographs can be given to the police should loss occur. Note the price paid, from whom purchased, the date of acquisition and the condition.

Storage and handling.   New collectors should get into the habit of handling coins by the edge. This is especially important as far as highly polished proof coins are concerned.

Collectors may initially keep their coins in paper or plastic envelopes housed in boxes, albums or special containers. Many collectors will eventually wish to own a hardwood coin cabinet in which the collection can be properly arranged and displayed. If a home-made cabinet is being constructed avoid oak and cedar wood; mahogany, walnut and rosewood are ideal. It is important that coins are not kept in a humid atmosphere; especial care must be taken with copper and bronze coins which are very susceptible to damp or condensation which may result in a green verdigris forming on the coins.

From beginner to numismatist

The new collector will feel that he has much to learn. He can best advance from tyro to experienced numismatist by examining as many coins as possible, noting their distinctive features and by learning to use the many books of reference that are available. It will be an advantage to join a local numismatic society, as this will provide an opportunity for meeting other enthusiasts and obtaining advice from more knowledgeable collectors. Most societies have a varied programme of lectures, exhibitions and occasional auctions of members' duplicates.

Those who become members of one or both of the national societies, the Royal Numismatic Society and the British Numismatic Society, can be sure of receiving an annual journal containing authoritative papers.

Many museums have coin collections available for study and a number of museum curators are qualified numismatists.

SOME COIN DENOMINATIONS

Gold

Angel	Eighty pence (6s. 8d.) from 1464; later 7s. 6d., 8s., 10s. and 11s.
Angelet or ½ Angel	Forty pence (3s. 4d.) from 1464, later 3s. 9d., 4s., 5s., 5s. 6d.
Aureus	Roman currency unit (originally $\frac{1}{60}$th lb), discontinued A.D. 324.
Britain Crown	Five shillings, 1604–12; 5s. 6d. (66d.) 1612–19.
Broad	Twenty shillings, Cromwell, 1656.
Crown	Five shillings, from 1544 (and see below and Britain crown above).
Crown of the Rose	Four shillings and 6 pence, 1526.
Crown of the Double Rose	Five shillings, 1526–44.
Florin (Double Leopard)	Six shillings, Edward III.
George Noble	Eighty pence (6s. 8d.) 1526.
Gold 'Penny'	Twenty to twenty-four pence, Henry III.
Guinea	Pound (20s.) in 1663, then rising to 30s. in 1694 before falling to 21s. 6d., 1698–1717; 21s., 1717–1813.
Halfcrown	Thirty pence, 1526 intermittently to 1612; 2s. 9d. (33d.), 1612–19.
Helm (Quarter Florin)	Eighteen pence, Edward III.
Laurel	Twenty shillings, 1619–25.
Leopard (Half florin)	Three shillings, Edward III.
Noble	Eighty pence (6s. 8d., or half mark), 1344–1464.
Pound	Twenty shillings, 1592–1600 (see also Unite, Laurel, Broad, Guinea and Sovereign).
Quarter Angel	Two shillings, 1544–7 and later 2s. 6d.
Rose Noble (Ryal)	Ten shillings, 1464–70.
Rose-Ryal	Thirty shillings, 1604–24.
Ryal	Ten shillings, Edward IV and Henry VII; fifteen shillings under Mary and Elizabeth I (see also Spur Ryal).
Solidus	Roman currency unit ($\frac{1}{72}$nd lb) from A.D. 312; the 's' of the £.s.d.
Sovereign	Twenty shillings or pound, 1489–1526 (22s. 6d., 1526–44), 1544–53, 1603–04 and from 1817 (see also Pound, Unite, Laurel, Broad and Guinea, and Fine Sovereign below).
'Fine' Sovereign	Thirty shillings, 1550–96 (see also Rose-Ryal).
Spur-Ryal	Fifteen shillings, 1605–12; 16s. 6d., 1612–25.
Stater	Name commonly given to the standard Celtic gold coin.
Third guinea	Seven shillings, 1797–1813.
Thistle Crown	Four shillings, 1604–12; 4s. 5d., 1612–19.
Thrymsa	Early Anglo-Saxon version of the late Roman tremissis (one-third solidus).
Triple Unite	Three pounds, Charles I (Shrewsbury and Oxford only, 1642–4).
Unite	Twenty shillings, 1604–12 and 1625–62; 22s., 1612–19.

Silver (and Cupro-Nickel)

Antoninianus	Roman, originally 1½ denarii in A.D. 214 (later debased to bronze).
Argenteus	Roman, a revived denarius.
Crown	Five shillings, 1551–1965.
Denarius	Roman, originally 10 then 16 asses (25 to the aureus), later debased: the 'd' of the £.s.d.

Farthing	Quarter penny, 1279–1553.
Florin	Two shillings, from 1849–1967.
Groat	Four pence, 1279–*c.* 1305 and 1351–1662 (Halfgroat from 1351). 'Britannia' groat, 1836–55 (and 1888 for Colonial use only). See also Maundy.
Halfcrown	Thirty pence (2s. 6d.), 1551–1967.
Halfpenny	Intermittently, *c.* 890–*c.* 970, *c.* 1108, short cross and, more generally, 1279–1660.
Maundy money	Four, three, two and one penny, from 1660.
New pence	Decimal coinage: 50p from 1969, 25p. (crown) 1972 and 1977, 80, 81, 10p. and 5p. from 1968. 'New' removed in 1982.
Quinarius	Roman, half denarius or 8 asses; later debased.
Penny (*pl.* pence)	Standard unit of currency from *c.* 775/780 A.D.
Sceat	Early Anglo-Saxon, small, thick penny.
Shilling	Twelve pence, 1548–1966.
Siliqua	Roman, $\frac{1}{24}$th solidus.
Sixpence	From 1551–1967.
Testern (Portcullis money)	One, two, four and eight testerns for use in the Indies (and equal to the Spanish 1, 2, 4 and 8 reales); 1600 only.
Testoon	Shilling, Henry VII and VIII.
Threefarthings	Elizabeth I, 1561–82.
Threehalfpence	Elizabeth I, 1561–82, and for Colonial use, 1834–62.
Threepence	From 1551–1944 (then see Maundy).
Twenty pence	Decimal coinage from 1982.

Copper, Bronze, Tin, Nickel-Brass, etc.

As	Roman, an early unit of currency; reduced in size and equal to $\frac{1}{16}$th denarius in Imperial times.
Centenionalis	Roman, replaced the depleted follis in A.D. 346.
Dupondius	Roman, brass two asses or one-eighth of a denarius.
Farthing	Quarter penny: Harrington, Lennox, Richmond, Maltravers and 'rose' farthings, 1613–49; regal issues, 1672–1956 (tin, 1684–92).
Follis	Roman, silver-washed bronze coin, $\frac{1}{5}$th argenteus, introduced *c.* A.D. 290, later debased.
Half Farthing	Victoria, 1839–56 (and for Colonial use 1828–37).
Halfpenny	From 1672 to 1967 (tin, 1685–92).
New Pence	Decimal coinage; 2p., 1p. and $\frac{1}{2}$p. from 1971. 'New' removed from 1982.
Penny	From 1797 to 1967 (previously a silver coin).
Pound	Decimal coin from 1983.
Quadrans	Roman, quarter as or $\frac{1}{64}$th denarius.
Quarter Farthing	For Colonial use only, 1839–53.
Semis	Roman, half as or $\frac{1}{32}$nd denarius.
Sestertius	Roman, brass four asses or quarter denarius.
Third Farthing	For Colonial use only, 1827–1913.
Threepence	Nickelbrass, 1937–67.
Twopence	George III, 'Cartwheel' issue, 1797 only.

SOME NUMISMATIC TERMS EXPLAINED

Obverse	That side of the coin which normally shows the monarch's head or name.
Reverse	The side opposite to the obverse.
Blank	The coin as a blank piece of metal, i.e. before it is struck.
Flan	The whole piece of metal after striking.
Type	The main, central design.
Legend	The inscription.
Field	That flat part of the coin between the main design and the inscription or edge.
Exergue	That part of the coin below the main design, usually separated by a horizontal line, and normally occupied by the date.

Die	The block of metal, with design cut into it, which actually impresses the coin blank with the design.
Die variety	Coin showing slight variation of design.
Mule	A coin with the current type on one side and the previous (and usually obsolete) type on the other side, or a piece struck from two dies that are not normally used together.
Graining	The crenellations around the edge of the coin, commonly known as 'milling'.
Proof	Carefully struck coin from special dies with a mirror-like or matt surface. (In this country 'Proof' is *not* a term used to describe the state of preservation, but the method of striking.)
Hammered	Refers to the old craft method of striking a coin between dies hammered by hand.
Milled	Coins struck by dies worked in a coining press.

ABBREVIATIONS

Archb.	Archbishop		*mm.*	mintmark
Bp.	Bishop		mon.	monogram
cuir.	cuirassed		*O., obv.*	obverse
d.	penny, pence		p.	new penny, pence
diad.	diademed		pl.	plume
dr.	draped		quat.	quatrefoil
ex.	exergue		qtr.	quarter
grs.	grains		rad.	radiate
hd.	head		R̟., *rev.*	reverse
i.c.	inner circle		r.	right
illus.	illustration		s.	shillings
l.	left		var.	variety
laur.	laureate		wt.	weight

CONDITIONS OF A COIN

(i.e. grade of preservation) in order of merit as generally used in England.

Proof. See above.

FDC = *Fleur-de-coin.* Flawless, unused, without any wear, scratches or marks. Usually only applied to proofs.

Unc. = *Uncirculated.* A coin in new condition as issued by the Mint but, owing to modern mass-production methods of manufacture and storage, not necessarily perfect.

EF = *Extremely Fine.* A coin that shows little sign of having been in circulation, but which may exhibit slight surface marks or faint wear on very close inspection.

VF = *Very Fine.* Some wear on the raised surfaces; a coin that has had only limited circulation.

F = *Fine.* Considerable signs of wear on the raised surfaces, or design weak through faulty striking.

Fair. A coin that is worn, but which has the inscriptions and main features of the design still distinguishable, or a piece that is very weakly struck.

Poor. A very worn coin, of no value as a collector's piece unless extremely rare.

EXAMPLES OF CONDITION GRADING

EXTREMELY FINE

VERY FINE

FINE

FAIR

Edward III groat   *George II halfcrown*   *Victoria halfcrown*

BRITISH MINTS

SCOTLAND

N.IRELAND

Isle of Man

IRISH SEA

ENGLAND

WALES

N

NORTH SEA

Berwick–on–Tweed
Bamburgh
Newcastle–upon–Tyne
✱● Carlisle   Corbridge
Durham

Scarborough

York ✱◎
Kingston–upon–Hull   Hedon
Pontefract ✱

Caistor
Torksey   Louth ?
Rhuddlan   ●◎ Chester   Lincoln   Horncastle
✱✱Newark
Derby
Stafford   Nottingham
WASH   Castle Rising
✱✱ Shrewsbury   Lichfield ✱ Ashby-de-la-Zouch   Kings Lynn   Norwich
Tamworth   Leicester   Stamford
Aberystwyth   Birmingham
✱ (Dovey)   ?   Kings Norton   Peterborough
✱ Furnace   Bridgnorth   Coventry   Thetford   Dunwich
Aberystwyth   Hartlebury   Heaton   Bury–St.–Edmunds
Castle ✱   Soho   Warwick   Huntingdon
Droitwich   Northampton   Cambridge   Ipswich
Worcester ✱   ● Pershore   Bedford   Sudbury
Hereford   Newport Pagnell   Colchester ✱✱
Winchcombe   Buckingham
Gloucester   Aylesbury   Maldon
Berkeley   Cricklade   ✱● Oxford   Hertford
Swansea   Malmesbury   Wallingford   Horndon
Pembroke   Llantrisant   Cardiff   Bristol ✱◎   Chippenham   London ◎
BRISTOL   Bath   Bedwyn   Reading   Tower
CHANNEL   Axbridge   Warminster   Marlborough   Tower Hill   Rochester
Watchet   ?Frome   Guildford   Southwark   Canterbury   Sandwich
Barnstable   Bruton   Wilton   Winchester   Durham House   Lympne   Dover
Langport   Cadbury   Salisbury   Steyning   Romney   Hythe   Calais
Taunton   Ilchester   Shaftesbury   Southampton   Lewes   Rye
Petherton   Milborne Port   Chichester   Bramber   Hastings
Crewkerne   Dorchester   Christchurch   Cissbury   Pevensey
Exeter ◎✱   Bridport
Launceston   Lydford   Wareham   FRANCE
Totnes   Isle of Wight
✱Truro   ENGLISH CHANNEL

SCALE
0   50 Miles

LEGEND

Anglo Saxon and Norman, including Angevin mints. (to 1279)	●
Edwardian and later mints. (after 1279)	○
Mints operating in both periods.	◎
Charles 1st. and Civil War mints.	✱

Map drawn by Alan Mi

CELTIC COINAGE

PERIOD OF BELGIC MIGRATION

The earliest uninscribed coins found in Britain were made in Gaul and brought to this country by trade and by the migration of Belgic peoples from the continent (Gallo-Belgic issues A to F). The earliest may date from some time late in the second century B.C., coinciding with Germanic tribes pushing westward across the Rhine and ending with refugees fleeing from the Roman legions of Julius Caesar. Certain of these coins became the prototypes for the first gold staters struck in Britain, their designs being ultimately derived from the gold staters (M) of Philip II, King of Macedonia (359–336 B.C.).

The following list is based on the 1975 edition of R. P. Mack, *The Coinage of Ancient Britain*, which now incorporates the classification for the uninscribed coins published by D. F. Allen, *The Origins of Coinage in Britain: A Reappraisal*, and from information kindly supplied by H. R. Mossop, Esq.

The new 'V' reference in this series equates to R. D. Van Arsdell, *Celtic Coinage of Britain*, in which are listed many more varieties and sub-varieties than are included here.

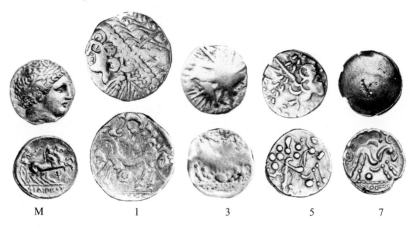

M   1   3   5   7

Gold Gallo-Belgic Issues £*

1   Gallo-Belgic A. (Ambiani), *c.* 125–100 B.C. *Stater.* Good copy of Macedonian stater, large flan. Laureate hd. of Apollo to l. or r. ℞. Horse to l. or r. *M. 1, 3; V. 10, 12* 850

2   — *Quarter stater.* As last. *M. 2, 4; V. 15, 20* 300

3   — B. (Ambiani), *c.* 115 B.C. *Stater.* Somewhat similar to 1, but small flan and "defaced" *obv.* die, some with lyre shape between horse's legs on *rev.* *M. 5, 7; V. 30, 33* 400

4   — — *Quarter stater.* As last. *M. 6, 8; V. 35, 37.* 250

5   — C. (Ambiani), *c.* 100–70 B.C. *Stater.* Disintegrated face and horse. *M. 26; V. 44* 325

6   — D. *c.* 80 B.C. *Quarter stater.* Portions of Apollo head. ℞. Unintelligible mixture of stars, crescents, pellets, zig-zag lines; often referred to as "Geometric" types. (See also British 'O', *S. 49*.) *M. 37, 39, 41, 41a, 42; V. 65/7/9/146.* 100

7   — E. (Ambiani), *c.* 57–45 B.C. *Stater.* Blank *obv.* ℞. Disjointed curved horse, pellet below. *M. 27; V. 52, 54* 225

8   — F. (Suessiones), *c.* 50 B.C. *Stater.* Disintegrated head and horse to r. *M. 34a; V. 85* 250

*The price in this section is for the condition in which the coin usually appears

£*

9 — Xc. *c.* 80 B.C. *Stater.* Blank except for VE monogram at edge of coin, ℞.
   S below horse to r. *M. 82; V. 87–1.* 400
10 — — *Quarter stater.* Similar, but horse to l. *M. 83; V. 355* 250
11 — Xd. *c.* 50 B.C. *Quarter stater.* Head l. of good style, horned serpent
   behind ear. ℞. Horse l. *M. 79; V. 78.* 500

12

13

18

Armorican (Channel Isles and N.W. Gaul), *c.* 75–50 B.C.   £*

12 *Stater.* Class I. Head r. ℞. Horse, boar below, remains of driver with
   Victory above, lash ends in one or two loops, or "gate"   45
13 Class II. Head r. ℞. Horse, boar below, remains of Victory only, lash ends
   in small cross of four pellets   40
14 Class III. Head r., anchor-shaped nose. ℞. Somewhat similar to Class I .   45
15 Class IV. Head r. ℞. Horse with reins, lyre shape below, driver holds
   vertical pole, lash ends in three prongs   50
16 Class V. Head r. ℞. Similar to last, lash ends in long cross with four pellets   50
17 Class VI. Head r. ℞. Horse, boar below, lash ends in "ladder"   60
18 *Quarter stater.* Similar types to above . . . .*from*   85
19 A. Westerham type, *c.* 95–65 B.C. As 5, but horse more disjointed. *M. 28,
   29; V. 200, 202.*   325

Celtic Coins Struck In Britain
Uninscribed gold staters

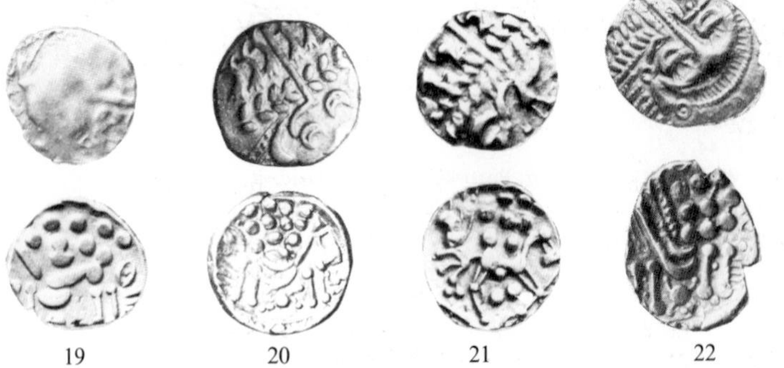

19   20   21   22

*The price in this section is for the condition in which the coin usually appears

£*

20 B. Chute type, *c.* 85–55 B.C. Similar but crab-like figure below horse.
   M. 32; V. 1205. 150
21 C. Yarmouth (I.O.W.) type, *c.* 80–70 B.C. Crude variety of 5. *M. 31; V.*
   1220 600
22 D. Cheriton type, *c.* 80–70 B.C. Variety of 20 with large crescent face.
   M. 33; V. 1215. 550
23 E. Waldingfield type, *c.* 90–70 B.C. Annulet and pellet below horse. *M. 48,*
   V. 1462. . . . . *Extremely rare*
24 F. Clacton type 1, *c.* 90–70 B.C. Similar to Westerham type but rosette
   below horse to l. *M. 47; V. 1458.* 400

25   26   28

25 G. Clacton type 2. Similar, but horse r., with pellet, or pellet with two
   curved lines below. *M. 46, 46a; V. 30, 1455.* 350
26 H. North East Coast type, *c.* 75–30 B.C. Variety of 5, pellet or rosette
   below horse to r. *M. 50, 50a, 51, 51a; V. 800.* 350
27 I. — — Similar, horse l., pellet, rosette or star with curved rays below.
   M. 52–57; V. 804, 805, 807 450
28 J. Norfolk wolf type, *c.* 65–45 B.C. ℞. Crude wolf to r. or l. *M. 49, 49a,*
   49b; V. 610. 650

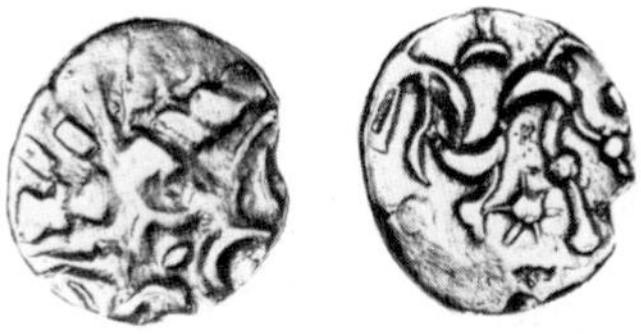

30    31

29 Ka. Coritani, South Ferriby type, *c.* 30 B.C.–A.D. 10. Crude wreath. ℞.
   Disjointed horse l., rectangular compartment enclosing four pellets above.
   M. 447–448; V. 825, 829 450
30 Kb. — — Similar, but star or rosette below horse. *M. 449–450a; V. 809,*
   811, 815, 817. 500
30A — — — Trefoil with central rosette of seven pellets. ℞. Similar to last.
   M. 450a; V. 821. In auction 1985 £5500. (this coin) . . . . *Unique*

*The price in this section is for the condition in which the coin usually appears

Uninscribed gold staters *continued* £*

31 L. Whaddon Chase type, *c.* 45–20 B.C. ℞. Spirited horse r. of new style,
    various symbols below. *M. 133–138a, 139a; V. 1470–6, 1485/7/91/93* . . . 350

32 — — *O.* Plain. ℞. Horse r., with ring ornament below or behind. *M. 140–*
    143; V. 1498–1505 325

33 Lx. North Thames group, *c.* 40–20 B.C. *O.* Blank apart from reversed SS.
    ℞. Similar to last. *M. 146; V. 1509* . . . . *Extremely rare*

34 Ly. North Kent group, *c.* 45–20 B.C. *O.* Blank. ℞. Horse l. or r., numerous
    ring ornaments in field. *M. 293, 294; V. 142, 157* 350

35 Lz. Weald group, *c.* 35–20 B.C. *O.* Blank. ℞. Horse l., panel below. *M. 84,*
    292; V. 150, 144 600

36 Lz. *O.* Blank with some traces of Apollo head. ℞. Horse r., large wheel
    ornament below. *M. 144–145; V. 1507.* 400

34

37

37 M. Wonersh type. *c.* 35–20 B.C. Crossed wreath design with crescents back
    to back in centre. ℞. Spiral above horse, wheel below. *M. 148; V. 1520* . 425

38

39

38 Na. Iceni, *c.* 30 B.C.–A.D. 10. Double crescent design. ℞. Horse r. *M. 397,*
    399; V. 620. 600

39 Nb. — Trefoil on cross design. ℞. Similar to last. *M. 401–403a; V. 626* . 600

40 Nc. — Cross of pellets. ℞. Similar to last. *M. 400; V. 624* 625

41

43

*The price in this section is for the condition in which the coin usually appears

£*

41 Qa. British "Remic" type, *c*. 45–25 B.C. Crude laureate head. ℞. Triple-tailed horse, wheel below. *M. 58, 60, 61; V. 210–14* 400
42 Qb. — Similar, but *obv*. blank. *M. 59, 62; V. 216, 1526* 250
43 R. Dobunni, *c*. 30 B.C.–A.D. 10. Similar, but branch emblem or ear of corn on *obv*. *M. 374; V. 1005*. 600

Uninscribed Quarter Staters

44   45   46

43A F. Clacton type. *O*. Plain, traces of pattern. ℞. Ornamental cross with pellets. *M. 35; V. 1460* 350
44 Lx. N. Thames group, *c*. 40–20 B.C. Floral pattern on wreath. ℞. horse l. or r. *M. 76, 151, 270–271; V. 234, 1608, 1623, 1688* 225
45 Ly. N. Kent group, *c*. 45–20 B.C. *O*. Blank. ℞. Horse r. *M. 78, 284–285; V. 158/163/170*. 225
46 Lz. Weald group, *c*. 35–20 B.C. Spiral design on wreath. ℞. Horse l. or r. *M. 77, 80–81; V. 250, 254, 366* 225
47 — — *O*. Blank. ℞. Horse l., panel below. *M. 85; V. 151*. 275
48 N. Iceni, *c*. 30 B.C.–A.D. 10. Floral pattern. ℞. Horse r. *M. 404; V. 628*. 275

49   50   51

49 O. Geometric type, Sussex group, *c*. 80–60 B.C. Unintelligible patterns (some blank on *obv*.). *M. 40, 43–45; V. 143, 1425/27/29* 85
50 P. Kentish group, *c*. 65–45 B.C. *O*. Blank. ℞. Trophy design. *M. 36, 38; V. 145–7* 175
51 Qc. British "Remic" type, *c*. 40–20 B.C. Head or wreath pattern, ℞. Triple-tailed horse, l. or r. *M. 63–67, 69–75; V. 220–32, 36, 42–6, 56, 1015* . . . 225
52 R. Dobunni, *c*. 30 B.C.–A.D. 10. *O*. Blank. ℞. Somewhat as last. *M. 68; V. 1010*. 325

Uninscribed Silver

53   55   56   58

*The price in this section is for the condition in which the coin usually appears

Uninscribed silver *continued*

52A North Thames group. Head l. with headband (or diadem) and flowing   £*
     hair. ℞. New style horse of Whaddon Chase type l. (See *S.* 31a). *M.* —;
     V. 80/1 . . . .   *Extremely rare*
52B — — Similar. ℞. Pegasos. *M.* —; *V.* —   200
53   Lx. Head l. or r. ℞. Horse l. or r. *M. 280, 435, 436, 438, 441; V. 80, 1546,*
     1549, 1555   125
54   — — Head l. ℞. Goat r., with long horns. *M. 437; V. 1552*   175
55   — — Two horses or two beasts. *M. 442, 443, 445; V. 474, 1626, 1948* . .   150
56   — — Star of four rays or wreath pattern. ℞. Horse or uncertain animal r.
     M. 272a, 414, 439; V. 164, 679, 1543.   125
56A — — Hd. r. with corded hair and headband. ℞. Horse l., leaf (?) below,
     ornaments in field. (Somewhat similar to *S.* 77).) *M.* — . . . .   *Extremely rare*
56B — — *Half unit.* Cruciform pattern with ornaments in angles. ℞. Horse l.,
     ear of corn between legs, crescent and pellets above. *M.* — . . . .   *Extremely rare*
56C — — *Quarter unit* (minim). Cross pattern. ℞. Two-tailed horse   120
57   Lz. South Thames group. Wreath or head of serpent. ℞. Horse *M.* 446B
     (*Allen L 28-10*).   125
58   — — Helmeted head r. ℞. Horse. *M. 89; V. 264*   200
58A — — Facing hd. of Celtic god with horns, wheel between. ℞. Triple-tailed
     horse. l., ornaments in field. *M.* — (May be Gaulish) . . . .   *Extremely rare*
58B — — Two swans (or cranes), boar and eel (?) below. ℞. Reindeer l., boar
     on hindquarters. *M.* — (May be Gaulish). . . . .   *Unique*
59   *Quarter unit* (3½ 4 grains). Similar to 58. *M. 90–91; V. 268–70* . . .   150

          60   61   61A

60   Durotriges, *c.* 60 B.C.–A.D. 20. Size and type of Westerham staters (nos.
     19 and 81). *M. 317; V. 1235* Quality of Æ varies, price for good Æ . . .   60
61   — Size and type of Sussex Geometric type (no. 49 above). *M. 319; V. 1242/*
     49.   50
61A — 'Starfish' design. ℞. 'Geometric' pattern. *M. 320; V. 1270*   100
62   — Very thin flans, *c.* 55 B.C. Crude hd. of lines and pellets. ℞. Horse
     similar. *M. 321; V. 1280.*   150
63   Dobunni, *c.* 30 B.C.–A.D. 10. Head r., with recognisable face. ℞. Triple-
     tailed horse l. or r. *M. 374a, b, 375, 376, 378; V. 1558, 1020, 1042*   125
64   — Very crude head. ℞. Similar to last. *M. 378a–384d; V. 1035, 37, 45, 49,*
     74, 75, 78, 85, 95.   75
65   — *Quarter unit.* As last. *M. 384c; V. 1080.* . . . .   *Extremely rare*

                            63   64

*The price in this section is for the condition in which the coin usually appears

66   69   72

£*

66	Coritani, *c.* 50 B.C.–A.D. 10. I. Prototype issue of good style and execution. Boar r., with rosette and ring ornaments. ℞. Horse. *M. 405, 405a, b, 406, 451; V. 855, 57, 60, 64*	150
67	— — *Half unit.* Similar. *M. 406a, 451a; V. 862/6.*	125
68	— II. South Ferriby type. Vestiges of boar on *obv.* ℞. Horse. *M. 410, 452, 453; V. 875/7.*	150
69	— — *O.* Plain. ℞. Horse. *M. 453a, 454; V. 884/7.*	100
70	— — *Half unit.* Similar. *M. 455–456; V. 879/89*	80
71	— — *Quarter unit.* Similar. *M. 456a; V. 881*	80

74   77   82

72	Iceni, *c.* 10 B.C.–A.D. 60. Boar r. ℞. Horse r. *M. 407–409; V. 655/7/9* . .	75
73	— *Half unit.* Similar. *M. 411; V. 661.*	75
73A	— — Antlered deer. ℞. Horse r. *M.* — (May be Gaulish)	*Unique*
73B	— Quarter unit. Similar to 73. *M.* — (May be Gaulish)	*Unique*
74	— Head r. ℞. Horse. *M. 412–413e; V. 665, 790, 792, 794*	100
74A	— Large bust of good style. ℞. Horse r.	125
74B	— Similar, but inverted ear of corn between legs of horse on *rev. M.* — *(413 variety)*	*Extremely rare*
75	— Double crescent and wreath pattern. ℞. Horse. *M. 414–415, 440; V. 675/79/1611*	40
76	— *Half unit.* Similar. *M. 417a; V. 683*	135
76A	— — Three crescents back to back. ℞. Horse r. *M. 417; V. 681.*	175

Uninscribed Bronze

77	Lx. North Thames group. Head l. with braided hair. ℞. Horse l. *M. 273, 274,* see also *M. 281; V. 1615, 1646*	90
78	— — Horned pegasus l. ℞. Pegasus l. *M. 446; V. 1629.*	*Extremely rare*
79	— — Other types . . . . *from*	225
80	Ly. North Kent group. Boar. ℞. Horse. *M. 295–296; V. 154*	150
81	Durotriges, *c.* A.D. 20–50. Debased form of Æ stater (no. 60). *M. 318; V. 1290.*	35
82	— Cast coins, *c.* A.D. 50–70. As illustration. *M. 322–370; V. 1322–70* . .	60

*The price in this section is for the condition in which the coin usually appears

Uninscribed Bronze *continued*

Potin (bronze with high tin content)   £*

83 Thames and South, *c.* 1st century B.C. Cast. Class I. Crude head. ℞. Lines
    representing bull. (*Allen*, types A–L.) *M. 9–22a; V. 104, 106, 108, 112, 114,
    115, 117, 119, 120, 122, 123, 125, 127, 129, 131, 133*   35
84 Kent and N. Thames, *c.* mid. 1st century A.D. Cast. Class II. Smaller flan,
    large central pellet. (*Allen*, types M–P.) *M. 23–25; V. 135–9*   80

CELTIC DYNASTIC ISSUES

The Celtic dynastic issues are among the most interesting and varied of all British coins. A great deal
is known about some of the issuers from Julius Caesar's *Commentaries* and other sources—chiefly
the kings of the Atrebates, Regni and Catuvellauni—while many are issues of kings quite unknown
to history bearing legends which defy interpretation.

Roman influence in coinage design is particularly noticeable in the reign of Cunobelin (*c.* A.D.
10–40), but the Icenian revolt of A.D. 61 in which Colchester and London were sacked with the
massacre of over 70,000 Romans resulted in the termination of British Celtic coinage which
previously had been allowed to circulate along with Roman coins.

The dates given for the various rulers are, in most cases, very approximate. Staters and quarter
staters are gold coins of varying quality.

N.B. Bronze coins in poor condition are worth very much less than the values given. All coins,
even good specimens, are worth less if they lack clear legends, are struck off-centre or have striking
cracks.

SOUTHERN BRITAIN

Atrebates and Regni. *Berks., Hants., Surrey and Sussex*

85 **Commius,** *c.* 35–20 B.C. *Stater.* Portions of laureate hd. r. ℞. COMMIOS
    around triple tailed horse r. *M. 92; V. 350*   2500
    Copied from the "Remic" type Qᴀ *(no. 41), this is the first inscribed British coin.*

85   86   88

86 **Tincommius,** *c.* 20 B.C.–A.D. 5. Celtic style. *Stater.* Similar, but TINC
    COMMI F, or TIN DV around horse. *M. 93, 94; V. 362, 363.*   850
87 — *Quarter stater.* TINCOM, zig-zag ornament below. ℞. Horse l. *M. 95;
    V. 365.*   650
88 Classical style. *Stater.* TINC or COM · F on tablet. ℞. Horseman with
    javelin. *M. 96, 98, 100; V. 375, 376, 385*   900
89 — *Quarter stater.* TINC on a tablet, C above, A or B below. ℞. Medusa
    hd. facing. *M. 97; V. 378*   550
90 — — *O.* As 88. ℞. Horse l. or r. *M. 99, 101–104; V. 379, 387–90*   325
91 — *Silver.* Head r., TINCOM. ℞. Eagle facing. *M. 105; V. 397*   300

*The price in this section is for the condition in which the coin usually appears

£*

91A — — Head l. R̨. Bull charging l., TINC. *M. 106; V. 396.* 225
92 — — Facing hd. with ornate hair. R̨. As last. *M. —; V. 370* 125
92A — — Laureate head l. R̨. Boar charging l., pentagram, TINCO in field.
V. 396. 225
92B — — Similar, but head r., C (?) behind. R̨. Bull charging r. *M. —; V. 381.* 225
92C — — — TINCOMMIVS. R̨. Horse l. *M. 131b; V. 473.* (Listed in Mack
under Verica.) 225
93 — — TINC. R̨. Animal prancing l. *M. 106a; V. 382* 150
93A — Victory r., TIN. R̨. CO.F. within wreath. *M. —.* 175
93B — — TINC in angles of four rays, pellets in centre. R̨. Lion on hippocamp
l. *M. —; V. 372* 150
93C — — Five pointed star, pellet in centre. R̨. Boy on a dolphin r., TIN below.
M. —; V. 371 75
94 — *Silver quarter unit.* C F within two interlinked squares. R̨. Dog to r.,
TINC. *M. 118; V. 383.* . . . . *Extremely rare*
94A — — Tablet contains CoF. R̨. Medusa hd 500

89   95

95 **Eppillus,** *c.* A.D. 5–10 (see also under Cantii). *Quarter stater.* Stars above
and below CALLEV *(Silchester).* R̨. EPPI over hound r. *M. 107; V.407* 175

96   98   99

95A — EPPILLV · COMM · F · around crescent. R̨. Horse r., star above and
below. *M. —; V. 409* 400
96 *Silver.* EPP over eagle. R̨. REX crescent CALLE. *M. 108; V. 415* 75
96A — Bearded hd. r. in wreath, no legend. R̨. Boar r., EPPI COM or EPPI F
CO. *M. —; V. 416.* 100
96C — Quarter unit. Crook-ended cross, pellets in angles. R̨. Horse r., EPP;
V. 421. . . . . *Extremely rare*
96D — — Bull's hd. facing. R̨. Ram (?)r., dividing EPPI CO. *M. —; V. 422* . 125
96E *Bronze.* Floral design of 8 petals surrounded by 4 crescents and 4 annulets.
R̨. Hound r., EPPI above, COM F below . . . . *Extremely rare*
97 **Verica,** *c.* A.D. 10–40. *Stater.* Group I. COM · F on tablet. R̨. VIR below
horseman r. *M. 109, 110; V. 460/1* 700
98 — II. Similar but title REX added. *M. 121; V. 500.* 600
99 — III. Vineleaf between VI–RI. R̨. Horseman r. *M. 125; V. 520* 750
100 *Quarter stater.* I. COM · F etc. R̨. Horse VIR etc. *M. 111–114; V. 465–8.* 300
101 — II. VERIC COM · F in two lines. R̨. Horse r., REX below. *M. 122;
V. 501.* 300
102 — III. Vineleaf, VERI below. R̨. Horseman as no. 97. *M. 124; V. 525* . . 300
103 — — Head or seated figure. R̨. Horseman r. *M. 126–127; V. 526/7.* 325

*The price in this section is for the condition in which the coin usually appears

Atrebates and Regni *continued*   £*
104   *Silver*. I. Crescents, COM · F. ℞. Boar. *M. 115; V. 470*   75
104A — — — ℞. Eagle l. VIR. *M. —; V. 471*.   75
104B — — VIRIC across field, ornaments above and below. ℞. Pegasus r., star
       design below (12.2 grs) . . . .   *Extremely rare*

       105   107   110

105   — II. Name around circles. ℞. Lion r. *M. 123; V. 505*   100
106   — III. Horseman with spear. ℞. Horseman with shield. *M. 128; V. 530* .   125
107   — — Seated figure. ℞. Two cornucopiae. *M. 129; V. 531*   75
108   — — Head r. ℞. Seated or standing figure. *M. 130–131; V. 532/3*   125
108A — — Head r. ℞. Eagle. *M. 131a; V. 534*   175
108B — — Bull dividing VERICA REX. ℞. Stg. fig. with head on a standard,
       COMMI F. *M. —; V. 506*   150
109   *Silver quarter unit.* I. *O*. Various. ℞. Animal. *M. 116–117; 119–120e;
       V. 480/2/4, 510/11, 552*   75
109A — — VIR in box. ℞. Boar's hd. r., CF. *M. —; cf. V. 564*   175
109B — Sphinx C.F. ℞. Dog or wolf curled head to tail. VERI; *V. 557*.   175
109C Eagle r. VERCA COMMI F. ℞. Wine krater. *M. —; V. 563*   150
110   — III. C · F in wreath. ℞. Head r., VERI. *M. 132; V. 551*.   75
111A — IV. VIR/VAR on tablet. ℞. Pegasus r., CO below. *M. —; V. 511*. . .   125
111B — — VERICA around bucranium. ℞. Tomb, or altar, C.F. *M. —; V. 552*.   125
111C — — 'Maltese cross' design, pellets in angles. ℞. Hand grasping trident,
       VER REX; *V. 487* (now attributed to Eppillus).   300
111D — Two cornucopiae. ℞. Eagle. *M.; V. 555*   125
111E Acorn pattern r. ℞. RVER CA, hippocamp; *V. 556*   125
111F Interlinked C's or crescents, standard between dividing CR at top. ℞.
       Hippocamp, VERICA. *M. —*   125
111G Human headed Sphinx, VERIC. ℞. Hd. r., SCF(?). *M. —*.   125
111H Helmeted bust r. in Roman style. ℞. Horse r., CF between legs. *M. —*,
       V. 558.   125
112   **Epaticcus**, *c.* A.D. 25–35. *Stater*. TASCI · F, ear of wheat. ℞. EPATICCV,
       horseman r. *M. 262; V. 575*.   1250
113   *Silver*. Head of Hercules r., EPATI. ℞. Eagle stg. on snake. *M. 263; V. 580*   50

       112   113

114   — Victory seated r. ℞. Boar. *M. 263a; V. 581*   100
114A — EPATI in panel. ℞. Lion r. *M. —; V. 583* . . . .   *Extremely rare*
115   *Silver quarter unit. O*. EPATI. ℞. Boar's head (?), TA below. *M. 264;
       V. 585*.   125

*The price in this section is for the condition in which the coin usually appears

£*

116 — Lion (?) r., EPA. ℞. TA in centre of double lozenge. *M.* — . . . . . .   *Rare*
117 **Caratacus,** *c.* A.D. 35–40. *Silver.* As 113, CARA. *M. 265; V. 593.*   400
    The above two rulers were brother and son of Cunoblin (see Catuvellauni), but their
    coins appear in the same area as Verica's.
117A *Silver quarter unit.* CARA around pellet in circle. ℞. Pegasus r., no legend.
    M. —*; V. 595*   175

Cantii *Kent*

118 **Dubnovellaunus,** *c.* 15–1 B.C. *(See also under Trinovantes.)* Stater. *O.* Blank.
    ℞. Horse r., DVBNOVELLAVNOS or DVBNOVI. *M. 282–283; V. 169/76.*   450
119 *Silver.* Griffin r. or horned animal. ℞. Horse l. or seated figure. *M. 286–*
    287; V. 171/8.   250
119A — Triangular or cruciform design. ℞. Horse r.; *cf. V. 164*   250
120 — Head l. ℞. Pegasus. *M. 288; V. 165.*   250
121 *Bronze.* Boar. ℞. Eagle, horseman or horse. *M. 289, 291, 291a, V. 173,*
    180/1   175
122 — Animal. ℞. Horse or lion l., DVBN on tablet below. *M. 290; V. 166* .   175

    117   117A   118

123 **Vosenios,** *c.* A.D. 5. *Stater. O.* Blank. ℞. Serpent below horse. *M. 297;*
    V. 184. . . . . *Extremely rare*
124 *Quarter stater.* Similar. VOSII below horse. *M. 298; V. 185*   450
125 *Silver.* Griffin and horse. ℞. Horse, retrograde legend. *M. 299a; V. 186* .   350
126 *Bronze.* Boar l. ℞. Horse l., SA below. *M. 299; V. 187*   250

    124   128

127 **Eppillus,** *c.* A.D. 10–25. *(See also under Atrebates.)* Stater. COM · F in
    wreath. ℞. Horseman l., EPPILLVS. *M. 300; V. 430.*   900
128 — Victory in wreath. ℞. Horseman r. Illustrated above. *M. 301; V. 431* .   1100
129 *Quarter stater.* EPPIL/COM · F. ℞. Pegasus. *M. 302; V. 435*   225
130 — EPPI around wreath, or COM · F. ℞. Horse. *M. 303–304; V. 436/7.* .   250
131 *Silver.* Head r. or l. ℞. Lion or horseman. *M. 305–306; V. 417/41*   175
132 — Diademed head l. or r., IOVIR. ℞. Victory or capricorn. *M. 307–308a;*
    V. 442/3   200
133 *Bronze.* Head l. ℞. Victory holding wreath. *M. 311; V. 452*   125
134 — Cruciform ornament or bull. ℞. Eagle. *M. 309–310; V. 450/1*   125
135 — Bearded head l. ℞. Horse r. *M. 312; V. 453*   125

    130   131

*The price in this section is for the condition in which the coin usually appears

Cantii *continued*   £*

136 **Amminus,** *c.* A.D. 15? *Silver.* Plant. ℞. Pegasus r. *M. 313; V. 192*   500
137 — A within wreath. ℞. Capricorn r. *M. 314; V. 194*   225
138 *Silver quarter unit.* A within curved lines. ℞. Bird. *M. 316; V. 561*   200
139 *Bronze.* Head r. ℞. Capricorn r. *M. 315; V. 195*   175
139A '‍B' within octagonal pattern. ℞. Bird. *M.—.* . . . .   *Extremely rare*

Unattributed coins of the Cantii

140 *Silver quarter unti.* Horseman. ℞. Seated figure wearing belt and holding
     spear or staff. *M. 316e; V. 153* . . . .   *Extremely rare*
141 *Bronze.* Boar or head. ℞. Lion to r. or l. *M. 316a, c; V. 154*   150
143 — *O.* Uncertain. ℞. Ring ornaments. *M. 316d; V. 154* . . . .   *Extremely rare*
144 *Bronze quarter unit.* Quatrefoil pattern. ℞. Horse r. *M. 316f; V. 154* . . .   150

136   145   148

Durotriges *W. Hants., Dorset, Somerset and S. Wilts*

145 **Crab.** *Silver.* CRAB in angles of cross. ℞. Eagle. *M. 371; V. 1285*   500
146 *Silver quarter unit.* CRAB on tablet. ℞. Star shape. *M. 372; V. 1286* . . .   400
147 **Uncertain.** *Silver.* Two boars back to back. ℞. Ring ornaments etc. in field.
     M. 373 (probably Gaulish) . . . .   *Unique*

NORTH THAMES

Trinovantes *Essex and counties to the West*

150   152   154

148 **Addedomaros,** *c.* 15–1 B.C. *Stater.* Crossed wreath or spiral. ℞. Horse,
     wheel or cornucopiae below. *M. 266–267; V. 1605/20*   650
149 — Double crescent ornament. ℞. Horse, branch below. *M. 268; V. 1635*.   650
150 *Quarter stater.* Similar, but rectangle or wheel below horse. *M. 269;
     V. 1638*   650
     *[Note. For uninscribed bronze, sometimes attributed to Addedomaros, see
     S. 77 (M. 273/274; V. 1646).]*
151 **Diras?,** *c.* A.D. 1? *Stater. O.* Blank. ℞. DIRAS and snake (?) over horse,
     wheel below. *M. 279; V. 162* . . . .   *Extremely rare*
152 **Dubnovellaunus,** *c.* A.D. 1–10. *(See also under Cantii.) Stater.* Wreath
     design. ℞. Horse l., branch below. *M. 275; V. 1650*.   550
153 *Quarter stater.* Similar. *M. 276; V. 1660*   275
154 *Bronze.* Head r. or l. ℞. Horse l. or r. *M. 277–278*, see also *M. 281; V. 1665,
     1667, 1669*   75

*The price in this section is for the condition in which the coin usually appears

£*

155 — Without legend but associated with the Trinovantes. Head or boar. ℞.
Horse or horseman. *M. 280a, b, d*   120

Catuvellauni *N. Thames, Herts., Beds., spreading East and South*

157

Tasciovanus, *c.* 20 B.C.–A.D. 10, and associated coins

157 *Stater.* Crescents in wreath. ℞. TASCIAV and bucranium over horse. *M.*
149–150; V. 1680/2   750
158 — Similar, sometimes with VER *(Verulamium).* ℞. Horseman r., TASC.
M. 154–156; V. 1730/2/4   700
159 — Similar, but T, or V and T. ℞. Similar to last. *M. 157; V. 1790*   750
160 — As 157. ℞. Horse, CAMV monogram *(Camulodunum). M. 186; V. 1684* .   800
161 — TASCIOV / RICON in panel. ℞. Horseman l. *M. 184; V. 1780*   1100
162 — TASCIO in panel. ℞. Horseman r., SEGO. *M. 194; V. 1845*   1100
163 *Quarter stater.* Wreath, TASCI or VERO. ℞. Horse, TAS or TASC. *M.*
152–153; V. 1690/2   350
164 —*O.* As 160. ℞. CAMVL mon. over horse. *M. 187; V. 1694*   350
165 — *O.* As 161, omitting RICON. ℞. Pegasus l. *M. 185; V. 1786*   350
166 — *O.* As 162. ℞. Horse l. omitting SEGO. *M. 195; V. 1848*   350
167 *Silver.* Bearded head l. ℞. Horseman r., TASCIO. *M. 158; V. 1745*   225
168 — Pegasus l., TAS. ℞. Griffin r., within circle of pellets. *M. 159; V. 1790*   225
169 — Eagle stg. l., TASCIA. ℞. Griffin r., *M. 160; V. 1792*   225
170 —VER in beaded circle. ℞. Horse r., TASCIA. *M. 161; V. 1699*   185
171 — — ℞. Naked horseman, no legend. *M. 162; V. 1747*   185

172   175   178

172 — Laureate hd. r., TASCIA. ℞. Bull butting l. *M. 163; V. 1794*   185
173 — Cruciform ornament, VERL. ℞. Boar, r. TAS. *M. 164; V. 1796*   185
173A — Saltire over cross within square, serpentine design around. ℞. Similar to
last. *M. —*   350
174 — TASC in panel. ℞. Pegasus l. *M. 165; V. 1798.*   175
175 — — ℞. Horseman l. carrying a long shield. *M. 166; V. 1800*   175
176 — SEGO on panel. ℞. Horseman. *M. 196; V. 1851*   300
177 — DIAS / C / O. ℞. Horse, VIR (?) below. *M. 188; V. 1877*   300
178 *Bronze.* Two heads in profile, one bearded. ℞. Ram l., TASC. *M. 167;*
V. 1705.   75
179 — Bearded head r. ℞. Horse l., VIIR, VER or TAS. *M. 168–169; V. 1707–9*   75
180 — Head r., TASC. ℞. Pegasus l., VER. *M. 170; V. 1711.*   75

*The price in this section is for the condition in which the coins usually appears

Tasciovanus *continued*   £*
181   — — TAS ANDO. ℞. Horse r. *M. 170a; V. 1873a*. . . . .   *Unique*
182   — Head r., TAS. ℞. Horseman r., VER. *M. 171; V. 1750*   75
183   — VERLAMIO between rays of star-shaped ornament. ℞. Bull l. *M. 172;*
       V. 1808   75

                185   190   191
184   *Bronze*. Similar, without legend. ℞. Sphinx l., legend SEGO? *M. 173;*
       V. 1855   75
185   — Similar. ℞. Bull r. *M. 174; V. 1810*   75
186   — Similar. ℞. Horse l., TASCI. *M. 175; V. 1812*   75
187   — Head r., TASC. . . ℞. Horse r. in double circle. *M. 175a; V. 1873* . . .   *Extremely rare*
188   — Laureate hd. r., TASCIO. ℞. Lion r., TASCIO. *M. 176; V. 1814* . . .   75
189   — Head r. ℞. Figure std. l., VER below. *M. 177; V. 1816*   85
190   — — TASCIAVA. ℞. Pegasus l., TAS. *M. 178; V. 1818 (double bronze*
       denomination) . . . .   *Extremely rare*
191   — Cruciform ornament of crescents and scrolls. ℞. Boar r., VER. *M. 179;*
       V. 1713   100
192   — Laureate head r. ℞. Horse l., VIR. *M. 180; V. 1820.*   80
193   — Raised band across centre, VER or VERL below, uncertain objects
       above. ℞. Horse grazing r. *M. 183a; V. 1717*   100
194   — RVII above lion r. within wide beaded circle. ℞. Eagle looking l.,
       sometimes reading RVE. *M. 189; V. 1890*   100
195   — Bearded head r., RVIIS. ℞. Horseman r., VIR. *M. 190; V. 1892.* . . .   90
196   — RVIIS on panel. ℞. Animal l. *M. 191; V. 1895*   100
197   — Head r., TASC DIAS. ℞. Centaur r. playing double pipe, or sometimes
       horses. *M. 192; V. 1882*   100
198   *Bronze half denomination*. Lion? r. ℞. Sphinx l. *M. 181; V. 1824* . . . . .   *Extremely rare*
199   — Bearded head l. or r., VER. ℞. Goat or boar r. *M. 182–183; V. 1715,*
       1826   100
200   — Head l. ℞. Animal l. with curved tail. *M. 183b, c; V. 1822*   100
201   — Annulet within square with curved sides. ℞. Eagle l., RVII. *M. 193;*
       V. 1903   100

                196   202   203
202   **Andoco**, *c*. A.D. 5–15. *Stater*. Crossed wreath design. ℞. Horse r., AND.
       M. 197; V. 1860   1250
203   *Quarter stater*. Crossed wreaths, ANDO. ℞. Horse l. *M. 198; V. 1863* . .   325
204   *Silver*. Bearded head l. in looped circle. ℞. Pegasus l., ANDOC. *M. 199;*
       V. 1868   300
205   *Bronze*. Head r., ANDOCO. ℞. Horse r., AND. *M. 200; V. 1871.*   150

*The price in this section is for the condition in which the coin usually appears

| 205 | 207 | 208 |

		£*
206	*Bronze half denomination.* Head l. ℞. Horse r., A between legs, branch in exergue. *M. —*	175
207	**Cunobelin** *(Shakespeare's Cymbeline). c.* A.D. 10–40. *Stater.* CAMVL on panel. ℞. Leaf above two horses galloping l., CVNOBELIN on curved panel below. *M. 201; V. 1910.*	1500
208	— Ear of corn dividing CA MV. ℞. Horse prancing r., CVNO below. *M. 203, 206, 210–213. V. 2010/25/1925/31/33/2020* Varying in style, from— .	650
209	— Similar, but horse l. *M. 208; V. 2029*	1250
210	*Quarter stater.* Similar to 207. *M. 202; V. 1913*	400
211	— Similar to 208. *M. 204, 209; V. 1927, 2015.*	275
212	— Similar to 208 but CAM CVN on *obv. M. 205; V. 2017*	400
213	*Silver.* Two bull headed snakes intertwined. ℞. Horse l., CVNO. *M. 214; V. 1947*	175
214	— Head l., CAMVL before. ℞. CVNO beneath Victory std. r. *M. 215; V. 2045.*	100
215	— CVNO BELI in two panels. ℞. CVN below horseman galloping r. (legends sometimes retrograde). *M. 216, 217; V. 1951/3*	150
216	— Two leaves dividing CVN. ℞. CAM below horseman galloping r. *M. 218; V. 2047*	175
217	— Flower dividing CA MV. ℞. CVNO below horse r. *M. 219; V. 2049* .	175
218	— CVNO on panel. ℞. CAMV on panel below griffin. *M. 234; V. 2051* .	150
219	— CAMVL on panel. ℞. CVNO below centaur l. carrying palm. *M. 234a; V. 1918*	150
219A	CAMVL on panel. ℞. Figure seated l. holding wine amphora, CVNOBE. *M. —*	175
219B	— Plant, CVNOBELINVS (see no. 136 Amminus). ℞. Hercules stg. r. holding club and thunderbolt, dividing CA MV. *M. —*	250
219C	— Laur. hd. r., CVNOBELINVS. ℞. Pegasus springing l., CAMV below. *M. —*	250
220	— CVNO on panel. ℞. TASC F below Pegasus r. *M. 235; V. 2053*	200

| 212 | 221 | 225 |

221	— Head r., CVNOBELINI. ℞. TASCIO below horse r. *M. 236; V. 2055*	300
222	— Winged bust r., CVNO. ℞. Sphinx std. l., TASCIO. *M. 237; V. 2057* .	90
223	— Draped female figure r., TASCIIOVAN. ℞. Figure std. r. playing lyre, tree behind. *M. 238; V. 2059*	200
224	— Male figure stg. dividing CV NO. ℞. Female std. side saddle on animal, TASCIIOVA. *M. 239; V. 2061*	200
224A	— Laur. hd. r., CVNOBELINVS. ℞. Victory r., TASCIO[VAN ...] ...	200

*The price in this section is for the condition in which the coin usually appears

Cunobelinus *continued*   £*

225 — Figure r. carrying dead animal, CVNOBELINVS. ℞. Figure stg.
holding bow, dog at side, TASCIIOVANI. *M. 240; V. 2063.*   225
226 — CVNO on panel, horn above, two dolphins below. ℞. Figure stg. r.,
altar behind. *M. 241a; V. 2065*   250
227 — CVNO on panel. ℞. Fig. walking r., CV N. *M. 254; V. 2067.*   225
228 — — ℞. Animal springing l. *M. 255; V. 1949.*   285
229 — CVN in centre of wreath. ℞. CAM below dog or she-wolf stg. r. *M. 256;
V. 2069*   285
230 — CVNO, animal l. ℞. CA below figure std. r. holding caduceus. *M. 258;
V. 2071*   425
231 — SOLIDV in centre of looped circle. ℞. Standing figure l., CVNO. *M.
259; V. 2073*   450
232 *Bronze.* Head l., CVNO. ℞. Boar l., branch above. *M. 220; V. 1969* . . .   65
233 — CVNOB ELINI in two panels. ℞. Victory std. l., TASC · F. *M. 221;
V. 1971*   65
234 — Winged animal l., CAM below. ℞. CVN before Victory stg. l. *M. 222a;
V. 1973*   65
235 — Bearded head facing. ℞. Similar to no. 232. *M. 223; V. 1963.*   100
236 — Ram-headed animal coiled up within double ornamental circle. ℞.
CAM below animal l. *M. 224; V. 1965*   125
237 — Winged animal r., CAMV. ℞. CVN below horse galloping r. *M. 225;
V. 2081*   80
238 — Bearded head l., CAMV. ℞. CVN or CVNO below horse l. *M. 226, 229,
V. 2085/2131*   75
239 — Laureate head r., CVNO. ℞. CVN below bull butting l. *M. 227; V. 2083.*   100
240 — Crude head r., CVN. ℞. Figure stg. l., CVN. *M. 228; V. 2135*   75
241 — CAMVL / ODVNO in two panels. ℞. CVNO beneath sphinx crouching
l. *M. 230; V. 1977*   80

242   247   251

242 — Winged beast springing l., CAMV. ℞. Victory stg. r. divides CV NO.
M. 231; V. 1979.   80
243 — Victory walking r. ℞. CVN below, horseman r. *M. 232; V. 1981.*   80
244 — Beardless head l., CAM. ℞. CVNO below eagle. *M. 233; V. 2087.* . . .   80
245 — Laureate head l., CVNOBELINI. ℞. Centaur r., TASCIOVANI · F.
M. 242; V. 2089   75
246 — Helmeted bust r. ℞. TASCIIOVANII above, sow stg. r., F below.
M. 243; V. 2091   75
247 — Horseman galloping r. holding dart and shield, CVNOB. ℞. Warrior
stg. l., TASCIIOVANTIS. *M. 244; V. 2093*   60
248 — Helmeted bust l., CVNOBII. ℞. TASC . FIL below boar l. std. on
haunches. *M. 245; V. 1983*   125
249 — Bare head r., CVNOBELINVS REX. ℞. TASC below bull butting r.
M. 246; V. 2095   75

*The price in this section is for the condition in which the coin usually appears

£*

250 — Bare head l., CVNO. R̟. TASC below bull stg. r. *M. 247; V. 1985.* . .   100
251 — Winged head l., CVNOBELIN. R̟. Metal worker std. r. holding hammer, working on a vase, TASCIO behind. *M. 248; V. 2097*   60
252 — Pegasus springing r., CVNO. R̟. Victory r., sacrificing bull, TASCI. *M. 249; V. 2099*   60
253 — CVNO on panel within wreath. R̟. CAMV below horse, full faced, prancing r. *M. 250; V. 2101.*   95

254   260

254 *Bronze.* Bearded head of Jupiter Ammon l., CVNOBELIN. R̟. CAM below horseman galloping r. *M. 251; V. 2103*   90
255 — Janus head, CVNO below. R̟. CAMV on panel below, sow std. r. beneath a tree. *M. 252; V. 2105* 150
256 — Bearded head of Jupiter Ammon r., CVNOB. R̟. CAM on panel below lion crouched r. *M. 253; V. 2107.*   90
257 — Sphinx r., CVNO. R̟. Fig. stg. l. divides CA *M. 260; V. 2109* . . . 175
258 — Animal stg. r. R̟. CVN below horseman r. *M. 261; V. 1987* 175
259 *Bronze half denomination.* Animal l. looking back. R̟. CVN below horse l. *M. 233a; V. 1967.* 200

S.W. MIDLANDS

Dobunni   *Glos., Here., Mon., Oxon., Som., Wilts. and Worcs.*

265   267

260 **Anted.** *Stater.* Ear of corn. R̟. ANTED or ANTEDRIG over triple-tailed horse r. *M. 385–386; V. 1062/6.* 750
261 *Silver.* Crude head r., as 64. R̟. AN TED over horse l. *M. 387; V. 1082* . 250
262 **Eisu.** *Stater.* Similar to 260 but EISV or EISVRIG. *M. 388; V. 1105* . . . 1350
263 *Silver.* Similar to 261 but EISV. *M. 389; V. 1110.* 200
264 **Inam.** (or Inara). *Stater.* Similar to 260 but INAM (or INARA). *M. 390; V. 1140.* . . . . *Extremely rare*
265 **Catti.** *Stater.* Similar to 260 but CATTI. *M. 391; V. 1130* 850
266 **Comux.** *Stater.* Similar to 260 but COMVX outwardly. *M. 392; V. 1092.* 1000
267 **Corio.** *Stater.* Similar to 260 but CORIO. *M. 393; V. 1035* 925
268 *Quarter stater.* COR in centre. R̟. Horse r. without legend. *M. 394; V. 1039* 1250

*The price in this section is for the condition in which the coin usually appears

Dobunni *continued*

269   270

£*

269 **Bodvoc.** *Stater.* BODVOC across field. ℞. As last. *M. 395; V. 1052.*   1200
270 *Silver.* Head l., BODVOC. ℞. As last. *M. 396; V. 1057*   200

EASTERN ENGLAND

Iceni *Cambs., Norfolk and Suffolk*   *c.* A.D. 10–61

272   273   279

271 **Duro.** *Silver.* Boar. ℞. Horse r., CAN(s) above, DVRO below. *M. 434;*
     V. 663.   500
272 **Anted.** *Stater.* Triple crescent design. ℞. ANTED in two monograms below
     horse. *M. 418; V. 705* . . . .   *Extremely rare*
273 *Silver.* Two crescents back to back. ℞. ANTED as last. *M. 419–421;*
     V. 710/11/15   40
274 *Silver half unit.* Similar to last. *M. 422; V. 720*   60
275 **Ecen.** *Silver.* As 273. ℞. Open headed horse r., ECEN below. *M. 424;*
     V. 730.   40
276 *Silver half unit.* Similar, but legends read ECE, EC, or ECN. *M. 431; V. 736* .   65
277 **Ed.** *Silver.* Similar to 275 but ED (also, E, EI and EDN) below horse. *M.*
     423, 425b; V. 734/40.   150
278 **Ece.** *Silver.* As 273. ℞. Stepping horse r., ECE below. *M. 425a; V. 761.* . .   60
279 — Similar, but "Y" headed horse r., ECE below. *M. 426–427; V. 762/4* .   50
280 — Similar, but horse l. *M. 428; V. 766*   50
281 **Saemu.** *Silver.* As 273. ℞. "Y" headed horse r., SAEMV below. *M. 433;*
     V. 770.   125
282 **Aesu.** *Silver.* As 273. ℞. As last, AESV. *M. 432; V. 775*   250

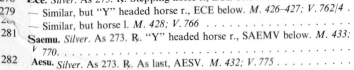

283

*The price in this section is for the condition in which the coin usually appears

£*

283 **Prasutagus,** Client King of the Iceni under Claudius; husband of Boudicca.
Silver. Head of good style l. SUB RII PRASTO. Ɍ. Rearing horse r.,
ESICO FECIT. *M. 434a; V. 780* 1100
    *The attribution by H. Mossop of these rare coins to King Prasutagus has
been made after a study of the legends on the ten known specimens and is
published in "Britannia", X. 1979.*

284 **Iat Iso.** *Silver.* IAT ISO (retrograde) on tablet, rosettes above and below.
Ɍ. Horse r., E above. *M. 416; V. 998* 600
285 **Ale Sca.** *Silver.* Boar r., ALE below. Ɍ. Horse, SCA below. *M. 469; V. 996.* 300

Coritani *Lincs., Yorks. and E. Midlands c. A.D. 10–61*

          291   292   294

286 **Aun Cost.** *Stater.* Crude wreath type. Ɍ. Disjointed horse l., AVN COST.
M. 457; V. 910 750
287 *Silver. O.* Blank or crude wreath design. Ɍ. AVN above horse l. *M. 458;
V. 914.* 300
288 *Silver half unit.* Similar. *Vide M. p. 166; V. 918* . . . . *Extremely rare*
289 **Esup Asu.** *Stater.* As 286 but IISVP ASV. *M. 456b; V. 920* 1100
290 *Silver.* Similar. *M. 456c; V. 924.* . . . . *Extremely rare*
291 **Vep Corf.** *Stater.* As 286. Ɍ. Disjointed horse, VEP CORF. *M. 459, 460;
V. 930.* 550
292 *Silver.* Similar. *M. 460b, 464; V. 934, 50.* 250
293 *Silver half unit.* Similar. *M. 464a; V. 938* . . . . *Extremely rare*
294 — Similar but VEPOC (M)ES, pellets below horse. *M. —; V. 955* 250
295 *Silver half unit.* Similar. *M. —; V. 958.* . . . . *Extremely rare*
296 **Vep.** *Stater. O.* Blank. Ɍ. VEP. (Only plated coins are known.) *M. 460a;
V. 905.* 375
297 *Silver.* As 286 or blank. Ɍ. VEP only. *M. —; V. 965* 200
298 *Silver half unit.* Similar. *M. 464b; V. 967* 250
299 **Dumno Tigir Seno.** *Stater.* DVMN (OC)? across wreath. Ɍ. Horse l.,
TIGIR SENO. *M. 461; V. 972.* 1000
300 *Silver. O.* DVMNO(C)? Ɍ. Horse r., legend as last. *M. 462; V. 974.* 350

  297   298   299

*The price in this section is for the condition in which the coin usually appears

Coritani *continued*

300   301   305

£*

301 **Volisios Dumnocoveros.** *Stater.* VOLI / SIOS in two lines. ℞. Horse,
     DVMNOCOVEROS across crude wreath. *M. 463; V. 978*   900
302 *Silver.* As last. *M. 463a; V. 978 or 80*   350
303 *Silver half unit.* As last but DVMNOCO. *M. 465; V. 984*   350
304 **Volisios Dumnovellaunos.** *Stater.* As 301. ℞. Horse, DVMNOVELAV-
     NOS. *M. 466; V. 988*   850
305 Silver half unit. As last but DVMNOVE. *M. 467; V. 992*   250
306 **Volisios Cartivel.** *Silver half unit.* As 301. ℞. Horse, CARTIVEL. *M. 468;*
     V. 994. . . . .   *Extremely rare*

*The price in this section is for the condition in which the coin usually appears

ROMAN BRITAIN

From the middle of the first century A.D. until the early part of the fifth century, Britannia was a province of the vast Roman Empire—a single state encompassing the whole of the Mediterranean basin. In common with other western provinces, no local coinage was officially produced in Britain during this period (unlike the Eastern part of the Empire where hundreds of towns were permitted to issue muncipal currency) until the latter part of the third century. It was, therefore, the regular Imperial coinage produced mainly at Rome until the mid-third century, that supplied the currency requirements of the province, and no representative collection of British coins is complete without some examples of these important issues.

Although Britain was on the fringe of the Roman World, and never entirely subdued by the legions, a surprisingly large number of coin types allude to events in the province—usually frontier wars in the north. In the closing years of the third century, the usurper Carausius established two mints in Britain; one in London, the other not yet certainly identified (either Camulodunum: Colchester or Clausentum: Bitterne, Southampton). After the defeat of the rebellion London became an official Roman mint, with a substantial output of bronze coinage until its closure, by Constantine the Great, in A.D. 325. Other coins were produced unofficially in Britain at various times: soon after the conquest (copies of bronze coins of Claudius, etc.), in the troubled times of the early 270s (copies of Claudius II and the Tetrici, i.e., "Barbarous radiates") and the final years of the occupation (mostly imitated from the bronze coinage of Constantius II—"soldier spearing fallen horseman" type).

The Roman legions were withdrawn to the continent by Honorius in A.D. 411, but a Romano-British civil administration continued to operate for some time afterward until disrupted by the Teutonic invasions.

For general information on Roman coinage see *Roman Coins and their Values* by D. R. Sear and *Roman Coins* by J. P. C. Kent; for more detailed works consult *Roman Imperial Coinage*, the British Museum Catalogues of Roman coins, *Roman Silver Coins* (5 vols.), the first four by H. A. Seaby and Vol. V by Dr C. E. King, and *The Coinage of Roman Britain* by G. Askew (2nd Edition).

An invaluable companion volume for anyone studying Roman coinage is S. W. Stevenson's *A Dictionary of Roman Coins.*

THE REPUBLIC

Only a few representative examples are listed. Many Republican coins circulated well into the Imperial period and found their way to Britain.

		F £	VF £
451	C. Naevius Balbus, moneyer, 79 B.C. Æ *denarius*. Diad. hd. of Venus r. Ŗ. Victory in triga r.	15	30

452 454

452	C. Calpurnius Piso, moneyer, 67 B.C. Æ *denarius*. Head of Apollo r. Ŗ. Horseman galloping r.	15	35
453	**Julius Caesar,** dictator, †44 B.C. Made two expeditions to Britain in 55 and 54 B.C. Æ *denarius*. Laur. head r. Ŗ. Venus stg. l.	130	325
454	Æ *denarius*. Elephant stg. r. Ŗ. Sacrifical implements	40	90
455	**Mark Antony,** triumvir, †30 B.C. Æ *denarius*. Galley r. Ŗ. Legionary eagle between two standards	35	80

Known for all Legions from I (PRI*mus*) *to XXIII, though only the following are known to have served in Britain during the Roman occupation—II Augusta, VI Victrix, IX Hispania, XIV Gemina Martia Victrix and XX Valeria Victrix.*

THE EMPIRE

456 461

	F £	VF £
456 **Augustus,** 27 B.C.–A.D. 14. Æ *denarius*. ℞. Caius and Lucius Caesars . .	25	65
457 Æ *as*. ℞. The altar of Lugdunum	30	65
458 **Divus Augustus Pater,** commemorative issue. Æ *as*. ℞. PROVIDENT S . C. Altar	25	65
459 **Livia,** wife of Augustus. Æ *dupondius*. ℞. Legend around S . C	65	200
460 **Agrippa,** general and statesman, †12 B.C. Æ *as*. ℞. Neptune stg. l. . . .	35	85
461 **Tiberius,** A.D. 14–37. Æ *denarius*. ℞. Livia seated r.	40	85
This coin is often referred to as the "Tribute Penny" of the Bible.		
462 **Drusus,** son of Tiberius, †A.D. 23. Æ *as*. ℞. Legend around S . C.	45	110
463 **Nero Claudius Drusus,** father of Claudius, †9 B.C. Æ *sestertius*. ℞. Claudius seated amidst arms	110	350
464 **Antonia,** mother of Claudius, †A.D. 37. Æ *dupondius*. ℞. Claudius stg. l.	65	150
465 **Germanicus,** father of Caligula, †A.D. 19. Æ *as*. ℞. Legend around S . C..	35	95
466 **Agrippina Senior,** wife of Germanicus, †A.D. 33. Æ *sestertius*. ℞. Two mules drawing covered carriage	150	500
467 **Caligula,** 37–41. Æ *as*. ℞. VESTA. Vesta seated l.	65	150

468 474

468 **Claudius,** 41–54. Invaded Britain A.D. 43. Æ *aureus*. ℞. DE BRITANN on triumphal arch.	500	1500
469 Æ *denarius*. Similar.	150	400
470 Æ *didrachm* of Caesarea. ℞. DE BRITANNIS below Emperor in quad- riga r.	110	350
471 Æ *sestertius*. ℞. SPES AVGVSTA S . C. Spes walking l., of barbarous style, struck in Britain.	65	220
472 Æ *dupondius*. ℞. CERES AVGVSTA S . C. Ceres seated l., of barbarous style, struck in Britain.	45	95
473 Æ *as*. ℞. S . C. Minerva brandishing javelin	35	85
474 **Nero,** 54–68. Æ *denarius*. ℞. SALVS. Salus seated l.	65	150
475 Æ *as*. ℞. S . C. Victory flying l.	35	95
476 **Galba,** 68–69. Æ *denarius*. ℞. DIVA AVGVSTA. Livia stg. l.	65	180

				F £	VF £
477	**Otho,** 69. Æ *denarius*. ℞. SECVRITAS P . R. Securitas stg. l.			110	280
478	**Vitellius,** 69. Æ *denarius*. ℞. XV . VIR SACR . FAC. Tripod with dolphin			65	150

479   483

479   **Vespasian,** 69–79. Commanded one of the legions in the Claudian invasion
of Britain. Æ *denarius*. ℞. ANNONA AVG. Annona seated l.   25   55

480   *Æ as*. ℞. PROVIDENT. S . C. Large altar   35   75

481   **Titus,** 79–81. Æ *denarius*. ℞. FORTVNA AVGVST. Fortuna stg. l. . . .   45   85

482   **Domitian,** 81–96. Æ *denarius*. ℞. IMP . XI. COS . XI . CENS . P . P . P.
Minerva fighting.   15   45

483   *Æ dupondius*. ℞. VIRTVTI AVGVSTI. S . C. Virtus stg. r.   20   50

484   **Nerva,** 96–98. Æ *denarius*. ℞. CONCORDIA EXERCITVVM. Clasped
hands.   25   65

485   489

485   **Trajan,** 98–117. Æ *denarius*. ℞. P . M . TR . P . COS . III . P . P. Victory
standing r. on prow   15   35

486   *Æ sestertius*. ℞. S . P . Q . R . OPTIMO PRINCIPI. S . C. Fortuna stg. l..   40   110

487   **Hadrian,** 117–138. Visited Britain *c*. A.D. 122 and constructed his famous
wall from the Tyne to the Solway. Æ *denarius*. ℞. FIDES PVBLICA.
Fides stg. r..   15   40

488   *Æ sestertius*. ℞. ADVENTVI AVG . BRITANNIAE. S . C. Emperor and
Britannia sacrificing over altar . . . . *Extremely rare*

489   — ℞. BRITANNIA. S . C. Britannia seated l. . . . . *Extremely rare*

490   — ℞. EXERC . BRITANNI. S . C. Emperor on horseback addressing
soldiers . . . . *Extremely rare*

491   *Æ as*. ℞. PONT . MAX . TR . POT . COS . III . BRITANNIA. S . C.
Britannia seated l..   120   330

		F £	VF £
492	**Sabina,** wife of Hadrian, Æ *denarius.* ℞. CONCORDIA AVG. Concordia seated l.	25	65
493	**Aelius Caesar,** 136–138. Æ *as.* ℞. TR . POT . COS . II . S . C. Fortuna stg. l.	35	95
494	**Antoninus Pius,** 138–161. His generals in Britain pushed the Roman frontier forward to the Forth–Clyde line (the Antonine Wall). *N aureus.* ℞. IMPERATOR II . BRITAN. Victory stg. on globe.	550	1250
495	Æ *denarius.* ℞. AEQVITAS AVG. Aequitas stg. l..	10	25

496   499

496	Æ *sestertius.* ℞. BRITANNIA. S . C. Britannia seated l. on rocks	350	1000
497	— ℞. IMPERATOR II . BRITAN. S . C. Victory stg. on globe	150	450
498	Æ *as.* ℞. Victory l. holding shield inscribed BRI · TAN	75	225
499	— ℞. BRITANNIA COS . III . S . C. Britannia seated l. in attitude of sadness.	45	135

This coin was very possibly struck at a temporary travelling mint in Britain.

500	**Faustina Senior,** wife of Antoninus Pius, Æ *denarius.* ℞. AVGVSTA. Ceres stg. r.	10	25
501	Æ *sestertius.* ℞. IVNO S . C. Juno stg. l.	18	55
502	**Marcus Aurelius,** 161–180. Æ *denarius.* ℞. COS III. Jupiter seated l.. . .	12	35
503	Æ *sestertius.* ℞. IMP . VI . COS . III. S . C. Roma seated l.	25	80

504   510   515

		F £	VF £
504	**Faustina Junior,** wife of Marcus Aurelius. Æ *denarius*. ℞. IVNONI REGINAE. Juno and peacock	10	25
505	Æ *as*. ℞. DIANA LVCIF . S . C. Diana stg. l.	10	30
506	**Lucius Verus,** 161–169. Æ *denarius*. ℞. CONCORD . AVG . COS . II. Concordia seated l.	20	50
507	**Lucilla,** wife of Lucius Verus. Æ *dupondius*. ℞. SALVS S . C. Salus stg. l..	15	40
508	**Commodus,** 177–192. There was considerable military activity in northern Britain in the early part of his reign. Æ *denarius*. ℞. MARTI VLTORI AVG. Mars stg. l.	15	45
509	Æ *sestertius*. ℞. BRITT . etc. Britannia stg., holding sword and wreath .	*Extremely rare*	
510	— ℞. VICT . BRIT . etc. Victory seated r., inscribing shield	75	225
511	**Crispina,** wife of Commodus, Æ *as*. ℞. IVNO LVCINA S . C. Juno stg. l	18	55
512	**Pertinax,** 193. One time governor of Britain, under Commodus. Æ *denarius*. ℞. LAETITIA TEMPOR COS . II. Laetitia stg. l	250	500
513	**Didius Julianus,** 193. Æ *sestertius*. ℞. CONCORD MILIT S . C. Concordia stg. l.	250	600
514	**Clodius Albinus,** 195–197. Proclaimed emperor while governor of Britain. Æ *denarius*. ℞. MINER . PACIF . COS . II. Minerva stg. l.	45	120
515	**Septimius Severus,** 193–211. Campaigned in Britain with his sons Caracalla and Geta; died at York. Æ *aureus*. ℞. VICTORIAE BRIT. Victory l., holding wreath and palm	850	2500
516	Æ *denarius*. ℞. Similar	25	60
517	— ℞. Similar, but Victory seated l.	25	65
518	— ℞. Similar, but Victory stg. beside palm tree.	30	70
519	— ℞. VIRT . AVG. Roma stg. l.	12	30

520   528

520	Æ *sestertius*. ℞. VICTORIAE BRITTANNICAE S.C. Two Victories affixing shield to palm tree, two captives below.	200	450
521	Æ *dupondius*. ℞. Similar, but Victory inscribing shield on palm tree . . .	85	250
522	Æ *as*. ℞. Similar, Victory stg. r. holding vexillum	85	250
524	**Julia Domna,** wife of Septimius Severus. Æ *denarius*. ℞. PIETAS PVBLICA. Pietas stg. l.	12	25
525	**Caracalla,** 198–217. Personally led the campaign of A.D. 210. Æ *aureus*. ℞. VICTORIAE BRIT. Victory seated l., holding shield	850	2500

		F	VF
		£	£
526	*AV quinarius*. ℞. VICTORIAE BRIT. Victory advancing l., holding wreath and palm	1100	3000
527	*AR denarius*. ℞. MARTI PACATORI. Mars stg. l.	12	30
528	— ℞. VICTORIAE BRIT. Victory advancing l., holding wreath and palm	25	65
529	— ℞. VICTORIAE BRIT. Victory advancing r., holding trophy	25	65
530	*Æ sestertius*. ℞. VICT . BRIT . P . M . TR . P . XIII . COS . III . P . P . S . C. Victory stg. r., erecting trophy	200	450
531	— ℞. VICT . BRIT . etc. Victory inscribing shield on tree.	200	450
532	— ℞. VICTORIAE BRITTANNICAE. S . C. Two Victories erecting shield on tree.	250	500
533	*Æ dupondius*. ℞. VICTORIAE BRITTANNICAE. S . C. Victory seated l., on shields	45	130
534	**Plautilla,** wife of Caracalla. *AR denarius*. ℞. PIETAS AVGG. Pietas stg. r..	20	50
535	**Geta,** 209–212. *AR denarius*. ℞. PONTIF . COS . II. Genius stg. l.	20	50
536	— ℞. VICTORIAE BRIT. Victory advancing r., holding wreath and palm	35	80
537	*Æ sestertius*. ℞. VICTORIAE BRITTANNICAE. S . C. Victory seated r., inscribing shield	250	500

537   541

538	— ℞. VICTORIAE BRITTANNICAE. S . C. Victory standing r., erecting trophy; Britannia stg. facing with hands tied	250	500
538A	**Geta,** 209–212. Billon *tetradrachm* of Alexandria, Egypt. ℞. NEIKH . KATA . BPET. Victory flying l.	300	700
539	**Macrinus,** 217–218. *AR denarius*. ℞. SALVS PVBLICA. Salus seated l., feeding snake	30	75
540	**Diadumenian,** *as Caesar*, 217–218. *AR denarius*. ℞. PRINC IVVENTVTIS. Diadumenian holding sceptre.	80	200
541	**Elagabalus,** 218–222. *AR denarius*. ℞. FIDES MILITVM. Fides stg. l., head r., holding standards	12	35
542	**Julia Paula,** wife of Elagabalus. *AR denarius*. ℞. CONCORDIA. Concordia seated l.	40	90
543	**Aquilia Severa,** wife of Elagabalus. *AR denarius*. ℞. CONCORDIA. Concordia stg. l..	65	140
544	**Julia Soaemias,** mother of Elagabalus. *AR denarius*. ℞. VENVS CAELESTIS. Venus stg. l.	30	65
545	**Julia Maesa,** grandmother of Elagabalus. *AR denarius*. ℞. IVNO. Juno stg. l.	18	40

546 550

	F £	VF £
546 **Severus Alexander**, 222–235. Æ *denarius*. ℞. PAX AVG. Pax advancing l.	12	25
547 Æ *sestertius*. ℞. FIDES MILITVM. S . C. Fides stg l.	15	35
548 **Orbiana**, wife of Severus Alexander. Æ *denarius*. ℞. CONCORDIA AVGG. Concordia seated l.	65	150
549 **Julia Mamaea**, mother of Severus Alexander. Æ *denarius*. ℞. VENVS VICTRIX. Venus stg. l.	12	25
550 **Maximinus I**, 235–238. Æ *denarius*. ℞. PAX AVGVSTI. Pax stg. l.	12	25
551 Æ *sestertius*. ℞. VICTORIA AVG. S . C. Victory advancing r.	18	50
552 **Maximus Caesar**, 235–238. Æ *sestertius*. ℞. PRINCIPI IVVENTVTIS. S . C. Maximus stg. l.	35	95
553 **Balbinus**, 238. Æ *denarius*. ℞. VICTORIA AVGG. Victory stg. l.	75	150
554 **Pupienus**, 238. Æ *denarius*. ℞. PAX PVBLICA. Pax seated l.	75	150
555 **Gordian III**, 238–244. Æ *denarius*. ℞. SALVS AVGVSTI. Salus stg. r. feeding serpent.	12	25
556 Æ *antoninianus*. ℞. ORIENS AVG. Sol stg. l.	8	15
557 Æ *sestertius*. ℞. AEQVITAS AVG. S . C. Aequitas stg. l.	12	25

558 563

558 **Philip I**, 244–249. Æ *antoninianus*. ℞. ROMAE AETERNAE. Roma seated l.	8	16
559 Æ *sestertius*. ℞. SECVRIT. ORBIS S . C. Securitas seated l.	15	35
560 **Otacilia Severa**, wife of Philip I. Æ *antoninianus*. ℞. PIETAS AVGV-STAE. Pietas stg. l.	10	22
561 **Philip II**, 247–249. Æ *antoninianus*. ℞. AETERNIT . IMPER. Sol advancing l.	10	25
562 **Trajan Decius**, 249–251. Æ *antoninianus*. ℞. DACIA. Dacia stg. l.	10	25
563 **Herennia Etruscilla**, wife of Trajan Decius. Æ *antoninianus*. ℞. PVDICI-TIA AVG. Pudicitia stg. l.	10	22
564 **Herennius Etruscus Caesar**, 251. Æ *antoninianus*. ℞. SPES PVBLICA. Spes advancing l.	18	45

	F	VF
	£	£

565   **Hostilian Caesar,** 251. Æ *antoninianus.* ℞. PIETAS AVGVSTORVM.
Sacrificial implements   25   65

566   **Trebonianus Gallus,** 251–253. Æ *antoninianus.* ℞. LIBERTAS AVGG.
Libertas stg. l.   8   22

567   **Volusian,** 251–253. Æ *antoninianus.* ℞. CONCORDIA AVGG. Concordia
seated l.   8   22

568   **Aemilian,** 252–253. Æ *antoninianus.* ℞. PACI AVG. Pax stg. l.   45   95

569   **Valerian I,** 253–260. Billon *antoninianus.* ℞. VICTORIA AVGG. Victory
stg. l.   5   10

570   576

570   **Gallienus,** 253–268. Æ *antoninianus.* ℞. DIANAE CONS . AVG. Antelope   3   8

571   **Salonina,** wife of Gallienus. Æ *antoninianus.* ℞. PIETAS AVG. Pietas stg.
l.   3   8

572   Valerian II Caesar, 253–255. Billon *antoninianus.* ℞. PIETAS AVGG.
Sacrificial implements   7   20

573   **Saloninus Caesar,** 259. Billon *antoninianus.* ℞. SPES PVBLICA. Spes
advancing l.   7   20

574   **Macrianus,** usurper in the East, 260–261. Billon *antoninianus.* ℞. SOL.
INVICTO. Sol stg. l.   30   80

575   **Quietus,** usurper in the East, 260–261. Billon *antoninianus.* ℞. ROMAE
AETERNAE. Roma seated l.   30   80

576   **Postumus,** usurper in the West, 259–268. Æ *antoninianus.* ℞. MONETA
AVG. Moneta stg. l.   5   15

577   **Laelianus,** usurper in the West, 268. Æ *antoninianus.* ℞. VICTORIA AVG.
Victory advancing r..   85   220

578   **Marius,** usurper in the West, 268. Æ *antoninianus.* ℞. VICTORIA AVG.
Victory advancing r..   30   70

579   **Victorinus,** usurper in the West, 268–270. Æ *aureus.* ℞. LEG . XX . VAL .
VICTRIX. Boar l   3,500   10,000

580   Æ *antoninianus.* ℞. SALVS AVG. Salus stg. l.   4   10

581   **Claudius II Gothicus,** 268–270. Æ *antoninianus.* ℞. MARTI PACIF. Mars
advancing l.   4   10

582   **Tetricus I,** usurper in the West, 270–273. Æ *antoninianus.* LAETITIA
AVG. Laetitia stg. l..   4   10

583   **Tetricus II Caesar,** usurper in the West, 270–273. Æ *antoninianus.* ℞. SPES
AVGG. Spes advancing l..   4   12

584A   584B   584C

		F £	VF £

584 **Barbarous radiates.** British and Continental copies of Æ *antoniniani*,
mostly of Claudius II (A), Tetricus I (B) and Tetricus II (C)   2   5
585 **Quintillus,** 270. Æ *antoninianus.* R̸. FIDES MILIT. Fides stg. l..   12   30
586 **Aurelian,** 270–275. Æ *antoninianus.* R̸. SECVRIT . AVG. Securitas stg. l..   5   12

587   596

587 **Severina,** wife of Aurelian. Æ *antoninianus.* R̸. PROVIDEN . DEOR.
Fides and Sol stg.   10   25
588 **Tacitus,** 275–276. Æ *antoninianus.* R̸. CLEMENTIA TEMP. Clementia
stg. l..   7   20
589 **Florianus,** 276. Æ *antoninianus.* R̸. SALVS AVG. Salus stg. l..   20   60
590 **Probus,** 276–282. Æ *antoninianus.* R̸. ABVNDANTIA AVG. Abundantia
stg. r..   5   12
591 **Carus,** 282–283. Æ *antoninianus.* R̸. PAX EXERCITI. Pax stg. l..   10   28
592 **Numerian,** 283–284. Æ *antoninianus.* R̸. ORIENS AVG. Sol advancing l..   10   25
593 **Carinus,** 283–285. Æ *antoninianus.* R̸. AETERNIT . AVG. Aeternitas stg.
l..   8   20
594 **Diocletian,** 284–305, London mint reopened *c.* 297. Æ *argenteus.* R̸.
VIRTVS MILITVM. Tetrarchs sacrificing before camp gate   80   220
595 Æ *antoninianus.* R̸. CLEMENTIA TEMP. Diocletian and Jupiter stg. . .   4   12
596 Æ *follis.* R̸. GENIO POPVLI ROMANI. Genius stg. l., LON (London)
mm..   8   28

597   600

Diocletian *continued*

		F £	VF £

597 Æ *follis*. ℞. Similar, no *mm*. (London) 8 25

598 — ℞. Similar, other *mms*.. . . . . 6 20

599 **Maximianus,** 286–310. Æ *argenteus*. ℞. VIRTVS MILITVM. Tetrarchs
sacrificing before camp gate 65 180

600 Æ *antoninianus*. ℞. SALVS AVGG. Salus stg. l. 4 12

601 Æ *follis*. ℞. GENIO POPVLI ROMANI. Genius stg. l., LON. *mm*. 10 30

602 — ℞. Similar, no *mm*.. . . . . 7 24

603 **Carausius,** commander of the Roman Channel fleet, who took power in
Britain and Northern Gaul, 287–293. *London mint* Æ *aureus*. ℞. PAX
AVG. Pax stg. l., no *mm*.. . . . . 7500 17500

604 623

604 Æ *denarius*. ℞. CONSER AVG. Neptune seated l. 550 1500

605 Æ *antoninianus*. ℞. ADVENTVS AVG. Emperor riding l.. . . . . 55 160

606 — ℞. COHR . PRAEF. Four standards 70 200

607 — ℞. COMES AVG. Victory stg. l. 25 70

608 — ℞. CONCORD . EXERCI. Four standards 40 120

609 — ℞. CONCORDIA MILITVM. Clasped hands. 40 120

610 — ℞. CONSERVAT . AVG. Sol stg. l. 55 160

611 — ℞. FELICIT . TEMP. Felicitas stg. l. 25 70

612 — ℞. FIDES MILITVM. Fides stg. l.. . . . . 55 160

613 — ℞. FORTVNA AVG. Fortuna stg. l.. 20 55

614 — ℞. GENIVS AVG. Genius stg. l. 55 160

615 — ℞. GERMANICVS MAX . V. Trophy between captives 130 360

616 — ℞. LAETITIA AVG. Laetitia stg. l. 20 55

617 — ℞. LEG . II . AVG. Capricorn l.. . . . . 55 160

618 — ℞. LEG XX . V . V. Boar r. 65 175

619 — ℞. MARS VLTOR. Mars walking r.. 55 160

620 — ℞. MONETA AVG. Moneta stg. l.. . . . . 20 55

621 — ℞. ORIENS AVG. Sol walking r. 25 70

622 Æ *antoninianus*. ℞. PACATOR ORBIS. Bust of Sol r.. . . . . 95 280

623 — ℞. PAX AVG. Pax stg. l. 16 50

624 — ℞. PIAETAS AVG. Pietas sacrificing at altar 25 70

625 — ℞. SALVS AVG. Salus feeding serpent 20 55

626 — ℞. SECVRIT . PERP. Securitas stg. l. 25 70

627 — ℞. VICTORIA AVG. Victory walking r. 25 70

628   643

	F £	VF £
628 Æ *antoninianus*. Struck in the name of Diocletian. ℟. PAX AVGGG. Pax stg. l.	20	60
629 Æ *antoninianus*. Struck in the name of Maximianus. ℟. PROVIDENTIA AVG. Providentia stg. l.	20	60
630 *Colchester or Clausentum mint.* Æ *denarius.* ℟. CONCORDIA MILITVM. Clasped hands	350	1000
631 Æ *antoninianus*. ℟. ABVNDANTIA AVG. Abundantia stg. l.	25	70
632 — ℟. APOLINI CON . AV. Griffin walking r.	90	240
633 — ℟. CONCORDIA AVGGG. Two emperors stg.	110	320
634 — ℟. CONSTANT . AVG. Nude male stg. r.	55	160
635 — ℟. EXPECTATE VENI. Britannia stg. r.	90	240
636 — ℟. FELICITAS AVG. Galley.	40	120
637 — ℟. GENIO BRITANNI. Genius stg. l.	120	340
638 — ℟. HILARITAS AVG. Hilaritas stg. l.	20	55
639 — ℟. IOVI CONSERV. Jupiter stg. l.	25	70
640 — ℟. LEG. I. MIN. Ram stg. r.	55	160
641 — ℟. LIBERALITAS AVG. Carausius seated with subordinates	70	200
642 — ℟. PAX AVG. Pax stg. l.	20	55
643 — ℟. PROVID . AVG. Providentia stg. l.	20	60
644 — ℟. RENOVAT . ROMA. She-wolf suckling Romulus and Remus.	65	175
645 — ℟. RESTIT . SAECVL. Carausius and Victory stg.	65	175
646 — ℟. ROMAE AETER. Roma seated l.	28	72
647 — ℟. SAECVLARES AVG. Lion walking r.	55	160
648 — ℟. SOLI INVICTE. Sol in quadriga	55	168
649 — ℟. SPES PVBLICA. Spes walking r.	20	60
650 — ℟. TEMP . FELICIT. Felicitas stg. l.	20	60
651 — ℟. VIRTVS AVG. Mars stg. r.	20	55
651A Æ *antoninianus*. Struck in the name of Diocletian. ℟. PAX AVGGG. Pax stg. l.	20	60
652 Æ *antoninianus*. Struck in the name of Maximianus. ℟. PAX AVGGG. Pax stg. l.	20	60

653   662

		F £	VF £
653	**Carausius, Diocletian and Maximianus.** Æ *antoninianus*. Struck by Carausius. CARAVSIVS ET FRATRES SVI. Jugate busts of three emperors l. ℞. PAX AVGGG. Pax stg. l.	600	1750
654	**Allectus,** chief minister and murderer of Carausius, 293–296. *London mint.* A/ *aureus*. ℞. PAX AVG. Pax stg. l.	7500	20,000
655	Æ *antoninianus*. ℞. AEQVITAS AVG. Aequitas stg. l.	25	65
656	— ℞. COMES AVG. Minerva stg. l.	25	65
657	— ℞. FORTVNA AVG. Fortuna seated l.	55	160
658	— ℞. HILARITAS AVG. Hilaritas stg. l.	20	60
659	— ℞. LAETITIA AVG. Laetitia stg. l.	28	70
660	— ℞. LEG . II. Lion walking l.	150	400
661	— ℞. ORIENS AVG. Sol stg. l.	60	175
662	— ℞. PAX AVG. Pax stg. l.	30	70
663	— ℞. PIETAS AVG. Pietas stg. l.	25	65
664	— ℞. PROVIDENTIA AVG. Providentia stg. l.	40	80
665	— ℞. SAECVLI FELICITAS. Emperor stg. r.	65	150
666	— ℞. SALVS AVG. Salus feeding serpent	25	65
667	— ℞. SPES PVPLICA. Spes holding flower	25	60
668	— ℞. TEMPORVM FELICI. Felicitas stg. l.	25	60
669	— ℞. VICTORIA AVG. Victory stg. r.	25	60
670	— ℞. VIRTVS AVG. Mars stg. r.	25	65
671	Æ *quinarius*. ℞. VIRTVS AVG. Galley	25	65
672	*Colchester or Clausentum mint.* Æ *antoninianus*. ℞. ABVND . AVG. Abundantia stg. l.	30	70
673	— ℞. ADVENTVS AVG. Emperor riding l.	90	220
674	— ℞. DIANAE REDVCI. Diana leading stag	70	180
675	— ℞. FELICITAS SAECVLI. Felicitas stg. l.	70	180
676	— ℞. FIDES EXERCITVS. Four standards	65	150
677	— ℞. IOVI CONSERVATORI. Jupiter stg. l.	70	180

678   681

678	— ℞. MONETA AVG. Moneta stg. l.	30	85
679	— ℞. PAX AVG. Pax stg. l.	28	70
680	— ℞. ROMAE AETERN. Roma in temple.	75	200
681	Æ *quinarius*. ℞. LAETITIA AVG. Galley.	30	70
682	— ℞. VIRTVS AVG. Galley	30	70

683   698

		F £	VF £
683	**Constantius I,** Caesar 293–305. Augustus 305–306, campaigned in Britain and died at York. Æ *follis.* R̟. GENIO POPVLI ROMANI. Genius stg. l., no *mm.*	9	28
684	Æ *follis.* R̟. MEMORIA FELIX. Eagles beside altar. PLN. *mm.*	8	25
685	Æ *radiate.* R̟. CONCORDIA MILITVM. Constantius and Jupiter stg.	7	20
686	**Galerius,** Caesar 293–305, Augustus 305–311. Æ *follis.* R̟. GENIO IMPERATORIS. Genius stg. l.	5	12
687	— R̟. GENIO POPVLI ROMANI. Genius stg. l., no *mm.*	6	16
688	**Galeria Valeria,** wife of Galerius. Æ *follis.* R̟. VENERI VICTRICI. Venus stg. l.	25	70
689	**Severus II,** 306–307. Æ *follis.* R̟. FIDES MILITVM. Fides seated l.	25	70
690	Æ *follis.* R̟. GENIO POPVLI ROMANI. Genius stg. l., no *mm.*	28	75
691	Æ *radiate.* R̟. CONCORDIA MILITVM. Severus and Jupiter stg.	20	55
692	**Maximinus II,** 309–313. Æ *follis.* R̟. GENIO AVGVSTI. Genius stg. l.	4	12
693	— R̟. GENIO POP . ROM. Genius stg. l., PLN. *mm.*	7	20
694	**Maxentius,** 306–312, Æ *follis.* R̟. CONSERV . VRB SVAE. Roma in temple	7	20
695	**Licinius I,** 308–324. Æ *follis.* R̟. GENIO POP . ROM. Genius stg. l., PLN. *mm.*	5	15
696	Æ 3. R̟. SOLI INVICTO COMITI. Sol stg. l.	3	8
697	**Licinius II Caesar,** 317–324. Æ 3. R̟. PROVIDENTIAE CAESS. Camp gate	4	12
698	**Constantine I, the Great,** 307–337. Came to power in Britain following his father's death at York. London mint closed 325. Æ *follis.* R̟. SOLI INVICTO COMITI. Sol stg. l., PLN *mm.*	8	25
699	Æ 3. R̟. BEATA TRANQVILLITAS. Altar. PLON *mm.*	4	12
700	Æ 3. R̟. VOT . XX. in wreath	2	5

701

701	**Commemorative issues,** Æ 3/4, commencing A.D. 330. Bust of Roma. R̟. She-wolf suckling Romulus and Remus	3	6
702	Æ 3/4. Bust of Constantinopolis. R̟. Victory stg. l.	3	6
703	**Fausta,** wife of Constantine. Æ 3. R̟. SPES REIPVBLICAE. Fausta stg.	8	25
704	— R̟. Similar. PLON *mm.*	45	120

		F	VF
		£	£
705	**Helena,** mother of Constantine. Æ 3. R. SECVRITAS REIPVBLICE. Helena stg. l.	10	25
706	— R. Similar. PLON *mm.*	35	100

707   714

707	**Theodora,** second wife of Constantius I, struck after her death. Æ 4. R. PIETAS ROMANA. Pietas holding child	5	15
708	**Crispus Caesar,** 317–326. Æ 3. R. CAESARVM NOSTRORVM VOT . V. Wreath	3	10
709	— R. PROVIDENTIAE CAESS. Camp gate. PLON *mm.*	5	12
710	**Delmatius Caesar,** 335–337. Æ 3. R. GLORIA EXERCITVS. Two soldiers stg.	10	25
711	**Hanniballianus Rex,** 335–337. Æ 4. R. SECVRITAS PVBLICA. Euphrates reclining	85	200
712	**Constantine II Caesar,** 317–337. Æ 3. R. BEAT . TRANQLITAS. Altar. PLON *mm.*.	5	12
713	Æ 3/4. R. GLORIA EXERCITVS. Two soldiers stg.	7	20
714	**Constans,** 337–350. Visited Britain in 343. Æ *centenionalis.* R. FEL . TEMP . REPARATIO. Constans stg. on galley	5	12

715   723   733   741

715	**Constantius II,** 337–361. Æ *centenionalis.* R. FEL . TEMP . REPARATIO. Soldier spearing fallen horseman.	4	10
716	Æ 3. R. PROVIDENTIAE CAESS. Camp gate. PLON *mm.*	30	60
717	**Magnentius,** usurper in the West, 350–353. Æ *centenionalis.* R. VICTOR- IAE DD . NN. AVG . ET CAE. Two Victories.	10	20

F	*VF*
£	£

718 **Decentius Caesar,** usurper in the West, 351–353. Æ *centenionalis.* R̥.
VICTORIAE DD . NN . AVG . ET . CAE. Two Victories   12   30

719 **Constantius Gallus Caesar,** 351–354. Æ *centenionalis.* R̥. FEL . TEMP
REPARATIO. Soldier spearing fallen horseman   8   22

720 **Julian II,** 360–363. Æ *siliqua.* R̥. VOT . X . MVLT . XX with wreath . .   25   55

721 Æ 3. R̥ Similar.   10   20

722 **Jovian,** 363–364. Æ 3. R̥. VOT . V . within wreath   25   55

723 **Valentinian I,** 364–375. Æ 3. R̥. SECVRITAS REIPVBLICAE. Victory
advancing l.   4   10

724 **Valens,** 364–378. Æ *siliqua.* R̥. VRBS ROMA. Roma seated l.   20   45

725 Æ 3. R̥. GLORIA ROMANORVM. Valens dragging captive.   4   10

726 **Gratian,** 367–383. Æ *siliqua.* R̥. VRBS ROMA. Roma seated l.   25   55

727 Æ 3. R̥. CONCORDIA AVGGG. Constantinopolis seated l.   7   18

728 **Valentinian II,** 375–392. Æ *siliqua.* R̥. VICTORIA AVGGG. Victory
advancing l.   30   65

729 Æ 2. R̥. GLORIA ROMANORVM. Valentinian stg. on galley.   9   22

730 Æ 4. R̥. SALVS REIPVBLICAE. Victory advancing l.   3   10

731 **Theodosius I,** 379–395. Æ 2. R̥. GLORIA ROMANORVM. Theodosius
stg. on galley.   9   22

732 Æ 4. R̥. SALVS REIPVBLICAE. Victory advancing l.   2   8

733 **Magnus Maximus,** usurper in the West, 383–388, proclaimed emperor by
the Roman army in Britain, N *solidus.* R̥. VICTORIA AVGG. Two
emperors seated. Victory between them; AVGOB *mm.* (London)   2750   8000

734 Æ *siliqua.* R̥. VICTORIA AVGG. Victory advancing l. AVGPS *mm.*
(London).   225   600

735 — R̥. VIRTVS ROMANORVM. Roma seated l..   25   65

736 **Flavius Victor,** usurper in the West, 387–388. Æ 4. R̥. SPES ROMA-
NORVM. Camp gate   25   55

737 **Eugenius,** usurper in the West, 392–394. Æ *siliqua.* R̥. VIRTVS ROMA-
NORVM. Roma seated l..   90   250

738 **Arcadius,** 383–408. Æ 2. R̥. GLORIA ROMANORVM. Arcadius stg. r..   9   22

739 **Honorius,** 393–423, during whose reign the so-called "Roman withdrawal"
from Britain took place. Æ *siliqua.* R̥. VIRTVS ROMANORVM. Roma
seated l.   25   65

740 Æ 3. R̥. VIRTVS EXERCITI. Honorius stg. r..   7   20

741 **Constantine III,** usurper in the West, proclaimed emperor in Britain, 407–
411. Æ *siliqua.* R̥. VICTORIA AVGGGG. Roma seated l.   100   300

742 **Valentinian III,** 425–455, during whose reign the last vestiges of Roman
rule in Britain disappeared. Æ 4. R̥. VOT . PVB. Camp gate   18   50

EARLY ANGLO-SAXON PERIOD, c. 600–c. 775

The withdrawal of Roman forces from Britain early in the 5th century A.D. and the gradual decline of central administration resulted in a rapid deterioration of the money supply. The arrival of Teutonic raiders and settlers hastened the decay of urban commercial life and it was probably not until late in the 6th century that renewed political, cultural and commercial links with the kingdom of the Merovingian Franks led to the appearance of small quantities of Merovingian gold *tremisses* (one-third solidus) in England. A purse containing such pieces was found in the Sutton Hoo ship-burial. Native Anglo-Saxon gold *thrymsas* were minted from about the 630s, initially in the style of their continental prototpyes or copied from obsolete Roman coinage and later being made in pure Anglo-Saxon style. By the middle of the 7th century the gold coinage was being increasingly debased with silver, and gold had been superseded entirely by about 675.

These silver coins, contemporary with the *deniers* or *denarii* of the Merovingian Franks, are the first English pennies, though they are commonly known today as *sceattas* (a term more correctly translated as "treasure" or "wealth"). They provide important material for the student of Anglo-Saxon art.

Though the earliest sceattas are a transition from the gold thrymsa coinage, coins of new style were soon developed which were also copied by the Frisians of the Low Countries. Early coins appear to have a standard weight of 20 grains (1.29 gms) and are of good silver content, though the quality deteriorates early in the 8th century. These coins exist in a large number of varied types, and as well as the official issues there are mules and other varieties which are probably contemporary imitations. Many of the sceattas were issued during the reign of Aethelbald of Mercia, but as few bear inscriptions it is only in recent years that research has permitted their correct dating and the attribution of certain types to specific areas. Some silver sceats of groups II and III and most types of groups IV to X were issued during the period (A.D. 716–757) when Aethelbald, King of Mercia, was overlord of the southern English. In Northumbria very debased sceattas or *stycas* continued to be issued until the middle of the ninth century. Though a definitive classification has not yet been developed, the arrangement given below follows the latest work on the series: this list is not exhaustive.

The reference "*B.M.C.*" is to the type given in *British Museum Catalogue: Anglo-Saxon Coins*, and *not* the item number.

North, J. J. *English Hammered Coinage*, Vol. 1, *c.* 650–1272 (1980).
Metcalf, D. M. "A stylistic analysis of the 'porcupine' sceattas". *Num. Chron.*, 7th ser., Vol. VI (1966).
Rigold, S. E. "The two primary series of sceattas", *B.N.J.*, xxx (1960).
Sutherland, C. H. V. *Anglo-Saxon Gold Coinage in the light of the Crondall Hoard* (1948).

ᚠ ᚪ Þ ᚻ ᚱ ᚲ · Χ ᚹ ᚺ ᚾ Ι Ϙ Ʃ Ɫ ᚤ ᛉ Ꞇ ᛒ Ϻ ᚻ Γ Ⴟ ᚻ ᚶ Ϝ Ꞙ Ʌ

f u th o r k · z w h n i j ih p x s t b e m l ng d œ a æ ea y

Early Anglo-Saxon Runes

GOLD

A. Anglo-Merovingian types

751	**Thrymsa** (*c.* 1.32 gms). Name and portrait of Bishop Leudard (chaplain to Q. Bertha of Kent). ℞. Cross. *N. 1.*	*Unique*
752	*Canterbury*. Bust r., moneyer's name. ℞. Cross, mint name. *N. 2*	*Extremely rare*

753	762	763

753	No mint name. Bust l. ℞. Cross. *N. 3–5, 7*	*Extremely rare*
754	Bust r. ℞. Cross. *N. 6–9, 12*	*Extremely rare*
755	Cross both sides. *N. 10*	*Extremely rare*
756	Bust r. ℞. Cross, runic letters, *N. 11*	*Extremely rare*

B. **Roman derivatives**

	F	VF
	£	£

757	**Solidus.** Bust r. copied from 4th cent. solidus. ℞. Various. *N. 13, 14* . . .		*Extremely rare*
758	— Runic inscription on reverse. *N. 15*		*Extremely rare*
759	**Thrymsa.** Radiate bust. r. ℞. Clasped hands. *N. 16.*		*Extremely rare*
760	Bust r., hands raised to cross. ℞. Camp gate. *N. 17*	1250	2500
761	Helmeted bust r. ℞. Cross, runic inscription. *N. 18.*	—	6500
762	Diad. bust r. ℞. "Standard", TOV / XX in centre. *N. 19. M.* —		*Extremely rare*
763	— Similar. ℞. Victory protecting "two emperors". *N. 20*	1250	2500

C. **"London" and derived issues**

764   765   767

764	**Thrymsa.** Facing bust, no legend. ℞. Greek cross, LONDVNIV. *N. 21.* .
765	Head r. or l. ℞. Plain cross, legend jumbled. *N. 22–24* . . . .

Extremely rare
Extremely rare

D. **"Witmen" group**

766	**Thrymsa.** Bust r. with trident centre. ℞. Cross with forked limbs, moneyer's name. *N. 25*		*Extremely rare*
767	— Similar, but blundered legend on reverse, *N. 25 var.*	1500	3000
768	— ℞. Cross potent. *N. 26.*	1500	3000

E. **"York" group**

769   771   772

769	**Thrymsa.** Three crosses with geometric squared design below. ℞. Small cross. *N. 27*		*Extremely rare*

F. **"Regal" coinages**

770	**Solidus** (4.12 gms). Diad.. bust r., moneyer's name around. ℞. Cross potent on steps. *N. 28.*		*Extremely rare*
771	**Thrymsa.** Diad. bust r., AVDVARLD REGES. ℞. Orb with cross, moneyer's name. *N. 29*	2000	4000
772	Diad. bust l., moneyer's name around. ℞. Cross and pellets, legend of Xs. *N. 30*		*Extremely rare*
773	Diad. bust r. ℞. Cross botonée, PADA in runes. *N. 31*	1650	3250

EARLY ANGLO-SAXON PERIOD, *c.* 600–*c.* 775

The withdrawal of Roman forces from Britain early in the 5th century A.D. and the gradual decline of central administration resulted in a rapid deterioration of the money supply. The arrival of Teutonic raiders and settlers hastened the decay of urban commercial life and it was probably not until late in the 6th century that renewed political, cultural and commercial links with the kingdom of the Merovingian Franks led to the appearance of small quantities of Merovingian gold *tremisses* (one-third solidus) in England. A purse containing such pieces was found in the Sutton Hoo ship-burial. Native Anglo-Saxon gold *thrymsas* were minted from about the 630s, initially in the style of their continental prototpyes or copied from obsolete Roman coinage and later being made in pure Anglo-Saxon style. By the middle of the 7th century the gold coinage was being increasingly debased with silver, and gold had been superseded entirely by about 675.

These silver coins, contemporary with the *deniers* or *denarii* of the Merovingian Franks, are the first English pennies, though they are commonly known today as *sceattas* (a term more correctly translated as "treasure" or "wealth"). They provide important material for the student of Anglo-Saxon art.

Though the earliest sceattas are a transition from the gold thrymsa coinage, coins of new style were soon developed which were also copied by the Frisians of the Low Countries. Early coins appear to have a standard weight of 20 grains (1.29 gms) and are of good silver content, though the quality deteriorates early in the 8th century. These coins exist in a large number of varied types, and as well as the official issues there are mules and other varieties which are probably contemporary imitations. Many of the sceattas were issued during the reign of Aethelbald of Mercia, but as few bear inscriptions it is only in recent years that research has permitted their correct dating and the attribution of certain types to specific areas. Some silver sceats of groups II and III and most types of groups IV to X were issued during the period (A.D. 716–757) when Aethelbald, King of Mercia, was overlord of the southern English. In Northumbria very debased sceattas or *stycas* continued to be issued until the middle of the ninth century. Though a definitive classification has not yet been developed, the arrangement given below follows the latest work on the series: this list is not exhaustive.

The reference "*B.M.C.*" is to the type given in *British Museum Catalogue: Anglo-Saxon Coins*, and *not* the item number.

North, J. J. *English Hammered Coinage*, Vol. 1, *c.* 650–1272 (1980).
Metcalf, D. M. "A stylistic analysis of the 'porcupine' sceattas". *Num. Chron.*, 7th ser., Vol. VI (1966).
Rigold, S. E. "The two primary series of sceattas", *B.N.J.*, xxx (1960).
Sutherland, C. H. V. *Anglo-Saxon Gold Coinage in the light of the Crondall Hoard* (1948).

f u th o r k · z w h n i j ih p x s t b e m l ng d œ a æ ea y

Early Anglo-Saxon Runes

GOLD

A. Anglo-Merovingian types

751 **Thrymsa** (*c.* 1.32 gms). Name and portrait of Bishop Leudard (chaplain to Q. Bertha of Kent). R̟. Cross. *N. 1.* . . . . *Unique*

752 *Canterbury.* Bust r., moneyer's name. R̟. Cross, mint name. *N. 2* . . . . . *Extremely rare*

753   762   763

753 No mint name. Bust l. R̟. Cross. *N. 3–5, 7* . . . . *Extremely rare*
754 Bust r. R̟. Cross. *N. 6–9, 12* . . . . *Extremely rare*
755 Cross both sides. *N. 10* . . . . *Extremely rare*
756 Bust r. R̟. Cross, runic letters, *N. 11* . . . . *Extremely rare*

B. **Roman derivatives**

		F	VF
		£	£
757	**Solidus.** Bust r. copied from 4th cent. solidus. ℞. Various. *N. 13, 14* . . .	*Extremely rare*	
758	— Runic inscription on reverse. *N. 15*	*Extremely rare*	
759	**Thrymsa.** Radiate bust. r. ℞. Clasped hands. *N. 16*	*Extremely rare*	
760	Bust r., hands raised to cross. ℞. Camp gate. *N. 17*	1250	2500
761	Helmeted bust r. ℞. Cross, runic inscription. *N. 18*	—	6500
762	Diad. bust r. ℞. "Standard", TOV / XX in centre. *N. 19. M.* —	*Extremely rare*	
763	— Similar. ℞. Victory protecting "two emperors". *N. 20*	1250	2500

C. **"London" and derived issues**

764   765   767

| 764 | **Thrymsa.** Facing bust, no legend. ℞. Greek cross, LONDVNIV. *N. 21.* . | *Extremely rare* | |
| 765 | Head r. or l. ℞. Plain cross, legend jumbled. *N. 22–24* . . . . | *Extremely rare* | |

D. **"Witmen" group**

766	**Thrymsa.** Bust r. with trident centre. ℞. Cross with forked limbs, moneyer's name. *N. 25*	*Extremely rare*	
767	— Similar, but blundered legend on reverse, *N. 25 var.*	1500	3000
768	— ℞. Cross potent. *N. 26*	1500	3000

E. **"York" group**

769   771   772

| 769 | **Thrymsa.** Three crosses with geometric squared design below. ℞. Small cross. *N. 27* . . . . | *Extremely rare* | |

F. **"Regal" coinages**

770	**Solidus** (4.12 gms). Diad.. bust r., moneyer's name around. ℞. Cross potent on steps. *N. 28*	*Extremely rare*	
771	**Thrymsa.** Diad. bust r., AVDVARLD REGES. ℞. Orb with cross, moneyer's name. *N. 29*	2000	4000
772	Diad. bust l., moneyer's name around. ℞. Cross and pellets, legend of Xs. *N. 30*	*Extremely rare*	
773	Diad. bust r. ℞. Cross botonée, PADA in runes. *N. 31*	1650	3250

	F £	VF £

Miscellaneous issues

774	**Thrymsa.** Crude bust r. ℞. Standing figure with arms outstretched. *N. 33*	*Extremely rare*
775	Crude bust or head r. ℞. Various. *N. 35, 38*	*Extremely rare*
776	Forked cross both sides, and other types. *N. 36, 37, 39*	*Extremely rare*

SILVER

I. **Transitional types struck in silver,** by thrymsa moneyers, *c.* 675–690

779   780   781

777	**Sceat.** *Kentish.* As 773, diad. bust r. ℞. *Pada* in runes across field. *N. 152*	600	1250
778	— Obv. Similar. ℞. Cross on steps. *B.M.C. type 2*	*Extremely rare*	
778A	As 763. ℞. Victory over two emperors. *B.M.C. 1*	*Extremely rare*	
779	— Diad. bust r., TNC to r. ℞. Cross with annulet in each angle, *Pada* in runes in legend. *B.M.C. 3*	600	1250
780	— "*Varimundus*". As 761, helmeted bust r. with sceptre. ℞. Cross pattée, TmVNVmVC, etc. *Rigold VB, 4–9*	650	1350

II. **Primary Sceattas,** *c.* 690–725

783   785   786

781	Series A, *Kentish.* Radiate bust r., usually of good style, TIC to r. ℞. "Standard". *B.M.C. 2a*	65	150
782	Series B, *Kentish.* Diad. bust r. ℞. Bird above cross on steps. *B.M.C. 26* .	100	225
783	— Diad. head r. within serpent-circle or bust r. ℞. Bird above cross and two annulets, serpent-circle around. *B.M.C. 27a*	65	150
784	— (Bz.) Diad. head r. of poorer style. ℞. Bird and cross larger and cruder. *B.M.C. 27b* (see also 791).	85	200
785	Series C, *East Anglian (?) Runic.* Radiate bust r. somewhat as 781. *Epa* (etc.) in runes to r. ℞. Neat "Standard" type. *B.M.C. 2b; Rigold R1* (see also 832, and for Frisian copies nos. 839 and 840)	60	100
786	Early "*porcupines*". Porcupine-like figure, body with annulet at one end, triangle at other. ℞. "Standard" with four pellets around central annulet. *Metcalf D*	45	90

787   789   790

	F £	VF £
787 — "Porcupine" has insect-like body with fore-leg. ℞. "Standard" with four lines and central annulet.. *Metcalf G*	40	75
788 — "Porcupine" with parallel lines in curve of body. ℞. "Standard" with VOIC-like symbols (and rarely with 5 crosses on *rev.*)	35	65
789 — Figure developed into plumed bird. ℞. "Standard" has groups of triple pellets. *B.M.C. type 6*	70	150
790 *Slightly later "porcupines" of reduced weight.* As 788 but various symbols in "standard" (some varieties are Frisian imitations—see 841–2 below) .	40	75

SILVER

III.   **"Mercian" types,** *c.* 705–730. More than one mint, possibly including London; the fineness dropping from good silver to under .500.

791   792   793

	F	VF
791 Derivative of 784, but bird and cross larger and cruder, no serpent circles. *B.M.C. 27b.*	75	175
792 Two heads face-to-face, cross with trident base between. ℞. Four birds clockwise around cross. *B.M.C. 37.*	100	250
793 Man holding two crosses. ℞. Bird and branch. *B.M.C. 23b*	125	250
794 Diad. bust r. with bird or cross. ℞. Hound and tree. *B.M.C. 42.*	150	400
795 Diad. bust r. with chalice. ℞. Man standing with cross and bird. *B.M.C. 20.*	125	275
796 Diad. bust r. with cross. ℞. Wolf curled head to tail. *B.M.C. 32a.*	125	275
797 — Similar, but wolf-headed serpent	125	275
798 — Similar, but wolf-serpent within torque. *B.M.C. 32b*	125	275
799 — Similar, but wolf's head r. or l. with long tongue. *B.M.C. 33.*	175	400
800 — Obv. Similar. ℞. Celtic cross or shield. *B.M.C. 34*	125	275

IV.   **Types of similar style or finess,** *of uncertain political attribution*

800A Kneeling archer r., tree behind. ℞. Bird on branch r., head turned l. *B.M.C. —*	*Extremely rare*	
801 As 791, but cross before head. ℞. Large and small bird. *B.M.C. 36.* . . .	200	400
802 Bust r., lettering around or with cable border. ℞. Bird r. in torque. *B.M.C. 38*	175	350
803 Bust l. within cable border. ℞. Man with two crosses. *B.M.C. 21*	200	400
804 Facing bust. ℞. Interlaced cruciform pattern, *B.M.C. 52.*	325	700

797   805   806

		F £	VF £

V. South Wessex types, *c.* 725–750. Found predominantly in excavations at Hamwic (Southampton)

805 Scutiform design (shield with bosses). ℞. Bird and branch as 794. *B.M.C. type 39* 120   200
806 Jewel-head, roundels around. ℞. Bird and branch. *B.M.C. 49.* 125   250
807 Scutiform design. ℞. Wolf-head whorl. *B.M.C. 48* 125   250

VI. South Saxon types, *c.* 720–750

808 Diad. bust r. cross before. ℞. "Standard". *B.M.C. 3a* 125   250
809 — Similar but crude style and of very base silver. 80   150

808   815   816

VII. "Dragon" types, *c.* 725–735?

810 Two standing figures, long cross between. ℞. Monster looking back to r. or l. *B.M.C. type 41b* 175   350
811 One standing figure, cross either side. ℞. As last. *B.M.C. 23a and 40* . . . 175   350
812 Four interlaced shields. ℞. As last. *B.M.C. 43* 175   350
813 Bust r., cross before. ℞. As last. *N. 114* . . . . *Extremely rare*
814 Wolf's head facing. ℞. As last. *N. 122.* 350   700
815 Wolf and twins. ℞. Bird in vine. *B.M.C. 7* 200   400
816 Diad. bust r. + LEV. ℞. "Porcupine" l. *B.M.C. 9.* 175   450
817 Facing head. ℞. Fantastic animal r. or l. *N. 143–146.* 250   625

VIII. "London issue" *of around .400 silver content or less, c.* 740–750

818 Diad. bust r., LVNDONIA (sometimes blundered). ℞. Man holding two long crosses. *B.M.C. type 12* 400   700
819 — Obv. As last. ℞. "Porcupine" to l. *B.M.C. 12/15* 350   800
820 — Obv. As last. ℞. Seated figure r. holding sceptre. *B.M.C. 13* . . . . . . *Unique*
821 — Obv. As last but bust l. ℞. Scutiform design. *B.M.C. 14* 300   650
822 Diad. bust r. with cross, no legend. ℞. As 818. *B.M.C. 15a* 150   300
823 — As last. ℞. Man standing with branch and cross, or two branches. *B.M.C. 15b.* 150   350
824 Diad. bust r. with floral scroll. ℞. As last 150   350
825 — As last. ℞. Man with two crosses. *B.M.C. 16* 120   275
826 As 813 but bust l. *B.M.C. 17.* 135   325
827 Diad. bust r. with cross. ℞. Man standing with cross and bird. *B.M.C. 18* 150   300

		F	VF
		£	£
828	Diad. bust l. with cross. ℞. As last. *B.M.C. 19*	150	350
829	Victory standing with wreath. ℞. Man with two crosses. *B.M.C. 22* . . .	250	550

818   831

IX.   **"Wolf-head whorl"** *types, mostly of about .300 silver or less, c.* 740–750

830	Man standing holding two crosses. ℞. Wolf-head whorl. *B.M.C. 23e.* . .	85	200
831	Sphinx or female centaur with outstretched wings. ℞. As above. *B.M.C. 47* See also No. 807.	110	225

832

X.   **East Anglian types,** *of about .500 silver or less, c.* 735–750. Struck to a standard of 15 grs./0.97 gm. or less

832	Crude radiate bust l. or r., *Epa, Wigraed,* or *Spi,* etc., in runes. ℞. "Standard". *Rigold R2* (compare with 785)	75	150
832A	Crude bust r. ℞. Porcupine modified into profile ½ moon face.	200	400
833	— Similar. ℞. Cross with each limb ending in annulet. *Rigold R2Z, N. 160.*	110	250
833A	Saltire in square. ℞. Cross ending in annulets. *B.M.C. 51*	75	150
834	Bird r. looking back. ℞. "Standard" with four annulets in saltire. *B.M.C. 46*	125	325
835	"Standard" both sides. *N. 55–57.*	150	325
836	Fantastic bird r. or l. ℞. Fantastic quadruped l. or r. *B.M.C. 44*	100	225
836A	— As above *rev.* on both sides	100	225
836B	— Hd. r. ℞. As 836 *obv.*	150	300
836C	— Quadruped r. ℞. Spiral	150	300

836   837   839

XI.   **Late sceattas,** *on a restored silver standard, c.* 750–775. These probably include some specimens of 830 and 831 and the following types:

837	"Porcupine". ℞. *Aethili/raed* in runes in two lines. *B.M.C. 4*	350	750
838	"Porcupine". ℞. Small cross, S E D E in angles. *N. 47.*	*Extremely rare*	

XII.   **Frisian sceattas,** *c.* 700–750. A number of large sceatta hoards have been found in the Netherlands and Lower Rhine area. Some of the coins are now known to have been minted in Frisia but some also circulated in England

839	Crude radiate bust l. or r., as 832, sometimes crude runes. ℞. Plain cross with pellets or annulets in angles. *Rigold R3. B.M.C. 2c*	35	65
839A	Helmeted head r. ℞. Cross with annulets	80	175

	F	VF
	£	£

840   "Standard". R. Cross and pellets. *B.M.C. 50*   45   125

840A Very crude facing bust. R. Similar   60   125

841   "Porcupine" with III, XII or XIII in curve. R. "Standard". *Metcalf A, B & C*   35   65

842   "Porcupine" has a triangle attached to curve or an outline of pellets. *Metcalf E & F*   40   70

843   844

843   Facing "Wodan" head. R. Monster. *B.M.C. 31*   100   225

843A Similar but "Standard" on *rev.*.   175   350

844   — Similar. R. Two men with staves or long cross. *B.M.C. 30a & b*. . . .   125   250

844A Good style bust l.; runic inscription. R. Annulet cross and pellets. . . . .   —   300

XIII.   Uncertain issues

847

846   **Ealdfrith** (? possibly sub-king of Lindsey, *c.* 790). Now considered to be Northumbria (see 846 below). . . . .

847   **Beonna**, King of East Anglia, *c.* 758. Æ *sceat*. Pellet in centre, Runic inscription. R. EFE in Roman characters around saltire cross.   400   800

847A — Similar. R. Name in Runic   650   1250

847B — Similar. R. Interlace pattern. . . . . *Extremely rare*

KINGS OF NORTHUMBRIA

In the North a series of silver sceats was struck with the king's name on the obverse and a fantastic animal on the reverse.

Towards the end of the eighth century the coinage degenerated to one of base silver and finally to copper or brass; from the second reign of Aethelred I the design becomes standardised with the king's name retained on the obverse but with the moneyer's name on the reverse and in the centre of both sides a cross, pellet or rosette., etc.

A parallel series of ecclesiastical coins was struck by the Archbishops of York. The coinage continued until the conquest of Northumbria by the Danes and the defeat of Osbert in 867, almost a century after introduction of the broad silver penny in Southern England.

846   **Aldfrith** (685–705). Æ *sceat*. Pellet in annulet. R. Fantastic animal l. with trifid tail . . . .

852   **Eadberht** (737–758). Æ *sceat*. . Small cross. R. Fantastic quadruped to l. or r.   750   1500

    Aethelwald Moll (759–765). See Archbishop Ecgberht of York   175   400

853　　　　　　　　　　859　　　　　　　　　861

		F £	VF £
853	**Alcred** (765–774). *Æ sceat*. As 852.	350	800
854	**Aethelred I,** first reign (774–779). *Æ sceat*. As last	350	800
855	**Aelfwald I** (779–788). *Æ sceat*. As last	400	950
856	— — Small cross. R. With name of moneyer CVDBEVRT	375	900
857	**Aethelred I,** second reign (789–796). *Æ sceat*. Similar. R. SCT CVD (St. Cuthbert), shrine	*Extremely rare*	
858	— Small cross. R. With moneyer's name	250	600

The last and the rest of the sceats, except where otherwise stated, have on the obv. *the king's name, and on the* rev. *the moneyer's name: in the centre on both sides is a cross, a pellet, a rosette, etc. During the following reign the silver sceat becomes debased and later issues are only brass or copper.*

859	**Eanred** (810–*c.* 854). Base *Æ sceat*.	30	65
859A	— *Æ penny*. Bust r. R. Cross, part moline part crosslet		*Unique*
860	— Æ *sceat*	20	40
861	**Aethelred II,** first reign (*c.* 854–858). Æ *sceat*	20	50
862	— R. Quadruped	200	600
863	**Redwulf** (*c.* 858). Æ *sceat.*.	45	90
864	**Aethelred II,** second reign (*c.* 858–*c.* 862). Æ *sceat*, mainly of the moneyer EARDWVLF	20	45
865	**Osbert** (*c.* 862–867). Æ *sceat*	70	140

Coins with blundered legends are worth less than those with normal readings, and to this series have been relegated those coins previously attributed to Eardwulf and Aelfwald II.

ARCHBISHOPS OF YORK

866　　　　　　　　　　868

866	**Ecgberht** (732 *or* 734–766). *Æ sceat*, with king Eadberht. As illustration, or holds cross and crozier	275	600
866A	— — with Aethelwald Moll. Cross each side	*Extremely rare*	
867	— — with Alchred. Cross each side.	*Extremely rare*	
868	**Eanbald II** (796–*c.* 830). *Æ sceat*. R. With name of moneyer	65	150
869	— Æ *sceat*, as last.	40	90

870   871

		F	VF
		£	£
870	**Wigmund** (837–854). Gold *solidus*. Facing bust. ℞. Cross in wreath. . . .		*Unique*
871	— Æ *sceat*, various	35	70
872	**Wulfhere** (854–900). Æ *sceat*	85	175

MIDDLE ANGLO-SAXON PERIOD, c. 780–973

In the kingdom of the Franks a reformed coinage of good quality *deniers* struck on broad flans had been introduced by Pepin in 755 and continued by his son Charlemagne and his descendants. A new coinage of *pennies* of similar size and weighing about 20 grains (1.3 gms) was introduced into England, probably by Offa, the powerful king of Mercia, about 755/780, though early pennies also exist of two little known kings of Kent, Heaberht and Ecgberht, of about the same period.

The silver penny (*Lat.* "denarius", hence the *d.* of our £ *s. d.*) remained virtually the sole denomination of English coinage for almost five centuries, with the rare exception of occasional gold coins and somewhat less rare silver halfpence. The penny reached a weight of 24 grains, i.e., a "pennyweight" during the reign of Aelfred the Great. Silver pennies of this period normally bear the ruler's name, though not always his portrait, and the name of the moneyer responsible for their manufacture.

Pennies were issued by various rulers of the Heptarchy for the kingdoms of Kent, Mercia, East Anglia and Wessex (and possibly Anglian Northumbria), by the Danish settlers in the Danelaw and the Hiberno-Norse kings of York, and also by the Archbishops of Canterbury and a Bishop of London. Under Eadgar, who became the sole ruler of England, a uniform coinage was instituted throughout the country, and it was he who set the pattern for the "reformed" coinage of the later Anglo-Saxon and Norman period.

Halfpence were issued by most rulers from Alfred to Eadgar between 871–973 for S. England, and although all are rare today, it is probable that reasonable quantities were made.

Nos. 873–1387 are all silver pennies except where stated.

NB. Many pennies of the early part of this period have chipped flans and prices should be reduced accordingly.

KINGS OF KENT

		F	VF
		£	£
873	**Heaberht** (*c.* 765). Monogram for REX. ℞. Five annulets, each containing a pellet, joined to form a cross		*Unique*
874	**Ecgberht** (*c.* 780). Similar. ℞. Varied. . . . . *from*	1350	3500
875	**Eadberht Praen** (796–798). As illustration. ℞. Varied.	1350	3500

875   877

876	**Cuthred** (798–807). *Canterbury.* Various types without portrait . . . *from*	425	1000
877	— As illustration	475	1100

878   879

878	**Anonymous** (*c.* 822–823). *Canterbury.* As illustration	650	1650
879	**Baldred** (*c.* 823–825). *Canterbury.* Head or bust r. ℞. Varied	1000	2500

		F	VF
		£	£
880	— Cross each side.	750	2000
881	*Rochester*. Diademed bust r. ℞. Varied	*Extremely rare*	

ARCHBISHOPS OF CANTERBURY

882   885

882	**Jaenberht** (765–792). His name around central ornament or cross and wedges. ℞. OFFA REX in two lines.	1500	3500
883	— His name in three lines. ℞. OFFA REX between the limbs of Celtic cross	2000	4500
884	**Aethelheard** (el. 792, cons. 793, d. 805). With Offa as overlord. First issue (792–793), with title *Pontifex*	1250	3500
885	— Second issue (793–796), with title *Archiepiscopus*	1200	3000
886	— With Coenwulf as overlord. Third issue (796–805)	1150	3250
886A	— Alone, as last. ℞. Moneyer, cross with pellets etc.	*Extremely rare*	
887	**Wulfred** (805–832). group I (805–*c*. 810). As illustration. ℞. Crosslet, alpha-omega. . . . . *from*	1200	4250
888	— Group II (*c*. 810). As last. ℞. DOROVERNIA C monogram	600	1450
889	— Group III (pre- 823). Bust extends to edge of coin. ℞. As last	550	1300
890	— Groups IV and V (*c*. 822–823). Anonymous under Ecgberht. Moneyer's name in place of the Archbishop's. ℞. DOROBERNIA CIVITAS in three or five lines.	575	1400
891	— Group VI (*c*. 823–825). Baldred type. Crude portrait. ℞. DRVR CITS in two lines.	600	2100
892	— Group VII (*c*. 832). Second monogram (Ecgberht) type. Crude portrait r., PLFRED. ℞. DORIB C. Monogram as 1035	600	2100

287   894

893	**Ceolnoth** (833–870). Group I with name CIALNOD. Tonsured bust facing. ℞. Varied . . . . *from*	275	750
894	— Group II. Similar but CEOLNOD. ℞. Types of Aethelwulf of Wessex.	300	600
895	— Group III. Diad. bust r. ℞. Moneyer's name in and between lunettes .	400	900

Archbishops of Canterbury *continued*

896

			F £	VF £
896	**Aethered** (870–889). Bust r. ℞. As illustration or with long cross with lozenge panel	1750	4500
897	— Cross pattée. ℞. ELF / STAN		*Unique*

898

			F £	VF £
898	**Plegmund** (890–914). DORO in circle. ℞. As illustration above, various moyeners. . . . *from*	350	850
899	— Similar, but title EPISC, and XDF in centre	550	1300
900	— Small cross pattée. ℞. Somewhat as last	300	750
901	— Crosses moline and pommée on *obv.*	550	1300

KINGS OF MERCIA

Until 825 Canterbury was the principal mint of the Kings of Mercia and some moneyers also struck coins for the Kings of Kent and Archbishops.

GOLD

902   903

902	**Offa** (757–796). Gold *dinar*. Copy of Arabic dinar of Caliph Al Mansur, dated 157 A.H. (A.D. 774), with OFFA REX added on *rev.*	*Unique*
903	Gold *penny*. Bust r., moneyer's name. ℞. Standing figure, moneyer's name.	*Unique*

SILVER

904   905

	F £	VF £
904 *Canterbury*. Group I (*c.* 784–*c.* 787). Early coins without portraits, small flans. Various types . . . . *from*	500	1300
905 — Group II (*c* 787–*c.* 792). Various types with portrait, small flans *from*	850	2100
906 — — — Various types without portraits, small flans. . . . . *from*	450	1100

907   909

907 *Canterbury*. Group III (*c.* 792–796). Various types without portrait, large flans . . . . *from*	600	1300
908 *East Anglia*. Copies of Group II and III, possibly struck *c.* 790. Ornate, crude, and sometimes with runic letters	650	1600
909 **Cynethryth** (wife of Offa). Coins as Group II of Offa. As illustration . . .	3000	6000
910 — *O*. As *rev.* of last. ℞. EOBA on leaves of quatrefoil.	2500	5000
911 **Eadberht** (Bishop of London, died 787/789). EADBERHT EP in three lines. ℞. Name of Offa	1650	3500
The attribution to this particular cleric is uncertain.		
912 **Coenwulf** (796–821). Group I (796–805). *Canterbury* and *London*. Without portrait. His name in three lines. ℞. Varied	450	1100
913 — *Canterbury*. Name around m as illus. below. ℞. Moneyer's name in two lines.	*Unique*

914   915

914 — *Both mints*. Tribrach type as illustration	275	650
915 — Group II (*c.* 805–810). *Canterbury*. With portrait. Small flans. ℞. Varied but usually cross and wedges	400	900

		F	VF
		£	£
916	— Groups II and IV (*c.* 810–820). *Canterbury.* Similar but larger flans. ℞. Varied	350	750
917	— *Rochester.* Large diad. bust of coarse style. ℞. Varied. (Moneyers: Dun, Ealhstan)	475	1100
918	— *London.* With portrait generally of Roman style. ℞. Crosslet.	450	1000
919	— *E. Anglia.* Crude diad. bust r. ℞. Moneyer's name LVL on leaves in arms of cross.	450	1050
920	— — *O.* as last. ℞. Various types . . . . *from*	400	900

921   929

921	**Ceolwulf I** (821–823). *Canterbury.* Group I. Bust r. ℞. Varied. (Moneyers: Oba, Sigestef)	575	1350
922	— — Group II. Crosslet. ℞. Varied	500	1250
923	— — Group III. Tall cross with MERCIORŬ. ℞. Crosslet. SIGESTEF DOROBERNIA.		*Unique*
924	— *Rochester.* Group I. Bust r. ℞. Varied	500	1250
925	— — Group IIA. As last but head r.	550	1350
926	— — Group IIB. Ecclesiastical issue by Bp. of Rochester. With mint name, DOROBREBIA, but no moneyer	*Extremely rare*	
927	— *East Anglia.* Crude style and lettering with barbarous portrait. ℞. Varied.	500	1250
928	**Beornwulf** (823–825). Bust r. ℞. Moneyer's name in three lines	1350	3250
929	— ℞. Cross crosslet in centre	1100	2500
930	Crude copy of 928 but moneyer's name in two lines with crosses between.	*Extremely rare*	

931   933

931	**Ludica** (825–827). Bust r. ℞. Moneyer's name in three lines as 928	*Extremely rare*	
932	— Similar. ℞. Moneyer's name around cross crosslet in centre, as 929 . .	*Extremely rare*	
933	**Wiglaf,** first reign (827–829). Crude head r. ℞. Crosslet	1750	4500

934

	F £	VF £
934 Second reign (830–840). Cross and pellets. ℞. Moneyer's name in and between lunettes of pellets	1750	4500

935

		F	VF
935	**Berhtwulf** (840–852). Various types with bust . . . . *from*	700	1650
936	— Cross potent over saltire. ℞. Cross potent	750	1850
937	Berhtwulf with Aethelwulf of Wessex. As before. ℞. IAETHELWLF REX. cross pommée over cross pattée.		*Unique*
938	**Burgred** (852–874). *B.M.C. type A.* Bust r. ℞. Moneyer's name in and between lunettes.	100	175
939	— — B. Similar but lunettes broken in centre of curve.	110	230

938   939   940   941

940	— — C. Similar but lunettes broken in angles	110	230
941	— — D. Similar but legend divided by two lines with a crook at each end	100	185
942	— — E. As last, but m above and below	350	900
943	**Ceolwulf II** (874–*c.* 880). Bust r. ℞. Two emperors seated. Victory above.		*Unique*

944

944	— ℞. Moneyer's name in angles of long cross with lozenge centre	3000	7500

KINGS OF EAST ANGLIA

946 948

	F £	VF £
Beonna (*c.* 760). See no. 847		
946 **Aethelberht** (d. 794). As illustration	*Only 3 known*	
947 **Eadwald** (*c.* 798). King's name in three lines. ℞. Moneyer's name in quatrefoil or around cross	1500	3500
948 **Aethelstan I** (*c.* 825–840). Bust r. or l. ℞. Crosslet or star	850	2250
949 Bust r. ℞. Moneyer's name in three or four lines	850	2250
950 Alpha or A. ℞. Varied	400	850
951 *O.* and *rev.* Cross with or without wedges or pellets in angles	400	950
952 — Similar, with king's name both sides	550	1350
952A Name around ship in centre. ℞. Moneyer Eadgar, pellets in centre. (Possibly the earliest of his coins.)	*Unique*	
953 **Aethelweard** (*c.* 840–*c.* 855), A. Omega or cross and crescents. ℞. Cross with pellets or wedges.	600	1500

953 954

954 **Edmund** (855–870). Alpha or A. ℞. Cross with pellets or wedges	350	650
955 — *O.* Varied. ℞. Similar	350	650

For the St. Edmund coins and the Danish issues struck in East Anglia bearing the name of Aethelred I of Wessex, see Danish East Anglia.

VIKING COINAGES

Danish East Anglia, c. 885–915

956   957

		F £	VF £
956	**Aethelstan II** (878–890), originally named Guthrum? Cross pattée. ℞. Moneyer's name in two lines	1000	2500
957	**Oswald** (unknown except from his coins). Alpha or A. ℞. Cross pattée. .	*Extremely rare*	
958	— Copy of Carolinigian "temple" type. ℞ Cross and pellets	*Unique fragment*	
959	**Aethelred I.** As last, with name of Aethelred I of Wessex. ℞. As last, or cross-crosslet.	*Extremely rare*	
960	**St. Edmund**, memorial coinage, Æ *penny*, type as illus. below, various legends of good style	75	125
961	— Similar, but barbarous or semi-barbarous legends.	70	110
962	*Halfpenny.* Similar.	400	1000

961   963

963	**St. Martin of Lincoln.** As illustration	1500	3750
964	**Alfred.** (Viking imitations, usually of very barbarous workmanship.) Bust r. ℞. *Londonia* monogram	550	1500
965	— Similar, but *Lincolla* monogram	*Extremely rare*	

966   970

966	— Small cross, as Alfred group II (*Br. 6*), various legends, some read REX DORO . . . *from*	200	500
967	— Similar. ℞. 'St. Edmund type' A in centre	500	1500
968	— Two emperors seated. ℞. As 964. (Previously attributed to Halfdene.)	*Unique*	

		F £	VF £
969	*Halfpenny.* As 964 and 965 . . . . *from*	500	1500
970	— As 966	450	1350

Danelaw, *c.* 898–915

971	**Alfred** (Imitations). ELFRED between ORSNA and FORDA. ℞. Moneyer's name in two lines (occasionally divided by horizontal long cross).	250	650
972	— *Halfpenny.* Similar, of very crude appearance	*Extremely rare*	

971   975

973	**Alfred/Plegmund.** *Obv.* ELFRED REX PLEGN	*Extremely rare*	
974	**Plegmund.** Danish copy of 900	300	750
975	**Earl Sihtric.** Type as 971. SCELDFOR between GVNDI BERTVS. ℞ SITRIC COMES in two lines	*Extremely rare*	

Viking Coinage of York?
References are to "The Classification of Northumbrian Viking Coins in the Cuerdale hoard", by C. S. S. Lyon and B. H. I. H. Stewart, in Numismatic Chronicle, 1964, p. 281ff.

976	**Siefred.** C . SIEFRE DIIS REX in two lines. ℞. EBRAICE CIVITAS (or contractions), small cross. *L. & S. Ia, Ie, Ii*	200	550
977	— Cross on steps between. ℞. As last. *L. & S. If, Ij*	275	750
978	— Long cross. ℞. As last. *L. & S. Ik*	*Extremely rare*	
979	SIEFREDVS REX, cross crosslet within legend. ℞. As last. *L. & S. Ih.* .	130	325
980	SIEVERT REX, cross crosslet to edge of coin. ℞. As last. *L. & S. Ic, Ig, Im*	130	325
981	— Cross on steps between. ℞. As last. *L. & S. Il*	240	650
982	— Patriarchal cross. ℞. DNS DS REX, small cross. *L. & S. Va*	150	400
983	— — ℞. MIRABILIA FECIT, small cross. *L. & S. VIb*	185	500
984	REX, at ends of cross crosslet. ℞. SIEFREDVS, small cross. *L. & S. IIIa, b*	140	385
985	— Long cross. ℞. As last. *L. & S. IIIc.*	120	325
986	*Halfpenny.* Types as 977, *L. & S. Ib*; 980, *Ic*; and 983, *VIb*	*Extremely rare*	

980   993

987	**Cnut.** CNVT REX, cross crosslet to edge of coin. ℞. EBRAICE CIVITAS, small cross. *L. & S. Io, Iq.*	70	150
988	— — ℞. CVNNETTI, small cross. *L. & S. IIc*	80	175

		F £	VF £
989	— Long cross. ℞. EBRAICE CIVITAS, small cross. *L. & S. Id, In, Ir* . .	65	120
990	— — ℞. CVNNETTI, small cross. *L. & S. IIa, IId*.	65	120
991	— Patriarchal cross. ℞. EBRAICE CIVITAS, small cross. *L. & S. Ip, Is.*	65	120
992	— — ℞.—*Karolus* monogram in centre. *L. & S. It*	400	1000
993	— — ℞. CVNNETTI, small cross. *L. & S. IIb, IIe*.	65	110
994	*Halfpenny.* Types as 987, *L. & S. Iq*; 989, *Id*; 991, *Is*; 992, *Iu*; 993, *IIb and e* . . . . *from*	400	850
995	As 992, but CVNNETTI around *Karolus* monogram. *L. & S. IIf*	400	875

995   998

996	**Cnut and/or Siefred.** CNVT REX, patriarchal cross. ℞. SIEFREDVS, small cross. *L. & S. IIId*.	110	235
997	— — ℞. DNS DS REX, small cross. *L. & S. Vc*.	150	325
998	— — ℞. MIRABILIA FECIT. *L. & S. VId*	140	200
999	EBRAICE C, patriarchal cross. ℞. DNS DS REX, small cross. *L. & S.* *Vb*.	120	250
1000	— — ℞. MIRABILIA FECIT. *L. & S. VIc*	140	275
1001	DNS DS REX in two lines. ℞. ALVALDVS, small cross. *L. & S. IVa* .		1500
1002	DNS DS O REX, similar. ℞. MIRABILIA FECIT. *L. & S. VIa*	250	550
1003	*Halfpenny.* As last. *L. & S. VIa*	*Extremely rare*	
1004	**"Cnut".** Name blundered around cross pattée with extended limbs. ℞. QVENTOVICI around small cross. *L. & S. VII*	300	600
1005	— *Halfpenny.* Similar. *L. & S. VII*.	450	1000
	Possibly not Northumbrian; the reverse copied from the Carolingian coins *of Quentovic, N. France.*		

York, early tenth century issues

1006	**St. Peter coinage.** Early issues. SCI PETRI MO in two lines. ℞. Cross pattée.	175	400
1007	— similar. ℞. "Karolus" monogram.	*Extremely rare*	
1008	*Halfpenny.* Similar. ℞. Cross pattée	1000	2250

1006   1009

| 1009 | **Regnald** (blundered types). RAIENALT, head to l. or r. ℞. EARICE CT,
"Karolus" monogram. . . . . | 1250 | 3000 |

		F	VF
		£	£
1010	— Open hand. ℞. Similar.	1000	2500
1011	— Hammer. ℞. Bow and arrow	1250	3000
1012	— Similar. ℞. Sword	*Extremely rare*	

English Coins of the Hiberno-Norse Vikings

Early period, *c.* **919–925**

| 1013 | **Sihtric** (921–927). SITRIC REX, sword. ℞. Cross or T | 1500 | 3750 |

1015   1016

1014	**St. Peter coinage.** Late issues SCI PETRI MO, sword and hammer. ℞. EBORACEI, cross and pellets	350	850
1015	— Similar. ℞. Voided hammer	450	1000
1016	— Similar. ℞. Solid hammer	700	1600

Modern coins of this type are sold at the Jorvic Centre, York
St. Peter coins with blundered legends are rather cheaper.

Later period, 939–954 (after the battle of Brunanburh). Mostly struck at York.

1017	**Anlaf Guthfrithsson,** 939–941. Flower type. Small cross, ANLAF REX TO D. ℞. Flower above moneyer's name	2500	6000
1018	**Olaf Guthfrithsson.** Circumscription type, with small cross each side, ANLAF CVNVNC, M in field on reverse (*Derby*)	2500	6000
1018A	— Two line type. ONLAF REX. Large letter both sides (*Lincoln?*)	2000	5000
1019	— Raven type. As illustration, ANLAF CVNVNC	2000	5000

1019   1020

1020	**Olaf Sihtricsson,** first reign, 941–944. Triquetra type. As illus., CVNVNC. ℞. Danish standard	2000	5000
1021	— Circumscription type (a). Small cross each side, CVNVNC	2000	5000
1022	— Cross moline type, CVNVNC. ℞. Small cross	*Extremely rare*	
1023	— Two line type. Small cross. ℞. ONLAF REX. ℞. Name in two lines	2000	5000
1024	**Regnald Guthfrithsson,** 943–944. Triquetra type. As 1020. REGNALD CVNVNC	3000	7500
1025	— Cross moline type. As 1022, but REGNALD CVNVNC	2500	6000
1026	**Sihtric Sihtricsson,** *c.* 942. Triquetra type. As 1020, SITRIC CVNVNC	*Unique*	

1025   1030

		F £	VF £
1027	— Circumscription type. Small cross each side		*Unique*
1028	**Eric Blood-axe,** first reign, 948. Two line type. Small cross, ERICVC REX A; ERIC REX AL; or ERIC REX EFOR. ℞. Name in two lines.	2500	6000
1029	**Olaf Sihtricsson,** second reign, 948–952. Circumscription type (b). Small cross each side. ONLAF REX	2750	6500
1029A	— Flower type. small cross ANLAF REX ℞. Flower above moneyer's name.	2500	6000
1029B	— Two line type. Small cross, ONLAF REX. ℞. Moneyer's name in two lines.	2000	5000
1030	**Eric Blood-axe,** second reign, 952–954. Sword type. ERIC REX in two lines, sword between. ℞. Small cross.	2750	6500

KINGS OF WESSEX

Later, KINGS OF ALL ENGLAND

All are silver pennies unless otherwise stated

BEORHTRIC, 786—802

Beorhtric was dependent on Offa of Mercia and married a daughter of Offa.

1031

1031	As illustration	*Extremely rare*
1032	Alpha and omega in centre. ℞. Omega in centre	*Extremely rare*

ECGBERHT, 802—839

King of Wessex only, 802–825; then also of Kent, Sussex, Surrey, Essex and East Anglia, 825–839, and of Mercia also, 829–830.

1033	*Canterbury.* Group I. Diad. hd. r. within inner circle. ℞. Various *. from*	1450	3500
1034	— II. Non-portrait types. ℞. Various . . . . *from*	750	2250

1035

		F £	VF £
1035	— III. Bust r. breaking inner circle. R̟. DORIB C	1100	2500
1036	*London.* Cross potent. R̟. LVN / DONIA / CIVIT		*Unique*
1037	— — R̟. REDMVND MONE around TA	1500	4250
1038	*Rochester,* royal mint. Non-portrait types with king's name ECGBEORHT . . . . *from*	1150	3250
1039	— — Portrait types, ECGBEORHT . . . . *from*	1350	4000
1040	*Rochester,* bishop's mint. Bust r. R̟. SCS ANDREAS (APOSTOLVS) . .	1450	4600
1041	*Winchester.* SAXON monogram or SAXONIORVM in three lines. R̟. Cross.	1150	3250

AETHELWULF, 839—858

Son of Ecgberht; sub-King of Essex, Kent, Surrey and Sussex, 825–839; King of all southern England, 839–855; King of Essex, Kent and Sussex only, 855–858. No coins are known of his son Aethelbald who ruled over Wessex proper, 855–860

1042

1042	*Canterbury.* Phase I (839–*c.* 843). Head within inner circle. R̟. Various. *Br. 3*	225	600
1043	— — Larger bust breaking inner circle. R̟. A. *Br. 1 and 2*	225	600
1044	— — Cross and wedges. R̟. SAXONIORVM in three lines in centre. *BR. 10*	225	550
1045	— — Similar, but OCCINDENTALIVM in place of moneyer. *Br. 11* . .	225	750
1046	— Phase II (*c.* 843–848?). Cross and wedges. R̟. Various, but chiefly a form of cross or a large A. *Br. 4*	225	500
1047	— — New portrait, somewhat as 1043. R̟. As last. *Br. 7*	225	500
1048	— — Smaller portrait. R̟. As last, with *Chi/Rho* monogram. *Br. 7*	250	500
1049	— Phase III (*c.* 848/851–*c.* 855). DORIB in centre. R̟. CANT mon. *Br. 5*	225	500
1050	— — CANT mon. R̟. CAN M in angles of cross. *Br. 6*	250	500

1044   1051

	F £	VF £
1051 — Phase IV (c. 855–859). Type as Aethelberht. New neat style bust R. Large voided long cross. Br. 8	225	450
1052 Winchester. SAXON mon. R. Cross and wedges. Br. 9	350	750

AETHELBERHT, 858–865/866

Son of Aethelwulf; sub-King of Kent, Essex and Sussex, 858–860; King of all southern England, 860–865/6

1053 As illustration below	200	400
1054 O. Similar, R. Cross fleury over quatrefoil	700	1500

1053

AETHELRED I, 865/866–871

Son of Aethelwulf; succeeded his brother Aethelberht.

1055 As illustration	250	700
1056 Similar, but moneyer's name in four lines	600	1500

For another coin with the name Aethelred see 959 under Viking coinages.

1055

ALFRED THE GREAT, 871—899

Brother and successor to Aethelred, Alfred had to contend with invading Danish armies for much of his reign. In 878 he and Guthrum the Dane divided the country, with Alfred holding all England south and west of Watling Street. Alfred occupied London in 886.

		F £	VF £
Types with portraits			
1057	Bust r. R̝. As Aethelred I. *Br. 1 (name often* AELBRED)	300	650
1058	— R̝. Long cross with lozenge centre, as 9544, *Br. 5*	1500	4000
1059	— R̝. Two seated figures, as 943. *Br. 2*		*Unique*
1060	— R̝. As Archbp. Aethered; cross within large quatrefoil. *Br. 3*		*Unique*

1057 1062

1061	*London.* Bust. r. R̝. LONDONIA monogram	600	1400
	Copies made in tin at the Wembley Exhibition are common		
1062	— R̝. Similar, but with moneyer's name added	750	1600
1063	— *Halfpenny.* Bust r. R̝. LONDONIA monogram as 1061	1000	2500
1064	*Gloucester.* R̝. ÆT GLEAPA in angles of three limbed cross		*Unique*

Types without portraits

1065	King's name on limbs of cross, trefoils in angles. R̝. Moneyer's name in quatrefoil. *Br. 4*		*Unique*

1066 1069

1066	Cross pattée. R̝. Moneyer's name in two lines. *Br. 6*	175	350
1067	— As last, but neater style, as Edw, the Elder	185	375
1068	— *Halfpenny.* As 1066	650	1650
1069	*Canterbury.* As last but DORO added on *obv. Br. 6a*	250	550
	For other pieces bearing the name of Alfred see under the Viking coinages.		
1070	*Exeter?* King name in four lines. R̝. EXA vertical		5000
1071	*Winchester?* Similar to last, but PIN		*Extremely rare*
1072	"Offering penny". Very large and heavy. AELFRED REX SAXORVM in four lines. R̝. ELIMO in two lines i.e. (*Elimosina,* alms)		*Extremely rare*

EDWARD THE ELDER, 899–924

Eadward, the son of Alfred, aided by his sister Aethelflaed 'Lady of the Mericians', annexed all England south of the Humber and built many new fortified boroughs to protect the kingdom.

1074

		F £	VF £
1073	**Rare types**. *Br. 1. Bath?* R. BA	*Extremely rare*	
1074	— 2. *Canterbury.* Cross moline in pommée. R. Moneyer's name	800	2000
1075	— 3. *Chester?* Small cross. R. Minster	825	2500
1076	— 4. — Small cross. R. Moneyer's name in single line	700	1800
1077	— 5. — R. Two stars	950	2250

1078   1082

1078	— 6. — R. Flower above central line, name below	900	2500
1079	— 7. — R. Floral design with name across field	900	2400
1080	— 8. — R. Bird holding twig	*Extremely rare*	
1081	— 9. — R. Hand of Providence	1500	3000
1082	— 10. — R. City gate of Roman style	*Extremely rare*	
1083	— 11. — R. Anglo-Saxon burg	800	1850

1084   1087

1084	**Ordinary types**. *Br. 12.* Bust l. R. Moneyer's name in two lines . . . *from*	400	900
1085	— — As last, but in *gold*	*Unique*	
1086	— 12a. Similar, but bust r. of crude style	350	1250
1087	— 13. Small cross. R. Similar (to 1084)	140	260
1088	*Halfpenny.* Similar to last	*Extremely rare*	

AETHELSTAN, 924–939

Aethelstan, the eldest son of Eadward, decreed that money should be coined only in a borough, that every borough should have one moneyer and that some of the more important boroughs should have more than one moneyer.

1089   1094

1089	**Main issues**. Small cross. ℞. Moneyer's name in two lines	225	450
1090	Diad. bust r. ℞. As last	650	1500
1091	— ℞. Small cross	550	1350
1092	Small cross both sides	185	400
1093	— Similar, but mint name added	200	450
1094	Crowned bust r. As illustration. ℞. Small cross	450	1000
1095	— Similar, but mint name added	400	850

1100   1104

1096	**Local Issues**. *N. Mercian mints*. Star between two pellets. ℞. As 1089. . .	550	1250
1097	— Small cross. ℞. Floral ornaments above and below moneyer's name .	550	1250
1098	— Rosette of pellets each side	275	550
1099	— Small cross one side, rosette on the other side	300	650
1100	*N.E. mints*. Small cross. ℞. Tower over moneyer's name	550	1500
1101	— Similar, but mint name added	750	1750
1102	— Bust in high relief r. or l. ℞. Small cross	500	1150
1103	— Bust r. in high relief. ℞. Cross-crosslet	500	1150
1104	"Helmeted" bust r. ℞. As last	600	1500
1104A	Halfpenny, small cross. ℞. Moneyer's name in two lines	*Extremely rare*	

EADMUND, 939–946

Eadmund, the brother of Aethelstan, extended his realm over the Norse kingdom of York.

1105   1107

		F £	VF £
1105	Small cross or rosette. ℞. Moneyer's name in two lines with crosses or rosettes between . . . . *from*	160	350
1106	Crowned bust r. ℞. Small cross	300	650
1107	Similar, but with mint name	400	850
1108	Small cross either side, or rosette on one side	175	375
1109	Cross of five pellets. ℞. Moneyer's name in two lines	200	425
1110	Small cross. ℞. Flower above name	750	1750
1111	"Helmeted" bust r. ℞. Cross-crosslet	750	1750

1112

		F £	VF £
1112	*Halfpenny*. As 1105 . . . . *from*	950	2000

EADRED, 946–955

Eadred was another of the sons of Eadward. He lost the kingdom of York to Eric Bloodaxe.

1113   1115

		F £	VF £
1113	As illustration. ℞. Moneyer's name in two lines	135	275
1114	— Similar, but mint name after REX	300	750
1115	Crowned bust r. As illustration.	350	700
1116	— ℞. Similar, with mint name added	400	950

	F	VF
	£	£
1117 Rosette. ℞. As 1113.	125	250
1118 Small cross. ℞. Rosette	135	285
1119 — ℞. Flower enclosing moneyer's name. *B.M.C. II*		*Extremely rare*
1120 *Halfpenny.* Similar to 1113 . . . . *from*		2000

HOWEL DDA, d. 949–950

Grandson of Rhodri Mawr, Howel succeeded to the kingdom of Dyfed *c.* 904, to Seisyllog *c.* 920 and became King of Gwynedd and all Wales, 942.

1121

1121 HOPÆL REX, small cross or rosette. ℞. Moneyer's name in two lines. .   *Unique*

EADWIG, 955–959

Elder son of Eadmund, Eadwig lost Mercia and Northumbria to his brother Eadgar in 957.

1122

1122 *Br. 1.* Type as illustration.	200	400
1123 — — Similar, but mint name in place of crosses	350	1000
1123A — Similar to 1122, but star in place of cross on *obv.*		*Unique*
1124 — 2. As 1122, but moneyer's name in one line	600	2200
1125 — 3. Similar. ℞. Floral design	675	2250
1126 — 4. Similar. ℞. Rosette or small cross	250	550
1127 — 5. Bust r. ℞. Small cross (*possibly an altered coin of Eadgar*)		*Extremely rare*

1128

1128 *Halfpenny.* Small cross. ℞. Flower above moneyer's name.		*Unique*
1128A — Similar. ℞. PIN (Winchester) across field		*Extremely rare*

EADGAR, 959–975

King in Mercia and Northumbria from 957; King of all England 959–975.

It is now possible on the basis of the lettering to divide up the majority of Eadgar's coins into issues from the following regions: N.E. England, N.W. England, York, East Anglia, Midlands, S.E. England, Southern England, and S.W. England. (*See* "Anglo-Saxon Coins", ed. R. H. M. Dolley.)

1129   1135

		F	VF
		£	£
1129	*Br. I.* Small cross. R̸. Moneyer's name in two lines, crosses between, trefoils top and bottom	100	185
1130	— — R̸. Similar, but rosettes top and bottom (a N.W. variety)	100	210
1131	— — R̸. Similar, but annulets between	150	300
1132	— — R̸. Similar, but mint name between (a late N.W. type)	125	325
1133	— 2. — R̸. Floral design	750	2000
1134	— 4. Small cross either side	110	250
1135	— — Similar, with mint name	250	500
1136	— — Rosette either side	150	275
1137	— — Similar, with mint name	225	475
1138	— 5. Large bust to r. R̸. Small cross	400	900
1139	— — Similar, with mint name	600	1300
1140	*Halfpenny.* (8½ grains.) *Br. 3.* Small cross. R̸. Flower above name	*Extremely rare*	
	For 'reform' issues see 1141 below.		
1140A	— — R̸. Mint name around cross (Chichester)	*Unique*	
1140B	— Bust r. R̸. 'Londonia' monogram	4500	

LATE ANGLO-SAXON PERIOD

In 973 Eadgar introduced a new coinage. A royal portrait now became a regular feature and the reverses normally have a cruciform pattern with the name of the mint in addition to that of the moneyer. Most fortified towns of burghal status were allowed a mint, the number of moneyers varying according to their size and importance: some royal manors also had a mint and some moneyers were allowed to certain ecclesiastical authorities. In all some seventy mints were active about the middle of the 11th century (see list of mints pp. 65–67).

The control of the currency was retained firmly in the hands of the central government, unlike the situation in France and the Empire where feudal barons and bishops controlled their own coinage. Coinage types were changed at intervals to enable the Exchequer to raise revenue from new dies and periodic demonetization of old coin types helped to maintain the currency in a good state. No halfpence were minted during this period. During the latter part of this era, full pennies were sheared into 'halfpennies' and 'farthings'. They are far rarer than later 'cut' coins.

1141

	F	VF
EADGAR, 959–975 *continued*	£	£
1141 **Penny.** Type 6. Small bust l. ℞. Small cross, name of moneyer and mint .	500	950

EDWARD THE MARTYR, 975–978

Son of Eadgar and Aethelflaed, Eadward was murdered at Corfe, reputedly on the orders of his stepmother Aelfthryth.

1142

1142 Type as illustration above	650	1300

AETHELRED II, 978–1016

He was the son of Eadgar and Aelfthryth. His reign was greatly disturbed by incursions of Danish fleets and armies which massive payments of money failed to curb. His later by-name 'the Unready' come from *Unrede*, 'no counsel', a play on his given name.

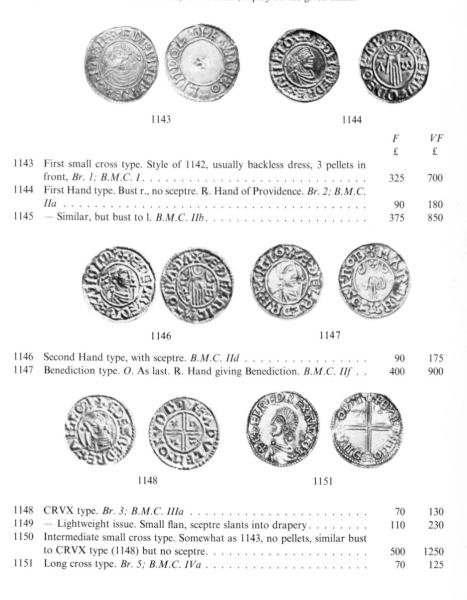

1143   1144

		F	VF
		£	£
1143	First small cross type. Style of 1142, usually backless dress, 3 pellets in front, *Br. 1; B.M.C. 1*	325	700
1144	First Hand type. Bust r., no sceptre. R. Hand of Providence. *Br. 2; B.M.C. IIa*	90	180
1145	— Similar, but bust to l. *B.M.C. IIb*	375	850

1146   1147

1146	Second Hand type, with sceptre. *B.M.C. IId*	90	175
1147	Benediction type. *O.* As last. R. Hand giving Benediction. *B.M.C. IIf*	400	900

1148   1151

1148	CRVX type. *Br. 3; B.M.C. IIIa*	70	130
1149	— Lightweight issue. Small flan, sceptre slants into drapery	110	230
1150	Intermediate small cross type. Somewhat as 1143, no pellets, similar bust to CRVX type (1148) but no sceptre.	500	1250
1151	Long cross type. *Br. 5; B.M.C. IVa*	70	125

1152

		F	VF
		£	£
1152	Helmet type. *Br. 4; B.M.C. VIII*	70	135
1153	— — Similar, but struck in **gold**		*Unique*
1154	Last small cross type. As 1143, but different style	70	115
1154A	Similar, but bust r.	200	500
1155	— Similar, but bust to edge of coin. *B.M.C. Id*	250	550

1154   1156

1156 Agnus Dei type. *Br. 6; B.M.C. X* . . . .   *Extremely rare*

CNUT, 1016–1035

Son of Swegn Forkbeard, King of Denmark, Cnut was acclaimed King by the Danish fleet in
England in 1014 but was forced to leave. He returned in 1015 and in 1016 agreed on a division of the
country with Eadmund Ironsides, the son of Aethelred. No coins of Eadmund are known and on his
death in November 1016 Cnut secured all England, marrying Emma of Normandy, widow of
Aethelred.

Main types

1157   1158   1159   1160

		F £	VF £
1157	Quatrefoil type. *BR. 2; B.M.C. VIII*	85	145
1158	Helmet type. *Br. 3; B.M.C. XIV*	75	125
1159	Short cross type. *BR. 4; B.M.C. XVI*	75	125
1159A	— Similar, but with banner in place of sceptre..	250	500
1160	Jewel cross type. *Br. 6; B.M.C. XX.* Type as 1163	500	1100

[*This type is now considered to be a posthumus issue struck under the auspices of his widow, Aelgifu Emma.*]

HAROLD I, 1035–1040

Harold, the son of Cnut and Aelgifu of Northampton, initially acted as regent for his half-brother Harthacnut on Cnut's death, was then recognised as King in Mercia and the north, and King throughout England in 1037.

1163   1165

1163	Jewel cross type, as illustration. *Br. 1; B.M.C. 1*	160	330
1164	Long cross and trefoils type. *Br. 2; B.M.C. V.*	160	340
1165	— Similar, but fleur de lis in place of trefoils. *B.M.C. Vc*	150	320

HARTHACNUT, 1035–1042

He was heir to Cnut but lost the throne to his half-brother Harold owing to his absence in Denmark. On Harold's death he recovered his English realm.

1167   1168

1166	**Early period, 1036**. Jewel cross type, as 1163; bust l. *Br. 1; B.M.C. I* ...	700	1500
1167	— Similar, but bust r. *B.M.C. Ia*.	650	1400
1168	**Restoration, 1040–1042**. Arm and sceptre type, with name Harthacnut. *Br. 2; B.M.C. II*	800	1650
1169	— Similar, but with name "Cnut"	500	1000

1169   1170

	F	VF
	£	£

1170   **Danish types**, of various designs, some of English type mostly struck at
Lund, Denmark (now Sweden). . . . . *from*   175   350

EDWARD THE CONFESSOR, 1042–1066

Edward was the son of Aethelred II and Emma of Normandy. A number of new mints were opened
during his reign.

1171   1173

1171   PACX type, cross extends to edge of coin. *Br. 4; B.M.C. IVa*.   150   325
1172   — Similar, but cross ends at legend. *B.M.C. IV*   150   325
1173   Radiate type. *Br. 2; B.M.C. I*   80   140

1174   1175

1174   Trefoil quadrilateral type. *Br. 1; B.M.C. III*.   75   135
1175   Short cross type, small flans. *Br. 3; B.M.C. II*   70   120

1176   1179

1176   Expanding cross type; light issue (18 grs.). *Br. 5; B.M.C. V*   80   135

		F	VF
		£	£
1177	— — Heavy issue (27 grs.)	75	140
1178	— — Similar, but struck in **gold**		*Unique*
1179	Helmet type. *Br. 6; B.M.C. VII*	70	120
1180	— — Similar but bust l.	350	900

1181   1182

| 1181 | Sovereign type. *Br. 7; B.M.C. IX* . . . . | 95 | 150 |
| 1182 | Hammer cross type. *Br. 8; B.M.C. XI* . . . . | 75 | 130 |

1183   1184

| 1183 | Facing bust type. *Br. 9; B.M.C. XIII* . . . . | 70 | 125 |
| 1184 | Pyramids type. *Br. 10; B.M.C. XV* . . . . | 90 | 160 |

1185

| 1185 | Large facing bust with sceptre. ℞. Similar. . . . . | 950 | 2000 |

Most York coins of this reign have an annulet in one quarter of the reverse.

HAROLD II, 1066

Harold was the son of Godwin Earl of Wessex. He was the brother-in-law of Edward the Confessor and was recognised as King on Edward's death. He defeated and killed Harald of Norway who invaded the north, but was himself defeated and killed at the Battle of Hastings by William of Normandy.

1186   1187

		F	VF
		£	£
1186	Bust l. with sceptre. ℞. PAX across centre of *rev. B.M.C. I*	300	550
1187	Similar, but without sceptre. *B.M.C. Ia*	325	700
1188	Bust r. with sceptre	600	1250

ANGLO-SAXON, NORMAN AND EARLY PLANTAGENET MINTS

In Anglo-Saxon times coins were struck at a large number of towns. The place of mintage is normally given on all coins from the last quarter of the 10th century onwards, and generally the name of the person responsible (e.g. BRVNIC ON LVND). Below we give a list of the mints, showing the reigns (Baronial of Stephen's reign omitted), of which coins have been found. After the town names we give one or two of the spellings as found on the coins, although often they appear in an abbreviated or extended form. On the coins the Anglo-Saxon and Norman *w* is like a P or Γ and the *th* is Đ. We have abbreviated the kings' names, etc.:

Alf	—	Alfred the Great	Wi	—	William I
EE	—	Edward the Elder	Wii	—	William II
A'stan	—	Aethelstan	He	—	Henry I
EM	—	Edward the Martyr	St	—	Stephen (regular issues)
Ae	—	Aethelred II	M	—	Matilda
Cn	—	Cnut	HA	—	Henry of Anjou
Hi	—	Harold I	WG	—	William of Gloucester
Htr	—	Harthacnut	T	—	"Tealby" coinage
ECfr	—	Edward the Confessor	SC	—	Short cross coinage
Hii	—	Harold II	LC	—	Long cross coinage

Axbridge (ACXEPO, AGEPOR) Ae, Cn, Ht.
Aylesbury (AEGEL) Ae, Cn, ECfr.
Barnstaple (BEARDA, BARDI), Edwig, Ae-Hi, ECfr, Wi, He.
Bath (BADAN) EE-Edmund, Edwig-ECfr, Wi, He, St.
Bedford (BEDANF, BEDEF) Edwig-T.
Bedwyn (BEDEΓIN) ECfr, Wi.
Berkeley (BEORC) ECfr, Wi.
Bramber ? (BRAN) St.
Bridport (BRIPVT, BRIDI) A'stan, Ae, Cn, Ht, ECfr, Wi.
Bristol (BRICSTO) Ae-T, M. HA, LC.
Bruton (BRIVT) Ae-Cn, ECfr.
Buckingham (BVCIN) EM-Hi, ECfr.
Bury St. Edmunds (EDMVN, SEDM, SANTEA) A'stan?, ECfr, Wi, He-LC.
Cadbury CADANB) Ae, Cn.
Caistor (CASTR) EM, Ae, Cn.
Cambridge (GRANTE) Edgar-Wii.
Canterbury (DORO, CAENT, CANTOR, CANTΓAR) Alf, A'stan, Edgar-LC.
Cardiff (CAIRDI, CARDI, CARITI) Wi, He, St, M.
Carlisle (CAR, CARDI, EDEN) He-LC.
Castle Gotha ? (GEOĐA, IOĐA) Ae-Ht.
Castle Rising (RISINGE) St.
Chester (LEIGECES, LEGECE, CESTRE) A'stan, Edgar-T.
Chichester (CISSAN CIV, CICES, CICST) A'stan, Edgar-St, SC.
Chippenham ? (CIPEN) St.
Christchurch, see Twynham.
Cissbury (SIĐEST) Ae, Cn.
Colchester (COLEAC, COLECES) Ae-Hi, ECfr-T.
Crewkerne (CRVCERN) Ae, Cn.
Cricklade (CROCGL, CRIC, CREC) Ae-Wii.
Derby (DEOR, DIORBI, DERBI) A'stan, Edgar-ECfr, Wi-St.
Dorchester (DORCE, DORECES) Ae-ECfr, Wi-He, WG.
Dover (DOFER) A'stan, Edgar-St.
Droitwich (PICC, PICNEH) ECfr. Hii.
Dunwich (DVNE) St.
Durham (DVRE DVRHAN) Wi, St-LC.
Exeter (EAXANC, EXEC, XECST) Alf, A'stan, Edwig-LC.
Eye (EI, EIE) St.
Frome ? (FRO) Cn-ECfr.
Gloucester (GLEAΓEC, GLEΓ, GΓ) Alf, A'stan, Edgar-St, HA, T, LC.
Guildford (GILDEF) EM-Cn, Ht-Wii.

Hastings (HAESTIN) Ae-St.
Hedon, near Hull (HEDVN) St.
Hereford (HEREFOR) A'stan, Ae-St, HA, T, LC.
Hertford (HEORTF) A'stan, Edwig-Hi, ECfr, Wi, Wii.
Horncastle ? (HORN) EM, Ae.
Horndon ? (HORNIDVNE) ECfr.
Huntingdon (HVNTEN) Edwig-St.
Hythe (HIÐEN) ECfr, Wi, Wii.
Ilchester (IVELCE, GIFELCST, GIVELC) Edgar, EM-He, T, LC.
Ipswich (GIPESΓIC) Edgar-SC.
Kings Lynn (LENN, LENE) SC.
Langport (LANCPOR) A'stan, Cn, Hi, ECfr.
Launceston (LANSTF, SANCTI STEFANI) Ae, Wi, Wii, St. T.
Leicester (LIGER, LIHER, LEHRE) A'stan, Edgar-T.
Lewes (LAEPES) A'stan, Edgar-T.
Lichfield (LIHFL) SC.
Lincoln (LINCOLNE, NICOLE) Edgar-LC.
London (LVNDENE) Alf-LC.
Louth ? (LVD) Ae.
Lydford (LYDAN) EM-Hi, ECfr.
Lympne (LIMEN) A'stan, Edgar-Cn.
Maldon (MAELDVN, MAELI) A'stan, Ae-Hi, ECfr, Wii.
Malmesbury (MALD, MEALDMES) Ae-Wii, HA.
Marlborough (MAERLEB) Wi, Wii.
Milbourne Port (MYLE) Ae, Cn.
Newark (NEPIR, NIPOR) Edwig, Eadgar, Ae, Cn.
Newcastle (NEWEC, NIVCA) St, T, LC.
Newport (NIPAN, NIPEP) Edgar, ECfr.
Northampton (HAMTVN, NORHANT) Edwig, Edgar-Wi, He-LC.
Norwich (NORPIC) A'stan-LC.
Nottingham (SNOTINC) A'stan, Ae-St.
Oxford (OXNAFOR, OXENEF) A'stan, Edmund, Edred, Edgar-St, M, T-LC.
Pembroke (PAN, PAIN) He-T.
Pershore (PERESC) ECfr.
Peterborough (MEDE, BVR) Ae, Cn, Wi.
Petherton (PEDÐR) ECfr.
Pevensey (PEFNESE, PEVEN) Wi, Wii, St.
Reading (READIN) ECfr.
Rhuddlan (RVDILI, RVLA) Wi, SC.
Rochester (ROFEC) A'stan, Edgar-He, SC.
Romney (RVME, RVMNE) Ae-Hi, ECfr-He.
Rye (RIE) St.
Salisbury (SAEREB, SALEB) Ae-ECfr, Wi- T.
Sandwich (SANPIC) ECfr, Wi-St.
Shaftesbury (SCEFTESB, SCEFITI) A'stan, Ae-St.
Shrewsbury (SCROBES, SALOP) A'stan, Edgar-LC.
Southampton (HAMWIC, HAMTVN) A'stan, Edwig-Cn.
Southwark (SVDGE, SVDΓEEORC) Ae-St.
Stafford (STAFF, STAEF) A'stan, Ae-Hi, ECfr, Wi, Wii, St, T.
Stamford (STANFOR) Edgar-St.
Steyning (STAENIG) Cn-Wii.
Sudbury (SVDBI, SVB) Ae, Cn, ECfr, Wi-St.
Swansea (SWENSEI) HA?
Tamworth (TOMPEARÐGE, TAMPRÐ) A'stan, Edwig-Hi, ECfr, Wi-St.
Taunton (TANTVNE) Ae, Cn, Ht-St.
Thetford (ÐEOTFOR,, TETFOR) Edgar-T.
Torksey (TORC, TVRC) EM-Cn.
Totnes (DARENT VRB, TOTANES, TOTNESE) A'stan, Edwig-Cn, Wii.
Twynham, now Christchurch (TPIN, TVEHAM) Wi, He.
Wallingford (PELING, PALLIG) A'stan, Edgar-He, T, LC.
Wareham (PERHAM) A'stan, Ae, Cn, Ht-St, M, WG.
Warminster (PORIME) Ae-Hi, ECfr.
Warwick (PAERING, PERPIC) A'stan, Edgar-St.
Watchet (PECEDPORT, PICEDI) Ae-ECfr, Wi-St.
Wilton (PILTVNE) Edgar-LC.

Winchcombe (PINCELE, PINCL) Edgar-Cn, Ht-Wi.
Winchester (PINTONIA, PINCEST) Alf-A'stan, Edwig-LC.
Worcester (PIHRAC, PIHREC) Ae-Hi, ECfr-Sc.
York (EBORACI, EOFERPIC) A'stan, Edmund, Edgar-LC.

The location of the following is uncertain.
AESTHE *(? Hastings)* Ae.
BRYGIN *(? Bridgnorth,* but die-links with NIPAN and with *Shaftesbury)* Ae.
DERNE, DYR (E. Anglian mint) ECfr.
DEVITVN *(? Welsh Marches* or *St. Davids)* Wi.
EANBYRIG, Cn.
MAINT, Wi.
ORSNAFORDA *(? Horsforth or Orford)* Alf.
WEARDBYRIG *(? Warborough)* A'stan, Edgar.

EDWARDIAN AND LATER MINTS

London, Tower: Edw. I–GEO. III.
London, Tower Hill: Geo. III–Eliz. II.
London, Durham House: Hen. VIII (posth.)–Edw. VI.
Ashby de la Zouche: Chas. I.
Aberystwyth: Chas. I.
Aberystwyth: -Furnace: Chas. I.
Bridgnorth: Chas. I.
Berwick-on-Tweed: Edw. I–Edw. III.
Birmingham, Heaton: Vic., Geo. V.
Birmingham, King's Norton: Geo. V.
Birmingham, Soho: Geo. III.
Bombay, India (branch mint): Geo. V.
Bristol: Edw. I, Edw. IV, Hen. VI rest., Hen. VIII–Edw. VI, Chas. I, Wm. III.
Bury St. Edmunds: Edw. I–Edw. III.
Calais: Edw. III–Hen. IV, Hen. VI.
Canterbury: Edw. I–Edw. III, Edw. IV, Hen. VII–Edw. VI.
Carlisle: Chas. I.
Chester: Edw. I, Chas. I, Wm. III.
Colchester: Chas. I.
Coventry: Edw. IV.
Durham: Edw. I–Edw. IV, Rich. III–Hen. VIII.
Exeter: Edw. I, Chas. I, Wm. III.
Hartlebury Castle, Worcs.: Chas. I.
Kingston-upon-Hull: Edw. I.
Lincoln: Edw. I.
Llantrisant: Eliz. II (decimal coinage).
Melbourne, Australia (branch mint): Vic.–Geo. V.
Newark: Chas. I.
Newcastle-upon-Tyne: Edw. I.
Norwich: Edw. IV, Wm. III.
Ottawa, Canada (branch mint): Edw. VII–Geo. V.
Oxford: Chas I.
Perth, Australia (branch mint): Vic.–Geo. V.
Pontefract: Chas. I.
Pretoria, South Africa (branch mint): Geo. V.
Reading: Edw. III.
Scarborough: Chas. I.
Shrewsbury: Chas. I.
Southwark: Hen. VIII–Edw. VI.
Sydney, Australia (branch mint): Vic.–Geo. V.
Tournai, Belgium: Hen. VIII.
Truro: Chas. I.
Worcester: Chas I.
York: Edw. I, Edw. III–Edw. IV, Rich. III–Edw. VI, Chas. I, Wm. III.

NORMAN KINGS AND THEIR SUCCESSORS

There were no major changes in the coinages following the Norman conquest. The controls and periodic changes of the type made in the previous reigns were continued. Nearly seventy mints were operating during the reign of William I; these had been reduced to about fifty-five by the middle of the 12th century and, under Henry II, first to thirty and later to eleven. By the second half of the 13th century the issue of coinage had been centralized at London and Canterbury, with the exception of two ecclesiastical mints. Of the thirteen types with the name PILLEMVS, PILLELM, etc. (William), the first eight have been attributed to the Conqueror and the remaining five to his son William Rufus.

From William I to Edward II inclusive all are silver pennies unless otherwise stated.

Cut 'halfpennies' and 'farthings' were still made in this period and are scarce until the later issues of Henry I and Stephen.

WILLIAM I, 1066–1087

William Duke of Normandy was the cousin of Edward the Confessor. After securing the throne of England he had to suppress several rebellions.

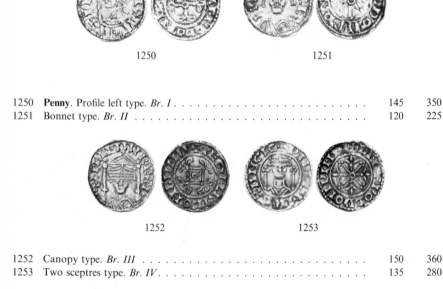

1250   1251

1250	**Penny.** Profile left type. *Br. I*	145	350
1251	Bonnet type. *Br. II*	120	225

1252   1253

1252	Canopy type. *Br. III*	150	360
1253	Two sceptres type. *Br. IV.*	135	280

1254   1255

1254	Two stars type. *Br. V.*	100	185
1255	Sword type. *Br. VI*	185	385

1256 1257

		F	VF
		£	£
1256	Profile right type. *Br VII*	250	550
1257	PAXS type. *Br. VIII*	80	125

WILLIAM II, 1087–1100

William Rufus was the second son of William I, his elder brother Robert succeeding to the Dukedom of Normandy. He was killed hunting in the New Forest.

1258 1259

1258	**Penny**. Profile type. *Br. 1*	225	500
1259	Cross in quatrefoil type. *Br. 2*	225	450

1260 1261

1260	Cross voided type. *Br. 3*	225	460
1261	Cross pattée and fleury type. *Br. 4*	250	575

1262

1262	Cross fleury and piles type. *Br. 5*	350	650

HENRY I, 1100–1135

Fifteen types were minted during this reign. In 1108 provision was made for minting round halfpence again, none having been struck since the time of Eadgar, but relatively few can have been made. The standard of coinage manufacture was now beginning to deteriorate badly. Many genuine coins were being cut to see if they were plated counterfeits and there was a reluctance by the public to accept such damaged pieces. About 1108–9 an extraordinary decision was taken ordering the official mutilation of all new coins by snicking the edges, thus ensuring that cut coins had to be accepted. Pennies of types VII to XII (Nos. 1268–1273) usually have a cut in the flan that sometimes penetrated over a third of the way across the coin.

At Christmas 1124 the famous 'Assize of the Moneyers' was held at Winchester when all the moneyers in England were called to account for their activities and a number are said to have been mutilated for issuing coins of inferior quality.

Note. Academic opinion is now agreed that the order of types II to XI is in doubt. A new chronology for these types was published in Spinks' *Numismatic Circular*, Sept. 1990. We have put the new proposed dates against the original types in our text. The principal changes are: type III precedes type II, and types VII to XI now have the following order: IX, VIII, VII, XI, X.

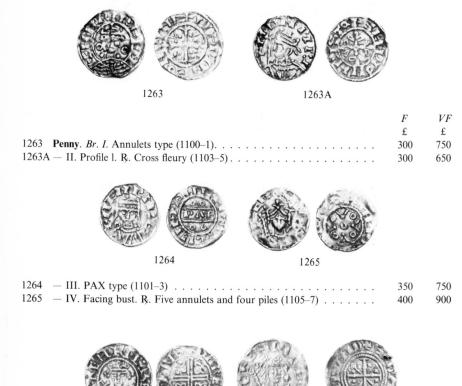

1263   1263A

1264   1265

1266   1267

		F	VF
		£	£
1263	**Penny.** *Br. I.* Annulets type (1100–1)	300	750
1263A	— II. Profile l. ℞. Cross fleury (1103–5)	300	650
1264	— III. PAX type (1101–3)	350	750
1265	— IV. Facing bust. ℞. Five annulets and four piles (1105–7)	400	900
1266	— V. — ℞. Voided cross with fleur in each angle (1107–8)	500	1100
1267	— VI. Pointing bust and stars type (1108–9)	900	1850

1268

		F £	VF £

1268 — VII. Facing bust. ℞. Quatrefoil with piles (1111–13)   250   500

1269   1270

1269 *Br*. VIII. Large bust 1. ℞. Cross with annulet in each angle (1110–11) . .   600   1450
1270 — IX. Facing bust. ℞. Cross in quatrefoil (1109–10).   450   1000

1271   1272

1271 — X. Small facing bust in circle. ℞. Cross fleury (1115–18)   225   475
1272 — XI. Very large bust 1. ℞. "Double inscription" around small cross pattée
(1113–15).   600   1100

1273   1274

1273 — XII. Small bust 1. ℞. Cross with annulet in each angle (1118–20) . . .   350   750
1274 — XIII. Star in lozenge fleury type (1120–2)   250   550

1275   1276

	F	VF
	£	£
1275 — XIV. Pellets in quatrefoil type (1122–5)	120	275
1276 — XV. Quadrilateral on cross fleury type (1125–35)	85	200

*Full flan pieces with good legends may be worth more than the price stated.

1277

1277* *Halfpenny*. Facing head. R̸. Cross potent with pellets in angles	2000	4000
1277A — As above R̸. Similar to penny die of type IX		*Unique*

*A number of specimens have appeared lately in new finds.

STEPHEN, 1135–1154
and the Civil War and Anarchy, 1138–1153

Stephen of Blois, Count of Boulogne and a nephew of Henry I, hastily crossed the Channel on his uncle's death and secured the throne for himself, despite Henry's wishes that his daughter Matilda should succeed him. She was the widow of the German emperor Henry V, and was then married to Geoffrey, Count of Anjou. Two years later Matilda arrived in England to claim the throne, supported by her half-brother Robert of Gloucester. During the protracted civil war that ensued Matilda and later her son, Henry of Anjou, set up an alternative court at Bristol and held much of the west of England, striking coins at mints under their control. Many irregular coins were struck during this troubled period, some by barons in their own name. Particularly curious are the coins from the Midlands and E. Anglia which have Stephen's head defaced, now believed to have been issued during the Interdict of 1148. In 1153, following the death of Stephen's son, Eustace, a treaty between the two factions allowed for the succession of Matilda's son Henry and a uniform coinage was once more established throughout the kingdom.

    B.M.C.—British Museum Catalogue: *Norman Kings*, 2 vols. (1916). *M.*—Mack, R. P., "Stephen and the Anarchy 1135–54", *BNJ*, XXXV (1966), pp. 38–112.

STEPHEN

Regular regal issues

1278   1280

	F £	VF £

1278	**Penny**. Cross moline (Watford) type. Bust r., with sceptre. R. Cross moline with lis in angles. *B.M.C. I; M. 3–42*	80	170
1279	— Similar, but obv. reads PERERIC or PERERICM. *M. 43–50*	350	800
1280	Voided cross type. Facing bust with sceptre. R. Voided cross pattée with mullets in angles. *East and South-east mints only. B.M.C. II; M. 53–66.* .	150	325

1281   1282

| 1281 | Cross fleury type. Bust l. with sceptre. R. Cross fleury with trefoils in angles. *East and South-east mints only. B.M.C. VI; M. 77–99* . . . . | 350 | 800 |
| 1282 | Cross pommée (Awbridge) type. Bust half-left with sceptre. R. Voided cross pommée with lis in angles. *B.M.C. VII; M. 99z–135b* . . . . *For B.M.C. types III, IV & V, see 1300–1302.* | 150 | 325 |

Local and irregular issues of the Civil War

A. Coins struck from erased or defaced dies (interdict of 1148)

1283   1288

1283	As 1278, with king's bust defaced with long cross. *East Anglian Mints. M. 137–147*	400	950
1284	— Similar, but king's bust defaced with small cross. *Nottingham. M. 149*	400	800
1285	— Similar, but sceptre defaced with bar or cross. *Nottingham, Lincoln and Stamford. M. 148 and 150–154*	300	800
1286	— Similar, but king's name erased. *Nottingham. M. 157*	500	1000
1286A	— Other defacements	*Extremely rare*	

B. South-Eastern variant

| 1287 | As 1278, but king holds mace instead of sceptre. *Canterbury. M. 158.* . . . | *Extremely rare* | |

C. Eastern variants

| 1288 | As 1278, but roundels in centre or on limbs of cross or in angles. *Suffolk mints. M. 159–168.* . . . . | 600 | 1200 |
| 1288A | As 1278, but star before sceptre and annulets at tips of fleurs on reverse. *Suffolk mints. M. 188* . . . . | 1000 | 2500 |

| | F | VF |
| | £ | £ |

1289   As 1278, but thick plain cross with pellet at end of limbs, lis in angles.
       Lincoln. M. 169–173.   600   1200
1290   — Similar, but thick plain cross superimposed on cross moline. *M. 174* .   *Extremely rare*
1290A As 1278. ℞. Quadrilateral over voided cross. *M. 176*. . . . .   *Extremely rare*
1290B As 1278. ℞. Long cross to edge of coin, fleurs outwards in angles. *Lincoln.*
       M. 186–187 . . . .   *Extremely rare*

D.   Southern variants
1291   As 1278, but with large rosette of pellets at end of obverse legend. *M. 184–*
       185 . . . .   *Extremely rare*
1292   — Similar, but star at end of obverse legend. *M. 187y*. . . . .   *Extremely rare*
1293   Crowned bust r. or l. with rosette of pellets before face in place of sceptre.
       ℞. As 1280, but plain instead of voided cross. *M. 181–183* . . . .   *Extremely rare*

1295

1295   As 1278, but usually collar of annulets. ℞. Voided cross moline with
       annulet at centre. *Southampton. M. 207–212*   600   1500

E.   Midland variants

1296

1296   As 1278, but cross moline on reverse has fleured extensions into legend.
       Leicester. M. 177–178.   1000   2500
1297   As 1278 but crude work. ℞. Voided cross with lis outwards in angles.
       Tutbury. M. 179. . . . .   *Extremely rare*
1298   Somewhat similar. ℞. Voided cross with martlets in angles. *Derby. M. 175*   1200   3000

1298   1300

	F	VF
	£	£

1299   As 1278. R̩. Plain cross with T-cross in each angle. *M. 180* . . . .   *Extremely rare*

1300   Facing bust with three annulets on crown. R̩. Cross pattée, fleurs inwards
in angles. *Northampton or Huntingdon (?). B.M.C. III; M.67–71*   1200   3000

1301   1302

1301   Facing bust with three fleurs on crown. R̩. Lozenge fleury, annulets in
angles. *Lincoln or Nottingham. B.M.C. IV; M. 72–75*   1250   3250

1302   Bust half-right with sceptre. R̩. Lozenge with pellet centre, fleurs inwards
in angles. *Leicester. B.M.C. V; M. 76*   1250   3250

1303   **Robert**, Earl of Leicester(?). As 1280, but reading ROBERTVS. *M. 269* .   *Extremely rare*

F.   North-east and Scottish border variants

1304   As 1278, but star before sceptre and annulets at tips of fleurs on reverse.
M. 188   1000   2500

1305   As 1278, but a voided cross extending to outer circle of reverse. *M. 189–192*

Extremely rare

1306   As 1278, but crude style, with Stephen's name. *M. 276–279 and 281–282.*   700   1750

1307   — Similar. R̩. Cross crosslet with cross-pattée and crescent in angles.
M. 288 . . . .   *Extremely rare*

1308   **David I** (K. of Scotland). As 1305, but with name DAVID REX. *M. 280*   1500   —

1309   **Henry** (Earl of Northumberland, son of K. David). hENRIC ERL. As
1278. *M. 283–285*   1200   3000

1310   — Similar. R̩. Cross fleury. *M. 286–287*   1000   2500

1311   — As 1307, but with name NENCI : COM on obverse. *M. 289.*   1200   2750

G.   "Ornamented" series. *So-called 'York Group' but probably minted in Northern France*

1312   As 1278, with obverse inscription NSEPEFETI, STEFINEI or RODBDS.
R̩. WISÐ. GNETA, etc., with ornament(s) in legend (sometimes retro-
grade). *M. 215–216 and 227* . . . .   *Extremely rare*

1313   1315

1313   Flag type. As 1278, but king holds lance with pennant, star to r. R̩. As
1278, mostly with four ornaments in legend. *M. 217*   1250   2500

1313A — Similar, but with eight ornaments in reverse inscription. *M. 217.*   1250   2500

	F £	VF £

1314 As 1278, but STIEN and ornaments, sceptre is topped by pellet in lozenge. R̵. Cross fleury over plain cross, ornaments in place of inscription. *M. 218.* — *Extremely rare*

1314A King stg. facing, holding sceptre and long standard with triple-tailed pennon. R̵. Cross pattée, crescents and quatrefoils in angles, pellets around, ornaments in legend . . . . — *Unique*

1315 **Stephen and Queen Matilda.** Two standing figures holding sceptre, as illustration. R̵. Ornaments in place of inscription. *M. 220* . . . . — 2500 — 5000

1316   1320

1316 **Eustace.** EVSTACIVS, knight stg. r. holding sword. R̵. Cross in quatrefoil, EBORACI EDTS (or EBORACI TDEFL). *M. 221–222.* . . . . — *Extremely rare*

1317 — Similar, but ThOMHS FILIuS VIF. *M. 223.* . . . . — *Extremely rare*

1318 — Similar, but mixed letters and ornaments in rev. legend. *M. 224.* . . . . — 1500

1319 [EVSTA] CII . FII . IOANIS, lion passant r, collonnade (or key?) below. R̵. Cross moline with cross-headed sceptres in angles, mixed letters and ornaments in legend. *M. 225* . . . . — *Unique*

1320 Lion rampant r., looped object below, EISTAOhIVS. R̵. Cross fleury with lis in angles, mostly, ornaments in legend. *M. 226* . . . . — 1400 — 3250

1321 **Rodbert.** Knight on horse r., RODBERTVS IESTV (?). R̵. As 1314. *M. 228* — *Extremely rare*

1321   1322

1322 **Bishop Henry.** Crowned bust r., crozier and star to r., HENRICVS EPC. R̵. Somewhat as last, STEPhANVS REX. *M. 229* . . . . — *Extremely rare*

H. Uncertain issues

1323 Crowned bust r. with sceptre, -NEPᚱ:. R̵. Cross pattée with annulets in angles (as Hen. I type XIII). *M. 272.* . . . . — *Extremely rare*

1324 Crowned facing bust with sceptre, star to r. (as Hen. I type XIV). R̵. As last. *M. 274* . . . . — *Extremely rare*

1325 Other types. . . . . — *Extremely rare*

ANGEVINS

1326   1331

1326	**Matilda**, Dowager Empress, Countess of Anjou (in England 1139–1148). As 1278, but cruder style, MATILDI IMP. etc. *M. 230–240*	750	1750
1326A	Obv. similar. ℞. Cross pattée over cross fleury (Cardiff hoard)	750	1750
1326B	Similar, but triple pellets or plumes at end of cross (Cardiff hoard)	*Extremely rare*	
1327	**Duke Henry**, son of Matilda and Geoffrey of Anjou, Duke of Normandy from 1150 (in England 1147–1149–1150 and 1153–1154). As 1278 but hENRICVS, etc. *M. 241–245*	2250	5000
1327A	As 1295 but hENRIC. *M. 246*	*Extremely rare*	
1327B	As 1326B, but hENNENNVS R, etc	*Extremely rare*	
1328	Obverse as 1278. ℞. Cross crosslet in quatrefoil. *M. 254*	*Extremely rare*	
1329	Crowned bust r. with sceptre. ℞. Cross fleury over quadrilateral fleury. *M. 248–253*	2250	4500
1330	Crowned facing bust, star each side. ℞. Cross botonnée over a quadrilateral pommée. *M. 255–258*	2250	5000
1331	Obverse as 1330. ℞. Voided cross botonnée over a quadrilateral pommée. *M. 259–261*	2250	5000
1332	**William**, Earl of Gloucester (succeeded his father, Earl Robert, in 1147). Type as Henry of Anjou, no. 1329. *M. 262*	*Unique*	
1333	Type as Henry of Anjou, no. 1330. *M. 263*	*Unique*	
1334	Type as Henry of Anjou, no. 1331. *M. 264–268*	2500	5500
1335	**Brian Fitzcount**, Lord of Wallingford (?). Type as Henry of Anjou, no. 1330. *M. 270*	*Unique*	
1336	**Patrick**, Earl of Salisbury (?). Helmeted bust r. holding sword, star behind. ℞. As Henry of Anjou, no. 1329. *M. 271*	*Extremely rare*	

HENRY II, 1154–1189

Cross-and-crosslets ("Tealby") Coinage, 1158–1180

Coins of Stephen's last type continued to be minted until 1158. Then a new coinage bearing Henry's name replaced the currency of the previous reign which contained a high proportion of irregular and sub-standard pennies. The new Cross and Crosslets issue is more commonly referred to as the "Tealby" coinage, as over 5000 of these pennies were discovered at Tealby, Lincolnshire, in 1807. Thirty mints were employed in this re-coinage, but once the re-minting had been completed not more than a dozen mints were kept open. The issue remained virtually unchanged for twenty-two years apart from minor variations in the king's portrait. The coins tend to be poorly struck.

Cut coins occur with varying degrees of frequency during this issue, according to the type and local area.

A   B   C

Penny

	F £
1337 Class A. No hair.	35
1338 — B. Similar but mantle varies.	40
1339 — C. Decorated collar, curl of hair	35

D   E   F

1340 — D. Decoration continues along shoulder	40
1341 — E. Similar bust, but shoulder not decorated	45
1342 — F. Hair in long ringlet to r. of bust.	45

Mints and classes of the Cross-and-Crosslets coinage

Approximate dates for the various classes are as follows:

A 1158–1161, B and C 1161–1165, D 1165–1168, E 1168–1170 and F 1170–1180.

Bedford . . . . .A – – – – –	Ilchester . . . . .A B C D – F	Pembroke. . . . .A – – – – –
Bristol. . . . . .A B C D E F	Ipswich . . . . . .– B C D E F	Salisbury . . . . .A – – – – –
Bury St. Edmunds . .A B C D E F	Launceston. . . .A – – – – –	Shrewsbury. . . .A – – – – –
Canterbury . . . . . .A B C D E F	Leichester. . . . .A – – – – –	Stafford. . . . . .A – C – – –
Carlisle . . . . .A – C D E F	Lewes. . . . .– – – – ? F	Thetford . . . . .A – C D – F
Chester . . . . .A – – D – –	Lincoln . . . . . .A B C D E F	Wallingford . . .A – – – – –
Colchester. . . . . . .A – C – E –	London. . . . . .A B C D E F	Wilton . . . . . .A – – – – –
Durham. . . . . . . .A B C – – –	Newcastle. . . . .A – C D E F	Winchester . . . .A – C D ? –
Exeter . . . . .A B C D – –	Northampton . .A – C ? – –	York . . . . .A – C D – –
Gloucester . . . . . .A – – – – –	Norwich . . . . .A B C D – F	
Hereford . . . . . . .A – C – – –	Oxford . . . . .A – – D E –	

*The Fine price allows for the usual poor-quality strike.

"Short Cross" coinage of Henry II (1180–1189)

In 1180 a coinage of new type, known as the Short Cross coinage, replaced the Tealby issue. The new coinage is remarkable in that it covers not only the latter part of the reign of Henry II, but also the reigns of his sons Richard and John and his grandson Henry III, and the entire issue bears the name "hENRICVS". There are no English coins with names of Richard or John. The Short Cross coins can be divided chronologically into various classes: eleven mints were operating under Henry II and tables of mints, moneyers and classes are given for each reign.

Cut coins continue and although less common than after 1247, they are still up to ten times commoner than during the Anglo-Saxon period.

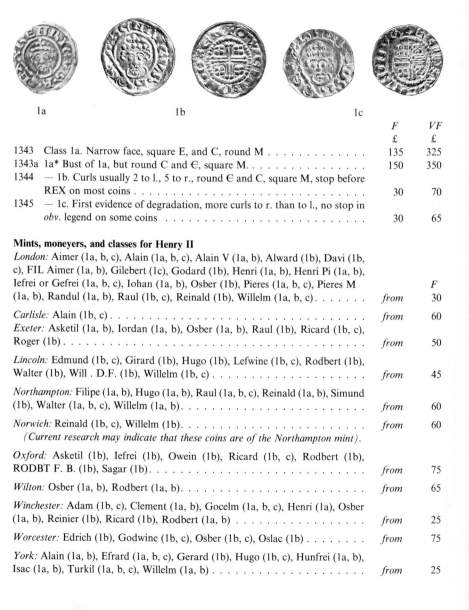

1a   1b   1c

			F	VF
			£	£
1343	Class 1a. Narrow face, square E, and C, round M		135	325
1343a	1a* Bust of 1a, but round C and E, square M.		150	350
1344	— 1b. Curls usually 2 to l., 5 to r., round E and C, square M, stop before REX on most coins		30	70
1345	— 1c. First evidence of degradation, more curls to r. than to l., no stop in *obv.* legend on some coins		30	65

Mints, moneyers, and classes for Henry II

London: Aimer (1a, b, c), Alain (1a, b, c), Alain V (1a, b), Alward (1b), Davi (1b, c), FIL Aimer (1a, b), Gilebert (1c), Godard (1b), Henri (1a, b), Henri Pi (1a, b), Iefrei or Gefrei (1a, b, c), Iohan (1a, b), Osber (1b), Pieres (1a, b, c), Pieres M (1a, b), Randul (1a, b), Raul (1b), Reinald (1b), Willelm (1a, b, c) . . . . . .   *from*   **F** 30

Carlisle: Alain (1b, c) . . . .   *from*   60

Exeter: Asketil (1a, b), Iordan (1a, b), Osber (1a, b), Raul (1b), Ricard (1b, c), Roger (1b) . . . .   *from*   50

Lincoln: Edmund (1b, c), Girard (1b), Hugo (1b), Lefwine (1b, c), Rodbert (1b), Walter (1b), Will . D.F. (1b), Willelm (1b, c) . . . .   *from*   45

Northampton: Filipe (1a, b), Hugo (1a, b), Raul (1a, b, c), Reinald (1a, b), Simund (1b), Walter (1a, b, c), Willelm (1a, b). . . . .   *from*   60

Norwich: Reinald (1b, c), Willelm (1b). . . . .   *from*   60
   (Current research may indicate that these coins are of the Northampton mint).

Oxford: Asketil (1b), Iefrei (1b), Owein (1b), Ricard (1b, c), Rodbert (1b), RODBT F. B. (1b), Sagar (1b). . . . .   *from*   75

Wilton: Osber (1a, b), Rodbert (1a, b). . . . .   *from*   65

Winchester: Adam (1b, c), Clement (1a, b), Gocelm (1a, b, c), Henri (1a), Osber (1a, b), Reinier (1b), Ricard (1b), Rodbert (1a, b) . . . .   *from*   25

Worcester: Edrich (1b), Godwine (1b, c), Osber (1b, c), Oslac (1b) . . . .   *from*   75

York: Alain (1a, b), Efrard (1a, b, c), Gerard (1b), Hugo (1b, c), Hunfrei (1a, b), Isac (1a, b), Turkil (1a, b, c), Willelm (1a, b) . . . .   *from*   25

RICHARD I, 1189–1199

Pennies of Short Cross type continued to be issued throughout the reign, all bearing the name hЄNRICVS. The coins of class 4, which have very crude portraits, continued to be issued in the early years of the next reign. The only coins bearing Richard's name are from his territories of Aquitaine and Poitou in western France.

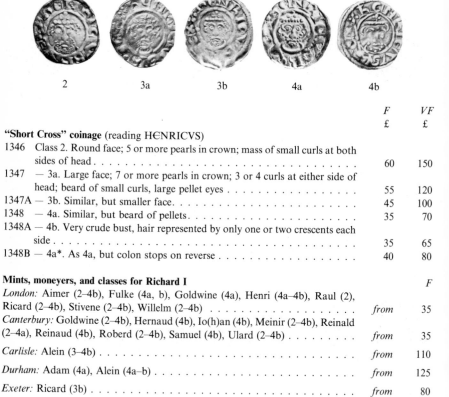

	2	3a	3b	4a	4b

	F	VF
	£	£

"Short Cross" coinage (reading HЄNRICVS)

		F	VF
1346	Class 2. Round face; 5 or more pearls in crown; mass of small curls at both sides of head	60	150
1347	— 3a. Large face; 7 or more pearls in crown; 3 or 4 curls at either side of head; beard of small curls, large pellet eyes	55	120
1347A	— 3b. Similar, but smaller face	45	100
1348	— 4a. Similar, but beard of pellets	35	70
1348A	— 4b. Very crude bust, hair represented by only one or two crescents each side	35	65
1348B	— 4a*. As 4a, but colon stops on reverse	40	80

Mints, moneyers, and classes for Richard I *F*

London: Aimer (2–4b), Fulke (4a, b), Goldwine (4a), Henri (4a–4b), Raul (2), Ricard (2–4b), Stivene (2–4b), Willelm (2–4b) . . . . *from* 35

Canterbury: Goldwine (2–4b), Hernaud (4b), Io(h)an (4b), Meinir (2–4b), Reinald (2–4a), Reinaud (4b), Roberd (2–4b), Samuel (4b), Ulard (2–4b) . . . . *from* 35

Carlisle: Alein (3–4b) . . . . *from* 110

Durham: Adam (4a), Alein (4a–b) . . . . *from* 125

Exeter: Ricard (3b) . . . . *from* 80

Lichfield: Ioan (2) . . . . *Extremely rare*

Lincoln: Edmund (2), Lefwine (2), Willelm (2) . . . . *from* 45

Northampton: Geferi (4a), Roberd (3), Waltir (3) . . . . *from* 90

Norwich: Randul (4a–b), Willelm (4a–b) . . . . *from* 90

Shrewsbury: Ive (4b), Reinald (4a, 4b), Willelm (4a) . . . . *from* 150

Winchester: Adam (3a), Gocelm (2–3), Osbern (3–4a), Pires (4a), Willelm (2–4) . *from* 50

Worcester: Osbern (2) . . . . *Extremely rare*

York: Davi (4b?), Everard (2–4b), Hue (2–4a), Nicole (4b), Turkil (2–4b) . . . . *from* 40

JOHN, 1199–1216

"Short Cross" coinage *continued.* All with name hЄNRICVS

The Short Cross coins of class 4 will have continued during the early years of John's reign, but in 1205 a re-coinage was initiated and new Short Cross coins of better style replaced the older issues. Coins of classes 5a and 5b were issued in the re-coinage in which sixteen mints were employed. Only ten of these mints were still working by the end of class 5. The only coins to bear John's name are the pennies, halfpence and farthings issues for Ireland.

| 4c | 5a | 5b | 5c | 6a1 | 6a2 |

			F	VF
			£	£
1349	Class 4c. Somewhat as 4b, but letter S is reversed		30	70
1350	— 5a. New coinage of neat style and execution; realistic face; 5 or more pearls to crown; letter S is reversed; *mm* cross pommée		30	65
1350A	— — with ornamented letters		35	110
1350B	— 5a/5b or 5b/5a mules		35	80
1351	— 5b. Similar, but S normal and *mm* reverts to cross pattée.		25	50
1352	— 5c. Similar, but letter X composed of 4 strokes in the form of a St. Andrew's cross.		25	50
1353	— 6a1. Coarser style; letter X composed of 2 wedges in the form of a St. Andrew's cross.		20	45
1353A	— 6a2. Similar, but letter X has arms at right angles and with rounded ends		20	45

Mints, moneyers and classes for John

	F

London: Abel (5c–6a), Adam (5b–c), Arnaud (5b), Beneit (5b–c), Fulke (4c–5a), Henri (4c–5b), Ilger (5b–6a), Iohan (5b), Rauf (5c–6a), Rener (5b–c), Ricard (4c–5b), Ricard B (5b–c), Ricard T (5b), Walter (5c–6a), Willelm (4c–5c), Willelm B (5b–c), Willelm L (5b–c), Willelm T (5b–c) . . . . *from* 20

Bury St. Edmunds: Fulke (5b–c) . . . . *from* 50

Canterbury: Arnaud (5a–c), Coldwine (4c–5c), (H)ernaud (5a–c), Hue (4c–5c), Io(h)an (4c–5c), Iohan B (5b–c), Iohan M (5b–c), Rauf (Vc?), Roberd (4c–5c), Samuel (4c–5c), Simon (5a or c), Simun (4c–5b) . . . . *from* 15

Carlisle: Tomas (5b) . . . . *from* 90

Chichester: Pieres (5b), Rauf (5a–b), Simon (5a–b), Willelm (5b) . . . . *from* 50

Durham: Pieres (4c–6a) . . . . *from* 70

Exeter: Gilebert (5a–b), Iohan (5a–b), Ricard (5a–b) . . . . *from* 45

Ipswich: Alisandre (5b, c), Iohan (5b–c) . . . . *from* 50

Kings Lynn: Iohan (5b), Nicole (5b), Willelm (5b) . . . . *from* 135

Lincoln: Alain (5a), Andreu (5a–c), Hue (5b–c), Iohan (5a), Rauf (5a–b), Ricard (5a), Tomas (5a, b) . . . . *from* 40

Northampton: Adam (5b–c), Randul (4c), Roberd (5b), Roberd T (5b). . . . . . . *from* 45

		F
Norwich: Gifrei (5a–c), Iohan (5a–c), Renald (5a), Renaud (5a–c)	*from*	45
Oxford: Ailwine (5b), Henri (5b), Miles (5b)	*from*	50

Rhuddlan: An irregular issue probably struck during this reign. Halli, Henricus,
Tomas, Simond . . . . *from* 80

Rochester: Alisandre (5b), Hunfrei (5b) . . . . *from* 100

Winchester: Adam (5a–c), Andreu (5b–c), Bartelme (5b–c), Henri (5a), Iohan (5a–
c), Lukas (5b, c), Miles (5a–c), Rauf (5b–c), Ricard (5a, b) . . . . *from* 25

York: Davi (4c–5b), Nicole (4c–5c), Renaud (5b), Tomas (5b) . . . . *from* 30

HENRY III, 1216–72

"Short Cross" coinage *continued* (1216–47)

The Short Cross coinage continued for a further thirty years during which time the style of portraiture and workmanship deteriorated. By the 1220s minting had been concentrated at London and Canterbury, one exception being the mint of the Abbot of Bury St. Edmunds.

Halfpenny and farthing dies are recorded early in this issue (1221–30); a few halfpennies and now one farthing have been discovered. See nos 1357 D–E.

6b	6c	7 early	7 middle	7 late

"Short Cross" coinage, 1216–47

		F	VF
		£	£
1354	Class 6b. Very tall lettering; early coins have a head similar to 6a, but later issues have a long thin face	18	40
1355	— 6c. Pointed face	18	40
1355A	— — Ornamental lettering	50	135
1355B	— 6x. Large face, two curls each side of hd., pellet on chin, letter X only by sceptre	—	—
1355C	— 6d. Tall, straight-sided letter, pellet on crossbar of N on most coins. .	—	—
1356	— 7. No stops between words in rev. legend; no neck	15	35

8a	8b1	8b2	8b3

1357	— 8a. New style; *mm* cross pattée; letter X curule shaped	*Extremely rare*
1357A	— 8b1. Similar; *mm* cross pommée.	20 75
1357B	— 8b2. Cruder version; wedge-shaped letter X	20 75
1357C	— 8b3. Very crude version; letter X is cross pommée	20 75

1357D

| | | | F |
| | | | £ |

1357D **"Short Cross" coinage.** (*c.* 1221–30). Cl. 7. Halfpenny. hENRICVS REX.
Ɍ. TER.RI ON LUND or ELIS ON LUND (London) . . . . *Extremely rare*
1357E — —Farthing. Similar. Ɍ. TERRI ON LUND . . . . *Unique*

Mints, moneyers, and classes for Henry III "Short Cross" coinage

London: Abel (6b–7), Adam (7), (H)elis (7), Giffrei (7), Ilger (6b–7), Ledulf (7), Nichole (7–8), Rau(l)f (6b–7), Ricard (7), Terri (7), Walter (6b–6c). . . . . *from* 15
Bury St. Edmunds: Io(h)an (7–8), Norman (7), Rauf (6b–7), Simund (7), Wil-lelm (7). . . . . *from* 30

Canterbury: Arnold (6x), Henri (6b–7), Hiun (6b–7), Iun (7), Io(h)an (6b–8), Ioan Chic (7), Ioan F. R. (7), Nicole (7–8), Norman (7), Osmund (7), Roberd (6b), Robert (7), Robert Vi (7), Roger (6b–7), Roger of R (7), Salemun (6x, 7), Samuel (6b–7), Simon (7), Simun (6b–7), Tomas (6d, 7), Walter (6b–7), Willem (7–8), Willem Ta (7) . . . . *from* 12

Durham: Pieres (7) . . . . *from* 100

Winchester: Henri (6c) . . . . *from* 20

York: Iohan (6c), Peres (6c), Tomas (6c), Wilam (6c) . . . . *from* 120

"Long Cross" coinage (1247–72)

By the middle of Henry's reign the coinage in circulation was in a poor state, being worn and clipped. In 1247 a fresh coinage was ordered, the new pennies having the reverse cross extended to the edge of the coin to help safeguard the coins against clipping. The earliest of these coins have no mint or moneyers' names. A number of provincial mints were opened for producing sufficient of the Long Cross coins, but these were closed again in 1250, only the royal mints of London and Canterbury and the ecclesiastical mints of Durham and Bury St. Edmunds remaining open.

In 1257, following the introduction of new gold coinages by the Italian cities of Brindisi (1232), Florence (1252) and Genoa (1253), Henry III issued a gold coinage in England. This was a gold "Penny" valued at 20 silver pence and twice the weight of the silver penny. The coinage was not a success, being undervalued, and coinage ceased after a few years—few have survived.

Cut halfpennies and farthings are common for this period, with a greater concentration in the early part. They are up to 100 times commoner than in late Anglo-Saxon times.

Without sceptre

Ia   Ib

		F	VF
		£	£
1358	Class Ia. hENRICVS: REX. Ɍ. ANGLIE TERCI.	75	150
1359	Ib. hENRICVS REX. ANG. Ɍ. LIE TERCI LON *(London)*, CAN *(Canterbury)* or AED *(Bury St. Edmunds)* . . . . *from*	40	65
1360	— — I/II mule	45	75

II	IIIa	IIIb	IIIc

			F	VF
			£	£
1361	Class II. hENRICVS REX TERCI. R. Moneyer and mint		25	50
1362	— IIIa. hENRICVS REX · III, thin face as class II		15	28
1363	— IIIb. Smaller, rounder face		15	28
1364	— IIIc. Face with pointed chin, neck indicated by two lines, usually REX: III.		15	28

With sceptre

IVa	IVb	Va	Vb	Vc

1365	Class IVa. Similar to last, but with sceptre	50	110
1366	— IVb. Similar, but new crown with half-fleurs and large central fleur . .	60	130
1367	— Va. With class IV bust, round eyes, from now on legend begins at 10 o'clock	17	30
1368	— Vb. Narrower face, wedge-tailed R, round eyes	15	28
1369	— Vc. As last, but almond-shaped eyes	15	28

Vd	Ve	Vf	Vg	Vh

1370	— Vd. Portrait of quite different style; new crown with true-shaped fleur	35	85
1371	— Ve. Similar, with jewelled or beaded crown	90	225
1372	— Vf. New style larger face, double-banded crown.	17	40
1373	— Vg. Single band to crown, low central fleur, curule chair shaped X . .	16	35
1374	— Vh. Crude copy of Vg, with pellets in lieu of fleur	20	50
1375	— Vi. Similar to last, but triple line of pellets for beard	*Extremely rare*	

Vi   1376

| | F | VF |
| | £ | £ |

1376 **Gold penny** of 20d. As illustration . . . . *Extremely rare*
    A very fine specimen sold at auction in June 1985 for £65,000.

Mints, Moneyers, and classes for Henry III "Long Cross" coinage

London: Davi or David (IIIc–Vf), Henri (IIIa–Vd, f, g), Ion, Ioh, Iohs or Iohan (Vc–g), Nicole (Ib/II mule, II–Vc), Renaud (Vg–i), Ricard (IIIc–Vg), Robert (Vg), Thomas (Vg), Walter (Vc–g), Willem (Vc–g and gold penny) . . . .   *from* 15

Bristol: Elis (IIIa, b, c), Henri (IIIb), Iacob (IIIa, b, c), Roger (IIIa, b, c), Walter (IIIb, c). . . . .   *from* 22

Bury St. Edmunds: Ion or Iohs (II–Va, Vg, h, i), Randulf (Va–f), Renaud (Vg), Stephane (Vg) . . . .   *from* 20

Canterbury: Alein (Vg, h), Ambroci (Vg), Gilbert (II–Vd/c mule, Vf, g), Ion, Ioh, Iohs, or Iohanes (IIIe–Vd, f, g), Nicole or Nichole (Ib/II mule, II–Vh), Ricard (Vg, h), Robert (Vc–h), Walter (Vc–h), Willem or Willeme (Ib/II mule, II–Vd, f, g)   *from* 15

Carlisle: Adam (IIIa, b), Ion (IIIa, b), Robert (IIIa, b), Willem (IIIa, b) . . . . .   *from* 50

Durham: Philip (IIIb), Ricard (V, b, c), Roger (Vg), Willem (Vg) . . . .   *from* 60

Exeter: Ion (II–IIIc), Philip (II–IIIc), Robert (II–IIIc), Walter (II–IIIb) . . . . .   *from* 35

Gloucester: Ion (II–IIIc), Lucas (II–IIIc), Ricard (II–IIIc), Roger (II–IIIc) . . . .   *from* 25

Hereford: Henri (IIIa, b), Ricard (IIIa, b, c), Roger (IIIa, b, c), Walter (IIIa, b, c).   *from* 40

Ilchester: Huge (IIIa, b, c), Ierveis (IIIa, b, c), Randulf (IIIa, b, c), Stephe (IIIa, b, c) . . . .   *from* 60

Lincoln: Ion (II–IIIc), Ricard (II–IIIc), Walter (II–IIIc), Willem (II–IIIc) . . . .   *from* 25

Newcastle: Adam (IIIa, b), Henri (IIIa, b, c), Ion (IIIa, b, c), Roger (IIIa, b, c) .   *from* 22

Northampton: Lucas (II–IIIb), Philip (II–IIIc), Tomas (II–IIIc), Willem (II–IIIc)   *from* 25

Norwich: Huge (II–IIIc), Iacob (II–IIIc), Ion (II–IIIc), Willem (II–IIIc) . . . . .   *from* 35

Oxford: Adam (II–IIIc), Gefrei (II–IIIc), Henri (II–IIIc), Willem (II–IIIc) . . . .   *from* 35

Shrewsbury: Lorens (IIIa, b, c), Nicole (IIIa, b, c), Peris (IIIa, b, c), Ricard (IIIa, b, c) . . . .   *from* 45

Wallingford: Alisandre (IIIa, b), Clement (IIIa, b), Ricard (IIIa, b), Robert (IIIa, b) . . . .   *from* 35

Wilton: Huge (IIIb, c), Ion (IIIa, b, c), Willem (IIIa, b, c) . . . .   *from* 40

Winchester: Huge (II–IIIc), Iordan (II–IIIc), Nicole (II–IIIc), Willem (II–IIIc) .   *from* 22

York: Alain (II–IIIb), Ieremie (II–IIIb), Ion (II–IIIc), Rener (II–IIIc), Tomas (IIIb, c). . . . .   *from* 25

EDWARD I, 1272–1307

"Long Cross" coinage *continued* (1272–79). With name hЄNRICVS

The earliest group of Edward's Long Cross coins are of very crude style and known only of Durham and Bury St. Edmunds. Then, for the last class of the type, pennies of much improved style were issued at London, Durham and Bury, but in 1279 the Long Cross coinage was abandoned and a completely new coinage substituted.

Cut halfpennies and farthings also occur for this issue, and within this context are not especially rare.

	VI	VII	

		F	VF
		£	£
1377	Class VI. Crude face with new realistic curls, Є and N ligate	15	45
1378	— VII. Similar, but of improved style, usually with Lombardic U	70	125

Mints, moneyers, and classes for Edward I "Long Cross" coinage

		F
London: Phelip (VII), Renaud (VII)	*from*	85
Bury St. Edmunds: Ioce (VII), Ion or Ioh (VI, VII)	*from*	15
Durham: Roberd (VI), Robert (VII)	*from*	175

New Coinage (from 1279).

A major re-coinage was embarked upon in 1279 which introduced new denominations. In addition to the penny, halfpence and farthings were also minted and, for the first time, a fourpenny piece called a "Groat" (from the French *Gros*).

As mint administration was now very much centralized, the practice of including the moneyer's name in the coinage was abandoned (except for a few years at Bury St. Edmunds). Several provincial mints assisted with the re-coinage during 1279–81, then minting was again restricted to London, Canterbury, Durham and Bury.

The provincial mints were again employed for a subsidiary re-coinage in 1299–1302 in order to re-mint lightweight coins and the many illegal *esterlings* (foreign copies of the English pennies or *Sterlings*, mainly from the Low Countries, are usually poorer quality than the English coins).

1379

		F	VF
		£	£
1379	**Groat**. (= 4d.; wt. 89 grs.). Type as illustration but several minor varieties.	1000	2250

Extant specimens often show traces of having been mounted on the obverse and gilded on the reverse; unmounted coins are worth more.

1a 1b 1c

	F	VF
	£	£

1380 **Penny**. *London*. Class 1a. Crown with plain band, ЄDW RЄX; Lombardic N on obv. 300 650

1381 — 1b. — ЄD RЄX; no drapery on bust, Roman N 350 750

1382 — 1c. — ЄDW RЄX; Roman N, normal or reversed; small lettering ... 14 35

1383 — 1d. — ЄDW R;—; large lettering and face................ 12 30

1384 — — — Annulet below bust (for the Abbot of Reading) 135 325

1d(1384) 2a 2b

1385 — 2a. Crown with band shaped to ornaments; large face and short neck similar to 1d; usually broken left petal to central fleur of crown. 16 40

1386 — 2b. — tall bust; long neck; N reversed 12 33

3a 3b 3c

1387 — 3a. Crescent-shaped contraction marks; pearls in crown, drapery is foreshortened circle 35 65

1388 — 3b. — — drapery is segment of a circle 25 45

1389 — 3c. — normal crown; drapery in one piece, hollowed in centre. 8 25

3e　　　　　　　　3f　　　　　　　　3g

		F	VF
		£	£
1390	— 3d. — — drapery in two pieces, broad face	10	30
1391	— 3e. — long narrow face (mostly Northern mints)	12	32
1392	— 3f. — broad face, large nose, rougher work, late S first used	25	60
1393	— 3g. — small neat bust, narrow face.	7	25

4a　　　　4b　　　　4c　　　　4d　　　　4e

		F	VF
		£	£
1394	— 4a. Comma-shaped contraction mark, late S always used, C and Є open	10	30
1395	— 4b. Similar, but face and hair shorter.	7	25
1396	— 4c. Larger face with more copious hair; unbarred A first used	7	25
1397	— 4d. Pellet at beginning of *obv.* and/or *rev.* inscription	10	30
1398	— 4e. Three pellets on breast; pellet in *rev.* legend	12	32

5a　　　　　　　　　　　5b

		F	VF
1399	— 5a. Well spread coins, pellet on breast, A normally unbarred	35	85
1400	— 5b. Coins more spread, tall lettering, long narrow face, pellet on breast.	35	85

6a　　　　　　6b　　　　　　7a

		F £	*VF* £
1401	— 6a. Smaller coins, initial cross almost plain, crown with wide fleurs . .	90	200
1402	— 6b. Initial cross well pattée; lettering of good style; closed Є (from now on)	50	100
1403	— 7a. Rose on breast; almond-shaped eyes, double barred N	40	100

7b   8a   8b   9a   9b

		F	*VF*
1404	— 7b. — — longer hair, new crown	40	100
1404A	Type as 7, but no rose	*Extremely rare*	
1405	— 8a. Smaller crown; top-tilted S; longer neck	25	60
1406	— 8b. Not unlike 9a, but top-tilted S	25	55
1407	— 9a. Narrow face, flatter crown, star on breast	14	35
1408	— 9b. Small coins; Roman N, normal, un-barred, or usually of pot-hook form; often star or pellet on breast.	8	23

10ab   10cf   10cf

		F	*VF*
1409 1410	10ab. Read ЄDWARR, ЄDWARD, ЄDWR'R'. Ornate Rs. Usually bi-foliate crown from now on	15	35
1411 1412 1413 1414	10cf. Read ЄDWA. Plain Rs	7	15

For further classification of Class 10, see "Sylloge of British Coins, 39, The J. J. North Collection, Edwardian English Silver Coins 1279–1351", Chapter 10, Class 10, c. 1301–10, by C. Wood.

Prices are for full flan, well struck coins.

The prices for the above types are for London. For coins of the following mints (see over page); types struck in brackets. Prices are for the commonest type of each mint.

| Berwick Type I | Type II | Type III | Type IV |

	F	*VF*
	£	£

1415	*Berwick-on-Tweed.* (Blunt types I–IV) . . . . *from*	20	55
1416	*Bristol.* (2; 3b; c, d; 3f, g; 9b) . . . . *from*	18	40
1417	*Bury St. Edmunds.* Robert de Hadelie (3c, d, g; 4a, b, c) . . . . . . *from*	50	120
1418	— Villa Sci Edmundi (4e; 5b; 6b; 7a; 8a–10f) . . . . *from*	20	50
1419	*Canterbury.* (2; 3b–g; 4; 5; 7a; 9;10) . . . . *from*	8	25
1420	*Chester.* (3g; 9b) . . . . *from*	35	70
1421	*Durham.* King's Receiver (9b; 10a, b, e, f) . . . . *from*	16	35
1422	— Bishop de Insula (2; 3b, c, e, g; 4a) . . . . *from*	18	40
1423	— Bishop Bec (4b, c, d; 5b; 6b; 7a; 8b; 9; 10b–f) mostly with *mm.* cross moline . . . . *from*	18	40
1424	— — (4b) cross moline in one angle of *rev.* . . . . *from*	120	250
1425	*Exeter.* (9b)	40	110
1426	*Kingston-upon-Hull.* (9b)	40	110
1427	*Lincoln.* (3c, d, f, g) . . . . *from*	16	34
1428	*Newcastle-upon-Tyne.* (3e; 9b; 10) . . . . *from*	20	50
1429	*York.* Royal mint (2; 3b, c, d, f; 9b) . . . . *from*	15	40
1430	— Archbishop's mint (3e, f; 9b). R̃. Quatrefoil in centre . . . . . . *from*	25	70

1433   1436

1431	**Halfpenny,** *London.* Class IIIb. Drapery as segment of circle	30	75
1432	—IIIc. Normal drapery as two wedges	30	75
1433	— IIIg. Similar, larger letters, wider crown	25	65
1433A	— — IV c. Comma abbreviation mark, thick waisted s.	30	75
1433B	— — Pellet before LON	35	85
1434	IVe. Usually three pellets on breast, one on *rev.*	40	90
1434A	— VI. Double barred N, small lettering	35	85
1435	— VII. Double barred N, large lettering.	32	80
1436	IX. Pot-hook N, usually no star on breast, crown band curved at fleurs .	20	55
1437	— X.ЄDWAR R ANGL DNS hYB, thick waisted letters	20	55

The above prices are for London; halfpence of the mints given below were also struck.

| 1438 | *Berwick-on-Tweed.* (Blunt types II and III) . . . . *from* | 60 | 150 |
| 1439 | *Bristol.* (IIIc; IIIg) . . . . | 50 | 150 |

		F £	VF £
1440	*Lincoln.* (IIIc)	70	175
1441	*Newcastle.* (IIIe). With single pellet in each angle of *rev.*	135	360
1442	*York.* (IIIb)	60	150

1443   1445   1446

		F £	VF £
1443	**Farthing**, *London.* Class I. Heavy weight (6.65 grains), ЄDWARDVS REX. Ŗ. LONDONIЄNSIS, bifoliate crown	25	100
1443A	— — — trifoliate crown	30	100
1444	— II. Similar, but reversed N's (6.62 grs.).	20	80
1445	— IIIc. As class I, but different bust.	20	70
1446	— IIIg. Lighter weight (5.5 grs.) Є R ANGLIЄ, no inner circle on *obv.* (5.5 grs.)	20	80
1446A	— IV Reads CIVITAS LONDON, narrow crown	45	120
1446B	— V — Wider crown	45	120
1447	— VI + VII. Similar, double barred N, pellet eyes	70	160
1448	VIII. Є R ANGL DN, closed Є	50	120
1449	— IX. Unbarred Ns.	45	110
1450	— X or XI. (Edward II) ЄDWARDVS REX A or AN inner circle both sides	25	70

Types 1449 and 1450 often appear on oval flans.

The above prices are for London; farthings of the mints given below were also struck.

1452

1451	*Berwick-on-Tweed.* (Blunt type III).		140	275
1452	*Bristol.* (II, IIIc (heavy), III (light))	*from*	85	225
1453	*Lincoln.* (III)	*from*	120	300
1453A	*Newcastle* (IIIe), triple pellet in *rev.* quarters		*Extremely rare*	
1454	*York.* (II; III)	*from*	125	300

For further information on the pennies of Edward I and II see the articles by K. A. Jacob in "Notes on English Silver Coins, 1066–1648", and for the mint of Berwick-on-Tweed, see the article by C. E. Blunt, in the Num. Chron., 1931.

EDWARD II, 1307–27

The coinage of this reign differs only in minor details from that of Edward I. No groats were issued in the years c. 1282–1351.

11a   12   13   14

15a   15b   15c

		F £	VF £
1455	**Penny,** *London.* Class 11a. Broken spear-head or pearl on l. side of crown; long narrow face, straight-sided N	10	30
1456	— 11b. — Є with angular back (till 15b), N with well-marked serifs . . .	10	30
1457	— 11c. — — A of special form.	30	65
1458	— 12. Central fleur of crown formed of three wedges	20	45
1459	— 13. Central fleur of crown as Greek double axe	16	40
1460	— 14. Crown with tall central fleur; large smiling face with leering eyes .	12	35
1461	— 15a. Small flat crown with both spear-heads usually bent to l.; face of 14.	16	40
1462	— 15b. — very similar, but smaller face.	16	40
1463	— 15c. — large face, large Є	18	45

The prices of the above types are for London. We can sometimes supply coins of the following mints; types struck in brackets.

Berwick Type V   Type VI   Type VII

			F	VF
1464	*Berwick-on-Tweed.* (Blunt types V, VI and VII).	*from*	50	95
1465	*Bury St. Edmunds.* (11; 12; 13; 14; 15)	*from*	16	40
1466	*Canterbury.* (11; 12; 13; 14; 15).	*from*	16	40
1467	*Durham.* King's Receiver (11a), *mm.* plain cross	*from*	25	55
1468	— Bishop Bec. (11a), *mm.* cross moline		25	60
1469	— Bishop Kellawe (11; 12; 13), crozier on *rev.*	*from*	25	55
1470	— Bishop Beaumont (13; 14; 15), *mm.* lion with lis.	*from*	30	70
1471	Sede Vacante (15c); *mm.* plain cross		55	135

*Prices are for full flan, well struck coins.

1469

1470

		F	VF
		£	£
1472	**Halfpenny** of *London.* ЄDWARDVS REX A(NG)	55	135
1473	— — *Berwick-on-Tweed.* (Blunt type V)	80	200
1474	**Farthing** of *London.* ЄDWARDVS REX (ANG)	65	160
1475	— *Berwick-on-Tweed.* (Blunt type V)	150	—

EDWARD III, 1327–77

During Edward's early years small quantities of silver coin were minted following the standard of the previous two reigns, but in 1335 halfpence and farthings were produced which were well below the .925 Sterling silver standard. In 1344 an impressive gold coinage was introduced comprising the Florin or Double Leopard valued at six shillings, and its half and quarter, the Leopard and the Helm. The design of the Florin was based on the contemporary gold of Philip de Valois of France. The first gold coinage was not successful and it was replaced later the same year by a heavier coinage, the Noble, valued at 6s. 8d, i.e., 80 pence, half a mark or one third of a pound, together with its fractions. The Noble was lowered in weight in two stages over the next few years, being stabilized at 120 grains in 1351. With the signing of the Treaty of Bretigni in 1360 Edward's title to the Kingdom of France was omitted from the coinage, but it was resumed again in 1369.

In 1344 the silver coinage had been re-established at the old sterling standard, but the penny was reduced in weight to just over 20 grains and in 1351 to 18 grains. Groats were minted again in 1351 and were issued regularly henceforth until the reign of Elizabeth.

Subsequent to the treaty with France which gave England a cross-channel trading base at Calais, a mint was opened there in 1363 for minting gold and silver coins of English type. In addition to coins of the regular English mints, the Abbot of Reading also minted silver pence and a halfpence with a scallop shell badge while coins from Berwick display one or two boars' heads.

There is evidence of re-use of dies at later periods, e.g. 3rd coinage halfpennies.

Mintmarks

6	1	2	3	74	4	5	7a

1334–51	Cross pattée (6)	1356	Crown (74)
1351–2	Cross 1 (1)	1356–61	Cross 3 (4)
1351–7	Crozier on cross end (76a, *Durham*)	1361–9	Cross potent (5)
1352–3	Cross 1 broken (2)	1369–77	Cross pattée (6)
1354–5	Cross 2 (3)		Plain cross (7a)
			Cross potent and four pellets

The figures in brackets refer to the plate of mintmarks on page 351.

GOLD

Third coinage, 1344–51
First period, 1344

1476 1477 1478

	F £	VF £

1476 **Florin** or **Double Leopard**. (= 6s.; wt. 108 grs.). King enthroned beneath
canopy; crowned leopard's head each side. ℞. Cross in quatrefoil. . . . . *Extremely rare*

1477 **Half-florin** or **Leopard**. Leopard sejant with banner l. ℞. Somewhat as last. *Extremely rare*

1478 **Quarter-florin** or **Helm**. Helmet on fleured field. ℞. Floriate cross. . . . . *Extremely rare*

Second period, 1344–46

1479 **Noble** (= 6s. 8d., wt. 138$\frac{6}{13}$ grs.). King stg. facing in ship with sword and
shield. ℞. L in centre of royal cross in tressure . . . . *Extremely rare*

1480 **Quarter-noble**. Shield in tressure. ℞. As last. 1250 2750

Third period, 1346–51

1481 **Noble** (wt. 128$\frac{4}{}$ grs.). As 1479, but Є in centre; large letters 600 1400

1482 **Half-noble**. Similar 6000

1483 **Quarter-noble**. As 1480, but Є in centre 250 550

Fourth coinage, 1351–77
    Reference: L. A. Lawrence, *The Coinage of Edward III from 1351.*
    Pre-treaty period, 1351–61. With French title.

1488 1498

1484 **Noble** (wt. 120 grs.), series B (1351). Open Є and C, Roman M; *mm*. cross 1
(1). 325 600

1485 — — *rev.* of series A (1351). Round lettering, Lombardic M and N; closed
inverted Є in centre 350 675

		F	VF
		£	£
1486	C (1351–1352). Closed Є and C, Lombardic M; *mm.* cross 1 (1)	275	500
1487	D (1352–1353). *O.* of series C. R̩. *Mm.* cross 1 broken (2).	400	700
1488	E (1354–1355). Broken letters, V often has a nick in r. limb; *mm.* cross 2 (3).	275	500
1489	F (1356). *Mm.* crown (74)	325	600
1490	G (1356–1361). *Mm.* cross 3 (4). Many varieties	250	475
1491	**Half-noble**, B. As noble with *rev.* of series A, but closed Є in centre not inverted.	225	475
1492	C. *O.* as noble. *Rev.* as last	250	500
1493	E. As noble	450	800
1494	G. As noble. Many varieties	175	375
1495	**Quarter-noble**, B. Pellet below shield. R̩. Closed Є in centre	135	225
1496	C. *O.* of series B. *Rev.* details as noble.	140	275
1497	E. *O.* as last. *Rev.* details as noble, pellet in centre	160	300
1498	G. *Mm.* cross 3 (4). Many varieties	110	200

Transitional treaty period, 1361. French title omitted, replaced by that of Aquitaine on the noble and (rarely) on the half-noble, but not on the quarter-noble; irregular sized letters; *mm.* cross potent (5).

1499	**Noble**. R̩. Pellets or annulets at corners of central panel	300	600
1500	**Half-noble**. Similar	150	360
1501	**Quarter-noble**. Similar. Many varieties.	140	250

1499

1500

1503

Treaty period, 1361–69. Omits FRANC, new letters, usually curule-shaped X; *mm.* cross potent (5).

1502	**Noble**. *London*. Saltire or nothing before ЄDWARD	235	500
1503	— Annulet before ЄDWARD (with, rarely, crescent on forecastle)	235	500
1504	*Calais*. C in centre of *rev.*, flag at stern of ship	275	625
1505	— — without flag	275	625

1506   1508

			F	VF
			£	£
1506	**Half-noble**. *London*. Saltire before ЄDWARD	165	325
1507	— Annulet before ЄDWARD	175	350
1508	*Calais*. C in centre of *rev.*, flag at stern of ship	250	575
1509	— — without flag................................	250	575
1510	**Quarter-noble**. *London*. As 1498. ℞. Lis in centre.............	100	200
1511	— — annulet before ЄDWARD...................	100	200
1512	*Calais*. ℞. Annulet in centre	125	225
1513	— — cross in circle over shield...................	135	275
1514	— ℞. Quatrefoil in centre; cross over shield.............	135	275
1515	— — crescent over shield.....................	225	475

Post-treaty period, 1369–1377. French title resumed.

			F	VF
1516	**Noble**. *London*. Annulet before ЄD. ℞. Treaty period die	275	525
1517	— — — crescent on forecastle	300	575
1518	— — post-treaty letters. ℞. Є and pellet in centre	250	500
1519	— — — ℞. Є and saltire in centre...................	325	600
1520	*Calais*. Flag at stern. ℞. Є in centre..................	275	550

1521

			F	VF
1521	— — *Rev.* as 1518, with Є and pellet in centre	235	500
1522	— As 1520, but without flag. ℞. C in centre	250	575
1523	**Half-noble**. *London*. *O*. Treaty die. *Rev.* as 1518	*Extremely rare*	
1524	*Calais*. Without AQT, flag at stern. ℞. Є in centre	325	700
1525	— — ℞. Treaty die with C in centre.................	350	725

SILVER

First coinage, 1327–35 (.925 fineness)

1526   1530   1535

		F	VF
		£	£
1526	**Penny**. *London*. As Edw. II; class XVd with Lombardic n's	275	650
1527	*Bury St. Edmunds*. Similar	*Extremely rare*	
1528	*Canterbury; mm.* cross pattée with pellet centre................	200	450
1529	— — three extra pellets in one quarter	200	475
1530	*Durham*. ℞. Small crown in centre......................	400	850
1531	*York*. As 1526, but quatrefoil in centre of *rev*....................	175	400
1532	— — — pellet in each quarter of *mm*.....................	175	400
1533	— — — three extra pellets in one quarter................	175	400
1534	— — — Roman N on *obv*.............................	175	400
1535	*Berwick* (1333–1342, Blunt type VIII). Bear's head in one quarter of *rev*..	250	600
1536	**Halfpenny**. *London*. If struck then indistinguishable from EDWARD II (cf. 1472)......	100	225
1537	*Berwick* (Bl. VIII). Bear's head in one or two quarters............	50	125
1538	**Farthing**. *London*. EDWARDVS REX A*, flat crown	85	175
1539	*Berwick* (Bl. VIII). As 1537.........................	70	150

1537   1540

Second coinage, 1335–43 (.833 fineness)

1540	**Halfpenny**. *London*. EDWARDVS REX A(NG)*, rough work, tall crown.	20	50
1541	*Reading*. Escallop in one quarter.......................	300	550
1542	**Farthing**. *London*. As halfpenny	50	125

Third or florin coinage, 1344–51. Bust with bushy hair. (.925 fine, 18 grs.)

1543   1555

		F £	VF £
1543	**Penny.** *London.* Class 1. ЄDW, Lombardic n's	13	45
1544	— 2, ЄDWA, n's, but sometimes N's on *rev.*.	12	35
1545	— 3, ЄDW, N's, sometimes reversed or n's on *rev.*	12	35
1546	— 4, ЄDW, no stops, reversed N's, but on *rev.* sometimes n's, N's or double-barred N's	12	35
1547	*Canterbury.* ЄDWA, n's	45	105
1548	— ЄDW, reversed N's	40	95
1549	*Durham,* Sede Vacante (1345). A, ЄDW R. ℞. No marks	50	125
1550	— — B, similar, ЄDWAR R	125	275
1551	— Bp. Hatfield. C, similar, but pellet in centre of *rev.*	75	175
1552	— — — — Crozier on *rev.*.	75	225
1553	— — — — — with pellet in centre of *rev.*	75	225
1554	— — D, ЄDWARDVS RЄX AIn, crozier on *rev.*	150	325
1555	*Reading.* *O.* as 1546. ℞. Escallop in one quarter	200	475
1556	*York.* *O.* as 1546. ℞. Quatrefoil in centre	35	80
1557	**Halfpenny.** *London.* ЄDWARDVS RЄX(An).	20	40
1558	— — pellet either side of crown sometimes	25	65
1559	— — saltire either side of crown and in one quarter of *rev.*, or pellet in each quarter	25	60
1560	*Reading.* *O.* Similar. ℞. Escallop in one quarter	275	500
1561	*Continental imitation.* Mostly reading ЄDWARDIENSIS	18	45
1562	**Farthing.** *London.* ЄDWARDVS REX	50	135
1562A	*Reading.* As last. ℞. As halfpenny		*Unique*

Fourth coinage, 1351–77
    Reference: L. A. Lawrence, *The Coinage of Edward III from 1351.*
    Pre-treaty period, 1351–61. With French title.

1567

		F £	VF £
1563	**Groat** (=4d., 72 grs.). *London,* series B (1351). Roman M, open C and Є; *mm.* cross 1	110	275
1564	— — — crown in each quarter.		*Unique*
1565	— C (1351–2). Lombardic m, closed C and Є, R with wedge-shaped tail; *mm.* cross 1	20	60
1566	— D (1352–3). R with normal tail; *mm.* cross 1 or cross 1 broken (2) . .	25	80
1567	— E (1354–5). Broken letters, V often with nick in r. limb; *mm.* cross 2 (3)	18	50
1568	— — — lis on breast	20	70

1570   1571

		F	VF
		£	£
1569	— F (1356). *Mm.* crown (74)	25	90
1570	— G (1356–61). Usually with annulet in one quarter and sometimes under bust, *mm.* cross 3 (4). Many varieties	20	60
1571	*York*, series D. As London	50	130
1572	— E. As London	40	115

1573   1574

1573	**Halfgroat**. *London*, series B. As groat	50	140
1574	— C. As groat	15	45
1575	— D. As groat	17	50
1576	— E. As groat	15	45
1577	— F. As groat	20	55
1578	— G. As groat	17	50
1579	— — — annulet below bust	25	70
1580	*York*, series D. As groat	30	85
1581	— E. As groat	25	65
1582	— — — lis on breast	35	100

1584   1587   1591

1583	**Penny**. *London*. Series A (1351). Round letters, Lombardic m and n, annulet in each quarter; *mm.* cross pattée	60	110
1584	— C. Details as groat, but annulet in each quarter	10	30
1585	— D. Details as groat, but annulet in each quarter	10	30
1586	— E. Sometimes annulet in each quarter	10	30
1587	— F. Details as groat	12	35

		F	VF
		£	£
1588	— G. Details as groat.	10	30
1589	— — — annulet below bust	15	45
1590	— — — saltire in one quarter	25	55
1591	*Durham*, Bp. Hatfield. Series A. As 1583, but extra pellet in each quarter,		
	VIL LA crozier DVRRЄM.	150	350
1592	— C. Details as groat. ℞. Crozier, CIVITAS DVNЄLMIЄ	30	80
1593	— D — — —	35	85
1594	— E — — —	25	65
1595	— F — Є. Crozier, CIVITAS DVRЄMЄ.	30	75
1596	— G — — —	20	50
1597	— — — — — annulet below bust	20	55
1598	— — — — — saltire in one quarter	20	55
1599	— — — — — annulet on each shoulder	20	55
1600	— — — — — trefoil of pellets on breast	25	65
1601	— — — ℞. Crozier, CIVITAS DVRЄLMIЄ	30	75
1602	*York*, Royal Mint. Series D.	30	65
1603	— — E.	15	40
1604	— Archb. Thorsby. Series D. ℞. Quatrefoil in centre.	25	55
1605	— — G —	17	40
1606	— — — annulet or saltire on breast.	17	40
1607	**Halfpenny**. *London*. Series E. ЄDWARDVS RЄX An	100	250
1608	— G, but with *obv.* of F (*mm.* crown). Annulet in one quarter	—	400
1609	**Farthing**. *London*. Series E. ЄDWARDVS RЄX	150	300
1609A	— — Series G. Annulet in one quarter	*Extremely rare*	

Transitional treaty period, 1361. French title omitted, irregular sized letters; *mm.* cross potent (5).

		F	VF
1610	**Groat**. *London*. Annulet each side of crown	100	350
1611	**Halfgroat**. Similar, but only seven arches to tressure	90	225

|1611|1612|

		F	VF
1612	**Penny**, *London*. Omits RЄX, annulet in two upper qtrs. of *mm*	40	110
1613	*York*, Archb. Thoresby. Similar, but quatrefoil enclosing pellet in centre of		
	rev.	40	110
1614	*Durham*. Bp. Hatfield. Similar. ℞. Crozier, CIVITAS DORЄLMЄ	55	125
1615	**Halfpenny**. Two pellets over *mm.*, ЄDWARDVS RЄX An	75	150

Treaty period, 1361–69. French title omitted, new letters, usually "Treaty" X; *mm.* cross potent (5).

		F	VF
1616	**Groat**, *London*. Many varieties	25	90
1617	— Annulet before ЄDWARD	30	100
1618	— Annulet on breast	60	175

1619

		F £	VF £
1619	*Calais*. As last	85	200

1621   1635

1620	**Halfgroat**, *London*. As groat	20	50
1621	— — Annulet before ЄDWARDVS	20	50
1622	— — Annulet on breast.	45	120
1623	*Calais*. As last	90	200
1624	**Penny**, *London*. ЄDWARD AnGL R, etc.	15	40
1625	— — — pellet before ЄDWARD	20	50
1626	*Calais*. Ŗ. VILLA CALЄSIE.	65	160
1627	*Durham*. Ŗ. DIVITAS DVNЄLMIS.	40	90
1628	— Ŗ. Crozier, CIVITAS DVRЄMЄ.	30	75
1629	*York*, Archb. Thoresby. Quatrefoil in centre of *rev.*, ЄDWARDVS DЄI G RЄX An.	35	75
1630	— — — ЄDWARDVS RЄX ANGLI.	15	45
1631	— — — — quatrefoil before ЄD and on breast	20	50
1632	— — — — annulet before ЄD.	25	55
1633	— — — ЄDWARD AnGL R DnS HYB	30	70
1634	**Halfpenny**. ЄDWARDVS RЄX An, pellet stops	25	55
1635	— Pellet before ЄD, annulet stops.	25	70
1636	**Farthing**. ЄDWARDVS RЄX, pellet stops	80	180

Post-treaty period, 1369–77. French title resumed, X like St. Andrew's cross; *mm.* 5, 6, 7a.

1637   1639

1637	**Groat**. Various readings, *mm.* cross pattée.	85	250
1638	— — row of pellets across breast (chain mail)	165	500
1639	— row of annulets below bust (chain mail); *mm.* cross potent with four pellets.	190	600

		F	VF
		£	£
1640	**Halfgroat**. Various readings	85	250
1640A	— Thin portrait of Richard II		*Rare*
1641	— row of pellets one side of breast (chain mail)	165	525
1642	**Penny**, *London*. No marks on breast	38	95
1643	— Pellet or annulet on breast	50	120
1644	— Cross or quatrefoil on breast	43	110
1645	*Durham*, Bp. Hatfield. *Mm.* 7a, CIVITAS DVnOLM, crozier	43	110
1646	— — — — annulet on breast	50	120
1647	— — — — lis on breast	38	95
1648	*York*. Archb. Thoresby or Neville. R̩. Quatrefoil in centre	25	65
1649	— — — lis on breast	50	105
1650	— — — annulet on breast	30	70
1651	— — — cross on breast	30	70

1652

| 1652 | **Farthing**. EDWARD REX ANGL, large head without neck . . . . | 150 | 325 |

RICHARD II, 1377–99

There was no significant change in the coinage during this reign. Noteworthy is the first appearance of symbols on the ship's rudder on some of the gold coins. The earlier silver coins have a portrait like that on the coins of Edward III, but the king's head and the style of lettering were altered on the later issues.

Reference: *Silver coinages of Richard II, Henry IV and V.* (B.N.J. 1959–60 and 1963).

Mintmark: cross pattée (6)

GOLD

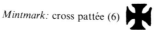

1655

1657

1653	**Noble,** *London.* With altered *obv.* and/or *rev.* die of Edw. III . . . . *from*	550	1250
1654	— Lettering as Edw. III, lis over sail	450	1100
1655	— Straight-sided letters, annulet over sail.	400	1000
1656	— Late issue, fish-tail lettering; no marks, or trefoil by shield.	450	1050
1657	— — — lion or lis on rudder.	575	1250
1658	— — small dumpy lettering; escallop or crescent on rudder and/or trefoil over sail or by shield . . . . *from*	525	1150

1658

1662

		F £	VF £
1659	*Calais.* Flag at stern, otherwise as 1653 .... *from*	500	1025
1660	— — as 1655, but quatrefoil over sail	475	1000
1661	— — as 1656; no marks	500	1025
1662	— — — lion on rudder	600	1350
1663	— — as 1658	475	1000

1664   1672/3   1677

		F £	VF £
1664	**Half-noble**, *London.* As 1653	525	1200
1665	— as 1655	450	1000
1666	— as 1656; lion on rudder	475	1100
1667	— as 1658; crescent on rudder	525	1200
1668	*Calais.* Flag at stern, otherwise as 1653	550	1500
1669	— — as 1655; quatrefoil over sail	550	1500
1670	— — as 1656; lion on rudder	525	1400
1671	— — as 1658, but one var. has saltire behind rudder	700	1600
1672	**Quarter-noble**, *London.* R in centre of *rev.*	225	425
1673	— Lis or pellet in centre of *rev.*	225	425
1674	— — *obv.* die of Edw. III altered	240	475
1675	— — escallop over shield	250	500
1676	— — trefoil of annulets over shield	235	450
1677	— — quatrefoil, cross or slipped trefoil over shield .... *from*	215	425

SILVER

		F £	VF £
1678	**Groat.** I. Style of Edw. III, F (*i.e. et*) before FRANC, etc.	250	750
1679	II. New lettering, retrograde Z before FRANC, etc.	175	475
1680	III. Bust with bushy hair, "fishtail" serifs to letters.	250	700
1681	IV. New style bust and crown, crescent on breast	850	2000

1679   1682

	F	VF
	£	£
1682 **Halfgroat**. II. New lettering.	200	550
1683 III. As 1680	225	600
1684 — — with *obv*. die of Edw. III (1640A)	400	850
1685 IV. As 1681, but no crescent	550	1200
1685A *Obv*. as Edw. III (1640A). ℞. As Type IV		*Rare*
1686 **Penny**, *London*. I Lettering as 1678, RICARDVS REX AnGLIE	175	450
1688 — II. As 1679, Z FRAnC lis on breast	175	450
1689 — III. As 1680, RICARD REX AnGLIE, fish-tail letters.	200	500

1689   1692

1690 *York*. I. Early style, usually with cross or lis on breast,		
quatrefoil in centre of *rev*.	60	
1691 — II. New bust and letters, no marks on breast	55	
1692 — Local dies. Pellet above each shoulder, cross on breast,		
REX AnGLIE	35	100
1693 — — — REX DNS EB.	45	110
1694 — — — REX AnG FRAnC	45	110
1695 — III. As 1680, REX AnGL Z FRANC (scallop after TAS)	75	125
1696 — IV. Very bushy hair, new letters, no crescent. ℞. R in centre of		
quatrefoil.	225	475
1697 *Durham*. Cross or lis on breast, DVnOLM	250	625

1699   1701   1704

1698 **Halfpenny**. Early style. LONDON, saltire or annulet on breast	50	120
1699 Intermediate style. LOnDOn, no marks on breast.	25	65
1700 Type III. Late style. Similar, but fishtail letters	35	85
1700A Type IV. Short, stubby lettering	35	85
1701 **Farthing**. Small bust and letters	200	450
1702 — — rose after REX	225	500
1703 Large head, no bust.	250	550
1704 Rose in each angle of *rev*. instead of pellets	450	900

HENRY IV, 1399–1413

In 1412 the standard weights of the coinage were reduced, the noble by 12 grains and the penny by 3 grains, partly because there was a scarcity of bullion and partly to provide revenue for the king, as Parliament had not renewed the royal subsidies. As in France, the royal arms were altered, three fleur-de-lis taking the place of the four or more lis previously displayed.

Mintmark: cross pattée (6)

Heavy coinage, 1399–1412　　　　　　GOLD

1707　　　　　　　　　　　　1708

		F	VF
		£	£
1705	**Noble** (120 grs.), *London.* Old arms with four lis in French quarters; crescent or annulet on rudder	—	6000
1706	— New arms with three lis; crescent, pellet or no marks on rudder....	—	6000
1707	*Calais.* Flag at stern, old arms; crown on or to l. of rudder	*Extremely rare*	
1708	— — new arms; crown or star on rudder	*Extremely rare*	
1709	**Half-noble**, *London.* Old arms	*Extremely rare*	
1710	— new arms	*Extremely rare*	
1711	*Calais.* New arms	*Extremely rare*	
1712	**Quarter-noble**, *London.* Crescent over old arms	800	1750
1713	— — — new arms.	700	1600
1714	*Calais.* New arms. ℞. *Mm.* crown	900	1900

1710

                                                    1715   F   VF
                                                                  £   £

Light coinage, 1412–13

1715 **Noble** (108 grs.). Trefoil, or trefoil and annulet, on side of ship. ℞. Trefoil
      in one quarter   700   1600
1716 **Half-noble**. Similar, but always with annulet   6000   —

                                    1717

1717 **Quarter-noble**. Trefoils, or trefoils and annulets beside shield, lis above. ℞.
      Lis in centre   375   800

SILVER

Heavy coinage, 1399–1412

         1718   1722   1723

1718 **Halfgroat** (36 grs.). Star on breast   1000   2500
1718A — Muled with Edw. III (1640A) . . . .   Rare
1719 **Penny**, *London*. Similar, early bust with long neck   500   1250
1720 — later bust with shorter neck, no star   500   1250
1721 *York*. Early bust with long neck   350   800
1722 — later bust with broad face, round chin   350   800
1723 **Halfpenny**. Early small bust   170   375
1724 Later large bust, with rounded shoulders, annulets by neck   185   375
1725 **Farthing**. Face without neck   400   800

Light coinage, 1412–13

1728   1731   1737

		F £	VF £
1726	**Groat** (60 grs.). I. Pellet to l., annulet to r. of crown; altered die of Richard II	1500	3500
1727	New dies; II. Annulet to l., pellet to r. of crown, 8 or 10 arches to tressure	1250	3000
1728	— III. Similar but 9 arches to tressure.	1250	3000
1729	**Halfgroat**. Pellet to l., annulet to r. of crown	*Extremely rare*	
1730	Annulet to l., pellet to r. of crown	650	1500
1731	**Penny**, *London*. Annulet and pellet by crown; trefoil on breast and before CIVI	400	950
1732	— — annulet or slipped trefoil before LON.	400	950
1733	— Pellet and annulet by crown.	*Unique*	
1734	*York*. Annulet on breast. ℞. Quatrefoil in centre	375	750
1735	*Durham*. Trefoil on breast, DVnOLM.	325	700
1736	**Halfpenny**. Struck from heavy dies.	160	325
1737	New dies; annulet either side of crown or none	160	325
1738	**Farthing**. Face, no bust; ?trefoil after REX	475	950

HENRY V, 1413–22

There was no change of importance in the coinage of this reign. There was, however, a considerable development in the use of privy marks which distinguished various issues, except for the last issue of the reign when most marks were removed. The Calais mint, which had closed in 1411, did not reopen until early in the next reign.

Mintmarks

Cross pattée (4). Pierced cross with Pierced cross (18).
pellet centre (20).

GOLD

1756

1744

		F £	VF £
1739	**Noble.** A. Quatrefoil over sail and in second quarter of *rev.* Short broad letters, no other marks	*Extremely rare*	
1740	— B. Ordinary letters; similar, or with annulet on rudder	500	900
1741	— C. Mullet by sword arm, annulet on rudder	450	750
1742	— — — broken annulet on side of ship	300	525
1743	—D. Mullet and annulet by sword arm, trefoil by shield, broken annulet on ship	325	625
1744	— E. Mullet, or mullet and annulet by sword arm, trefoil by shield, pellet by sword point and in one quarter, annulet on side of ship	350	650
1745	— — Similar, but trefoil on ship instead of by shield	400	700
1746	— F. Similar, but no pellet at sword point, trefoil in one quarter	350	700
1747	— G. No marks; annulet stops, except for mullet after first word	625	1150
1748	**Half-noble.** B. As noble; Hen. IV *rev.* die	*Extremely rare*	
1749	— C. Broken annulet on ship, quatrefoil below sail	375	800
1750	— — Mullet over shield, broken annulet on *rev.*	350	700

1750

1751	— F. Similar, but no annulet on ship, usually trefoil by shield	400	850
1752	— F/E. As last, but pellet in 1st and annulet in 2nd quarter.	450	1000

		F £	VF £
1753	— G. As noble, but quatrefoil over sail, mullet sometimes omitted after first word of *rev.*.	500	1150
1754	**Quarter-noble.** A. Lis over shield and in centre of *rev.* Short broad letters; quatrefoil and annulet beside shield, stars at corners of centre on rev. . . .	225	425
1755	— C. Ordinary letters; quatrefoil to l., quat. and mullet to r. of shield . .	150	300
1756	— — — annulet to l., mullet to r. of shield	145	280
1757	— F. Ordinary letters; trefoil to l., mullet to r. of shield	175	350
1758	— G. — no marks, except mullet after first word.	175	350

SILVER

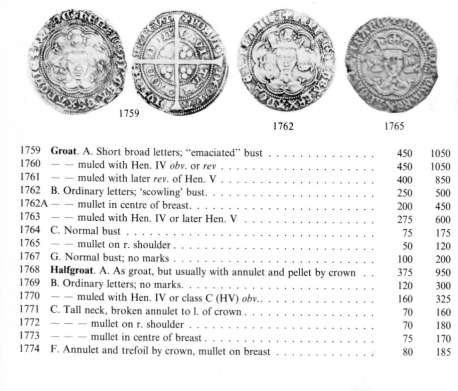

1759

1762   1765

		F £	VF £
1759	**Groat.** A. Short broad letters; "emaciated" bust	450	1050
1760	— — muled with Hen. IV *obv.* or *rev*	450	1050
1761	— — muled with later *rev.* of Hen. V	400	850
1762	B. Ordinary letters; 'scowling' bust.	250	500
1762A	— — mullet in centre of breast.	200	450
1763	— — muled with Hen. IV or later Hen. V	275	600
1764	C. Normal bust	75	175
1765	— — mullet on r. shoulder	50	120
1767	G. Normal bust; no marks	100	200
1768	**Halfgroat.** A. As groat, but usually with annulet and pellet by crown . .	375	950
1769	B. Ordinary letters; no marks.	120	300
1770	— — muled with Hen. IV or class C (HV) *obv.*.	160	325
1771	C. Tall neck, broken annulet to l. of crown	70	160
1772	— — — mullet on r. shoulder	70	180
1773	— — — mullet in centre of breast	75	170
1774	F. Annulet and trefoil by crown, mullet on breast	80	185

1773   1774

		F	VF
		£	£
1775	G. New neat bust: no marks	70	180
1776	**Penny.** *London.* A. Letters, bust and marks as 1768	175	450
1777	— B. Altered A *obv.*, with mullet and broken annulet added by crown. R. Ordinary letters	140	375

1778   1791

1778	— C. Tall neck, mullet and broken annulet by crown	20	60
1779	— D. Similar, but whole annulet.	25	75
1780	— F. Mullet and trefoil by crown	27	80
1781	— G. New neat bust, no marks, DI GRA.	25	75
1782	*Durham.* C. As 1778 but quatrefoil at end of legend	45	135
1783	— D. As 1779	40	125
1784	— G. Similar, but new bust. R. Annulet in one qtr.	50	160
1785	*York.* C. As 1778, but quatrefoil in centre of *rev.*	20	60
1786	— D. Similar, but whole annulet by crown	20	60
1787	— E. As last, but pellet above mullet	40	110
1788	— F. Mullet and trefoil by crown	27	80
1789	— — Trefoil over mullet to l., annulet to r. of crown	25	70
1790	— G. Mullet and trefoil by crown (London dies).	25	70
1791	— — Mullet and lis by crown, annulet in one qtr. (usually local dies and muled with Henry VI).	25	70

1796   1798

1792	**Halfpenny.** A. Emaciated bust, annulets by crown	30	75
1793	— altered dies of Hen. IV	75	200
1794	C. Ordinary bust, broken annulets by crown	20	40
1795	D. Annulets, sometimes broken, by hair.	20	40
1796	F. Annulet and trefoil by crown	20	45
1797	G. New bust; no marks, usually muled with Henry VI.	75	175
1798	**Farthing.** G. Small face with neck	150	325

HENRY VI, First Reign, 1422–61

The supply of gold began to dwindle early in the reign, which accounts for the rarity of gold after 1426. The Calais mint was reopened in 1424 and for some years a large amount of coin was struck there. It soon stopped minting gold; the mint was finally closed in 1440. A royal mint at York was opened for a short time in 1423/4.

Marks used to denote various issues become more prominent in this reign and can be used to date coins to within a year or so.

Reference: *Heavy Coinage of Henry VI*, by C. A. Whitton (B.N.J. 1938–41).

Mintmarks

7a	105	18	133	8	9	15

1422–60	Plain cross (7a, intermittently)	1427–34	Cross patonce (8)
	Lis (105, on gold)		Cross fleurée (9)
1422–27	Pierced cross (18)	1434–35	Voided cross (15)
1422–34	Cross pommée (133)	1435–60	Cross fleury (9)
		1460	Lis (105, on *rev.* of some groats)

For Restoration marks see p. 121.

GOLD

Annulet issue, 1422–7

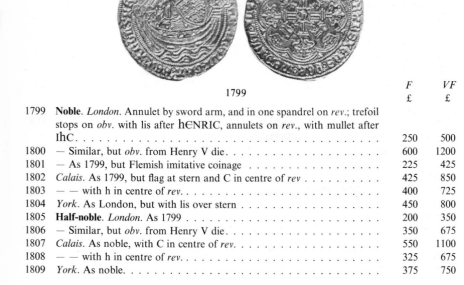

1799

		F £	VF £
1799	**Noble**. *London*. Annulet by sword arm, and in one spandrel on *rev.*; trefoil stops on *obv.* with lis after hENRIC, annulets on *rev.*, with mullet after IhC.	250	500
1800	— Similar, but *obv.* from Henry V die.	600	1200
1801	— As 1799, but Flemish imitative coinage	225	425
1802	*Calais*. As 1799, but flag at stern and C in centre of *rev*	425	850
1803	— — with h in centre of *rev*.	400	725
1804	*York*. As London, but with lis over stern	450	800
1805	**Half-noble**. *London*. As 1799	200	350
1806	— Similar, but *obv.* from Henry V die.	350	675
1807	*Calais*. As noble, with C in centre of *rev*.	550	1100
1808	— — with h in centre of *rev*.	325	675
1809	*York*. As noble.	375	750

		F £	*VF* £
1810	**Quarter-noble**. *London*. Lis over shield; *mm*. large lis.	130	240
1811	— — — trefoil below shield	175	400
1812	— — — pellet below shield.	*Extremely rare*	
1813	*Calais*. Three lis over shield; *mm*. large lis.	200	400
1814	— Similar but three lis around shield	225	450
1815	— As 1810, but much smaller *mm*..	175	375
1816	*York*. Two lis over shield.	225	400

1814   1819

Rosette-mascle issue, 1427–30

		F £	*VF* £
1817	**Noble**. *London*. Lis by sword arm and in *rev*. field; stops, rosettes, or rosettes and mascles.	525	1150
1818	*Calais*. Similar, with flag at stern.	530	1350
1819	**Half-noble**. *London*. Lis in *rev*. field; stops, rosettes and mascles.	750	1500
1820	*Calais*. Similar, flag at stern; stops, rosettes	800	1600
1821	**Quarter-noble**. *London*. As 1810; stops, as noble	225	475
1822	— without lis over shield	200	450
1823	*Calais*. Lis over shield, rosettes r. and l., and rosette stops.	325	500

Pinecone-mascle issue, 1430–4

		F £	*VF* £
1824	**Noble**. *London*. Stops, pinecones and mascles	550	1200
1825	**Half-noble**. *London*. O. Rosette-mascle die. ℞. As last	*Extremely rare*	
1826	**Quarter-noble**. As 1810, but pinecone and mascle stops	*Unique*	

Leaf-mascle issue, 1434–5

		F £	*VF* £
1827	**Noble**. Leaf in waves; stops, saltires with two mascles and one leaf	1000	2500
1828	**Half-noble**. (Fishpool Hoard).	*Unique*	
1829	**Quarter-noble**. As 1810; stops, saltire and mascle; leaf on inner circle of *rev*. .	1000	2250

Leaf-trefoil issue, 1435–8

			£
1830	**Noble**. Stops, leaves and trefoils		4000
1830A	**Half-noble**. Mule with Annulet Issue reverse die		*Unique*
1831	**Quarter-noble**. Similar.		*Unique*

Trefoil issue, 1438–43

		£	£
1832	**Noble**. Trefoil below shield and in *rev*. legend.	1000	3000

Leaf-pellet issue, 1445–54

		£	£
1833	**Noble**. Annulet, lis and leaf below shield	1000	3000

Cross-pellet issue, 1454–60

			£
1834	**Noble**. Mascle at end of *obv*. legend		*Unique*

SILVER

Annulet issue, 1422–7

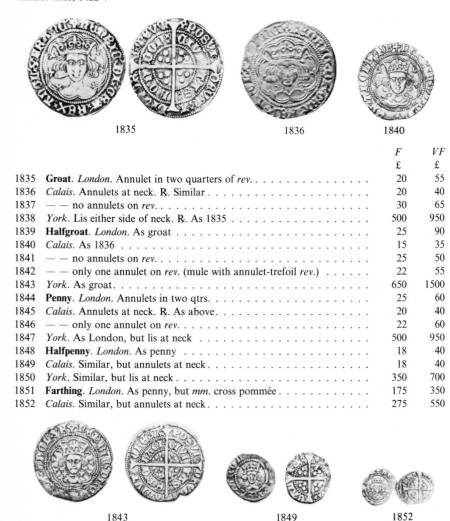

	1835	1836	1840

		F	VF
		£	£
1835	**Groat**. *London*. Annulet in two quarters of *rev*.	20	55
1836	*Calais*. Annulets at neck. ℞. Similar	20	40
1837	— — no annulets on *rev*.	30	65
1838	*York*. Lis either side of neck. ℞. As 1835	500	950
1839	**Halfgroat**. *London*. As groat	25	90
1840	*Calais*. As 1836	15	35
1841	— — no annulets on *rev*.	25	50
1842	— — only one annulet on *rev*. (mule with annulet-trefoil *rev*.)	22	55
1843	*York*. As groat.	650	1500
1844	**Penny**. *London*. Annulets in two qtrs.	25	60
1845	*Calais*. Annulets at neck. ℞. As above.	20	40
1846	— — only one annulet on *rev*.	22	60
1847	*York*. As London, but lis at neck	500	950
1848	**Halfpenny**. *London*. As penny	18	40
1849	*Calais*. Similar, but annulets at neck.	18	40
1850	*York*. Similar, but lis at neck.	350	700
1851	**Farthing**. *London*. As penny, but *mm*. cross pommée	175	350
1852	*Calais*. Similar, but annulets at neck.	275	550

	1843	1849	1852

Many mules exist which span two or even three issues, dating from the Annulet-trefoil issue to the Pinecone-mascle issue inclusive.

Annulet-trefoil sub-issue

1853	**Groat**. *London*. As 1835, but trefoil of pellets to l. of crown (*North*)	100	200
1854	*Calais*. Similar, but annulets by neck also.	50	120
1855	**Halfgroat**. *Calais*. Similar, but usually with ann. or ros.-mas. *rev*.	50	125
1856	**Penny**. *Calais*. Similar	60	150
1857	— — only one annulet on *rev*	75	185

Rosette-mascle issue, 1427–30. All with rosettes (early) or rosettes and mascles somewhere in the legends.

		F	VF
		£	£
1858	**Groat**. *London.*	40	90
1859	*Calais.*	25	65
1860	mascle in two spandrels (as illus. 1863).	50	125

1861   1863   1872

1861	**Halfgroat**. *London.*	30	70
1862	*Calais.*	20	40
1863	— mascle in two spandrels, as illustrated	35	90
1864	**Penny**. *London.*	50	100
1865	*Calais.*	30	60
1866	*York.* Archb. Kemp. Crosses by hair, no rosette	30	70
1867	— — Saltires by hair, no rosette...........................	30	70
1868	— — Mullets by crown......................................	30	70
1869	*Durham,* Bp. Langley. Large star to l. of crown, no rosette, DVnOLMI.	60	160
1870	**Halfpenny,** *London*	25	55
1871	*Calais.*	20	50
1872	**Farthing,** *London*	110	225
1873	*Calais. Mm.* cross pommée	120	250

1875   1879   1884

Pinecone-mascle issue, 1430–4. All with pinecones and mascles in legends.

1874	**Groat,** *London*	30	70
1875	*Calais.*	25	60
1876	**Halfgroat,** *London*	25	60
1877	*Calais.*	25	55
1878	**Penny,** *London*	50	100
1879	*Calais.*	24	70
1880	*York,* Archb. Kemp. Mullet by crown, quatrefoil in centre of *rev.*	20	55
1881	— — rosette on breast, no quatrefoil	18	50
1882	— — mullet on breast, no quatrefoil	40	90
1883	*Durham,* Bp. Langley. DVnOLMI.	60	160
1884	**Halfpenny,** *London*	25	45
1885	*Calais.*	25	45

Full flan coins are difficult to find in the smaller denominations.

		F	*VF*
		£	£
1886	**Farthing**, *London*	100	225
1887	*Calais*. *Mm.* cross pommée	175	425

Leaf-mascle issue, 1434–5. Usually with a mascle in the legend and a leaf somewhere in the design.

1888	**Groat**. *London*. Leaf below bust	75	150
1889	— — *rev.* of last or next coinage.	40	125
1890	*Calais*. Leaf below bust, and usually below MЄVM	35	110
1891	**Halfgroat**. *London*. Leaf under bust, pellet under TAS and DON.	30	70
1892	*Calais*. Leaf below bust, and sometimes on *rev.*.	32	75
1893	**Penny**. *London*. Leaf on breast, no stops on *rev.*	35	80
1894	*Calais*. Leaf on breast and below SIЄ	40	80
1895	**Halfpenny**. *London*. Leaf on breast and on *rev.*.	20	50
1896	*Calais*. Leaf on breast and below SIЄ	45	100

1892   1897

Leaf-trefoil issue, 1435–8. Mostly with leaves and trefoil of pellets in the legends.

1897	**Groat**. *London*. Leaf on breast	37	95
1898	— without leaf on breast	30	100
1899	*Calais*. Leaf on breast.	*Extremely rare*	
1900	**Halfgroat**. *London*. Leaf on breast; *mm.* plain cross	30	85
1901	— *O. mm.* cross fleury; leaf on breast	30	85
1902	— — without leaf on breast	30	85
1903	**Penny**. *London*. Leaf on breast	30	65
1903A	*Calais*. Similar	*Unique*	
1904	*Durham*, Bp. Neville. Leaf on breast. ℞. Rings in centre, no stops, DVnOLM	80	200
1905	**Halfpenny**. *London*. Leaf on breast.	17	40
1906	— without leaf on breast	22	50
1907	**Farthing**. *London*. Leaf on breast; stops, trefoil and saltire on *obv.*	100	325

Trefoil issue, 1438–43. Trefoil of pellets either side of neck and in legend, leaf on breast.

1908	**Groat**. *London*. Sometimes a leaf before LON	50	125

1908

		F	*VF*
		£	£
1909	— Fleurs in spandrels, sometimes extra pellet in two qtrs.........	50	135
1910	— Trefoils in place of fleurs at shoulders, none by neck, sometimes extra pellets................	40	125
1911	*Calais*..	100	350
1911A	**Halfgroat.** Similar, but trefoil after DEUM. Mule only with leaf trefoil *obv.* .	*Extremely rare*	
1912	**Halfpenny,** *London*	30	70

1912

Trefoil pellet issue, 1443–5

1913	**Groat.** Trefoils by neck, pellets by crown, small leaf on breast; sometimes extra pellet in two quarters......................	50	150

Leaf-pellet issue, 1445–54. Leaf on breast, pellet each side of crown, except where stated.

1914	**Groat.** AnGL; extra pellet in two quarters	35	90
1915	Similar, but AnGLI..............................	25	75
1916	— — trefoil in *obv.* legend	50	110
1917	Leaf on neck, fleur on breast, often extra pellet in two quarters......	30	85
1918	As last, but two extra pellets by hair....................	75	175
1919	**Halfgroat.** As 1914 *mm.*8	25	70
1920	Similar, but *mm.* plain cross, sometimes no leaf on breast, no stops ...	25	80
1921	**Penny.** *London.* Usually extra pellets in two quarters...........	30	70
1922	— — pellets by crown omitted	30	70
1923	— — trefoil in legend...........................	35	90
1924	*York,* Archb. Booth. ℞. Quatrefoil and pellet in centre	24	60
1925	— — two extra pellets by hair (local dies)................	18	55
1926	*Durham,* Bp. Neville. Trefoil in *obv.* legend. B. Two rings in centre of cross.	75	225
1927	— — Similar, but without trefoil......................	75	225
1928	**Halfpenny.** Usually extra pellet in two quarters..............	20	45
1929	— *mm.* plain cross............................	20	45
1930	**Farthing.** As last............................	150	325

1915   1927

Unmarked issue, 1453–4

1931	**Groat.** No marks on *obv.*; two extra pellets on *rev*.............	200	500
1932	— four extra pellets on *rev*.......................	350	750
1933	**Halfgroat.** As 1931	175	400

	F	VF
	£	£

Cross-pellet issue, 1454–60

1934 **Groat**. Saltire either side of neck, pellets by crown, leaf and fleur on breast,
extra pellets on *rev*. 75 200

1935 Saltire on neck, no leaf, pellets by crown, usually mullets in legend; extra
pellets on *rev*. 70 165

1936 — Similar, but mascles in place of mullets on *obv*. 75 175

1937 — — pellets by hair instead of by crown 60 200

1938 **Halfgroat**. Saltire on neck, pellets by crown and on *rev*., mullets in legend. 175 400

1939 **Penny**. *London*. Saltire on neck, pellets by crown and on *rev*., mascle(s), or
mullet and mascle in legend 75 175

1940 *York*, Archb. Wm. Booth. Saltires by neck, usually leaf on breast, pellets
by crown. ℞. Cross in quatrefoil in centre. Illustrated below 40 90

1941 *Durham*, Bp. Laurence Booth. Saltire and B at neck, pellets by crown. ℞.
Rings in centre. 100 250

1942 **Halfpenny**. Saltires by neck, usually two extra pellets on *rev*. 50 110

1943 Similar, but saltire on neck, sometimes mullet after hЄnRIC 80 165

1944 **Farthing**. Saltire on neck, usually pellets by crown and on *rev*., but known
without either. 150 325

1935    1940    1945

Lis-pellet issue, 1456–60

1945 **Groat**. Lis on neck; pellets by crown. ℞. Extra pellets 150 325

Full flan coins are difficult to find in the smaller denominations.

EDWARD IV, First Reign, 1461–70

In order to increase the supply of bullion to the mint the weight of the penny was reduced to 12 grains in 1464, and the current value of the noble was raised to 8s. 4d. Later, in 1465, a new gold coin was issued, the Ryal or "Rose Noble", weighing 120 grains and having a value of 10s. However, as 6s. 8d. had become the standard professional fee the old noble was missed, and a new coin was issued to take its place, the Angel of 80 grains.

Royal mints were opened at Canterbury and York to help with the re-coinage, and other mints were set up at Bristol, Coventry and Norwich, though they were not open for long.

Reference: C. E. Blunt and C. A Whitton, *The Coinage of Edward IV and Henry VI (Restored),* B.N.J. 1945–7.

Mintmarks

| 105 | 9 | 7a | 33 | 99 | 28 | 74 | 11 |

1461–4	Lis (105)		1467–70	Lis (105, *York*)	
	Cross fleury (9)		1467–8	Crown (74)	often
	Plain cross (7a)			Sun (28)	combined
1464–5	Rose (33 and 34)		1468–9	Crown (74)	sometimes
1464–7	Pall (99, *Canterbury*)			Rose (33)	combined
1465–6	Sun (28)		1469–70	Long cross	often
1466–7	Crown (74)			fitchée (11)	combined
				Sun (28)	

GOLD

Heavy coinage, 1461–4

		F	VF
		£	£
1946	**Noble** (= 6s. 8d., wt. 108 grs.). Normal type, but *obv.* legend commences at top left, lis below shield; *mm.* -/lis	4000	8000
1947	— Quatrefoil below sword arm; *mm.* rose/lis	*Extremely rare*	
1948	— ℞. Roses in two spandrels; *mm.* rose	*Extremely rare*	
1949	**Quarter-noble**	*Unique*	

1946    1950

Light coinage, 1464–70

1950	**Ryal** or rose-noble (= 10s., wt. 120 grs.), *London.* Type as next illus. Large fleurs in spandrels; *mm.* 33–74	275	475
1951	— — Small trefoils in spandrels; *mm.* 74–11	275	475

Light coinage, *continued.*

1952

		F	VF
		£	£
1952	— Flemish imitative coinage (mostly 16th cent.)	215	450
1953	*Bristol.* B in waves, large fleurs; *mm.* 28, 74	350	725
1954	— — small fleurs in spandrels; *mm.* 74, 28	350	725
1955	*Coventry.* C in waves; *mm.* sun	650	1400
1956	*Norwich.* N in waves; *mm.* sun, rose?	800	1600
1957	*York.* Є in waves, large fleurs in spandrels, *mm.* 28, 105	350	750
1958	— — small fleurs, *mm.* 105, 28	350	750
1959	**Half-ryal.** *London.* As 1950	250	425
1960	*Bristol.* B in waves; *mm.* 28–28/74	325	850
1961	*Coventry.* C in waves; *mm.* sun	*Extremely rare*	
1962	*Norwich.* N in waves; *mm.* rose	1200	2500

1963   1965

1963	*York.* Є in waves; *mm.* 28, 105, 33/105	275	500
1963A	Similar but lis instead of Є in waves (probably York)	*Extremely rare*	
1964	**Quarter-ryal.** Shield in tressure of eight arcs, rose above. ℞. Somewhat as half ryal; *mm.* 28/33		*Unique?*
1965	Shield in quatrefoil, ℞. Є above, rose on l., sun on r.; *mm.* 33/28–74/33 .	175	425
1966	— — sun on l., rose on r.; *mm.* 74–11	190	475

1967

	F £	VF £

1967 **Angel** (= 6s. 8d., wt. 80 grs.). St. Michael spearing dragon. ℞. Ship, rays of
sun at masthead, large rose and sun beside mast; *mm.* -/33 . . . . *Extremely rare*

1968 — — small rose and sun at mast; *mm.* -/74 . . . . *Extremely rare*

First reign

SILVER

1972   1978

Heavy coinage, 1461–4

		F	VF
1969	**Groat** (60 grs.). Group I, lis on neck, pellets by crown; *mm.* 9, 7a, 105, 9/105	55	150
1970	— Lis on breast, no pellets; *mm.* plain cross, 7a/105	55	175
1971	— — with pellets at crown; *mm.* plain cross	55	175
1972	II, quatrefoils by neck, crescent on breast; *mm.* rose	60	150
1973	III, similar but trefoil on breast; *mm.* rose.	55	140
1974	— — — eye in *rev.* inner legend, *mm.* rose	50	125
1975	— Similar, but no quatrefoils by bust	65	165
1976	— — Similar, but no trefoil on breast	65	165
1977	IV, annulets by neck, eye after TAS; *mm.* rose	80	200
1978	**Halfgroat.** I, lis on breast, pellets by crown and extra pellets in two qtrs.; *mm.* 9, 7a.	150	450
1979	II, quatrefoils at neck, crescent on breast; *mm.* rose	170	425
1980	III, similar, but trefoil on breast, eye on *rev.*; *mm.* rose	170	425
1981	— Similar, but no mark on breast	160	400
1982	IV, annulets by neck, sometimes eye on *rev.*; *mm.* rose	150	375
1983	**Penny** (15 grs.), *London.* I, marks as 1978, but mascle after RЄX; *mm.* plain cross	150	425
1984	— II, quatrefoils by neck; *mm.* rose	*Extremely rare*	

1985

		F	*VF*
		£	£
1985	— III, similar, but eye after TAS; *mm.* rose	150	350
1986	— IV, annulets by neck; *mm.* rose	200	400
1987	*York*, Archb. Booth. Quatrefoils by bust, voided quatrefoil in centre of *rev.*; *mm.* rose	120	250
1988	*Durham. O.* of Hen. VI. ℞. DVnOLIn	160	350

> Some of the Durham pennies from local dies may belong to the heavy coinage period, but if so they are indistinguishable from the light coins.

		F	*VF*
1989	**Halfpenny**. I, as 1983, but no mascle.	100	200
1990	II, quatrefoils by bust; *mm.* rose	60	140
1991	— saltires by bust; *mm.* rose	80	160
1992	III, no marks by bust; *mm.* rose	65	150
1993	IV, annulets by bust; *mm* rose	65	160
1994	**Farthing**. I, as 1989	500	1250

Light coinage, 1464–70. There is a great variety of groats and we give only a selection. Some have pellets in one quarter of the reverse, or trefoils over the crown; early coins have fleurs on the cusps of the tressure, then trefoils or no marks on the cusps, while the late coins have only trefoils.

		F	*VF*
1995	**Groat** (48 grs.), *London*. Annulets at neck, eye after TAS; *mm.* 33 (struck from heavy dies, IV).	45	120
1996	— — — Similar, but new dies, eye after TAS or DOn	40	105
1997	— Quatrefoils at neck, eye; *mm.* 33 (heavy dies, III)	45	115
1998	— — — Similar, but new dies, eye in *rev.* legend	35	100
1999	— No marks at neck, eye; *mm.* 33	60	140

2000   2002

		F	*VF*
2000	— Quatrefoils at neck, no eye; *mm.* 33, 74, 28, 74/28, 74/33, 11/28	22	45
2001	— — — rose or quatrefoil on breast; *mm.* 33, 74/28	25	55
2002	— No marks at neck; *mm.* 28, 74, 11/28, 11.	25	65
2003	— Trefoils or crosses at neck; *mm.* 11/33, 11/28, 11	25	65

Light coinage, silver, *continued.*

		F	VF
		£	£
2004	*Bristol.* B on breast, quatrefoils at neck; *mm.* 28/33, 28, 28/74, 74, 74/28 .	30	70
2005	— — trefoils at neck; *mm.* 28	30	90
2006	— — no marks at neck; *mm.* 28	35	110
2007	— Without B, quatrefoils at neck; *mm.* 28	28	100
	Bristol is variously rendered as BRESTOLL, BRISTOLL, BRESTOW, BRISTOW.		
2008	*Coventry.* C on breast, quatrefoils at neck, COVETRE; *mm.* 28/33, 28 . .	50	125
2009	— — Local dies, similar; *mm.* rose.	65	160
2010	— — — as last, but no C or quatrefoils.	70	200
2011	*Norwich.* n on breast, quatrefoils at neck, nORWIC or nORVIC, *mm.* 28/33, 28	50	125
2012	*York.* Є on breast, quatrefoils at neck, ЄBORACI; *mm.* 28, 105/74, 105, 105/28	30	75
2013	— Similar, but without Є on breast, *mm.* 105.	40	100
2014	— Є on breast, trefoils at neck; *mm.* 105/28, 105	30	90
2015	**Halfgroat.** *London.* Annulets by neck (heavy dies); *mm.* 33		*Unique*
2016	— Quatrefoils by neck; *mm.* 33/-, 28/-, 74, 74/28	45	95
2017	— Saltires by neck; *mm.* 74, 74/28	45	95
2018	— Trefoils by neck; *mm.* 74, 74/28, 11/28	40	85
2019	— No marks by neck; *mm.* 11/28	90	180
2020	— *Bristol.* Saltires or crosses by neck; *mm.* 33/28, 28, 74, 74/-.	80	210
2021	— Quatrefoils by neck; *mm.* 28/-, 74, 74/-.	70	200
2022	— Trefoils by neck; *mm.* 74	95	225
2023	— No marks by neck; *mm.* 74/28	95	225
2024	*Canterbury,* Archb. Bourchier (1464–7). Knot below bust; quatrefoils by neck; *mm.* 99/-, 99, 99/33, 99/28	15	40
2025	— — — quatrefoils omitted *mm.* 99.	15	40
2026	— — — saltires by neck; *mm.* 99/-, 99/28	20	45
2026A	— — — trefoils by neck; *mm.* 99.	40	90

2027   2030

2027	— — — wedges by hair and/or neck; *mm.* 99, 99/33, 99/28	20	60
2028	— — As 2024 or 2025, but no knot	25	70
2029	— Royal mint (1467–9). Quatrefoils by neck; *mm.* 74, 74/-	15	45
2030	— — Saltires by neck; *mm.* 74/-, 74	20	45
2031	— — Trefoils by neck; *mm.* 74, 74/-, 74/28, 33	20	45
2032	— No marks by neck; *mm.* 28	50	125
2033	*Coventry.* Crosses by neck; *mm.* sun		*Unique*
2034	*Norwich.* Saltires by neck; *mm.* sun		*Extremely rare*

		F	VF
		£	£

Light coinage, silver, *continued.*

2035	*York.* Quatrefoils by neck; *mm.* sun, lis, lis/-	50	130
2036	— Saltires by neck; *mm.* lis	45	100
2037	— Trefoils by neck; *mm.* lis, lis/-	45	100
2038	— Є on breast, quatrefoils by neck; *mm.* lis/-	50	105
2039	**Penny** (12 grs.), *London.* Annulets by neck (heavy dies); *mm.* 33	70	160
2040	— Quatrefoils by neck; *mm.* 28, 74	30	60
2041	— Trefoil and quatrefoil by neck; *mm.* 74	35	75
2042	— Saltires by neck; *mm.* 74	35	75
2043	— Trefoils by neck; *mm.* 74, 11	25	50
2044	— No marks by neck; *mm.* 11	*Extremely rare*	
2045	*Bristol.* Crosses, quatrefoils or saltires by neck, BRISTOW; *mm.* crown .	85	225
2046	— Quatrefoils by neck; BRI(trefoil)STOLL	100	260
2047	— Trefoil to r. of neck BRISTOLL	125	275
2048	*Canterbury,* Archb. Bourchier. Quatrefoils or saltires by neck, knot on breast; *mm.* pall	70	160
2049	— — Similar, but no marks by neck	80	175
2050	— — As 2048, but no knot	75	170
2051	— — Crosses by neck, no knot	75	170
2052	— Royal mint. Quatrefoils by neck; *mm.* crown	125	300
2053	— *Durham,* King's Receiver (1462–4). Local dies, mostly with rose in centre of *rev.*; *mm.* 7a, 33	20	60
2054	— Bp. Lawrence Booth (1465–70). B and D by neck, B on *rev.*; *mm.* 33 .	22	65
2055	— — Quatrefoil and B by neck; *mm.* 28	24	70
2056	— — B and quatrefoil by neck; *mm.* 74	*Extremely rare*	
2057	— — D and quatrefoil by neck; *mm.* 74	26	75
2058	— — Quatrefoils by neck; *mm.* crown	30	90
2059	— — Trefoils by neck; *mm.* crown	30	90
2060	— — Lis by neck; *mm.* crown	30	90
2061	*York,* Sede Vacante (1464–5). Quatrefoils at neck, no quatrefoil in centre of *rev.*; *mm.* 28, 33	50	125
2062	— Archb. Neville (1465–70). Local dies, G and key by neck, quatrefoil on *rev.*; *mm.* 33, 7a	35	75

2063   2068

2063	— — London-made dies, similar; *mm.* 28, 105, 11	20	70
2064	— — Similar, but no marks by neck; *mm.* large lis	*Extremely rare*	
2065	— — — Quatrefoils by neck; *mm.* large lis	15	50
2066	— — — Trefoils by neck; *mm.* large lis	30	65
2067	**Halfpenny,** *London.* Saltires by neck; *mm.* 34, 28, 74	30	70
2068	— Trefoils by neck; *mm.* 28, 74, 11	25	55
2069	— No marks by neck; *mm.* 11	*Unique?*	
2070	*Bristol.* Crosses by neck; *mm.* 74	125	275
2071	— Trefoils by neck; *mm.* 74	90	200

Light coinage, silver, *continued.*

		F	VF
		£	£
2072	*Canterbury*, Archb. Bourchier. No marks; *mm.* pall	100	225
2072A	— — — Trefoils by neck, *mm.* pall	100	225
2073	— Royal mint. Saltires by neck; *mm.* crown	65	140
2074	— — Trefoils by neck; *mm.* crown.	60	125
2075	*York*, Royal mint. Saltires by neck; *mm.* lis/-, sun/-	65	140
2076	— — Trefoils by neck; *mm.* lis/-	60	125
2077	**Farthing**, *London*. ЄDWARD DI GRA RЄX, no marks at neck, *mm.* 33	*Extremely rare*	
2077A	— Trefoils by neck, *mm.* 74	600	—

Full flan coins are difficult to find in the smaller denominations.

134

HENRY VI RESTORED, Oct. 1470–Apr. 1471

The coinage of this short restoration follows closely that of the previous reign. Only angel gold was issued, the ryal being discontinued. Many of the coins have the king's name reading hⒺnRICV—a distinguishing feature.

Mintmarks

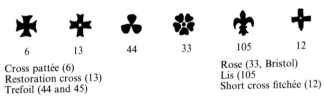

| 6 | 13 | 44 | 33 | 105 | 12 |

Cross pattée (6)
Restoration cross (13)
Trefoil (44 and 45)

Rose (33, Bristol)
Lis (105
Short cross fitchée (12)

GOLD

2079

		F	VF
		£	£
2078	**Angel**, *London*. As illus. but no B; *mm.* -/6, 13, -/105, none	400	900
2079	*Bristol*. B in waves; *mm.* -/13, none	650	1500
2080	**Half-angel**, *London*. As 2078; *mm.* -/6, -/13, -/105.	1400	3000
2081	*Bristol*. B in waves; *mm.* -/13		*Unique*

SILVER

2082   2084

		F	VF
2082	**Groat**, *London*. Usual type; *mm.* 6, 6/13, 6/105, 13, 13/6, 13/105, 13/12. .	125	200
2083	*Bristol*. B on breast; *mm.* 13, 13/33, 13/44, 44, 44/13, 44/33, 44/12	150	325
2084	*York*. Ⓔ on breast; *mm.* lis, lis/sun	125	265
2085	**Halfgroat**, *London*. As 2082; *mm.* 13, 13/-.	225	500
2086	*York*. Ⓔ on breast; *mm.* lis	*Extremely rare*	
2087	**Penny**, *London*. Usual type; *mm.* 6, 13, 12.	300	650

		F	*VF*
		£	£
2087A	*Bristol.* Similar; *mm.* 12		*Unique?*
2088	*York.* G and key by neck; *mm.* lis	175	400
2089	**Halfpenny,** *London.* As 2087; *mm.* 12	200	400
2090	*Bristol.* Similar; *mm.* cross		*Unique?*

EDWARD IV, Second Reign, 1471–83

The Angel and its half were the only gold denominations issued during this reign. The main types and weight standards remained the same as those of the light coinage of Edward's first reign. The use of the "initial mark" as a mintmark to denote the date of issue was now firmly established.

Mintmarks

| 33 | 105 | 12 | 55 | 44 | 55 | 28 | 56 | 17 |

| 37 | 6 | 18 | 19 | 20 | 31 | 11 | 38 |

1471–83	Rose (33, *York & Durham*)	1473–7	Cross pattée (6)
	Lis (105, *York*)		Pierced cross 1 (18)
1471	Short cross fitchée (12)	1477–80	Pierced cross and
1471–2	Annulet (large, 55)		pellet (19)
	Trefoil (44)		Pierced cross 2 (18)
	Rose (33, *Bristol*)		Pierced cross, central
1471–3	Pansy (30, *Durham*)		pellet (20)
1472–3	Annulet (small, 55)		Rose (33, *Canterbury*)
	Sun (28, *Bristol*)	1480–3	Heraldic cinquefoil (31)
1473–7	Pellet in annulet (56)		Long cross fitchée
	Cross and four pellets (17)		(11, *Canterbury*)
	Cross in circle (37)		Halved sun and rose (38)?

GOLD

2091   2093

		F	*VF*
		£	£
2091	**Angel.** *London.* Type as illus.; *mm.* 12, 55, 56, 17, 18, 19, 31	200	400
2092	*Bristol.* B in waves; *mm.* 55	650	1400
2093	**Half-angel.** As illus.; *mm.* 55, cross in circle, 19, 20/19, 31	185	350
2094	King's name and title on *rev.*; *mm.* 12/-	375	700
2095	King's name and the title both sides; *mm.* 55/-	300	550

SILVER

2101   2106

		F £	VF £
2096	**Groat**, *London*. Trefoils on cusps, no marks by bust; *mm*. 12–37	25	70
2097	— — roses by bust; *mm*. 56	35	95
2098	— Fleurs on cusps; no marks by bust; *mm*. 18–20	25	65
2099	— — pellets by bust; *mm*. 18 (2)	60	175
2100	— — rose on breast; *mm*. 31	25	60
2101	*Bristol*. B on breast; *mm*. 33, 33/55, 28/55, 55, 55/-, 28	60	165
2102	*York*. Є on breast; *mm*. lis	65	175
2103	**Halfgroat**, *London*. As 2096; *mm*. 12–31	30	80
2104	*Bristol*. B on breast; *mm*. 33/12	*Extremely rare*	
2105	*Canterbury* (Royal mint). As 2103; *mm*. 33, 11, 11/31, 31	25	65
2106	— C on breast; *mm*. rose	20	55
2107	— — R̟. C in centre; *mm*. rose	20	55
2108	— — R̟. Rose in centre; *mm*. rose	20	60
2109	*York*. No. Є on breast; *mm*. lis	75	200
2110	**Penny**, *London*. No marks by bust; *mm*. 12–31	30	70
2111	*Bristol*. Similar; *mm*. rose	*Extremely rare*	
2112	*Canterbury* (Royal). Similar; *mm*. 33, 11	65	140
2113	— C on breast; *mm*. 33	80	175

2115   2116   2123

		F £	VF £
2114	*Durham*, Bp. Booth (1471–6). No marks by neck; *mm*. 12, 44	18	60
2115	— — D in centre of *rev*.; B and trefoil by neck; *mm*. 44, 33, 56	18	65
2116	— — — two lis at neck; *mm*. 33	18	60
2117	— — — crosses over crown, and on breast; *mm*. 33	15	55
2118	— — — crosses over crown, V under CIVI; *mm*. 33, 30	15	55
2119	— — — B to l. of crown, V on breast and under CIVI	15	55
2120	— — — As last but crosses at shoulders	15	55
2121	— Sede Vacante (1476). R̟. D in centre; *mm*. 33	35	125
2122	— Bp. Dudley (1476–83). V to r. of neck; as last	18	60
2123	— — D and V by neck; as last, but *mm*. 31	15	55

Nos. 2117–2123 are from locally-made dies.

2125　　　　　　　　　2134

		F £	VF £
2124	*York*, Archb. Neville (1471–2). Quatrefoils by neck. ℞. Quatrefoil; *mm.* 12 (over lis)	90	225
2125	— — Similar, but G and key by neck; *mm.* 12 (over lis)	13	35
2126	— Neville suspended (1472–5). As last, but no quatrefoil in centre of *rev.*.	15	37
2126A	— — no marks by bust, similar; *mm.* annulet.	90	225
2127	— — No marks by neck, quatrefoil on *rev.*; *mm.* 55, cross in circle, 33. .	15	40
2128	— — Similar but Є and rose by neck; *mm.* 33	15	40
2129	— Archb. Neville restored (1475–6). As last, but G and rose	18	45
2130	— — Similar, but G and key by bust	15	40
2131	— Sede Vacante (1476). As 2127, but rose on breast; *mm.* 33	18	45
2132	— Archb. Lawrence Booth (1476–80). B and key by bust, quatrefoil on *rev.*; *mm.* 33, 31	13	40
2133	— Sede Vacante (1480). Similar, but no quatrefoil on *rev.*; *mm.* 33	15	45
2134	— Archb. Rotherham (1480–3). T and slanting key by neck, quatrefoil on *rev.*; *mm.* 33	13	40
2135	— — — Similar, but star on breast	150	350
2136	— — — Star on breast and to r. of crown	80	175
2137	**Halfpenny**, *London*. No marks by neck; *mm.* 12-31	25	65
2138	— Pellets at neck; *mm.* 18	30	70
2139	*Canterbury* (Royal). C on breast and in centre of *rev.*; *mm.* rose	70	150
2140	— C on breast only; *mm.* rose	60	130
2141	— Without C either side; *mm.* 11	70	160
2142	*Durham*, Bp. Booth. No marks by neck. ℞. DERAM, D in centre; *mm.* rose.	90	200
2142A	— — Lis either side of neck. ℞. D or no mark in centre.	*Extremely rare*	
2143	— — — Similar, but V to l. of neck	90	200

Full flan coins are very difficult to find in the small denominations.

EDWARD IV or V

Mintmark: Halved sun and rose.

The consensus of opinion now favours the last year of Edward IV for the introduction of the halved-sun-&-rose mintmark, but it is suggested that the earliest coins of Edward V's reign were struck from these Edw. IV dies. The coins are very rare.

	GOLD	F	VF
		£	£
2144	**Angel.** As 2091.	700	1750
2145	**Half-angel.** As 2093	*Extremely rare*	

2145   2146

SILVER

2146	**Groat.** As 2098.	300	750
2147	**Penny.** As 2110	600	1200
2148	**Halfpenny.** As 2137	300	700

EDWARD V, 1483

On the death of Edward IV, 9th April, 1483, the 12-year-old Prince Edward was placed under the guardianship of his uncle, Richard, Duke of Gloucester, but within eleven weeks Richard usurped the throne and Edward and his younger brother were confined to the Tower and were never seen alive again. The boar's head was a personal badge of Richard, Edward's 'Protector'.

Recent research indicates that the mint marks previously thought to be for this reign are now attributable to Edward IV, Edward IV or V, or Richard III. On the publication of this research paper in the near future, it is expected we will remove coins of specifically Edward V.

Mintmarks: Boar's head on *obv.*, halved sun and rose on *rev.*

GOLD

2149	**Angel.** As 2091.	*Extremely rare*
2150	**Half-angel.** Similar	*Unique*

SILVER

2151

	F	*VF*
	£	£
2151 **Groat**. As 2098.		*Rare*
2152 **Halfgroat**. As 2103		*Unique*
2153 **Penny**. As 2110	?	*Unknown?*

RICHARD III, 1483–5

Richard's brief reign was brought to an end on the field of Bosworth. His coinage follows the pattern of the previous reigns. The smaller denominations of the London mint are all rare.

Mintmarks

    38   62   63   105   33

Halved sun and rose, 3 styles (38, 39 and another with the sun more solid, see *North*).
Boar's head, narrow (62) wide (63).
Lis (105, *Durham*)
Rose only (33).

GOLD

2154	**Angel**. Reading ЄDWARD but with R and rose by mast; *mm.* sun and rose.		*Unique*
2155	— Similar, but boar's head *mm.* on *obv*		*Unique*

2156   2158

2156	Reading RICARD or RICAD. Ŗ. R and rose by mast; *mm.* various combinations.	600	1050
2157	— Similar, but R by mast over rose (?)	650	1200
2158	**Half-angel**. Ŗ. R and rose by mast; *mm.* boar's head		*Extremely rare*

SILVER

2159　　　　　　　　　　2160

		F	VF
		£	£
2159	**Groat**, *London*. *Mm*. various combinations	225	425
2160	— Pellet below bust	250	475
2161	*York*. *Mm*. Sun and rose (*obv*.)	350	800
2162	**Halfgroat**. *Mm*. sun and rose on *obv*. only	750	1500
2163	Pellet below bust; *mm*. sun and rose		Unique
2164	— *mm*. boar's head (*obv*.)	850	1750
2165	**Penny**. *London*. *mm*. boar's head (*obv*.)		Unique

　　　　This was the R. Carlyon-Britton specimen. It was stolen from our premises
　　　　Feb. 1962.

2168　　　　　　　　　　2169

2166	*York*, Archb. Rotherham. ℞. Quatrefoil in centre; *mm*. sun and rose . . .	300	550
2167	— — T and upright key at neck; *mm*. rose	150	350
2168	— — — *mm*. boar's head	150	350
2169	*Durham*, Bp. Sherwood. S on breast. ℞. D in centre; *mm*. lis	125	300
2170	**Halfpenny**, *London*. *Mm*. sun and rose	325	600
2171	— *Mm*. boar's head	400	800

Most small denomination coins are short of flan and unevenly struck.

HENRY VII, 1485–1509

For the first four years of his reign Henry's coins differ only in name and mintmark from those of his predecessors, but in 1489 radical changes were made in the coinage. Though the pound sterling had been a denomination of account for centuries, a pound coin had never been minted. Now a magnificent gold pound was issued, and, from the design of the king enthroned in majesty, was called a 'Sovereign'. The reverse had the royal arms set in the centre of a Tudor rose. A few years later the angel was restyled and St. Michael, who is depicted about to thrust Satan into the Pit with a cross-topped lance, is no longer a feathered figure but is clad in armour of Renaissance style. A gold ryal of ten shillings was also minted again for a brief period.

The other major innovation was the introduction of the Shilling in the opening years of the 16th century. It is remarkable for the very fine profile portrait of the King which replaces the representational image of a monarch that had served on the coinage for the past couple of centuries. This new portrait was also used on groats and halfgroats but not on the smaller denominations.

Mintmarks

39	41	40	42	33	11	7a	123
105	76b	31	78	30	91	43	57
85	94	118	21	33	53		

1485–7	Halved sun and rose (39)	1495–8	Pansy (30)
	Lis upon sun and rose (41)		Tun (123, *Canterbury*)
	Lis upon half rose (40)		Lis (105, *York*)
	Lis-rose dimidiated (42)	1498–9	Crowned leopard's head (91)
	Rose (33, *York*)		Lis issuant from rose (43)
1487	Lis (105)		Tun (123, *Canterbury*)
	Cross fitchy (11)	1499–1502	Anchor (57)
1487–8	Rose (33)	1502–4	Greyhound's head (85)
	Plain cross (7a, *Durham*)		Lis (105, profile issue only)
1488–9	No marks		Martlet (94, *York*)
1489–93	Cinquefoil (31)	1504–5	Cross-crosslet (21)
	Crozier (76b, *Durham*)	1504–9	Martlet (94, *York* and
1492	Cross fitchy (11, gold only)		*Canterbury*)
1493–5	Escallop (78)		Rose (33, *York* and
	Dragon (118, gold only)		*Canterbury*)
	Lis (105, *Canterbury* and *York*	1505–9	Pheon (53)
	Tun (123, *Canterbury*)		

The coins are placed in groups, as in Brooke, *English Coins*, to correspond to the classification of the groats.

GOLD

		F	VF
		£	£
2173	**Sovereign** (20s; wt. 240 grs.). Group I. Large figure of king sitting on backless throne. ℞. Large shield crowned on large Tudor rose. *mm.* 31'. .		*Unique*
2172	— Group II. Somewhat similar but throne has narrow back, lis in background. ℞. Large Tudor rose bearing small shield. *mm.* -/11		*Extremely rare*

Gold

2174

		F £	VF £
2174	**Sovereign** III. King on high-backed very ornamental throne, with grey-hound and dragon on side pillars. ℞. Shield on Tudor rose; *mm.* 118. . .	5550	13,000
2175	IV. Similar but throne with high canopy breaking legend and broad seat, *mm.* 105/118, (also with no *obv.* i.c. *mm.* 105/118, very rare).	5000	10,500
2176	— Narrow throne with a portcullis below the king's feet (like Henry VIII); *mm.* 105/21, 105/53	5250	11,000
2177	**Double-sovereign** and **Treble-sovereign** from same dies as 2176. These *piedforts* were probably intended as presentation pieces *mm.* 105/21, 105/53. .	*Extremely rare*	

2178

2178	**Ryal** (10s.). As illustration: *mm.* -/11.	6500	15,000

2181   2183

		F £	VF £
2179	**Angel** (6s. 8d). I. Angel of old type with one foot on dragon. ℞. PЄR CRVCЄM. etc., *mm.* 39, 40, (also muled both ways).	235	700
2179A	— With Irish title, and legend over angel head. *mm.* 33/–	*Extremely rare*	
2180	— — Name altered from RICARD? and h on *rev.* from R. *mm.* 41/39, 41/40, 41/–, 39/?	500	1100
2181	II. As 2179, but *mm.* none. 31/-.	200	500
2181A	II/III mule. *mm.* 31/78, ℞. PER CRUC or AVTEM TRANS	275	575
2182	As 2181. ℞. IhC AVTЄM TRANSIЄnS etc.; *mm.* none, 31/-.	275	575
2183	III. New dies, angel with both feet on dragon; (large straight lettering) *mm.* 78–85 except 91 (many mules exist)	200	400
2183A	— Angel with very small wings. *mm.* 78	*Rare*	
2184	— — ℞. IhC AVTЄM TRANSIЄnS, etc.; *mm.* 78	250	550
2185	IV. Small square lettering; *mm.* 85 (also muled with 2183).	200	475
2186	— Tall thin lettering; *mm.* 21 (also muled with 2185 *obv.*)	200	400
2187	V. Large crook-shaped abbreviation after hЄNRIC; *mm.* 21 and 53 (combinations and mules exist).	200	375
2188	**Half-angel or angelet.** I. *Mm.* 39, 41, (old dies RIII altered)	250	700
2189	III. Angel with both feet on dragon: *mm.* 30, 57/30, –/85	175	375
2190	IV. Small square lettering; *mm.* 33.	*Extremely rare*	
2191	— *Obv.* as last. ℞. Tall thin lettering; *mm.* 33/21	*Extremely rare*	
2192	V. As angel; *mm.* pheon.	165	350

SILVER

Facing bust issues. Including "Sovereign" type pennies.

2194   2195

2193	**Groat.** I. Open crown; *mm.* 40 (rose on bust), 39–42 and none (combinations)	60	140
2194	— — crosses or saltires by neck, 41, 40, 105–33 and none (combinations)	70	165
2195	IIa. Large bust with out-turned hair, crown with two plain arches; *mm.* none, 31, 31/-, 31/78.	30	75
2196	— — similar but crosses by neck; *mm.* none, -/105	35	90
2197	— — ℞. Portcullis over long cross; *mm.* -/lis	*Extremely rare*	

	2198	2199	2201

		F £	VF £
*2198	**Groat.** IIIa. Bust as IIa. Crown with two jewelled arches, *mm.* 31, 78. . .	35	85
*2198A	IIIb. Similar, but new bust with hair turning inwards; *mm.* 78, 30	25	55
*2199	IIIc. Bust as IIIb, but crown with one plain and one jewelled arch, new realistic hair; *mm.* 30–21 and none.	35	60
*2199A	IIId. As last, but plainer letters. *mm* 57, 85, 33 and none	30	85
2200	IVa. Wide single arch crown; arch is single or double bar with 4 crockets; *mm.* 85, 85/33, 21	35	65
2201	IVb. — Similar, but arch is double bar with 6 uprights or crockets as jewels; *mm.* 85, 21/85, 21	30	60
	* *mm.*s muled.		
2202	**Halfgroat,** *London.* I. Open crown, tressure unbroken; *mm.* 40/-, 40/39 (R. III mule)	350	750
2203	— IIIa. Double arched crown, rosettes on tressure; *mm.* 78		*Rare*
2204	— IIIb. Similar, nothing on tressure. R. Lozenge panel in centre; *mm.* lis	40	100
2205	— — Similar, but also with lis on breast; *mm.* lis.	40	100
2206	— IIIc. Unarched crown with tressure broken. R. Lozenge panel in centre; *mm.* lis	25	55
2206A	— — — Similar but smaller dies and much smaller lettering	25	55

	2211		2214	

		F £	VF £
2207	*Canterbury,* Archb. Morton. I. Open crown, crosses by neck. R. m in centre; *mm.* tun/-	30	75
2208	— — II. Similar, but double-arched crown; *no mm.*	30	50
2209	III King and Archb. jointly. As last but without m; (a) early lettering, trefoil stops; *mm.* lis, tun and lis/lis	15	40
2209A	*Obv.* as last. R. As 2207; *mm.* lis/-	25	50
2210	— — (b) ornate lettering, rosette stops; *mm.* tun, lis in combinations. . .	15	40
2211	— — (c) — saltire or no stops; *mm.* 123, 123 & 30/123	15	40
2212	*York,* Royal mint. (a) Double-arched crown, lis on breast (rarely omitted). R. Lozenge panel in centre; *mm.* lis	25	55
2213	— — (b) Similar, but unarched crown, tressure broken, *mm.* lis.	20	45

		F £	VF £
2214	— Archb. Savage. (a) Double-arched crown, keys at neck, no tressure; ornate lettering; *mm.* martlet	20	45
2215	— — (b) Similar, but fleured tressure, small square lettering; *mm.* 94. . .	20	45
2216	— — (c) As last, but tall thin lettering; *mm.* 94	20	45
2217	— As last but no keys; *mm.* 94	20	50

2221   2226

2218	**Penny.** Old type. *London; mm.* 40/-		750
2219	— — — crosses by bust, *mm.* small cross (*obv.*)		*Extremely rare*
2220	— *Canterbury*, Archb. Morton. Open crown, *mm.* tun/- R. ᛗ in centre .		*Extremely rare*
2221	— — King and Archb. jointly, arched crown; *mm.* tun, tun/-	40	100
2222	— *Durham*, Bp. Sherwood. S on breast. R. D in centre; *mm.* 7a/-	75	175
2223	— *York*, Archb. Rotherham. With or without cross on breast, *mm.* 33/-, T and cross or key at neck. R. h in centre	35	90
2224	— — — T and trefoil at neck. R. Quatrefoil in centre and two extra pellets; *mm.* 41/-	40	100
2225	"Sovereign" type. *London.* Early lettering, no stops, no pillars to throne; no *mm.*		*Extremely rare*
2226	— — — single pillar on king's right side, trefoil stops; no *mm.* or 31/- . .	17	60
2227	— — Ornate letters, rosette stops, single pillar; *mm.* lis (can be muled with above)	20	70
2228	— — — saltire stops or none, two pillars; *mm.* none, -/30	17	60
2229	— — Similar, but small square lettering; no *mm.*	17	60
2230	— — Similar, but lettering as profile groats two double pillars; *mm.* 21, 53, none (sometimes on one side only)	20	70
2231	— *Durham*, Bp. Sherwood. Crozier to r. of king, throne with one pillar. R. D and S beside shield	25	70
2232	— — Throne with two pillars, no crozier. R. As last	25	70
2233	— — Bp. Fox. Throne with one pillar. R. Mitre above shield, RD or DR at sides, no *mm.*	25	60
2234	— — Similar, but two pillars	25	70
2235	*York*, Archb. Rotherham. Keys below shield; early lettering, trefoil stops, no pillars to throne, no *mm.*	20	55

2231   2233   2235

		F £	VF £
2236	**Penny.** — — single pillar	25	55
2237	— — — ornate lettering, rosette or no stops, single pillar	25	55
2238	— — — — — two pillars sometimes with crosses between legs of throne.	25	55

       2245   2248   2249

		F £	VF £
*2239	**Halfpenny,** *London.* I. Open crown; *mm.* 40, 42	75	150
2240	— — — trefoils at neck; no *mm.*, rose.	75	150
2241	— — — crosses at neck; *mm.* 33.	50	125
2242	— II. Double arched crown; *mm.* cinquefoil, none	25	60
2243	— — — saltires at neck; no *mm.*	20	55
2244	— III. Crown with single arch, ornate lettering; no *mm.*	25	60
2245	— V. Much smaller portrait; *mm.* pheon, lis, none	35	75
2246	*Canterbury,* Archb. Morton. I. Open crown. ℞. ℳ in centre	*Extremely rare*	
2247	— — II. Similar, but arched crown, saltires by bust; *mm.* profile eye (82)	*Extremely rare*	
2248	— King and Archb. III. Arched crown; *mm.* 105, none	75	200
2249	*York,* Archb. Savage. Arched crown, key below bust.	100	250
2250	**Farthing,** *London.* ҺЄПRIC DI GRA RЄX (A), arched crown	150	300

*No.s 2239–49 have *mm.* on *obv.* only.

Profile issue

                                   2253

		F £	VF £
2251	**Testoon** (ls.). Type as groat. ҺЄПRIC (VS); *mm.* lis	4000	8000
2252	— ҺЄПRIC VII; *mm.* lis	4500	9000
2253	— ҺЄПRIC SЄPTIM; *mm.* lis	5000	10,000

       2254   2258

| | | F | VF |
| | | £ | £ |

2254 **Groat,** *Tentative issue* (contemporary with full-face groats). Double band
to crown, hєnRIC VII; *mm.* none, 105/-, -/105: 105/85, 105, 85, 21 . . .   100   220

2255 — — — tressure on *obv.*; *mm.* 21   2750   5000

2256 — — hєnRIC (VS); *mm.* 105, -/105, 105/85, none   300   700

2257 — — hєnRIC SЄPTIM; *mm.* -/105   3250   6000

2258 *Regular issue.* Triple band to crown; *mm.* 21, 21 and 53/21, 21/21 and 53,
53 (both *mm.*s may occur on some *obv.* and *rev.*).   45   120

2261   2263

2259 **Halfgroat,** *London.* As last; *mm.* 105, 53/105, 105/53, 53   50   125

2260 — — no numeral after King's name, no *mm.*, -/lis . . . .   *Extremely rare*

2261 *Canterbury*, King and Archb. As London, but *mm.* 94, 33, 94/33   35   70

2262 *York*, Archb. Bainbridge. As London, but two keys below shield; *mm.* 94,
33, 33/94   30   65

2262A — Similar but no keys; *mm.* 94, 33/94   35   70

2263 — — XB beside shield; *mm.* 33/94   900   —

HENRY VIII, 1509–47

Henry VIII is held in ill-regard by numismatists as being the author of the debasement of England's gold and silver coinage; but there were also other important numismatic innovations during his reign. For the first sixteen years of the reign of the coinage closely followed the pattern of the previous issues, even to the extent of retaining the portrait of Henry VII on the larger silver coins.

In 1526, in an effort to prevent the drain of gold to continental Europe, the value of English gold was cried up by 10%, the sovereign to 22s. 0d. and the angel to 7s. 4d., and a new coin valued at 4s. 6d.—the Crown of the Rose—was introduced as a competitor to the French *écu au soleil*. The new crown was not a success and within a few months it was replaced by the Crown of the Double Rose valued at 5 shillings but made of gold of only 22 carat fineness, the first time gold had been minted below the standard 23¾ carat. At the same time the sovereign was again revalued to 22s. 6d. and the angel to 7s. 6d., with a new coin, the George Noble, valued at 6s. 8d. (one-third pound).

The royal cyphers on some of the gold crowns and half-crowns combine the initial of Henry with those of his queens: Katherine of Aragon, Anne Boleyn and Jane Seymour. The architect of this coinage reform was the Chancellor, Cardinal Thomas Wolsey, but besides his other changes he had minted at York a groat bearing his initials and cardinal's hat in addition to the other denominations normally authorized for the ecclesiastical mints.

In view of Henry's final break with Rome in 1534, followed by the Act of Supremacy of 1535, it was hardly surprising that the Church's coining privileges in England were finally terminated and the mints of Durham and York (ecclesiastical) were closed.

In 1544, to help finance the king's inordinate extravagances, it was decided to extend the process of debasement. Initially all the "fine" gold coins were reduced in quality to 23 carat, then in the following year gold was issued of 22 carat and later of 20 carat fineness. Concurrently the silver coins were reduced from the sterling standard fineness of 11 oz. 2 dwt. (i.e. .925 silver) to 9 oz. (.750), and later to 6 oz. (.500) and eventually 4 oz. (.333) fineness. Henry's nickname of "Old Coppernose" was earned not through his own personal characteristics but by his last poor 'silver' coins which soon displayed their two-thirds copper content once they became slightly worn.

Mintmarks

53
69
70
108
33
94
73
11

105
22
23
30
78
15
24
110

52
72a
44
8
65a
114
121
90

36
106
56
S
e
116

1509–26 Pheon (53)
Castle (69)
Castle with H (70, gold)
Portcullis crowned (108)
Rose (33, *Canterbury*)
Martlet (94, *Canterbury*)
Pomegranate (73, but broader, *Cant.*)
Cross fitchée (11, *Cant.*)

Lis (105, *Canterbury, Durham*)
1509–14 Martlet (94, *York*)
1509–23 Radiant star (22, *Durham & York*)
1513–18 Crowned T
1514–26 Star (23, *York & Durham*)
Pansy (30, *York*)
Escallop (78, *York*)
Voided cross (15, *York*)
1523–26 Spur rowel (24, *Durham*)

1526–44	Rose (33)	1526–32	Cross patonce (8, *Cant.*)
	Lis (105)		T (114, *Canterbury*)
	Sunburst (110)		Uncertain mark (121,
	Arrow (52)		*Canterbury*)
	Pheon (53)	1529–44	Radiant star (22, *Durham*)
	Lis (106)	1530–44	Key (90, *York*)
	Star (23, *Durham*)	1533–44	Catherine wheel (36,
1526–9	Crescent (72a, *Durham*)		*Canterbury*)
	Trefoil (44 variety,	1544–7	Lis (105 and 106)
	Durham)		Pellet in annulet (56)
	Flower of eight petals and		S
	circle centre (*Durham*)		Є or E
1526–30	Cross (7a, sometimes	1546–7	WS monogram (116, *Bristol*)
	slightly voided, *York*)		
	Acorn (65a, *York*)		

GOLD

First coinage, 1509–26

		F	VF
		£	£
2264	**Sovereign** (20s.). Similar to last sov. of Hen. VII; *mm.* 108.	3000	6500
2264A	**Ryal** (10s.) King in ship holding sword and shield. R̟. Similar to 1950, *mm.* -/108		*Unique*
2265	**Angel** (6s. 8d.). As Hen. VIII, but hЄnRIC? VIII DI GRA RЄX, etc.; *mm.* 53, 69, 70, 70/69, 108, R̟. May omit h and rose, or rose only; *mm.* 69, 108.	200	400
2266	**Half-angel.** Similar (sometimes without VIII), *mm.* 69, 70, 108/33, 108 . .	175	360

2265

Second coinage, 1526–44

2267

2267	**Sovereign** (22s. 6d.). As 2264, R̟. single or double tressure *mm.* 110, 105, 105/52	2500	5000
2268	**Angel** (7s. 6d.). As 2265, hЄnRIC VIII D(I) G(RA) R(EX) etc.; *mm.* 110, 105	250	600
2269	**Half-angel.** Similar; *mm.* 105	400	900

Second coinage gold

2270   2272

	F	VF
	£	£

2270   **George-noble** (6s. 8d.). As illustration; *mm.* rose . . . . | 2250 | 5500
2270A — Similar, but more modern ship with three masts, without initials hR. ℞.
    St. George brandishing sword behind head. . . . . *Unique*
2271   **Half-George-noble**. Similar to 2270. . . . . *Unique*
2272   **Crown of the rose** (4s. 6d., 23 ct). As illustration; *mm.* rose . . . . *Extremely rare*

2279   2285

		F	VF
2273	**Crown of the double-rose** (5s., 22 ct). Double-rose crowned, hK (Henry and Katherine of Aragon) both crowned in field. ℞. Shield crowned; *mm.* rose.	175	400
2274	— hK both sides; *mm.* rose/lis, lis, arrow	190	400
2275*	— hK / hA or hA / hK; *mm.* arrow	200	550
2276*	— hR / hK or hI / hR; *mm.* arrow	*Extremely rare*	
2277	— hA (Anne Boleyn); *mm.* arrow	225	575
2278	— hA / hR; *mm.* arrow	—	2250
2279	— hI (Jane Seymour); *mm.* arrow	200	450
2280*	— hK / hI; *mm.* arrow.	225	650
2281	— hR / hI; *mm.* arrow.	225	675
2282	— hR (Rex); *mm.* arrow	200	425
2283	— — but with hIBERIE REX; *mm.* pheon.	400	1000
2284	**Halfcrown**. Similar but king's name henric 8 on *rev.*, no initials; *mm.* rose	170	400
2285	— hK uncrowned on *obv.*; *mm.* rose	150	375
2286	— hK uncrowned both sides; *mm.* rose/lis, lis, arrow	160	385
2287	— hI uncrowned both sides; *mm.* arrow	225	500
2288	— hR uncrowned both sides; hIBREX; *mm.* pheon	325	750

*The hK initials may on later coins refer to Katherine Howard (Henry's fifth wife).

Third coinage, 1544–7

2291

		F £	VF £
2289	**Sovereign**, I (20s., Wt. 200 grs., 23 ct.). As illustration but king with larger face and larger design; *mm.* lis	4000	9500
2290	II (20s., wt. 200 or 192 grs., 23, 22 or 20 ct.). *Tower.* As illustration; *mm.* lis, pellet in annulet/lis	1150	3050
2291	— *Southwark.* Similar; *mm.* S, Є/S.	1200	2950
2292	— — Similar but Є below shield; *mm.* S/Є	*Extremely rare*	
2293	— *Bristol.* As London but *mm.* WS/-	2750	5000
2294	**Half-sovereign** (wt. 100 or 96 grs.), *Tower.* As illus.; *mm.* lis, pellet in annulet.	175	475
2295	— Similar, but with annulet on inner circle (either or both sides)	200	550
2296	*Southwark. Mm.* S.	200	550
2297	— Є below shield; *mm.* S, Є, S/Є, Є/S, (known without sceptre; *mm.* S) .	175	500
2298	*Bristol.* Lombardic lettering; *mm.* WS, WS/-	350	900

2294

2303   2304

		F	VF
2299	**Angel** (8s., 23 ct). Annulet by angel's head and on ship, hЄnRIC' 8; *mm.* lis.	175	350
2300	— Similar, but annulet one side only or none.	185	375
2301	**Half-angel.** Annulet on ship; *mm.* lis.	175	425
2302	— No annulet on ship; *mm.* lis.	200	475
2303	— Three annulets on ship; *mm.* lis	250	500
2304	**Quarter-angel** Angel wears armour; *mm.* lis	175	400
2304A	— Angel wears tunic; *mm.* lis.	200	450

Third coinage gold

		F £	VF £
2305	**Crown**, *London*. Similar to 2283, but hЄnRIC' 8; Lombardic lettering; *mm*. 56	160	350
2306	— without RVTILAnS; *mm*. 56	170	375
2307	— — — with annulet on inner circle.	180	400
2307A	— King's name omitted. DEI GRA both sides, *mm*. 56	*Extremely rare*	
2308	— *Southwark*. As 2306; *mm*. S, Є, E/S, Є/-, E/Є	225	425
2309	*Bristol*. hЄnRIC VIII. ROSA etc. ℞. D G, etc.; *mm*.-/WS	165	375
2310	— Similar but hЄnRIC(VS) 8 ℞. D(EI) G(RA); *mm*. -/WS, WS	165	375
2311	**Halfcrown**, *London*. Similar to 2288; *mm*. 56, 56/-	125	300
2312	— — with annulet on inner circle *mm*. 56	135	310
2313	*Southwark*. As 2311; *mm*. S	160	375
2314	— *O*. hЄnRIC 8 ROSA SINЄ SPIn. ℞. DЄI GRA, etc.; *mm*. Є	225	600
2315	*Bristol*. *O*. RVTILAnS, etc. ℞. hЄnRIC 8; *mm*. WS/-	250	450

For other gold coins in Henry's name see page 152.

SILVER

First coinage, 1509–26

2316   2327

2316	**Groat**. Portrait of Hen. VII. *London mm*. 53, 69, 108	45	110
2317	— *Tournai; mm*. crowned T. ℞. CIVITAS TORnACЄn *	160	500
2318	**Halfgroat**. Portrait of Hen. VII. *London; mm*. 108, 108/-.	90	180
2319	— *Canterbury*, Archb. Warham. POSVI *rev.; mm*. rose	70	180
2320	— — — WA above shield; *mm*. martlet	30	100
2321	— — — WA beside shield; *mm*. cross fitchée	40	120
2322	— — CIVITAS CAnTOR *rev.*, similar; *mm*. 73, 105, 11/105	40	90
2323	— *York*, POSVI *rev.*, Archb. Bainbridge (1508–14). Keys below shield; *mm*. martlet	40	90
2324•	— — — XB beside shield no keys; *mm*. martlet	55	125
2325	— — — Archb. Wolsey (1514–30). Keys and cardinal's hat below shield; *mm*. 94, 22	80	170
2326	— — CIVITAS ЄBORACI *rev*. Similar; *mm*. 22, 23, 30, 78, 15, 15/78 . .	35	70
2327	— — As last with TW beside shield; *mm*. voided cross.	40	80
2327A	— *Tournai*. As 2317	*Unique*	

*Other non-portrait groats and half-groats exist of this mint, captured during an invasion of France in 1513. (Restored to France in 1518.)

2332   2335   2336

		F	VF
		£	£
2328	**Penny,** "Sovereign" type, *London; mm.* 69, 108/-.	25	60
2329	— *Canterbury.* WA above shield; *mm.* martlet	Extremely rare	
2330	— — — WA beside shield; *mm.* 73/-.	30	70
2331	— *Durham,* Bp. Ruthall (1509–23). TD above shield; *mm.* lis	30	60
2332	— — — TD beside shield; *mm.* lis, radiant star.	25	60
2333	— — Bp. Wolsey (1523–9). DW beside shield, cardinal's hat below; spur rowel	90	225
2334	**Halfpenny.** Facing bust, hЄnRIC DI GRA RЄX (AGL). *London; mm.* 69, 108/-	35	75
2335	— *Canterbury.* WA beside bust; *mm.* 73/-, 11	80	175
2336	**Farthing.** *O. Mm.* 108/-, hЄnRIC DI GRA RЄX, a portcullis as type. ℞. CIVITAS LOnDON, rose in centre of long cross	750	1250

Second coinage, 1526–44

2337   2337D   2337E

2337	**Groat.** His own young portrait. *London;* bust r., with heavy jowls; mainly *mm.* rose, Roman letters, both sides, roses in cross ends	85	260
2337A	*Obv.* as last. ℞. Lombardic letters, saltires in cross ends; *mm.* rose	50	150
2337B	Bust as 2337 but Lombardic letters. ℞. Lombardic letters but roses in cross ends; *mm.* rose.	45	110
2337C	*Obv.* as last. ℞. As 2337A; *mm.* rose.	50	125
2337D	Second bust, Greek profile, longer hair, less heavy jowls; *mm.* rose	35	75
2337E	Third bust, stereotyped as ill. 2337E; *mm.* 33–53 (muling occurs)	30	60
2338	— — with Irish title HIB; larger flan, saltires in cross ends; *mm.* 53, 105 (also muled), 53/105, 105/53, 105.	250	600
2339	— *York,* Archb. Wolsey. TW beside shield, cardinal's hat below; *mm.* voided cross, acorn, muled (both ways)	50	120
2340	— — — omits TW; *mm.* voided cross	150	375

Second coinage silver

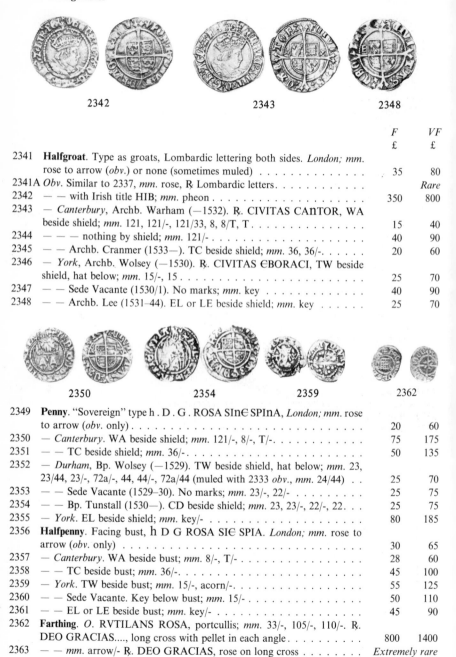

2342	2343		2348

		F	VF
		£	£

2341 **Halfgroat**. Type as groats, Lombardic lettering both sides. *London; mm.*
rose to arrow (*obv.*) or none (sometimes muled) 35 80
2341A *Obv.* Similar to 2337, *mm.* rose, ℞ Lombardic letters. . . . . *Rare*
2342 — — with Irish title HIB; *mm.* pheon 350 800
2343 — *Canterbury*, Archb. Warham (—1532). ℞. CIVITAS CAnTOR, WA
beside shield; *mm.* 121, 121/-, 121/33, 8, 8/T, T 15 40
2344 — — — nothing by shield; *mm.* 121/- 40 90
2345 — — Archb. Cranmer (1533—). TC beside shield; *mm.* 36, 36/-. 20 60
2346 — *York*, Archb. Wolsey (—1530). ℞. CIVITAS ЄBORACI, TW beside
shield, hat below; *mm.* 15/-, 15 . . . . 25 70
2347 — — Sede Vacante (1530/1). No marks; *mm.* key 40 90
2348 — — Archb. Lee (1531–44). EL or LE beside shield; *mm.* key 25 70

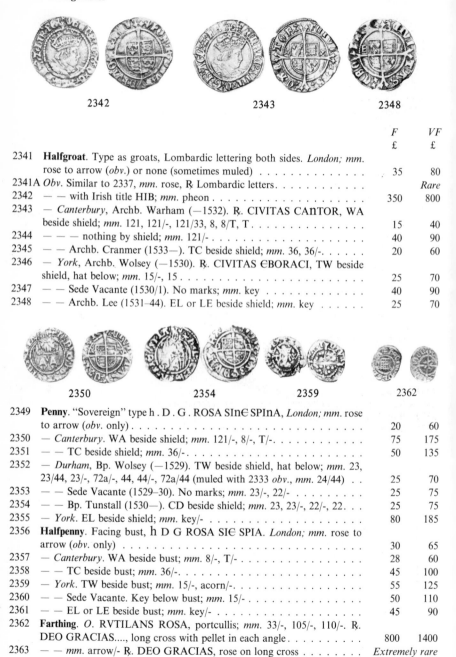

2350	2354	2359	2362

2349 **Penny**. "Sovereign" type h . D . G . ROSA SInЄ SPInA, *London; mm.* rose
to arrow (*obv.* only) 20 60
2350 — *Canterbury*. WA beside shield; *mm.* 121/-, 8/-, T/-. 75 175
2351 — — TC beside shield; *mm.* 36/- 50 135
2352 — *Durham*, Bp. Wolsey (—1529). TW beside shield, hat below; *mm.* 23,
23/44, 23/-, 72a/-, 44, 44/-, 72a/44 (muled with 2333 *obv.*, *mm.* 24/44) . . 25 70
2353 — — Sede Vacante (1529–30). No marks; *mm.* 23/-, 22/- 25 75
2354 — — Bp. Tunstall (1530—). CD beside shield; *mm.* 23, 23/-, 22/-, 22. . . 25 75
2355 — *York*. EL beside shield; *mm.* key/- 80 185
2356 **Halfpenny**. Facing bust, h D G ROSA SIЄ SPIA. *London; mm.* rose to
arrow (*obv.* only) 30 65
2357 — *Canterbury*. WA beside bust; *mm.* 8/-, T/- 28 60
2358 — — TC beside bust; *mm.* 36/-. 45 100
2359 — *York*. TW beside bust; *mm.* 15/-, acorn/-. 55 125
2360 — — Sede Vacante. Key below bust; *mm.* 15/- 50 110
2361 — — EL or LE beside bust; *mm.* key/- 45 90
2362 **Farthing**. *O.* RVTILANS ROSA, portcullis; *mm.* 33/-, 105/-, 110/-. ℞.
DEO GRACIAS...., long cross with pellet in each angle 800 1400
2363 — — *mm.* arrow/- ℞. DEO GRACIAS, rose on long cross . . . . *Extremely rare*
2363A — *Canterbury*. *O.* Similar. ℞. Similar. *mm.* 36/- . . . . *Extremely rare*

Third coinage, 1544–7 (Silver progressively debased. 9oz (.750), 6oz (.500) 4oz (.333).)

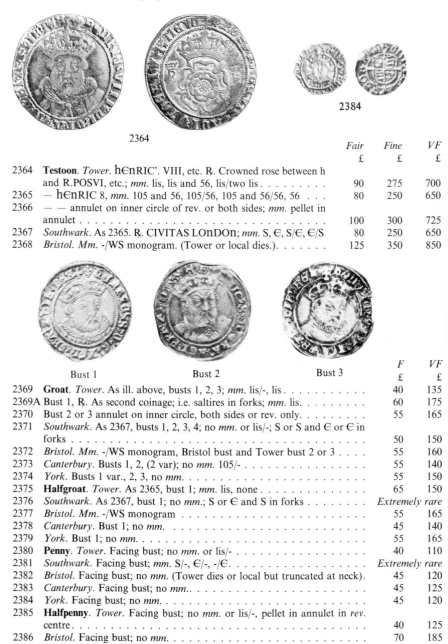

2384

2364

		Fair £	Fine £	VF £
2364	**Testoon**. *Tower*. hЄnRIC'. VIII, etc. R̥. Crowned rose between h and R.POSVI, etc.; *mm.* lis, lis and 56, lis/two lis	90	275	700
2365	— hЄnRIC 8, *mm.* 105 and 56, 105/56, 105 and 56/56, 56 . . .	80	250	650
2366	— — annulet on inner circle of rev. or both sides; *mm.* pellet in annulet	100	300	725
2367	*Southwark*. As 2365. R̥. CIVITAS LOnDOn; *mm.* S, Є, S/Є, Є/S	80	250	650
2368	*Bristol. Mm.* -/WS monogram. (Tower or local dies.).	125	350	850

Bust 1	Bust 2	Bust 3	F £	VF £
2369	**Groat**. *Tower*. As ill. above, busts 1, 2, 3; *mm.* lis/-, lis	40	135
2369A	Bust 1, R̥. As second coinage; i.e. saltires in forks; *mm.* lis.	60	175
2370	Bust 2 or 3 annulet on inner circle, both sides or rev. only.	55	165
2371	*Southwark*. As 2367, busts 1, 2, 3, 4; no *mm.* or lis/-; S or S and Є or Є in forks	50	150
2372	*Bristol. Mm.* -/WS monogram, Bristol bust and Tower bust 2 or 3	55	160
2373	*Canterbury*. Busts 1, 2, (2 var); no *mm.* 105/-.	55	140
2374	*York*. Busts 1 var., 2, 3, no *mm.*	55	150
2375	**Halfgroat**. *Tower*. As 2365, bust 1; *mm.* lis, none	65	150
2376	*Southwark*. As 2367, bust 1; no *mm.*; S or Є and S in forks	*Extremely rare*	
2377	*Bristol. Mm.* -/WS monogram	55	165
2378	*Canterbury*. Bust 1; no *mm.*	45	140
2379	*York*. Bust 1; no *mm.*	55	165
2380	**Penny**. *Tower*. Facing bust; no *mm.* or lis/-	40	110
2381	*Southwark*. Facing bust; *mm.* S/-, Є/-, -/Є.	*Extremely rare*	
2382	*Bristol*. Facing bust; no *mm.* (Tower dies or local but truncated at neck).	45	120
2383	*Canterbury*. Facing bust; no *mm.*.	45	125
2384	*York*. Facing bust; no *mm.*	45	120
2385	**Halfpenny**. *Tower*. Facing bust; no *mm.* or lis/-, pellet in annulet in *rev.* centre	40	125
2386	*Bristol*. Facing bust; no *mm.*	70	185
2387	*Canterbury*. Facing bust; no *mm.*, (some read H 8)	40	135
2388	*York*. Facing bust; no *mm.*	40	135

HENRY VIII POSTHUMOUS COINAGE, 1547–51

These coins were struck during the reign of Edward VI but bear the name and portrait of Henry VIII, except in the case of the half-sovereigns which bear the youthful head of Edward.

Mintmarks

◎	✠	⚓	K	E	W
56	105	52	K	E	116

(	Ⅱ	✿	⚭	t	🦅
66	115	33	122	t	94

1547	Annulet and pellet (56)	1549	TC monogram (115, *Bristol*)
1547–8	Lis (105)		Lis (105, *Canterbury*)
1547–9	Arrow (52)		Rose (33, *Canterbury*)
	K		Grapple (122)
	Roman E (*Southwark*)	1549/50	t (*Canterbury*)
	WS monogram (116, *Bristol*)	1550/1	Martlet (94)
1548–9	Bow (66, *Durham House*)		

GOLD

		F	VF
		£	£
2389	**Sovereign** (20 ct), *London*. As no. 2290, but Roman lettering; *mm.* lis. . .	1350	3750
2390	— *Bristol*. Similar but *mm.* WS	1700	4250

2391A   2395

2391	**Half-sovereign**. As 2294, but with youthful portrait with sceptre. *Tower*; *mm.* 52, 105, 94 (various combinations)	225	550
2391A	— Similar but no sceptre; *mm.* 52, 52/56	250	600
2392	— — — K below shield; *mm.* -/K, none,. E/-	240	575
2393	— — — grapple below shield; *mm.* 122, none, 122/-, -/122.	250	600
2394	— *Southwark*. Mm. E, E/-, -/E, Є/E. Usually Є or E (sometimes retrograde) below shield (sceptre omitted; *mm.* -/E)	225	550
2394A	— — — ℞. As 2296; *mm.*-/S	225	600
2395	**Crown**. Similar to 2305. *London; mm.* 52, 52/-, -/K, 122, 94, K	350	750

	F £	VF £
2396 — Similar but transposed legends without numeral; *mm.* -/arrow	375	775
2396A — As 2395, but omitting RVTILANS; *mm.* arrow	*Extremely rare*	
2396B Similar, but RVTILANS both sides; *mm.* arrow	*Extremely rare*	
2397 — *Southwark*. Similar to 2396; *mm.* E	*Extremely rare*	
2398 — — King's name on *obv.*; *mm.* E/-, E, -/E	—	400
2399 **Halfcrown**. Similar to 2311. *London; mm.* 52, K/-, 122/-, 94, -/52	250	600
2399A As last but E over h on *rev.*, *mm.* 56/52	*Extremely rare*	
2399B As 2399 but RUTILANS etc. on both sides, *mm.* arrow	*Extremely rare*	
2400 — *Southwark. Mm.* E, E/-, -/E	250	600

SILVER

AR (4oz .333)

	Fair	Fine
2401 **Testoon**. *Tower*. As 2365 with lozenge stops one side; -/56, 56	100	375
2402 *Southwark*. As 2367; *mm.* S/E	120	400

Some of the Bristol testoons, groats and halfgroats with WS *monogram were struck after the death of Henry VIII but cannot easily be distinguished from those struck during his reign.*

Bust 4   Bust 5   Bust 6

	F £	VF £
2403 **Groat**. *Tower*. Busts 4, 5, 6 (and, rarely, 2). ℞. POSVI, etc.; *mm.* 105–94 and none (frequently muled)	45	150
2404 *Southwark*. Busts 4, 5, 6. ℞. CIVITAS LONDON; no *mm.* -/E; lis/-, -/lis, K/E; roses or crescents or S and E in forks	50	160
2405 *Durham House*. Bust 6. ℞. REDDE CVIQUE QVOD SVVM EST; *mm.* bow	110	300
2406 *Bristol. Mm.* WS on *rev.* Bristol busts A and B, Tower bust 2 and 3	50	185
2407 — — *Mm.* TC on *rev.* Similar, Bristol bust B	90	300
2408 *Canterbury*. Busts 5, 6; no *mm.* or rose/-	45	140
2409 *York*. Busts 4, 5, 6; no *mm.* or lis/-, -/lis	55	160
2410 **Halfgroat**. Bust 1. *Tower*. POSVI, etc.; *mm.* 52, 52/-, 52/K, -/K, 52/122, 122, -/122	25	110
2411 — *Southwark*. CIVITAS LONDON; *mm.* E, -/E, none, 52/E, K/E	23	100
2412 — *Durham House*. ℞. REDD, etc.; *mm.* bow, -/bow	250	500
2413 — *Bristol. Mm.* WS on *rev.*	30	120
2414 — — *mm.* TC on *rev.*	50	150

2415

	F £	VF £
2415 **Halfgroat.** *Canterbury.* No *mm.* or t/-, -/t	25	100
2416 — *York.* No *mm.*, bust 1 and three quarter facing	30	120

2422　　　　2418　　　　2427

2417 **Penny.** *Tower.* CIVITAS LONDON. Facing bust; *mm.* 52/-, -/52, -/K, 122/-, -/122, none	30	100
2418 — — three-quarter bust; no *mm.*	30	100
2419 *Southwark.* As 2417; *mm.* E, -/E	75	225
2420 *Durham House.* As groat but shorter legend; *mm.* -/bow	135	400
2421 *Bristol.* Facing busts, as 2382, no *mm.*	35	120
2422 *Canterbury.* Similar	30	100
2423 — three-quarters facing bust; no *mm.*	30	100
2424 *York.* Facing bust; no *mm.*	30	100
2425 — three-quarters facing bust; no *mm.*	35	120
2426 **Halfpenny.** *Tower.* 52?, none	40	150
2427 *Canterbury.* No *mm.*, sometimes reads H8.	35	110
2428 *York.* No *mm.*	40	150

EDWARD VI, 1547–53

Coinage in his own name

While base coins continued to be issued bearing the name of Henry VIII, plans were made early in Edward's reign to reform the coinage. As a first step, in 1549, the standard of the gold was raised to 22 carat and "silver" was increased to 50% silver content. Baser shillings were issued in 1550, but finally, in 1551, it was decided to resume the coinage of some "fine" gold and a new silver coinage was ordered of 11 oz. 1 dwt. Fineness, i.e. almost up to the ancient standard. At the same time four new denominations were added to the coinage—the silver crown, halfcrown, sixpence and threepence. Pennies continued to be struck in base silver.

The first dates on English coinage appear in Roman numerals during this reign; MDXLVIII = 1548; MDXLIX = 1549; MDL = 1550; MDLI = 1551.

66	52	35	115	E	53	122
t	T	111	Y	126	94	91A
92	105	y	97	123	78	26

Mintmarks

1548–9	Bow (66, *Durham House*)	1549–50	6 (126 gold only)
1549	Arrow (52)	1550	Martlet (94)
	Grapple (122)	1550	Leopard's head (91A)
	Rose (35, *Canterbury*)	1550–1	Lion (92)
	TC monogram (115, *Bristol*)		Lis (105, *Southwark*)
	Roman E (*Southwark*)		Rose (33)
	Pheon (53)	1551	Yor y (117, *Southwark*)
	t or T (*Canterbury*)		Ostrich's head (97, gold only)
1549–50	Swan (111)	1551–3	Tun (123)
	Roman Y (*Southwark*)		Escallop (78)
		1552–3	Pierced mullet (26, *York*)

GOLD

First period, Apr. 1547–Jan. 1549

2429   2431

	F	VF
First period gold, *continued*	£	£

2429   **Half-sovereign** (20 ct). As 2391, but reading EDWARD 6. *Tower; mm.*
arrow   400   850

2430   — *Southwark* (Sometimes with E or Є below shield); *mm.* E   350   750

2431   **Crown.** RVTILANS, etc., crowned rose between E R both crowned. Ŗ.
EDWARD 6, etc., crowned shield between ER both crowned; *mm.* arrow,
E over arrow/- . . . .   *Extremely rare*

2431A   — *Obv.* as last. Ŗ. As 2305, *mm.* 52/56 . . . .   *Extremely rare*

2432   **Halfcrown.** Similar to 2431, but initials not crowned; *mm.* arrow . . . . .   *Extremely rare*

Second period, Jan. 1549–Apr. 1550

2433

2433   **Sovereign** (22 ct). As illustration; *mm.* arrow, Y, -/52.   1600   3250

2435   2438

2434   **Half-sovereign.** Uncrowned bust. *London.* TIMOR etc., MDXLIX on *obv.*;
mm. arrow . . . .   *Extremely rare*

2435   — — SCVTVM, etc., as illustration; *mm.* arrow, **6**, Y   400   900

2436   — *Durham House.* Uncrowned, ½ length bust with MDXLVIII at end of
obv. legend; *mm.* bow; SCVTVM etc.   *Extremely rare*

2437   — Normal, uncrowned bust. LVCERNA, etc., on *obv.*; *mm.* bow. . . . .   *Extremely rare*

2438   Crowned bust. *London.* EDWARD VI, etc. Ŗ. SCVTVM, etc.; *mm.* 52,
122, 111/52, 111, Y, 94   375   800

2439   — *Durham House.* Crowned, half-length bust; *mm.* bow . . . .   *Unique*

2440   — — King's name on *obv.* and *rev.*; *mm.* bow (mule of 2439/37)   4000   7500

2441   2444

* *Small denominations often occur creased or straightened.*

		F	VF
		£	£
2441	**Crown.** Uncrowned bust, as 2435; *mm*. 6, Y, 52/-, Y/-	700	1300
2442	Crowned bust, as 2438; *mm*. 52, 122, 111, Y (usually *obv*. only).	475	1000
2443	**Halfcrown.** Uncrowned bust; ℞. As 2441, *mm*. arrow, Y, Y/-, 52/-	550	1100
2444	Crowned bust, as illus. above; *mm*. 52, 52/111, 111, 122, Y, Y/-.	450	900
2445	Similar, but king's name on *rev*., *mm*. 52, 122.	550	1000

Third period, 1550–3

| 2446 | **"Fine" sovereign** (= 30s.). King on throne; *mm*. 97, 123 . . . . | 8000 | 20,000 |
| 2447 | **Double sovereign.** From the same dies, *mm*. 97 . . . . | *Extremely rare* | |

2448   2451

2448	**Angel** (= 10s.). As illustration; *mm*. 97, 123	3500	7000
2449	**Half-angel.** Similar, *mm*. 97.		*Unique*
2450	**Sovereign.** (= 20s.). Half-length figure of king r., crowned and holding sword and orb. ℞. Crowned shield with supporters; *mm*. y, tun	700	1750
2451	**Half-sovereign.** As illustration above; *mm*. y, tun	500	950
2452	**Crown.** Similar, but *rev*. SCVTVM etc., *mm*. y, tun	800	2000
2453	**Halfcrown.** Similar, *mm*. tun, y.	800	2000

SILVER

First period, Apr. 1547–Jan. 1549

| | 2459 | 2460 | F £ | VF £ |

2454	**Groat**. Cr. bust r. *Tower*. ℞. Shield over cross, POSVI, etc.; *mm*. arrow .		225	575
2455	— As last, but EDOARD 6, *mm*. arrow.		*Extremely rare*	
2456	— *Southwark*. *Obv*. as 2454. ℞. CIVITAS LONDON; *mm*.-/E or none, S in forks		300	700
2457	**Halfgroat**. *Tower*. *Obv*. as 2454; *mm*. arrow.		300	700
2458	*Southwark*. As 2456; *mm*. arrow, E		350	800
2459	*Canterbury*. Similar. No *mm*., also reads EDOARD (as ill.)		200	500
2460	**Penny**. *Tower*. As halfgroat, but E.D.G. etc. ℞. CIVITAS LONDON; *mm*. arrow.		225	700
2461	— *Southwark*. As last, but *mm*. -/E.		200	600
2462	*Bristol*. Similar, but reads ED6DG or E6DG no *mm*.		200	575
2463	**Halfpenny**. *Tower*. *O*. As 2460, *mm*. E (?). ℞. Cross and pellets		—	1000
2464	— *Bristol*. Similar, no *mm*. but reads E6DG or EDG		275	600

Second period, Jan. 1549–Apr. 1550

At all mints except Bristol, the earliest shillings of 1549 were issued at only 60 grains wt., but of 8 oz. standard. This weight and size were soon increased to 80 grains wt., but the fineness was reduced to 6 oz. so the silver content remained the same.

2465   2467

2465	**Shilling**. *Tower*. Broad bust with large crown. *Obv*. TIMOR etc. MDXLIX. ℞. Small, oval garnished shield (dividing ER). EDWARD VI etc., *mm*. 52, -/52, no *mm*.	60	250
2465A	*Southwark*. As last, *mm*. Y, EY/Y	100	300
2465B	*Canterbury*. As last, *mm*. -/rose.		*Rare*
2466	*Tower*. Tall, narrow bust with small crown. *Obv*. EDWARD VI etc. MDXLIX or MDL. ℞. As 2465 but TIMOR etc., *mm*. 52–91a (frequently muled)	60	225

The prices and rarity of nos. 2465–2473A are very much estimates, as they have not previously been divided thus.

	Fine £	VF £

2466A — *Obv.* as last, MDXLIX. ℞. Heavily garnished shield, Durham House style. *mm.* 122 . . . .   *Rare*

2466B *Southwark.* As 2466, *mm.* Y, Y/swan   70   250

2466C — — — ℞. as 2466A. *mm.* Y   75   275

2467 *Bristol. Obv.* similar to 2466. ℞. Shield with heavy curved garniture or as 2466, *mm.* TC/rose TC, rose TC . . . .   —   1250

2468 *Canterbury.* As 2466, *mm.* T, t, t/T.   90   275

2469 *Durham House.* Bust with elaborate tunic and collar TIMOR etc. MDXLIX. ℞. Oval shield, very heavily garnished in different style. EDWARD VI etc., *mm.* bow.   225   500

2469A As last but legends transposed   150   400

2470 — Bust as last. INIMICOS etc., no date. ℞. EDWARD etc.   135   350

2468   2470

2471 — — As last, but legends transposed   200   500

2472 — Bust similar to 2466. EDWARD VI etc. ℞. INIMICOS etc.   150   400

2472A As last but legends transposed   175   450

2472B *Tower.* Elegant bust with extremely thin neck. ℞. As 2466, *mm.* 94   110   300

2472C *Southwark.* As last, *mm.* Y   110   300

For coins of Edward VI countermarked, see p. 154.

2472   2472c

Third period, 1550–3

Very base issue 1550–1 (250 fine)

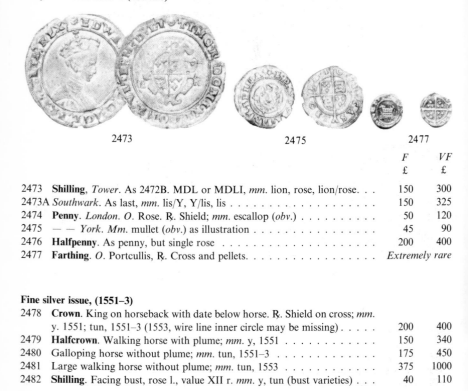

2473   2475   2477

| | F | VF |
	£	£
2473 **Shilling**, *Tower*. As 2472B. MDL or MDLI, *mm*. lion, rose, lion/rose. . .	150	300
2473A *Southwark*. As last, *mm*. lis/Y, Y/lis, lis	150	325
2474 **Penny**. *London*. O. Rose. ℞. Shield; *mm*. escallop (*obv*.)	50	120
2475 — — *York*. *Mm*. mullet (*obv*.) as illustration	45	90
2476 **Halfpenny**. As penny, but single rose	200	400
2477 **Farthing**. O. Portcullis, ℞. Cross and pellets.	*Extremely rare*	

Fine silver issue, (1551–3)

2478 **Crown**. King on horseback with date below horse. ℞. Shield on cross; *mm*.		
y. 1551; tun, 1551–3 (1553, wire line inner circle may be missing)	200	400
2479 **Halfcrown**. Walking horse with plume; *mm*. y, 1551	150	340
2480 Galloping horse without plume; *mm*. tun, 1551–3	175	450
2481 Large walking horse without plume; *mm*. tun, 1553	375	1000
2482 **Shilling**. Facing bust, rose l., value XII r. *mm*. y, tun (bust varieties) . . .	40	110

2478

2479

2482   2483   2486

			F £	VF £
2483	**Sixpence**. *London*. Similar, as illustration; *mm.* y/-, -/y, y, tun (bust varieties)	40	125
2484	*York*. As last, but CIVITAS ЄBORACI; *mm.* mullet	120	300
2485	**Threepence**. *London*. As sixpence, but III; *mm.* tun	125	325
2486	*York*. As 2484, but III by bust	175	500
2487	**Penny**. "Sovereign" type; *mm.* tun	—	1400

MARY, 1553–4

All Mary's gold coin was struck in 23 carat 3½ grain gold, the "crown" gold denominations being temporarily discontinued. The mintmarks appear at the end of the first or second word of the legends.

Pomegranate  Half-rose (or half-rose and castle)

GOLD

2488

		F £	VF £
2488	**"Fine" Sovereign** (= 30s.). Queen enthroned. ℞. Shield on rose, MDLIII, MDLIIII and undated, *mm.* pomegranate, half-rose (or mule)	1400	3000
2489	**Ryal** (= 15s.). As illus, MDLIII. ℞. As 1950 but ADNO etc. *mm.* pomegranate/-	*Extremely rare*	
	A very fine specimen sold at auction in November 1985 for £13,000.		
2490	**Angel** (= 10s.). Usual type; *mm.* pomegranate, half-rose, none? (Known with rose and M transposed)	450	900
2491	**Half-angel.** Similar; *mm.* pomegranate, pomegranate/-	1750	4500

2489   2492

2492	**Groat.** Crowned bust l. ℞. VERITAS, etc.; *mm.* pomegranate, pomegranate/-	40	110
2493	**Halfgroat.** Similar	*Extremely rare*	
2494	**Penny.** Similar, but M . D. G. ROSA, etc.	300	750
2495	— As last. ℞. CIVITAS LONDON; no *mm.*	300	750
2495A	— Base penny. Similar to 2474 but M.D.G. etc. . . . . *All late 19th cent. fabrications*		

PHILIP AND MARY, 1554–8

The groats and smaller silver coins of this period have Mary's portrait only, but the shillings and sixpences show the bust of the queen's husband, Philip of Spain.

Mintmarks

Lis (105)   Half-rose and castle

GOLD

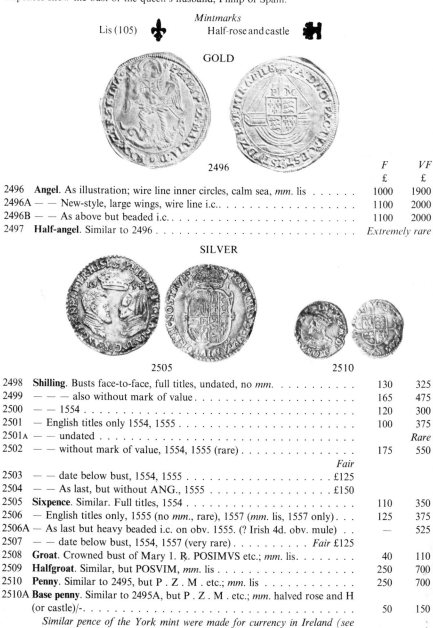

2496

		F	*VF*
		£	£
2496	**Angel**. As illustration; wire line inner circles, calm sea, *mm*. lis	1000	1900
2496A	— — New-style, large wings, wire line i.c..	1100	2000
2496B	— — As above but beaded i.c..	1100	2000
2497	**Half-angel**. Similar to 2496	*Extremely rare*	

SILVER

2505   2510

2498	**Shilling**. Busts face-to-face, full titles, undated, no *mm*.	130	325
2499	— — — also without mark of value.	165	475
2500	— — 1554	120	300
2501	— English titles only 1554, 1555	100	375
2501A	— — undated		*Rare*
2502	— — without mark of value, 1554, 1555 (rare)	175	550
		Fair	
2503	— — date below bust, 1554, 1555 . . . . £125		
2504	— — As last, but without ANG., 1555 . . . . £150		
2505	**Sixpence**. Similar. Full titles, 1554	110	350
2506	— English titles only, 1555 (no *mm*., rare), 1557 (*mm*. lis, 1557 only). . .	125	375
2506A	— As last but heavy beaded i.c. on obv. 1555. (? Irish 4d. obv. mule) . .	—	525
2507	— — date below bust, 1554, 1557 (very rare) . . . . *Fair* £125		
2508	**Groat**. Crowned bust of Mary 1. ℞. POSIMVS etc.; *mm*. lis.	40	110
2509	**Halfgroat**. Similar, but POSVIM, *mm*. lis	250	700
2510	**Penny**. Similar to 2495, but P . Z . M . etc.; *mm*. lis	250	700
2510A	**Base penny**. Similar to 2495A, but P . Z . M . etc.; *mm*. halved rose and H (or castle)/-.	50	150

Similar pence of the York mint were made for currency in Ireland (see Coins and Tokens of Ireland, no. 6502).

ELIZABETH I, 1558–1603

Elizabeth's coinage is particularly interesting on account of the large number of different denominations issued. 'Crown' gold coins were again issued as well as the 'fine' gold denominations. In 1559 the base shillings of Edward VI's second and third coinages were called in and countermarked for recirculation at reduced values. The normal silver coinage was initially struck at .916 fineness as in the previous reign but between 1560 and 1577 and after 1582 the old sterling standard of .925 was restored. Between 1578 and 1582 the standard was slightly reduced and the weights were reduced by 1/32nd in 1601. Gold was similarly reduced slightly in quality 1578–82, and there was a slight weight reduction in 1601.

To help alleviate the shortage of small change, and to avoid the expense of minting an impossibly small silver farthing, a threefarthing piece was introduced to provide change if a penny was tendered for a farthing purchase. The sixpence, threepence, threehalfpence and threefarthings were marked with a rose behind the queen's head to distinguish them from the shilling, groat, half-groat and penny.

Coins of exceedingly fine workmanship were produced in a screw press introduced by Eloye Mestrelle, a French moneyer, in 1561. With parts of the machinery powered by a horse-drawn mill, the coins produced came to be known as "mill money". Despite the superior quality of the coins produced, the machinery was slow and inefficient compared to striking by hand. Mestrelle's dismissal was engineered in 1572 and six years later he was hanged for counterfeiting.

Mintmarks

| 106 | 21 | 94 | 23 | 53 | 33 | 107 | 92 |

| 74 | 71 | 26 | 77 | 65b | 27 | 7 | 14 |

| 113 | 60 | 54 | 79 | 72b | 86 | 123 | 124 |

| 90 | 57 | 0 | 1 | 2 |

1558–60	Lis (106)	1578–9	Greek cross (7)
1560–1	Cross crosslet (21)	1580–1	Latin cross (14)
	Martlet (94)	1582	Sword (113)
1560–6	Star (23, milled)	1582–3	Bell (60)
1561–5	Pheon (53)	1582–4	A (54)
1565	Rose (33)	1584–6	Escallop (79)
1566	Portcullis (107)	1587–9	Crescent (72b)
1566–7	Lion (92)	1590–2	Hand (86)
1567–70	Coronet (74)	1591–5	Tun (123)
	Lis (105, milled)	1594–6	Woolpack (124)
1569–71	Castle (71)	1595–8	Key (90)
1570	Pierced mullet (26, milled)	1597–1600	Anchor (57)
1572–3	Ermine (77)	1600	0
1573–4	Acorn (65b)	1601–2	1
1573–7	Eglantine (27)	1602	2

N.B. *The dates for* mms *sometimes overlap. This is a result of using up old dies, onto which the new mark was punched.*

GOLD

Hammered Coinage
First to Third issues, 1559–78. ('Fine' gold of .979. 'Crown' gold of .916 fineness. Sovereigns of 240 grs. wt.). Mintmarks; lis to eglantine.

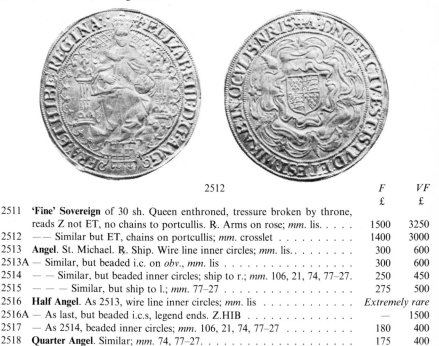

2512

		F £	VF £
2511	**'Fine' Sovereign** of 30 sh. Queen enthroned, tressure broken by throne, reads Z not ET, no chains to portcullis. R. Arms on rose; *mm.* lis.	1500	3250
2512	— — Similar but ET, chains on portcullis; *mm.* crosslet	1400	3000
2513	**Angel.** St. Michael. R. Ship. Wire line inner circles; *mm.* lis.	300	600
2513A	— Similar, but beaded i.c. on *obv.*, *mm.* lis	300	600
2514	— — Similar, but beaded inner circles; ship to r.; *mm.* 106, 21, 74, 77–27.	250	450
2515	— — — Similar, but ship to l.; *mm.* 77–27	275	500
2516	**Half Angel.** As 2513, wire line inner circles; *mm.* lis	*Extremely rare*	
2516A	— As last, but beaded i.c.s, legend ends. Z.HIB	—	1500
2517	— As 2514, beaded inner circles; *mm.* 106, 21, 74, 77–27	180	400
2518	**Quarter Angel.** Similar; *mm.* 74, 77–27.	175	400

2513   2520A

2519	**Half Pound** of 10 sh. Young crowned bust l. R. Arms. Wire line inner circles; *mm.* lis	400	900
2520	— Similar, but beaded inner circles; *mm.* 21, 33–107	300	600
2520A	— — Smaller bust; *mm.* 92	350	700
2520B	— — Broad bust, ear visible; *mm.* 92, 74, 71	350	700
2521	**Crown.** As 2519; *mm.* lis	*Extremely rare*	
2522	— Similar to 2520; *mm.* 21, 33–107	250	575
2522A	— Similar to 2520B; *mm.* 74, 71, 92	275	650
2523	**Half Crown.** As 2519; *mm.* lis.		2250
2524	— Similar to 2520; *mm.* 21, 33–107 (2 busts)	275	650
2524A	— Similar to 2520B; *mm.* 107–71.	300	700

	F	VF
	£	£

Fourth Issue, 1578–82 ('Fine' gold only of .976). Mintmarks: Greek cross, Latin cross and sword.

2525	**Angel.** As 2514; *mm.* 7, 14, 113.	250	475
2526	**Half Angel.** As 2517; *mm.* 7, 14, 113.	180	425
2527	— Similar, but without E and rose above ship; *mm.* 14	375	800
2528	**Quarter Angel.** As last; *mm.* 7, 14, 113.	175	350

Fifth Issue, 1583–1600 ('Fine' gold of .979, 'crown' gold of .916; pound of 174.5 grs. wt.).
Mintmarks: bell to **O**.

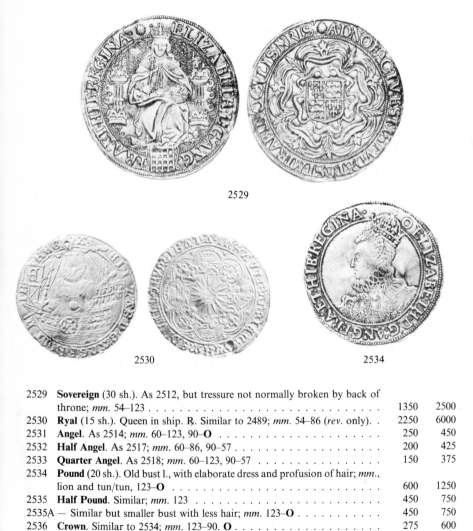

2529

2530   2534

2529	**Sovereign** (30 sh.). As 2512, but tressure not normally broken by back of throne; *mm.* 54–123	1350	2500
2530	**Ryal** (15 sh.). Queen in ship. ℞. Similar to 2489; *mm.* 54–86 (*rev.* only). .	2250	6000
2531	**Angel.** As 2514; *mm.* 60–123, 90–**O**	250	450
2532	**Half Angel.** As 2517; *mm.* 60–86, 90–57	200	425
2533	**Quarter Angel.** As 2518; *mm.* 60–123, 90–57	150	375
2534	**Pound** (20 sh.). Old bust l., with elaborate dress and profusion of hair; *mm.*, lion and tun/tun, 123–**O**	600	1250
2535	**Half Pound.** Similar; *mm.* 123	450	750
2535A	— Similar but smaller bust with less hair; *mm.* 123–**O**	450	750
2536	**Crown.** Similar to 2534; *mm.* 123–90. **O**	275	600
2537	**Half Crown.** Similar; *mm.* -/123, 123–90, **O**	250	550

Sixth Issue, 1601–3 ('Fine' gold of .979, 'crown' gold of .916; Pound of 172 grs. wt.). Mintmarks: **1** and **2**

		F £	VF £
2538	**Angel**. As 2531; *mm*. **1, 2**	300	650
2539	**Pound**. As 2534; *mm*. **1, 2**	650	1400
2540	**Half Pound**. As 2535A; *mm*. **1, 2**	600	1150

2541

2541	**Crown**. As 2536; *mm*. **1, 2**	Rare
2542	**Half Crown**. As 2537; *mm*. **1, 2**	Rare

Milled Coinage, 1561–70

2543	**Half Pound**. Crowned bust l.; *mm*. star, lis	650	1700
2544	**Crown**. Similar; *mm*. star, lis	800	2000
2545	**Half Crown**. Similar; *mm*. star, lis	1200	2500

For further details on both AV and AR milled coinage, *see* D. G. Borden 'An introduction to the Mill coinage of Elizabeth I'.

SILVER

Hammered Coinage
   Countermarked Edward VI base shillings (1559)

2546   2547

2546	**Fourpence-halfpenny**. Edward VI 2nd period 6 oz shillings countermarked on obverse with a portcullis; *mm*. 66, 52, t, 111, Y and 122	Extremely rare
2547	**Twopence-farthing**. Edward VI 3rd period 3 oz shillings countermarked on obverse with a seated greyhound; *mm*. 92. 105 and 35	Extremely rare

N.B. *Occasionally the wrong cmk. was used*

First Issue, 1559–60 (.916 fine, shillings of 96 grs.)

2548   2549

		F	VF
		£	£
2548	**Shilling**. Without rose or date. ELIZABET(H), wire line inner circles, pearls on bodice (three similar busts); *mm.* lis.	175	500
2549	— Similar, ELIZABETH, wire line and beaded inner circles, no pearls on bodice (several busts); *mm.* lis	100	350

2551   2555

2550	**Groat**. Without rose or date, wire line or no inner circles (two busts); *mm.* lis	100	250
2551	— Similar, wire line and beaded inner circles, large bust; circles *mm.* lis .	50	125
2551A	— — Small bust and shield (from halfgroat punch); *mm.* lis.	125	300
2552	**Halfgroat**. Without rose or date, wire line inner circles; *mm.* lis	150	350
2553	**Penny**. Without rose or date, wire line inner circles; *mm.* lis	115	275
2554	— Similar but dated 1558 on *obv.*; *mm.* lis	—	1500

Second Issue, 1560–1 (.925 fineness, shilling of 96 grs.)

2555	**Shilling**. Without rose or date, beaded inner circles. ET instead of Z (several bust varieties); *mm.* 21, 94.	50	150
2555A	— large bust with pearls on bodice as 2548; *mm.* 21, 94	75	200
2556	**Groat**. Without rose or date, bust as 2551; *mm.* 21, 94.	30	75
2557	**Halfgroat**. Without rose or date; *mm.* 21, 94	25	60
2558	**Penny**. Without rose or date (three bust varieties); *mm.* 21, 94	15	35

Third Issue, 1561–77 (Same fineness and weight as last)

| 2561 | 2562b | 2567 | 2571 |

		F	VF
		£	£
2559	**Sixpence**. With rose and date, large flan (27 mm. or more), large bust with hair swept back, 1561; *mm.* pheon	150	325
2560	— Similar, small bust, 1561; *mm.* pheon.	50	150
2561	— Smaller flan (26.5 mm.). Small regular bust, 1561–6; *mm.* 53–107	20	60
2561A	— Similar, without rose, 1561; *mm.* pheon	*Extremely rare*	
2561B	— Similar, very large bust, with rose, 1563–5; *mm.* pheon	50	150
2562	— intermediate bust, ear shows, 1566–74; *mm.* 92–65b (also 1567 mm. 71/74)	20	60
2562A	— Similar, without date; *mm.* lion, coronet, ermine	*Extremely rare*	
2563	— larger bust, 1573–7; *mm.* 77–27	20	60
2564	**Threepence**. With rose and date 1561, large flan (21 mm.); *mm.* pheon	25	75
2565	— smaller flan (19 mm.). Regular bust, 1561–7; *mm.* 53–92	15	45
2566	— taller bust, ear shows, 1566–77; *mm.* 92–27, 27/–, 27/65b	15	45
2566A	— Similar, without rose, 1568; *mm.* coronet	*Unique*	
2567	**Halfgroat**. Without rose or date; *mm.* 107–71	20	60
2568	**Threehalfpence**. With rose and date 1561, large flan (17 mm.) *mm.* pheon	40	100
2569	— — Smaller flan (16 mm.); 1561–2, 1564–70, 1572–7; *mm.* 53–107, 74–27.	20	55
2570	**Penny**. Without rose or date; *mm.* 33–71, 65b–27, 33/107, 92/107, 74/107.	15	45
2571	**Threefarthings**. With rose and date 1561–2, 1568, 1572–7; *mm.* 53, 74, 77–27	40	135

Fourth Issue, 1578–82 (.921 fineness, shilling of 95.6 grs.)

| 2572 | **Sixpence**. As 2563, 1578–82; *mm.* 7–113, 14/113, 14/7 | 20 | 60 |
| 2573 | **Threepence**. As 2566, 1578–82; *mm.* 7–113. | 18 | 55 |

2573

	F	VF
	£	£
2574 **Threehalfpence**. As 2569, 1578–9, 1581–2; *mm*. 7–113	20	60
2575 **Penny**. As 2570; *mm*. 7–113, 7/14, 14/7	20	50
2576 **Threefarthings**. As 2571, 1578–9, 1581–2; *mm*. 7–113	50	150

Fifth Issue, 1582–1600 (.925 fineness, shilling of 96 grs.)

2577 **Shilling**. Without rose or date, ELIZAB; ear concealed (two busts) *mm*. 60–72b, ear shows. *mm*. 79–0 (mules occur).	30	80
2578 **Sixpence**. As 2572, ELIZABETH, 1582; *mm*. bell.	30	65
2578A — Similar, ELIZAB, 1582–1600; *mm*. 60–0, also 1583 *mm*. 79/54	25	60
2579 **Halfgroat**. Without rose or date, two pellets behind bust. R̶. CIVITAS LONDON; *mm*. 60–0 (*mm*. bell sometimes without pellets)	12	45
2580 **Penny**. Without rose or date. R̶. CIVITAS LONDON; *mm*. 60–57, 90/-, 57/-, 0/–	10	40
2581 **Halfpenny**. Portcullis. R̶. Cross and pellets; *mm*. none, 54–0.	25	70

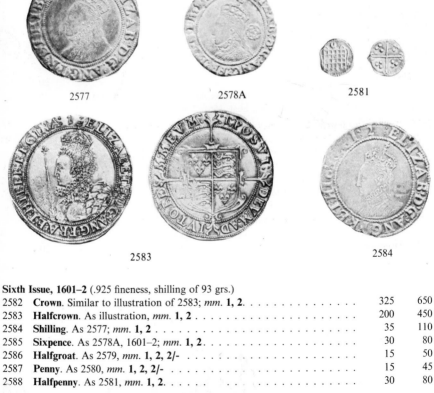

2577   2578A   2581

2583   2584

Sixth Issue, 1601–2 (.925 fineness, shilling of 93 grs.)

2582 **Crown**. Similar to illustration of 2583; *mm*. **1, 2**.	325	650
2583 **Halfcrown**. As illustration, *mm*. **1, 2**	200	450
2584 **Shilling**. As 2577; *mm*. **1, 2**	35	110
2585 **Sixpence**. As 2578A, 1601–2; *mm*. **1, 2**.	30	80
2586 **Halfgroat**. As 2579, *mm*. **1, 2, 2/-**	15	50
2587 **Penny**. As 2580, *mm*. **1, 2, 2/-**	15	45
2588 **Halfpenny**. As 2581, *mm*. **1, 2**.	30	80

Milled coinage

2592

				F	VF
				£	£
2589	**Shilling**. Without rose or date; *mm.* star. Plain dress, large size			325	800
2590	— decorated dress, large size (over 31 mm.).			130	400
2591	— — intermediate size (30–31 mm.)			85	275
2592	— — small size (under 30 mm.)			75	225
2593	**Sixpence**. Small bust, large rose. R. Cross fourchée, 1561–2; *mm.* star			30	90

2593   2594   2596   2597

2594	Tall narrow bust with plain dress, large rose, 1561–2; *mm.* star . . . *from*	30	90
2595	— similar, but decorated dress, 1561? 1562	30	90
2596	Large broad bust, elaborately decorated dress, small rose, 1562; *mm.* star	25	85
2597	— — cross pattée on *rev.*, 1562–4; *mm.* star	35	100
2598	— similar, pellet border, 1563–4	50	165
2598A	Bust with low ruff, raised rim, 1566 (over 4/3/2)	80	160
2599	Small bust, 1567–8, R. As 2593; *mm.* lis	40	115
2600	Large crude bust breaking legend; 1570, *mm.* lis; 1571/0, *mm.* castle (over lis)	90	250
2601	**Groat**. As illustration	75	275

2599   2601

		F	VF
		£	£
2602	**Threepence**. With rose, small bust with plain dress, 1561.	65	190
2603	Tall narrow decorated bust with medium rose, 1562	60	165
2604	Broad bust with very small rose, 1562.	80	210
2605	Cross pattée on *rev*., 1564/3	150	400
2606	**Halfgroat**. As groat	75	225
2607	**Threefarthings**. E . D . G . ROSA, etc., with rose. R̠. CIVITAS LONDON, shield with 1563 above	*Extremely rare*	

Portcullis money

Trade coins of 8, 4, 2, and 1 Testerns were coined at the Tower Mint in 1600/1 for the first voyage of the incorporated "Company of Merchants of London Trading into the East Indies". The coins bear the royal arms on the obverse and a portcullis on the reverse and have the *mm*. **O**. They were struck to the weights of the equivalent Spanish silver 8, 4, 2 and 1 reales.

		F	VF
		£	£
2607A	Eight testerns	650	1400
2607B	Four testerns.	350	725
2607C	Two testerns	425	900
2607D	One testern.	275	700

2607C

JAMES I, 1603–25

With the accession of James VI of Scotland to the English throne, the royal titles and coat of arms are altered on the coinage; on the latter the Scottish rampant lion and the Irish harp now appear in the second and third quarters. In 1604 the weight of the gold pound was reduced and the new coin became known as the 'Unite'. Fine gold coins of 23½ carat and crown gold of 22 carat were both issued, and a gold four-shilling piece was struck 1604–19. In 1612 all the gold coins had their values raised by 10%; but in 1619 the Unite was replaced by a new, lighter 20s. piece, the 'Laurel', and a lighter rose-ryal, spur-ryal and angel were minted.

In 1613 the King granted Lord Harrington a licence to coin farthings of copper as a result of repeated public demands for a low value coinage; this was later taken over by the Duke of Lennox. Towards the end of the reign coins made from silver sent to the mint from the Welsh mines had the Prince of Wales's plumes inserted over the royal arms.

Mintmarks

125	105	33	79	84	74	90

60	25	71	45	32	123	132

72b	7a	16	24	125	105	46

First coinage
| 1603–4 | Thistle (125) |
| 1604–5 | Lis (105) |

Second coinage
1604–5	Lis (105)
1605–6	Rose (33)
1606–7	Escallop (79)
1607	Grapes (84)
1607–9	Coronet (74)
1609–10	Key (90)
1610–11	Bell (60)
1611–12	Mullet (25)
1612–13	Tower (71)
1613	Trefoil (45)

1613–15	Cinquefoil (32)
1615–16	Tun (123)
1616–17	Closed book (132)
1617–18	Crescent (72b, gold)
1618–19	Plain cross (7a)
1619	Saltire cross (16, gold)

Third coinage
1619–20	Spur rowel (24)
1620–1	Rose (33)
1621–3	Thistle (125)
1623–4	Lis (105)
1624	Trefoil (46)

GOLD

First coinage, 1603–4 (Obverse legend reads D' . G' . ANG : SCO : etc.)

2610   2612

		F £	VF £
2608	**Sovereign** (= 20s.). King crowned r., half-length, first bust with plain armour. ℞. EXVRGAT, etc.; *mm.* thistle	600	1250
2609	— second bust with decorated armour; *mm.* 125, 105	650	1400
2610	**Half-sovereign.** Crowned bust r. ℞. EXVRGAT, etc.; *mm.* thistle	1500	3500
2611	**Crown.** Similar. ℞. TVEATVR, etc.; *mm.* 125, 105/125	700	2000
2612	**Halfcrown.** Similar; *mm.* thistle, lis.	200	600

N.B. *The Quarter-Angel of this coinage is considered to be a pattern (possibly a later strike), having the reverse of the half-crown although coin weights are known.*

Second coinage, 1604–19 (Obverse legend reads D' G' MAG : BRIT : etc.)

2613   2614

		F	VF
2613	**Rose-ryal** (= 30s., 33s. from 1612). King enthroned. ℞. Shield on rose; *mm.* 33–90, 25–132	700	1400
2614	**Spur ryal** (= 15s., 16s. 6d. from 1612). King in ship; *mm.* 33, 79, 74, 25–32, 132	1500	3000
2615	**Angel** (= 10s., 11s. from 1612). Old type but larger shield; *mm.* 33–74, 60–16.	350	700
2616	— — pierced for use as touch-piece	150	350
2617	**Half-angel** (= 5s., 5s. 6d. from 1612). Similar; *mm.* 71–132, 7a, 16	1300	3000

Second coinage gold

2620

2622   2627

		F £	VF £
2618	**Unite** (= 20s., 22s. from 1612). Half-length second bust r. ℞. FACIAM etc.; *mm.* lis or rose	225	425
2619	— fourth bust; *mm.* rose to cinquefoil	200	375
2620	— fifth bust; *mm.* cinquefoil to saltire	175	350
2621	**Double-crown.** Third bust r. ℞. HENRICVS, etc.; *mm.* lis or rose	135	325
2622	Fourth bust; *mm.* rose to bell	135	325
2623	Fifth bust; *mm.* key, mullet to saltire	150	340
2624	**Britain crown.** First bust r.; *mm.* lis to coronet	110	225
2625	Third bust; *mm.* key to cinquefoil	110	225
2626	Fifth bust; *mm.* cinquefoil to saltire	100	215
2627	**Thistle crown** (= 4s.). As illus.; *mm.* lis to plain cross	125	250
2628	— IR on only one side or absent both sides; *mm.* 79, 74, 71–123	140	275
2629	**Halfcrown.** I' D' G' ROSA SINE SPINA. First bust; *mm.* lis to key	115	210
2630	Third bust; *mm.* key to trefoil, 45/71	120	225
2631	Fifth bust; *mm.* cinquefoil to plain cross	110	185

Third coinage, 1619–25

2632	**Rose-ryal** (= 30s.; 196½ grs.). King enthroned. ℞. XXX above shield; lis, lion and rose emblems around; *mm.* 24, 125, 105	1000	1900
2633	Similar but plain back to throne; *mm.* 46	1100	2500
2634	**Spur-ryal** (= 15s.). As illus. ℞. Somewhat like 2530, but lis are also crowned. *mm.* 24–125, 46	1600	3250
2635	**Angel** (= 10s.) of new type; *mm.* 24–46	450	950
2636	— pierced for use as touch-piece	200	400

2634   2635

2638c

		F £	VF £
2637	**Laurel** (= 20s.; 140½ grs.). First (large) laur, bust l.; *mm*. 24, 24/-	225	485
2638	Second, medium, square headed bust, 'SS' tie ends; *mm*. 24, 33	200	375
2638A	Third, small rounded head, ties wider apart; *mm*. 33, 125	200	375
2638B	Fourth head, very small ties; *mm*. 105, 46.	200	375
2638C	Fourth head variety, tie ends form a bracket to value; *mm*. lis	225	400
2639	Fifth, small rather crude bust; *mm*. trefoil.	650	1750

2641   2642

2640	**Half-laurel**. First bust; *mm*. spur rowel	185	375
2641	— As 2638A; *mm*. rose	150	315
2641A	— As 2638B; *mm*. 33–46, 105/-	150	315
2642	**Quarter-laurel**. Bust with two loose tie ends; *mm*. 24–105	120	175
2642A	Bust as 2638C; *mm*. 105, 46, 105/46	120	175
2642B	As last but beaded, i.c. on *rev*. or both sides; *mm*. 105, 46.	130	200

Rev. mm. on ½ and ¼ laurels normally follows REGNA.

SILVER

2643

		F £	VF £
First coinage, 1603–4			
2643	**Crown**. King on horseback. ℞. EXVRGAT, etc., shield; *mm.* thistle, lis .	275	650
2644	**Halfcrown**. Similar.	250	750
2645	**Shilling**. First bust, square-cut beard. ℞. EXVRGAT, etc.; *mm.* thistle . .	50	160
2646	— Second bust, beard merges with collar; *mm.* thistle, lis	30	110

2646

2647 2648

2647	**Sixpence**. First bust; 1603; *mm.* thistle.	30	135
2648	Second bust; 1603–4; *mm.* thistle, lis	25	110
2649	**Halfgroat**. As illustration 2650 but II; *mm.* thistle, lis	25	70

		F	VF
		£	£
2650	**Penny**. First bust I behind head; *mm.* thistle, lis	25	65
2650A	— Second bust; *mm.* thistle.	40	110
2651	**Halfpenny**. As illustration; *mm.* thistle, lis	20	50

2650   2651

Second coinage, 1604–19

		F	VF
2652	**Crown**. King on horseback. ℞. QVAE DEVS, etc. *rev.* stops; *mm.* 105–84.	250	550
2653	**Halfcrown**. Similar; *mm.* 105–79	300	850
2654	**Shilling**. Third bust, beard cut square and stands out (*cf.* illus. 2657); *mm.*		
	lis, rose.	25	90
2655	— Fourth bust, armour plainer (*cf.* 2658); *mm.* 33–74, 60 over 74	20	80
2656	— Fifth bust, similar, but hair longer; *mm.* 74–7a (several bust varieties).	20	85

2657   2658

		F	VF
2657	**Sixpence**. Third bust; 1604–6; *mm.* lis, rose	25	85
2658	— Fourth bust; 1605–15; *mm.* rose to tun, 90/60, 25/60	20	90
2658A	— Fifth bust, 1618; *mm.* plain cross	*Unique*	

2660   2663

	F	VF
	£	£
2659 **Halfgroat**. As illus. but larger crown on *obv.*; *mm.* lis to coronet	12	30
2660 — — Similar, but smaller crown on *obv.*; *mm.* coronet to plain cross . . .	15	40
2660A As before, but TVEATVR legend both sides; *mm.* 7a	40	75
2661 **Penny**. As halfgroat but no crowns; *mm.* 105–32,7a and none, -/84, 32/- .	12	30
2662 — As before but TVEATVR legend both sides; *mm.* mullet	100	—
2663 **Halfpenny**. As illus.; *mm.* 105–25 (except 90), 32; all *mms* on *rev.* only . .	15	30

Third coinage, 1619–25

2664 **Crown**. As 2652, with plain or grass ground line, colon stops on *obv.*, no		
stops on *rev.*; *mm.* 33–46	160	360
2665 — — plume over shield; *mm.* 125–46	180	400

2666   2667

2666 **Halfcrown**. As 2664 but normally plain ground line only; all have bird-		
headed harp; *mm.* 33–46	100	235
2666A — — Similar but no ground line; *mm.* rose	120	300
2667 — — Plume over shield; groundline *mm.* 125–46	110	325
2668 **Shilling**. Sixth (large) bust, hair longer and very curly; *mm.* 24–46	25	80
2669 — — plume over shield; *mm.* 125–46	40	105
2670 **Sixpence**. Sixth bust; 1621–4; *mm.* 33–46	25	100
2671 **Halfgroat**. As 2660 but no stops on *rev.*; *mm.* 24–46 and none, 105 and 46,		
46/- *mm.* 24 with *rev.* stops known	12	25
2671A Similar but no inner circles; *mm.* lis, trefoil	30	90
2672 **Penny**. As illus.; *mm.* 24, 105, two pellets, none, many mule *mms*.	12	25
2672A — Similar but without inner circles on one or both sides; *mm.* lis, two		
pellets.	12	25
2673 **Halfpenny**. As 2663, but no *mm.*	15	30

2668   2670   2672

COPPER

For mintmarks see *English Copper, Tin and Bronze Coins in the British Museum, 1558–1958, by C. Wilson Peck.*

2675   2676   2679

		F £	VF £
2674	**Farthing**. "Harington", small size. 1a, letter or other mark below crown (originally tinned surface). . . . . *from*	15	40
2675	— — 1b, central jewel on circlet of crown with *mm.* below or crown unmodified.	20	45
2676	— 2, normal size of coin; *mm.* on *rev.*	10	20
2677	"Lennox". 3a; *mm. rev.* only	5	16
2678	— 3b; *mm.* both sides	4	15
2679	— — 3c; *mm. obv.* only	4	15
2680	— — 3d; larger crown	4	15
2681	— 4; oval type, legend starts at bottom l.	15	40

CHARLES 1, 1625–49

Numismatically, this reign is one of the most interesting of all the English monarchs. Some outstanding machine-made coins were produced by Nicholas Briot, a French die-sinker, but they could not be struck at sufficient speed to supplant hand-hammering methods. In 1637 a branch mint was set up at Aberystwyth to coin silver extracted from the Welsh mines. After the king's final breach with Parliament the parliamentary government continued to issue coins at London with Charles's name and portrait until the king's trial and execution. The coinage of copper farthings continued to be manufactured privately under licences held first by the Duchess of Richmond, then by Lord Maltravers and later by various other persons. The licence was finally revoked by Parliament in 1644.

During the Civil War coins were struck at a number of towns to supply coinage for those areas of the country under Royalist control. Many of these coins have an abbreviated form of the "Declaration" made at Wellington, Shropshire, Sept., 1642, in which Charles promised to uphold the Protestant Religion, the Laws of England and the Liberty of Parliament. Amongst the more spectacular pieces are the gold triple unites and the silver pounds and half-pounds struck at Shrewsbury and Oxford, and the emergency coins made from odd-shaped pieces of silver plate during the sieges of Newark, Scarborough, Carlisle and Pontefract.

Mintmarks

105	10	96	71	57	88	101	35

87	107	60	75	123	57	119a	23

119b	98	112	81	120	109

Tower Mint under Charles I

1625	Lis (105)
1625–6	Cross Cavalry (10)
1626–7	Negro's head (96)
1627–8	Castle (71)
1628–9	Anchor (57)
1629–30	Heart (88)
1630–1	Plume (101)
1631–2	Rose (35)
1632–3	Harp (87)
1633–4	Portcullis (107)
1634–5	Bell (60)
1635–6	Crown (75)
1636–8	Tun (123)
1638–9	Anchor (57)
1639–40	Triangle (119a)
1640–1	Star (23)
1641–3	Triangle in circle (119b)

Tower Mint under Parliament

1643–4	P in brackets (98)
1644–5	R in brackets (112)
1645	Eye (81)
1645–6	Sun (120)
1646–8	Sceptre (109)

Mint mark no. 57 is often horizontal to left or right.

59	B	58 var	58

Briot's Mint

1631–2	Flower and B (59)	1638–9	Anchor and B (58)
1632	B		Anchor and mullet

On mint mark no. 58 the 'B' below the anchor is sometimes shown as ᙖ

61	104	35	92	103	6	65b	71
89	91 *var.*	131	84	94 *var.*	64	93	34
102	67	127	128	129	25	83	100

134	71	A	B	75

Provincial Mints

1638–42	Book (61, *Aberystwyth*)	
1642	Plume (104, *Shrewsbury*)	
	Pellets or pellet (*Shrewsbury*)	
1642–3	Rose (35, *Truro*)	
	Bugle (134, *Truro?*)	
1642–4	Lion (92, *York*)	
1642–6	Plume (103, *Oxford*)	
	Pellet or pellets (*Oxford*)	
	Lis (105, *Oxford*)	
1643	Cross pattée (6, *Bristol*)	
	Acorn (65b, *Bristol*)	
	Castle (71, *Worcester* or	
	Shrewsbury)	
	Helmet (89, *Worcester*	
	and *Shrewsbury*)	
1643–4	Leopard's head (91 *var.*	
	Worcester)	
	Two lions (131, *Worcester*)	
	Lis (105, *Worcs.* or *Shrews.*)	
	Bunch of grapes (84, *Worcs.*	
	or *Shrews.*)	
	Bird (94 var., *Worcs.* or *Shrews.*)	

1643–4	Boar's head (*Worcs.* or *Shrews.*)
	Lion rampant (93, *Worcs.* or *Shrews.*)
	Rosette (34, *Worcs.* or *Shrews.*)
1643–5	Plume (102, *Bristol*)
	Br. (67, *Bristol*)
	Pellets (*Bristol*)
	Rose (35, *Exeter*)
	Rosette (34, *Oxford*)
1643–6	Floriated cross (127, *Oxford*)
1644	Cross pattée (6, *Oxford*)
	Lozenge (128, *Oxford*)
	Billet (129, *Oxford*)
	Mullet (25, *Oxford*)
1644–5	Gerb (83, *Chester*)
	Pear (100, *Worcester*)
	Lis (105, *Hereford?*)
	Castle (71, *Exeter*)
1645–6	Plume (102, *Ashby, Bridgnorth*)
1645	A (*Ashby*)
1646	B (*Bridgnorth*)
1648–9	Crown (75, Aberystwyth Furnace)

GOLD

Tower mint, under the King, 1625–42

2687

		F £	VF £

Tower Gold

2682 **Angel**. As for James I last issue, but *rev.* reads AMOR POPULI etc;
without mark of value; *mm.* lis and cross calvary. 550 1400
2683 — — pierced for use as touch-piece 200 350
2684 — X in field to r.; *mm.* 96–88, 71 and 96/71, 57 and 71/57. . . . . 450 1200
2685 — — — pierced for use as touch-piece 200 350
2686 — X in field to l.; *mm.* 96, 88, 35–119b 425 1100
2687 — — — pierced for use as touch-piece 200 350

2688   2697

2688 **Unite** (= 20s.). First bust with ruff and collar of order, high double-crown.
℞. Square-topped shield; *mm.* 105. . . . . 200 350
2688A — Similar, but extra garnishing to shield; *mm.* lis 225 425
2689 — Similar, but flat single-arched crown; *mm.* 105, 10 . . . . 200 375
2689A ℞. As 2688A. *mm.* 105 . . . . 200 400
2690 Second bust with ruff and armour nearly concealed with scarf; ℞. Square-
topped shield with slight garnishing *mm.* 10–88. . . . . 175 350
2690A Similar but more elongated bust, usually dividing legend. *mm.* 57–101,
88/101 . . . . 175 350
2691 — As 2690A but *mm.* anchor below bust 275 550
2691A *Obv.* as 2690A. ℞. As next: *mm.* plume 200 375
2692 Third bust, more armour visible. ℞. Oval shield with CR at sides; *mm.* 101, 35. . 185 400
2692A *Obv.* as next. ℞. As last, *mm.* plume 185 400
2693 Fourth bust, small lace collar with large high crown usually breaking i.c.,
long hair. Garter ribbon on breast. ℞. Oval shield with crowned CR at
sides; *mm.* 87, 107 . . . . 200 425
2693A Similar, but unjewelled crown, within or touching i.c.; *mm.* 107–23 . . . 200 400
2694 Sixth (Briot's) bust, large lace collar. ℞. Similar; *mm.* 119a–119b 225 450
2695 Briot's hammered issue, (square-topped shield); *mm.* 57 . . . . — 3000
2696 **Double-crown**. First bust. As 2688. ℞. Square-topped shield; *mm.* 105 . . 150 340
2696A Similar to last but wider flatter double-arched crown; *mm.* 105, 10 . . . . 150 340
*2697 Second bust. ℞. Similar to 2690; *mm.* 10–57 . . . . 145 320
*2697A Similar to 2690A: *mm.* 57–101 . . . . 150 330
2697B *Obv.* as last. ℞. As next: *mm.* plume 160 350

* For these coins inner circles are sometimes omitted on *obv.*, *rev.*, or both. *See also* 2704, 2704A and
2707.

Tower Gold

		F	VF
		£	£
2698	**Double-crown.** Third bust. Flat or domed crown. ℞. Oval shield with CR at sides; *mm.* 101, 35.	185	435
2699	Fourth bust, large head, high wide crown. ℞. Oval shield with crowned CR at sides; *mm.* 87	*Extremely rare*	
2699A	Similar to last, but flat crown, jewelled outer arch: *mm.* 87–123.	150	335
2699B	Similar, but smaller head, unjewelled crown: *mm.* 60–57.	150	335
2699C	Sim. to 2699, but bust within i.c.; *mm.* 60	*Extremely rare*	
2700	Fifth bust (Early Aberystwyth style). ℞. Similar; *mm.* 57	*Extremely rare*	
2700A	— (Late Aberystwyth style). ℞. *mm.* 57, 119a.	220	460
2701	Sixth bust. ℞. Normal; *mm.* 119a–119b	220	460
2702	— ℞. Briot's square-topped shield; *mm.* 57	*Extremely rare*	
2703	**Crown.** First bust with small round crown. ℞. Square-topped shield; *mm.* 105, 10.	115	200
2703A	As 2696A. *mm.* cross cavalry.	115	200
*2704	Second bust as 2690. ℞. Similar; *mm.* 10–71	105	200
*2704A	As 2690A. *mm.* 57–101, 88/-, 57/-, 101/-.	105	200
2704B	As 2691. Wire line i.c.s on *rev.*	*Rare*	
2705	*Obv.* as 2690A. ℞. As next; 101, 35, 101/-.	135	250
2706	Third bust. ℞. Oval shield with CR at sides; *mm.* 101	—	500
*2707	Fourth bust. ℞. Oval shield with crowned CR at sides; *mm.* -/87, 87–119b, 23/119a, 107/60	125	225
2708	Fifth (Aberystwyth style) bust. ℞. Similar; *mm.* anchor	165	350
2709	Sixth (Briot's) bust. ℞. Similar; *mm.* anchor.	*Unique*	

2703   2714

Tower mint, under Parliament, 1642–9. All Charles I types

2710	**Unite.** Fourth bust, as 2693A; *mm.* (P), (P)/-	200	500
2711	Sixth bust, as 2694 but crude style; *mm.* (P), (R), 119b.	325	700
2712	Seventh bust, cruder style; *mm.* eye, sun, sceptre	350	775
2713	**Double-crown.** Fourth bust, as 2699B; *mm.* eye	*Extremely rare*	
2714	Fifth bust, as 2700A; *mm.* sun, sceptre	325	750
2715	Sixth bust, as 2701; *mm.* (P)	400	925
2716	Eighth, dumpy bust with single flat-arched crown; *mm.* sun	*Unique*	
2717	**Crown.** Fourth bust, as 2707 jewelled crown; *mm.* -/98, 98/-, 98–120	150	375
2717A	Sim. but unjewelled crown. ℞. Small crude shield; *mm.* 81–109	150	375

Nicholas Briot's coinage, 1631–2

2718	**Angel.** Type somewhat as Tower but smaller and neater; *mm.* -/B.	*Extremely rare*	
2719	**Unite.** As illustration. ℞. FLORENT etc.; *mm.* flower and B/B	—	1750
2720	**Double-crown.** Similar but X. ℞. CVLTORES, etc. *mm.* flower and B/B .	550	1300
2720A	Similar but King's crown unjewelled: *mm.* flower and B/B, B	600	1400
2721	**Crown.** Similar; *mm.* B	*Extremely rare*	

* Inner circles sometimes omitted on obv. *or* rev. *or both.*

BRIOTS HAMMERED GOLD: See No. 2695.

2719

	F £	VF £

Provincial issues, 1638–49
Chester mint

2722 **Unite.** As Tower. Somewhat like a crude Tower sixth bust. ℞. Crowned,
oval shield, crowned CR, *mm.* plume . . . . *Extremely rare*

Shrewsbury mint, 1642 (See also 2749)

2723 **Triple unite,** 1642. Half-length figure l holding sword and olive-branch;
mm. : ℞. EXVRGAT, etc., around RELIG PROT, etc., in two wavy lines.
III and three plumes above, date below . . . . *Extremely rare*

Oxford mint, 1642–6

2724

2724 **Triple unite.** As last, but *mm.* plume, tall narrow bust, 1642 1750   3500
2725 Similar, but "Declaration" on continuous scroll, 1642–3 1850   3900
2725A Large bust of fine style. King holds short olive branch; *mm.* small lis. . . *Extremely rare*
    A good EF specimen fetched £48,000 in auction in May, 1989.
2726 As last, but taller bust, with scarf behind shoulder, 1643, *mm.* plume. . . 2050   4000
2727 Similar, but without scarf, longer olive branch, 1643 1750   3400
2728 Similar, but OXON below 1643, rosette stops. . . . . *Extremely rare*
2729 Smaller size, olive branch varies, bust size varies, 1644 OXON 1850   3750
2730 — Obv. as 2729, 1644 / OX 2050   4000

Gold

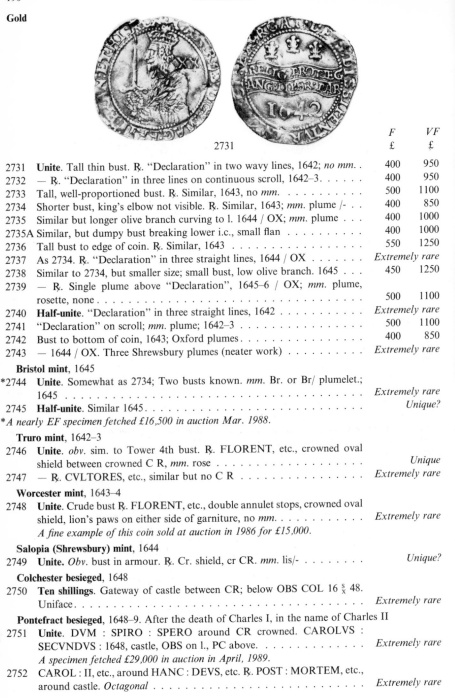

2731

		F £	VF £
2731	**Unite**. Tall thin bust. ℞. "Declaration" in two wavy lines, 1642; *no mm.* .	400	950
2732	— ℞. "Declaration" in three lines on continuous scroll, 1642–3.	400	950
2733	Tall, well-proportioned bust. ℞. Similar, 1643, no *mm*.	500	1100
2734	Shorter bust, king's elbow not visible. ℞. Similar, 1643; *mm*. plume /- .	400	850
2735	Similar but longer olive branch curving to l. 1644 / OX; *mm*. plume	400	1000
2735A	Similar, but dumpy bust breaking lower i.c., small flan	400	1000
2736	Tall bust to edge of coin. ℞. Similar, 1643	550	1250
2737	As 2734. ℞. "Declaration" in three straight lines, 1644 / OX	*Extremely rare*	
2738	Similar to 2734, but smaller size; small bust, low olive branch. 1645	450	1250
2739	— ℞. Single plume above "Declaration", 1645–6 / OX; *mm*. plume, rosette, none	500	1100
2740	**Half-unite**. "Declaration" in three straight lines, 1642	*Extremely rare*	
2741	"Declaration" on scroll; *mm*. plume; 1642–3	500	1100
2742	Bust to bottom of coin, 1643; Oxford plumes.	400	850
2743	— 1644 / OX. Three Shrewsbury plumes (neater work)	*Extremely rare*	

Bristol mint, 1645

*2744	**Unite**. Somewhat as 2734; Two busts known. *mm*. Br. or Br/ plumelet.; 1645	*Extremely rare*	
2745	**Half-unite**. Similar 1645.		*Unique?*

*A nearly EF specimen fetched £16,500 in auction Mar. 1988.

Truro mint, 1642–3

2746	**Unite**. *obv*. sim. to Tower 4th bust. ℞. FLORENT, etc., crowned oval shield between crowned C R, *mm*. rose	*Unique*
2747	— ℞. CVLTORES, etc., similar but no C R	*Extremely rare*

Worcester mint, 1643–4

2748	**Unite**. Crude bust ℞. FLORENT, etc., double annulet stops, crowned oval shield, lion's paws on either side of garniture, no *mm*.	*Extremely rare*
	A fine example of this coin sold at auction in 1986 for £15,000.	

Salopia (Shrewsbury) mint, 1644

2749	**Unite**. *Obv*. bust in armour. ℞. Cr. shield, cr CR. *mm*. lis/-	*Unique?*

Colchester besieged, 1648

2750	**Ten shillings**. Gateway of castle between CR; below OBS COL 16 $\frac{S}{X}$ 48. Uniface.	*Extremely rare*

Pontefract besieged, 1648–9. After the death of Charles I, in the name of Charles II

2751	**Unite**. DVM : SPIRO : SPERO around CR crowned. CAROLVS : SECVNDVS : 1648, castle, OBS on l., PC above.	*Extremely rare*
	A specimen fetched £29,000 in auction in April, 1989.	
2752	CAROL : II, etc., around HANC : DEVS, etc. ℞. POST : MORTEM, etc., around castle. *Octagonal*	*Extremely rare*

SILVER

Tower mint, under the King, 1625–42

2759

		F	VF
		£	£
2753	**Crown.** King on horseback with raised sword. 1a. Horse caparisoned with plume on head and crupper. ℞. Square-topped shield over long cross fourchée; *mm.* 105, 10.	150	475
2754	— 1b. Similar, but plume over shield, no cross; *mm.* 105, 10, 71	400	850
2755	— 2a. Smaller horse, plume on hd. only, cross on housings, king holds sword on shoulder. ℞. Oval garnished shield over cross fourchée, CR above; *mm.* harp.	150	400
2756	— 2b¹. — — plume divides CR, no cross; *mm.* 101, 35.	175	450
2757	— 2b². — — — with cross; *mm.* harp	250	650
2758	— 3a. Horse without caparisons. ℞. Oval shield without CR; *mm.* 60–23.	160	330
2759	— 3b. — — plume over shield; *mm.* 107, 75, 123.	190	450
2760	"Briot" horse with ground-line; *mm.* 119b	*Three known?*	

2762

2761	**Halfcrown.** As 2753. 1a¹. Rose on housings, ground-line; *mm.* lis	90	260
2761A	— Similar, but no rose on housings; *mm.* lis	*Very rare*	
2762	— 1a². Similar, but no rose or ground-line; *mm.* 105 (10/10 over 105) . .	90	275

Tower Silver

		F £	VF £
2763	**Halfcrown.** la³. As last but clumsier horse and shield not over cross; *mm.* 10–96.	60	160
2763A	— Sim. but only slight garnishing to shield; *mm.* 10, 71	60	160
2764	— la⁴. — — with ground-line; *mm.* lis.	450	1000
2765	— 1b. — — plume over shield; *mm.* 105, 10	500	1000
2765A	— Sim. but only slight garnishing; *mm.* 96–57	500	1000
2766	— 2/1b. As 2755 but rose on housings. ℞. As last; mm. heart, plume.	*Extremely rare*	
2767	— 2a. As 2755. ℞. Flattened oval garnished shield without cross; *mm.* 101/35 plume, rose, (CR above, divided by rose (rare), lis over rose, lis)	60	125
2768	— 2b. Similar, but large plume between the CR; *mm.* 101, 35.	125	300
2769	— 2c. As 2a, but differently garnished oval shield with CR at sides; *mm.* harp, portcullis, 107/87	45	110
2770	— 2d. Similar, but with plume over shield; *mm.* harp	225	550
2770A	— III/II mule, *mm.* portcullis.	*Extremely rare*	

2771   2775

2771	— 3a¹. No caparisons on horse, upright sword, scarf flies out from waist. ℞. Round garnished shield, no CR; *mm.* 60–119a, 60/75.	30	100
2772	— 3b. — — plume over shield; *mm.* 107–123	85	200
2773	— 3a². — cloak flies from king's shoulder; ℞. Shields vary; *mm.* 123–23, 119b, 119b over 119a	30	100
2774	— — — — rough ground beneath horse; ℞. Shields vary; *mm.* 119a, 23, 119b	30	100
2775	— 4. Foreshortened horse, mane before chest, tail between legs; *mm.* 23, 119b	30	100

Most late Tower halfcrowns have irregular flans.

2776A

2776	**Shilling.** l. Bust in ruff, high crown, jewelled arches. ℞. Square-topped shield over cross fourchée; *mm.* lis, (normal weight 92¾ grs.)	40	115
2776A	— Sim. but larger crown, plain inner arch; *mm.* 105, 10	40	115

		F	VF
		£	£
2777	**Shilling.** Sim. but light weight (81$\frac{33}{47}$ grs.); *mm.* 10	75	200
2778	— 1b^1. As 2776A, but plume over shield, no cross; *mm.* 105, 10.	100	250
2779	— 1a. Bust in ruff and armour concealed by scarf. ℞. As 2776; 10–71 . .	30	90
2780	— — — — light weight; *mm.* cross Calvary (often extremely small XII) .	75	210
2781	— 1b^2. As 2779, but plume over shield, no cross; *mm.* 10–101 (five bust varieties)	50	150
2781A	— — light weight 1b^2 *mm.* 10	75	200
2782	— 1b^3, — — — cross; *mm.* negro's head	350	750
2783	— 2a. More armour visible. ℞. Oval shield, CR above; *mm.* plume, rose.	25	80
2784	— 2b. — — plume over shield; *mm.* 101, 35, 101 over 88/101	100	300
2785	— 3^1. Bust with lace collar, (six bust varieties). ℞. Flattish oval shield, CR at sides; *mm.* harp, portcullis.	25	80
2786	— 3^2. — — plume over shield; *mm.* harp (three bust varieties)	200	400
*2787	— 3a. — no inner circles, rounder shield without CR; *mm.* 60–123 (five bust varieties)	20	70
2788	— 3b. — — plume over shield; *mm.* 60–123.	50	115

2787   2791   2793

		F	VF
2789	— 4^1. Large Aberystwyth bust, medium or small XII. ℞. Square-topped shield over cross fleury; *mm.* tun, small neat cross ends	50	125
2790	— 4^1. var. Similar, but rounder shoulders, large XII; *mm.* 123-, 119a, (cross ends vary)	20	65
2791	— 4^2. Smaller Aberystwyth bust with small double-arched crown, small XII; *mm.* tun, small neat cross ends	20	65
2792	— 4^3. — single-arches, large XII; *mm.* 123, 57, 119a, 119b (cross ends vary).	20	65
2793	— 4^4. Older (Briot's style) bust, very pointed beard; *mm.* 57–119b	20	60
2793A	*Obv.* as last. ℞. As Briots hammered issue; lozenge stops; *mm.* △ . . .		*Rare*

2797   2799

		F	VF
2794	**Sixpence.** 1. As 2776, but dated 1625–6; *mm.* 105, 10 (large bust *mm.* 10 noted, lightweight?)	45	175
2795	— 1a^1. As 2779, but dated 1625–9; *mm.* 10–88 (busts vary)	50	190
2796	— 1a^2. — no cross, 1630; *mm.* 88, 101.	55	200
2797	— 2a. As 2783, no date; *mm.* plume, rose	40	135
2798	— 2b. — plume dividing CR; *mm.* plume, rose, plume/rose	60	175
2799	— 3. As 2785; *mm.* harp, portcullis (busts and crowns vary).	40	150

Tower Silver

		F £	VF £
2800	**Sixpence.**— 3a. — no inner circles; *mm.* 60–123 (busts and crowns vary).	25	100
2801	— 4¹. As first Aberystwyth sixpence, double-arch crown, small VI. ℞. Square-topped shield over cross; *mm.* tun	30	100
2802	— 4¹. var. — similar, but large VI; *mm.* tun, anchor	35	120
2803	— 4². Second Aberystwyth bust, single-arched crown; *mm.* 57, 119a . . .	25	90
2804	— 4². larger bust, *mm.* 119a	45	125
2805	— 4³. Older (Briot's style) bust; *mm.* 119a–119b (moline cross ends) . . .	25	95

2806   2808   2818

		F £	VF £
2806	**Halfgroat.** 1. Crowned rose type; *mm.* 105–96, 105/-	10	25
2807	— 1a. — — without inner circles on one or both sides; *mm.* 96–101, 105, 105/-	10	30
2808	— 2a. King's 2nd bust in ruff and mantle. ℞. Oval shield; *mm.* plume, rose.	10	30
2809	— 2b. Similar, but with plume over shield; *mm.* plume, rose, plume/- . .	22	55
2809A	— — 2a Var. 3rd bust, with more armour. ℞. As last; *mm.* plume, rose .	10	25
2809B	— — Sim. but plume over shield; *mm.* 101	25	50
2810	— 3¹. Bust with lace collar. ℞. Oval shield between CR; no inner circles; *mm.* rose harp, crown, portcullis	10	35
2811	— 3²⁻⁴. — — inner circles sometimes only on one side; *mm.* harp, portcullis.	10	35
2814	— 3⁵. — — no CR, inner circles; *mm.* portcullis	10	35
2815	— 3⁶. — — — inner circles on *obv.*; *mm.* portcullis.	10	35
2816	— 3a¹. — ℞. Rounder shield, different garniture, no i.cs.; *mm.* 60–119a .	10	35
2817	— 3a². — — inner circles on *obv.*; *mm.* triangle.	10	35
2818	— 3a³. — — inner circles both sides; *mm.* 119a–119b	10	35
2819	— 3a⁴. Aberystwyth bust, no inner circles; *mm.* anchor	15	40
2820	— 3a⁵. — inner circle on *rev.*; *mm.* anchor	15	40
2821	— 3a⁶. Very small bust, no inner circles; *mm.* anchor.	15	40

2822   2828   2837

		F £	VF £
2822	**Penny.** 1. Rose each side; i.cs.; *mm.* 96, :/lis, lis/:, one or two pellets, lis .	10	30
2823	— 1a. — no i.cs.; *mm.* lis, one or two pellets, anchor.	10	30
2824	— 1b. — i.c. on *rev.*; *mm.* negro's head/two pellets.	12	35
2825	— 2. Bust in ruff and mantle. ℞. Oval shield; i.cs.; *mm.* plume, plume/rose	12	35
2826	— 2¹. — — no i.cs.; *mm.* plume, rose	15	40
2827	— 2a¹. More armour visible; no i.cs.; *mm.* plume, rose, plume/rose	12	30
2828	— 2a². — i.c. on *obv.*; *mm.* plume, rose, plume over rose	15	40
2829	— 2a³. — i.cs. both sides; *mm.* plume, rose	12	35

		F	VF
		£	£
2830	— 2a⁴. — i.c. on rev.; *mm.* rose over plume	20	55
2831	— 3¹. Bust in lace collar. ℞. CR at sides of shield; no i.cs.; *mm.* harp, one or two pellets. ¨/harp (also *obv.* i.c. *mm.* harp)	12	30
2832	— 3². — similar but no CR; *mm.* 87, 107, 107/¨, none	12	35
2833	— 3³. — — i.c. on *obv.*; *mm.* harp,¨,	12	35
2834	— 3⁴. — — i.c. on *rev.*; *mm.* harp	12	35
2835	— 3a¹. — similar, but shield almost round and with scroll garniture; no i.cs.; *mm.* bell, triangle, one to four pellets, none, bell/¨	10	25
2835A	— 3a¹ variety — i.c. on *obv.*, *rev.* or both sides; *mm.* triangle/two pellets, △,¨,	15	35
2836	— 3a³. Aberystwyth bust; i.c. on *obv.* or none; *mm.* one or two pellets or none, △/¨	13	25
2837	**Halfpenny.** Rose each side; no legend or *mm.*	12	30

Many small denominations have uneven irregular flans.

Tower mint, under Parliament, 1642–8. All Charles I type

		F	VF
2838	**Crown.** 4. Foreshortened horse; *mm.* (P) to sun	180	400
2839	— 5. Tall spirited horse; *mm.* sun	200	525
2840	**Halfcrown.** 3a³. As 2773, but coarse work; *mm.* (P) to sun, 81/120	30	95
2841	— 4. Foreshortened horse; *mm.* (P)	120	250
2842	— 5. Tall horse; *mm.* sun, sceptre	35	110
2843	**Shilling.** 4⁴. Briot style bust, *mm,* (P) (R), coarse work; *mm.* eye, sun	30	100

2844   2845A

		F	VF
2844	— 4⁵. Long narrow coarse bust; *mm.* sun, sceptre	35	100
2845	— 4⁶. Short bust with narrow crown; *mm.* sceptre	35	120
2845A	— — Short broad bust, as illus., broader crown; *mm.* sceptre	35	120
2846	**Sixpence.** 4³. Briot style bust; *mm.* (P) to sun	40	115
2847	— 4⁴. Late Aberystwyth bust modified; *mm.* (R) to sceptre	50	120
2848	— 4⁵. Squat bust of crude style; *mm.* eye and sun	150	350
2849	**Halfgroat.** 3a³. Sim. to 2818; *mm.* (P) to eye, sceptre, 98/119b	20	55
2850	— 3a⁷. Older, shorter bust, pointed beard; *mm.* eye to sceptre	18	45
2851	**Penny.** 3a². Older bust; *mm.* pellets, i.c. on *obv.* only	18	50

Nicholas Briot's coinage, 1631–9

  First milled issue, 1631–2

		F	VF
2852	**Crown.** King on horseback. ℞. Crowned shield between C R crowned; *mm.* flower and B / B	250	600

		F	*VF*
		£	£
2853	**Halfcrown**. Similar.	175	425
2854	**Shilling**. Briot's early bust with falling lace collar. ℞. Square-topped shield over long cross fourchée; ℞. Legend starts at top or bottom *mm.* flower and B/B, B	100	275
2855	**Sixpence**. Similar, but VI behind bust; *mm.* flower and B/B, flower and B/-	55	140

2855   2856

2856	**Halfgroat**. Briot's bust, B below, II behind. ℞. IVSTITIA, etc., square-topped shield over long cross fourchée	35	75
2856A	Pattern halfgroat. Uncrowned bust in ruff r. ℞. crowned, interlocked Cs. (North 2687). (Included because of its relatively regular appearance.) . .	45	80
2857	**Penny**. Similar, but I behind bust, no B; position of legend may vary. . .	25	60

Second milled issue, 1638–9

2858   2859

2858	**Halfcrown**. As 2853, but *mm.* anchor and B.	150	375
2859	**Shilling**. Briot's late bust, the falling lace collar is plain with broad lace border, no scarf. ℞. As 2854 but cross only to inner circle; *mm.* anchor and B, anchor or muled	50	130
2860	**Sixpence**. Similar, but VI; *mm.* 57, anchor and mullet/anchor	30	75

The two last often exhibit flan reduction marks.

Briot's hammered issue, 1638–9

| 2861 | **Halfcrown**. King on Briot's style horse with ground line. ℞. Square-topped shield; *mm.* anchor, triangle over anchor, also muled with Tower *rev.* . . | 450 | 1050 |
| 2862 | **Shilling**. Sim. to 2859; ℞. Square-topped shield over short cross fleury; usually *mm.* △/anchor. Each *mm.* alone is very rare, also muled with Tower *obv.* or *rev.* . . . . | 325 | 750 |

Provincial and Civil War issues, 1638–49 $\qquad$ F $\quad$ VF

York mint, 1643–4. *Mm.* lion $\qquad$ £ $\quad$ £

2863 **Halfcrown.** 1. Ground-line below horse. ℞. Square-topped shield between CR . . . . 140 $\quad$ 375

2864 — 2. — ℞. Oval shield as Tower 3a, groundline grass or dotted . . . . . 150 $\quad$ 450

2865 — 3. No ground-line. ℞. Similar. . . . . 125 $\quad$ 350

2866 *— 4. As last, but EBOR below horse with head held low. Base metal, often very base. . . . . 110 $\quad$ 300

2867 — 5. Tall horse, mane in front of chest, EBOR below. ℞. Crowned square-topped shield between CR, floral spray in legend. . . . . 90 $\quad$ 250

2868 — 6. As last, but shield is oval, garnished (*rev.* detail variations) . . . . . 80 $\quad$ 225

2868 $\qquad\qquad\qquad\qquad\qquad\qquad\qquad$ 2872

2869 — 7. Similar, but horse's tail shows between legs. ℞. Shield as last, but with lion's skin garniture, no CR or floral spray . . . . 70 $\quad$ 200

2870 **Shilling.** 1. Bust in scalloped lace collar 3[1]. ℞. EBOR above square-topped shield over cross fleury . . . . 60 $\quad$ 140

2871 — 2. Similar, but bust in plain armour, mantle; coarse work . . . . 70 $\quad$ 175

2872 — 3. *Obv.* as 2870. — ℞. EBOR below oval shield. . . . . 70 $\quad$ 175

2873 — 4. — Similar, but crowned oval shield (*obv.* finer style). . . . . 60 $\quad$ 140

2874 — 5. — As last, but lion's skin garniture . . . . 60 $\quad$ 140

2876 $\qquad\qquad\qquad\qquad\qquad$ 2877

2875 **Sixpence.** *Obv.* Sim. to 2870. Crowned oval shield . . . . 160 $\quad$ 425

2876 — — C R at sides. . . . . 135 $\quad$ 325

2877 **Threepence.** As type 4 shilling, but III behind bust. ℞. As 2870 . . . . . . 30 $\quad$ 70

These pieces are contemporary forgeries (BNJ1984).

Aberystwyth mint, 1638/9–42. *Mm.* book.
Plume 1 = with coronet and band. Plume 2 = with coronet only

		F £	VF £
2878	**Halfcrown.** Horseman similar to 2773, but plume 2 behind. ℞. Oval garnished shield with large plume above. *Obv.* plume 2, *rev.* plume 1. . .	300	750
2879	— Similar to 2774, plume 1 behind King, ground below horse. *Obv.* squat plume 1, *rev.* plume 1	350	850
2880	As 2773 but more spirited horse, no ground. FRAN ET HIB, plume 2/1	400	950
2881	**Shilling.** Bust with large square lace collar, plume 2 before, small XII. ℞. As before. No inner circles	150	425
2882	— inner circle on *rev.*	125	375
2883	As 2881, but large plume 1 or 2, large XII, inner circles	125	375
2884	As last, but small narrow head, square lace collar, large or square plume	135	400
2885	Small Briot style bust with round collar, plume 2.	165	450

2883   2886

2885A **Sixpence.** *Obv.* as Tower bust 3a, plume before. ℞. as 2889; *mm.* book (*obv.* only) . . . . — *Rare*

2886	Somewhat as 2881, but double-arched crown, small VI; no inner circles .	130	325
2887	Similar to 2886, but single arched crown, plume 2, inner circle *obv.* Large VI.	165	375
2888	Similar, but with inner circles both sides	130	325
2889	— — *Rev.* with small squat-shaped plume above, sometimes no *rev. mm.*	135	325
2890	Bust as the first Oxford sixpence; with crown cutting inner circle	165	375
2891	**Groat.** Large bust, lace collar, no armour on shoulder. Crown breaks or touches inner circle. ℞. Shield, plume 1 or 2	20	45
2892	— Similar, armour on shoulder, shorter collar. ℞. Similar.	30	60
2893	— Smaller, neater bust well within circle. ℞. Similar	20	45

2891   2894   2895–9

2894	**Threepence.** Small bust, large or small plume 2 before. ℞. Shield, plume 1 or 2 above, *obv.* legend variations	18	45
2895–9	— Similar, but squat pl. on *obv.*, crown cuts i.c. ℞. Pl. 2, *Obv.* legend variations.	22	55

Aberystwyth, *continued*

	F £	VF £
2900 **Halfgroat**. Bust as Tower type 3. ℞. Large plume. No i.cs, *mm.* pellet/book, book	55	115
2900A Bust as 2886. ℞. As last, no i.c.	45	135
2901 Bust with round lace collar; single arch crown, inner circles, colon stops.	40	100
2902 After Briot's bust, square lace collar: inner circles	40	100

2905   2907

2903	**Penny**. As 2901; CARO; no inner circles	65	135
2904	As 2901; CARO; inner circles	65	135
2905	As last but reads CAROLVS; inner circles	60	120
2906	*Obv.* similar to 2890, tall narrow bust, crown touches inner circle.	70	175
2907	**Halfpenny**. No legend. *O.* Rose. ℞. Plume.	100	250

Aberystwyth-Furnace mint, 1648/9. *Mm.* crown

2908	**Halfcrown**. King on horseback. ℞. Sim. to 2878	1000	2000
2909	**Shilling**. Aberystwyth type, but *mm.* crown	*Extremely rare*	
2910	**Sixpence**. Similar	*Extremely rare*	

2911   2913

2911	**Groat**. Similar	135	275
2912	**Threepence**. Similar	175	350
2913	**Halfgroat**. Similar. ℞. Large plume	185	425
2914	**Penny**. Similar	450	900

Uncertain mint (? Hereford)

2915

		Fair	Fine
2915	**Halfcrown**. As illustration, dated 1645 or undated	600	1500
2915A	— Scarf with long sash ends. CH below horse. ℞. Oval shield 1644 . . .		Rare
2915B	— ℞. Crowned oval shield, lion paws		Rare

Shrewsbury mint, 1642. Plume without band used as *mm.* or in field.

		F £	VF £
2917	**Pound**. King on horseback, plume behind, similar to Tower grp. 3 crowns. ℞. Declaration between two straight lines, XX and three Shrewsbury plumes above, 1642 below; *mm.* pellets, pellets/-	800	2250
2918	Similar, but Shrewsbury horse walking over pile of arms; no *mm.*, pellets.	750	1750
2919	As last, but cannon amongst arms and only single plume and XX above Declaration, no *mm.*.	1050	2600
2920	**Half-pound**. As 2917, but X; *mm.* pellets.	350	950
2921	Similar, but only two plumes on *rev.*; *mm.*, pellets	400	1000
2922	Shrewsbury horseman with ground-line, three plumes on *rev.*; *mm.*, none, pellets/-.	325	900
2923	— with cannon and arms or arms below horse; *mm.* pellets/-	300	850
2924	— no cannon in arms, no plume in *obv.* field; *mm.* plume/pellets, plume/-.	250	650

2926

2925	**Crown**. Aberystwyth horseman, no ground line	Extremely rare
2926	Shrewsbury horseman with ground-line; *mm.* -/pellets, pellets/-, none. . .	250 600
2927	**Halfcrown**. O. From Aberystwyth die; (S2880); *mm.* book. ℞. Single plume above Declaration, 1642	Extremely rare

		F £	VF £
2928	Sim. to Aberystwyth die, fat plume behind. ℞. Three plumes above Declaration; *mm.* pellets, pellets/-	165	400
2929	Shrewsbury horseman. ℞. As 2927, single plume, no *mm.*	185	475
2930	— ℞. 2: plume; 6, above Declaration	500	1100
2931	— with ground-line. ℞. Similar.........................	450	1000
2932	— — ℞. As 2927, single plume.........................	175	450
2933	— — ℞. Three plumes above Declaration; *mm.* none or pellets	135	300
2933A	*Obv.* as last. ℞. Aberystwyth die, plume over shield; *mm.* -/book		*Rare*
2934	— — — no plume behind king; *mm.* plume/pellets............	150	325
2935	**Shilling**. *O.* From Aberystwyth die; S2885 *mm.* book. ℞. Declaration type.	400	950
2936	*O.* From Shrewsbury die. ℞. Similar....................	450	1050

Oxford mint, 1642/3–6. *Mm.* usually plume with band, except on the smaller denominations when it is lis or pellets. There were so many dies used at this mint that we can give only a selection of the more easily identifiable varieties.

2937	**Pound**. Large horseman over arms, no exergual line, fine workmanship. ℞. Three Shrewsbury plumes and XX above Declaration, 1642 below; *mm.* plume/pellets..............................	1050	3000

2937

2938	— Similar, but three Oxford plumes, 1643; *mm.* as last	1050	3000
2939	Shrewsbury horseman trampling on arms, exergual line. ℞. As last, 1642.	650	2000
2940	— — cannon amongst arms, 1642–3; *mm.* similar	600	1850
2941	— as last but exergue is chequered, 1642; *mm.* similar	750	2450
2942	Briot's horseman, 1643; *mm.* similar....................	1500	4500
2943	*O.* As 2937. ℞. Declaration in cartouche, single large plume above, 1644 OX below	1500	4500
2944	**Half-pound**. As next. ℞. Shrewsbury die, 1642; *mm.* plume/-........	225	500
2945	Oxford dies both sides, 1642–3; *mm.* plume/pellets	200	400
2946	**Crown**. *O.* Shrewsbury die with ground-line. ℞. As last but V, 1642–3 ..	225	550
2947	Oxford horseman with grass below, 1643	350	900
2948	By Rawlins. King riding over a view of the city. ℞. Floral scrolls above and below Declaration, 1644 / OXON below (Beware forgeries!).		*Extremely rare*
	An extremely fine specimen sold at auction in May, 1989 for £24,750.		

Oxford Silver, *continued*

		F	*VF*
		£	£

2949	**Halfcrown**. *O*. From Shrewsbury die S2931 or 2934. ℞. 3 Ox plumes over 'Dec' 1642	135	375
2950	Ox plume, Shrewsbury horse. ℞. From Shrewsbury die, 1642	105	275
2951	Both Oxford dies, but Shrewsbury type horse, ground-line, 1642	70	200
2952	— — without ground-line, 1642	90	250
2953	Oxford type horse, ground-line, 1643	75	225

2954

2954	— without ground-line, 1643	70	190
2954A	— — ℞. 3 Shrewsbury plumes, 1642	100	300
2955	Briot's horse, grass below, 1643, 1643 / OX	80	225
2956	— — large central plume, 1643, 1643 / OX, 1644 / OX	90	275
2957	— lumpy ground, 1643, 1643 / OX	80	210
2958	— — large central plume, 1643–4 / OX	80	225
2959	— plain ground, 1644–5 / OX	80	225
2960	— — large central plume, 1644 / OX	80	225
2960A	Sim. but 2 very small Shrewsbury plumes at sides	100	300
2961	— — — Similar, but large date in script	105	325
2962	Rocky ground, two small plumes at date, 1644 / OX	225	500
2963	Large horse (as Briot's, but clumsier), plain ground, 1644–5 / OX	90	275
2964	— lumpy ground, 1644–5 / OX	90	275
2965	— — large central plume, 1644 / OX	90	275
2966	— pebbly ground, 1645–6 / OX	90	275
2967	— — pellets or annulets by plumes and at date, 1645–6 / OX	90	275
2968	— grass below, 1645–6 / OX	90	325
2969	— — rosettes by plumes and at date, 1645 / OX	110	400
2970	**Shilling**. *O*. From Shrewsbury die. ℞. Declaration type, 1642	100	275
2971	Both Oxford dies. Small bust, 1642–3	60	150
2972	Similar, but coarser work, 1643	60	150
2973	Large bust of fine work, 1643	60	150
2974	— 1644–6 / OX	75	200
2975	Bust with bent crown, 1643	90	250
2976	— 1644 / OX	90	250
2977	Rawlins' dies. Fine bust with R on truncation, 1644	125	300
2978	— — 1644 / OX	135	325
2979	Small size, 1646, annulets or pellets at date	105	275

2980

			F	VF
			£	£
2980	**Sixpence.** *O.* Aberystwyth die S2890. ℞. With three Oxford plumes, 1642– 3; *mm.* book/-.	110	250
2981	— ℞. With three Shrewsbury plumes, 1643; *mm.* book/-.	110	240
2982	— ℞. With Shrewsbury plume and two lis, 1644 / OX; *mm.* book/-.	*Extremely rare*	

2985   2991

2983	**Groat.** *O.* Aberystwyth die S2892. ℞. As 2985	35	110
2984	As last but three plumes above Declaration.	75	200
2985	As illustration, with lion's head on shoulder	50	120
2885A	*Obv.* as last ℞. 3 Shrewsbury plumes, 1644 / OX	75	170
2986	Large bust reaching to top of coin. ℞. As 2985.	60	150
2987	Large bust to bottom of coin, lion's head on shoulder, legend starts at bottom l. ℞. As last.	70	160
2988	Rawlins' die; similar, but no i.c., and with R on shoulder. ℞. As last.	70	160
2989	*O.* As 2985. ℞. Large single plume and scroll above Declaration, 1645.	60	140
2990	*O.* As 2987. ℞. As last	60	140
2991	*O.* As 2988. ℞. Large single plume above Declaration, which is in cartouche, 1645–6 (over 5)	80	200
2992	**Threepence.** *O.* Aberystwyth die; *mm.* book ℞. Declaration type, 1644 / OX	50	125
2993	Rawlins' die, R below shoulder; *mm.* lis. ℞. Aberystwyth die with oval shield; *mm.* book	45	125
2994	— ℞. Declaration type, three lis above, 1644 below; *mm.* lis/-.	40	115
2995	— Similar, without the R, 1646 (over 1644); no *mm.*	40	115
2996	**Halfgroat.** ℞. Aberystwyth type with large plume	75	175
2997	— ℞. Declaration type, 1644 / OX; *mm.* cross	110	200

2995   2999

Oxford Silver, *continued.*

		F	VF
		£	£
2998	**Penny.** *O.* Aberystwyth die S2904; *mm.* book. ℞. Type, small plume . . .	85	200
2999	As 2906 ℞. Type, large plume	85	200
3000	— Rawlins' die with R. ℞. Type, small plume	85	200
3001	— Wider bust similar to the halfgroat. ℞. Similar	100	275
3002	— — ℞. Declaration type, 1644	350	800

Bristol mint, 1643–5. *Mm.* usually plume or Br., except on small denominations

		F	VF
3003	**Halfcrown.** *O.* Oxford die with or without ground-line. ℞. Declaration, three Bristol plumes above, 1643 below	80	250
3004	— — Br. *mm.* on *rev.,* 1643.	70	240
3005	King wears unusual flat crown, *obv. mm.* acorn? between four pellets. ℞. As 3003, 1643	85	260
3006	— Br. *mm.* on *rev.,* 1643–4	85	225
3007	Shrewsbury plume behind king. ℞. As last	65	165
3008	— Br. below date, 1644	70	220
3009	Br. below horse and below date, 1644–5.	75	190
3010	Br. also *mm.* on *rev.,* 1644–5	75	210

3009   3024

		F	VF
3011	**Shilling.** *O.* Oxford die. ℞. Declaration, 1643	80	225
3012	— — Similar, but Br. as *rev. mm.,* 1643–4.	80	225
3013	Coarse bust. ℞. As 3011, 1643	90	275
3014	— — Similar, but Br. as *rev. mm.,* 1644	80	225
3015	Bust of good style, plumelet before. ℞. As last, 1644–5	80	225
3016	— — Similar, but Br. below date instead of as *mm.,* 1644	75	215
3016A	— — — Plume and two plumelets 1644.	90	225
3016B	Taller bust with high crown, no plumelets before. ℞. As last 1645	90	225
3017	Bust with round collar, *mm.* Br. on its side. ℞. As 3016, 1644–5	90	275
3018	Bust with square collar. ℞. Br. as *mm.,* 1645	80	215
3019	**Sixpence.** Small bust, nothing before. ℞. Declaration, 1643; *mm.* ·/Br. . . .	140	500
3020	Fine style bust. Plumelet before face, 1644; *mm.* ·/Br. (on its side)	125	400
3021	**Groat.** Bust l. ℞. Declaration, 1644	90	240
3022	— Plumelet before face, 1644.	110	300
3023	— Br. below date, 1644	100	260
3024	**Threepence.** *O.* As 2992. Aberystwyth die; *mm.* book. ℞. Declaration, 1644.	110	375
3025	Bristol die, plume before face, no *mm.,* 1644	125	450
3026	**Halfgroat.** Br. in place of date below Declaration	200	425
3027	**Penny.** Similar bust, I behind. ℞. Large plume with bands.	225	600

Late 'Declaration' issues, 1645–6
(Previously given as Lundy Island and/or Appledore and Barnstaple/Bideford, it seems likely that coins marked A, 1645 may be Ashby de la Zouch and the coins marked B or with plumes may be Bridgnorth on Severn.)

		F	VF
		£	£
3028	**Halfcrown.** A below horse and date and as *rev. mm.* 1645	700	2000
3029	Similar but *rev.* from altered Bristol die (i.e. the A's are over Br.).	525	1500
3030	As 3028 but without A below date 1645.	475	1450
3031	A below horse and as *rev. mm.* Scroll above Declaration, B below 1646 .	*Extremely rare*	
3032	Plumelet below horse struck over A. R. *Mm.* Shrewsbury plumes; scroll above Declaration, 1646	300	850
3033	— Similar, but plumelet below date	350	1000
3034	**Shilling.** Crowned bust l., *mm.* plume. R. Declaration type; *mm.* A and A below 1645.	350	850
3035	— Similar, but plumelet before face	350	850
3036	— — R. Scroll above Declaration. 1646, *mm.* plume/plumelet	135	285
3037	Shrewsbury plume before face. R. As last but *mm.* pellet	135	325

3039   3044

3038	**Sixpence.** O. Plumelet before face; *mm.* A ; R. 1645, 3 plumelets over 'Dec'	165	350
3039	O. Large Shrewsbury plume before face; *mm.* B. R. Scroll above Declaration, 1646, Shrewsbury plume and two plume plumelets	70	150
3040	**Groat.** As 3038.	*Extremely rare*	
3041	Somewhat similar, but *obv. mm.* plumelet; 1646.	80	175
3042	**Threepence.** Somewhat as last but only single plumelet above Declaration, no line below, 1645; no *mm.*	100	275
3043	— Scroll in place of line above, 1646 below.	65	150
3044	**Halfgroat.** Bust l., II behind. R. Large plume with bands dividing 1646; no *mm.*	250	600

The penny listed under Bristol may belong to this series.

Truro mint, 1642–3. *Mm.* rose

3045	**Half-pound.** King on horseback, face turned frontwards, sash in large bow. R. CHRISTO, etc., round garnished shield. Struck from crown dies on thick flan.	*Extremely rare*	
3046	**Crown.** Similar type	135	325
3047	— Shield garnished with twelve even scrolls.	160	375
3048	King's face in profile, sash flies out in 2 ends, well-shaped flan, finer workmanship	150	350

Truro Silver, *continued.*

3049

		F £	VF £
3049	**Halfcrown.** King on spirited horse galloping over arms. ℞. Oval garnished shield, 1642 in cartouche below	900	3000
3050	Similar, but no arms. ℞. Oblong shield, CR at sides	700	2500
3051	Galloping horse, king holds sword. ℞. Similar	650	2300
3052	— ℞. Similar, but CR above	600	1900
3053	Trotting horse. ℞. Similar, but CR at sides	300	750
3054	Walking horse, king's head in profile. ℞. Similar	275	725
3055	— ℞. Similar, but CR above	325	850
3055A	Similar, but groundline below horse. ℞. Similar, *mm.* bugle/-	*Extremely rare*	
3056	**Shilling.** Small bust of good style. ℞. Oblong shield	*Extremely rare*	
3057	Larger bust with longer hair. ℞. Round shield with eight even scrolls	600	1500
3058	— ℞. Oval shield with CR at sides	550	1400
3059	Normal bust with lank hair. ℞. As last	500	1100
3060	— ℞. As 3057	600	1500
3061	— ℞. Round shield with six scrolls	350	850

Truro or Exeter mint. *Mm.* rose

3064   3067-9

		F £	VF £
3062	**Halfcrown.** King on horseback, sash tied in bow. ℞. Oblong shield with CR at sides	110	300
3063	— ℞. Round shield with eight even scrolls	80	200
3064	— ℞. Round shield with six scrolls	70	175
3064A	— Angular garnish of triple lines to oblong shield	*Extremely rare*	
3065	King's sash flies out behind. ℞. As 3063	105	275
3066	— ℞. As 3064A	*Extremely rare*	
3067	Briot's horse with ground-line. ℞. As 3063	105	275
3068	— ℞. As 3066		*Unique*
3069	— ℞. As 3064	105	275

		F	*VF*
		£	£

Exeter mint, 1643–6. *Mm.* rose except where stated

3070	**Crown**. As 3046, but 1644 divided by *rev. mm.*	125	275
3071	Similar, but 1644 to l. of *mm.*	110	240
3072	Similar, but 1645 and *rev. mm.* EX.	125	275
3073	King's sash in two loose ends; *mm.* castle/rose, 1645	110	240
3074	— *mm.* castle/EX, 1645	150	325
3075	— *mm.* castle, 1645	110	240
3076	**Halfcrown**. As 3049, but 1644–5 in legend	*Extremely rare*	
3077	Similar, but *rev. mm.* castle, 1645	*Unique*	
3078	Short portly figure, leaning backwards on ill-proportioned horse, 1644, 16 rose 44	175	450
3079	Briot's horse and lumpy ground; 1644.	125	350

Larger denominations often have irregular flans.

3080

3080	Horse with twisted tail; 1644–5	120	325
3081	— ℞. *Mm.* castle, 1645	160	450
3082	— ℞. *Mm.* EX, 1645	160	450
3083	— ℞. Declaration type; *mm.* EX. 1644–5	750	2100
3084	— — — EX also below 1644.	800	1750
3085	**Shilling**. As 3061. 1644, 1645, *mm.* rose (may be before, after or middle of date)	125	265
3086	— ℞. Declaration type, 1645	350	1250
3087	**Sixpence**. Sim. to 3085, 1644, 16 rose 44.	150	400
3088	**Groat**. Somewhat similar but 1644 at beginning of *obv.* legend	55	125

3089   3091

3089	**Threepence**. As illustration, 1644	60	140
3090	**Halfgroat**. Similar, but II. ℞. Oval shield, 1644	80	275
3091	— ℞. Large rose, 1644	100	300
3092	**Penny**. As last but I behind head.	150	400

Worcester mint, 1643–4

3096

		F £	VF £
3093	**Halfcrown**. King on horseback l., W below; *mm.* two lions. ℞. Declaration type 1644; *mm.* pellets.	300	850
3094	— ℞. Square-topped shield; *mm.* helmet, castle.	225	850
3095	— ℞. Oval shield; *mm.* helmet	225	700
3096	Similar but grass indicated; *mm.* castle. ℞. Square-topped shield; *mm.* helmet or pellets. (Illustrated above).	225	700
3097	— ℞. Oval draped shield, lis or lions in legend	250	775
3098	— ℞. Oval shield CR at sides, roses in legend	275	850
3099	— ℞. FLORENT etc., oval garnished shield with lion's paws each side .	350	950
3100	Tall king, no W or *mm.* ℞. Oval shield, lis, roses, lions or stars in legend.	225	700
3101	— ℞. Square-topped shield; *mm.* helmet.	275	900
3102	— ℞. FLORENT, etc., oval shield; no *mm.*.	350	950
3103	Briot type horse, sword slopes forward, ground-line. ℞. Oval shield, roses in legend; *mm.* 91v, 105, none (combinations).	225	850
3104	— Similar, but CR at sides, 91v/-	275	850
3105	Dumpy, portly king, crude horse. ℞. As 3100; *mm.* 91v, 105, none	225	700

3106

3106	Thin king and horse. ℞. Oval shield, stars in legend; *mm.* 91v, none . . .	225	700

Worcester or Salopia (Shrewsbury)

3107	**Shilling**. Bust of king l., adequately rendered. ℞. Square-topped shield; *mm.* castle	400	1250
3108	— ℞. CR above shield; *mm.* helmet and lion	400	1250
3109	— ℞. Oval shield; *mm.* lion, pear	375	1250

3111 3117

		F	VF
		£	£
3110	**Shilling**. Bust a somewhat crude copy of last (two varieties); *mm.* bird, lis. ℞. Square-topped shield with lion's paws above and at sides; *mm.* boar's head, helmet	425	1250
3111	— — CR above	425	1250
3112	— ℞. Oval shield, lis in legend; *mm.* lis	400	1150
3113	— ℞. Round shield; *mm.* lis, 3 lis	425	1200
3114	Bust r.; *mm.* pear/-, pear/lis. ℞. Dr., oval shield with or without CR. (Halfcrown reverse dies)	*Extremely rare*	
3115	**Sixpence**. As 3110; *mm.* castle, castle/boar's hd	500	1250
3116	**Groat**. As 3112; *mm.* lis/helmet, rose/helmet	375	750
3117	**Threepence**. Similar; *mm.* lis *obv.*	175	400
3118	**Halfgroat**. Similar; *mm.* lis (*O.*) various (℞.)	350	750

Salopia (Shrewsbury) mint, 1644

		F	VF
3119	**Halfcrown**. King on horseback l. SA below; *mm.* lis. ℞. (*mm.*s lis, helmet, lion rampant, none). Cr. oval shield; *mm.* helmet	*Extremely rare*	
3120	— ℞. FLORENT, etc., crowned oval shield, no *mm.*	*Extremely rare*	
3121	— SA erased or replaced by large pellet or cannon ball; *mm.* lis in legend, helmet. ℞. As last	1200	2750
3122	Tall horse and king, nothing below; *mm.* lis. ℞. Large round shield with crude garniture; *mm.* helmet	525	1250
3123	— ℞. Uncrowned square-topped shield with lion's paw above and at sides; *mm.* helmet	575	1400
3124	— ℞. Small crowned oval shield; *mm.* various	525	1250
3125	— ℞. As 3120	550	1300
3126	Finer work with little or no mane before horse. ℞. Cr. round or oval shield	525	1250
3127	Grass beneath horse. ℞. Similar; *mm.* lis or rose	650	1400
3128	Ground below horse. ℞. As 3120	575	1400

Hartlebury Castle (Worcs.) mint, 1646

3129

	F	VF
	£	£

3129 **Halfcrown**. *O. Mm*. pear. ℞. HC (Hartlebury Castle) in garniture below
shield; *mm*. three pears 1100 2700

Chester mint, 1644

3130

	F	VF
3130 **Halfcrown**. As illus. ℞. Oval shield; *mm*. three gerbs and sword . . . . . . | 375 | 850 |
3131 — Similar, but without plume or CHST; ℞. Cr. oval shield with lion skin; *mm*. prostrate gerb; -/cinquefoil, -/ .·. | 450 | 900 |
3132 — ℞. Crowned square-topped shield with CR at sides both crowned *rev*.; *mm*. cinquefoil . . . . | 475 | 1200 |
3133 As 3130, but without plume or CHST. ℞. Declaration type, 1644 *rev*.; *mm*. plume. . . . . | 425 | 1050 |
3133A **Shilling**. Bust l. ℞. Oval garnished shield; *mm*. .·. (obv. only) . . . . | *Extremely rare* |
3133B — ℞. Square-topped shield; *mm*. as last . . . . | *Extremely rare* |
3133C — ℞. Shield over long cross. . . . . | *Extremely rare* |
3134 **Threepence**. ℞. Square-topped shield; *mm*.-/ prostrate gerb . . . . | 300 | 650 |

Coventry (or Corfe Castle) mint? *Mm*. two interlocked C's
3135 **Halfcrown**. King on horseback l. ℞. Oval shield. *(Now considered to be
probably a contemporary forgery)

Carlisle besieged, 1644–5
3136 **Three shillings**. Large crown above C . R / . III . S. ℞. OBS . CARL / · 1645. 1500 3200
3137 Similar but : OBS :/-: CARL :·/·1645 . . . . 1500 3700

3138

	F £	VF £
3138 **Shilling.** As illustration	850	2500
3139 ℞. Legend and date in two lines	900	2750

Note. *(3136–39) Round or Octagonal pieces exist.*

Newark besieged, several times 1645–6, surrendered May 1646

3140

	F	VF
3140 **Halfcrown.** Large crown between CR ; below, XXX. ℞. OBS / NEWARK / 1645 or 1646	200	425
3141 **Shilling.** Similar but curious flat shaped crown, NEWARKE, 1645	175	350
3142 Similar but high arched crown, 1645	150	300
3143 — NEWARK, 1645 or 1646	140	275
3144 **Ninepence.** As halfcrown but IX, 1645 or 1646	150	350
3145 — NEWARKE, 1645	140	325
3146 **Sixpence.** As halfcrown but VI, 1646	150	375

Pontefract besieged, June 1648–March 1648–9

	F	VF
3147 **Two shillings** (lozenge shaped). DVM : SPIRO : SPERO around CR crowned. ℞. Castle surrounded by OBS, PC, sword and 1648	*Extremely rare*	
3148 **Shilling** (lozenge shaped, octagonal or round). Similar	325	725
3149 — Similar but XII or r. dividing PC	325	700

After the death of Charles I (30 Jan. 1648/9), in the name of Charles II

Pontefract besieged, *continued*

3149   3150

	F £	VF £
3150 **Shilling** (octagonal). *O*. As last. ℞. CAROLVS : SECVNDVS : 1648, castle gateway with flag dividing PC, OBS on l., cannon protrudes on r.	325	725
3151 CAROL : II : etc., around HANC : DE / VS : DEDIT 1648. ℞. POST : MORTEM : PATRIS : PRO : FILIO around gateway etc. as last	325	725

Scarborough besieged, July 1644–July 1645

3165   3168

£

Type I. Castle with gateway to left, value punched below or to side

3152 **Five shillings and eightpence**.	*Extremely rare*
3153 **Crown**. Similar but SC also punched.	*Extremely rare*
3154 **Three shillings and fourpence**. As 3152	*Extremely rare*
3155 **Three shillings**. Similar	*Extremely rare*
3156 **Two shillings and tenpence**. Similar.	5500
3157 **Halfcrown**. Similar.	4750
3158 **Two shillings and fourpence**. Similar	*Extremely rare*
3159 **Two shillings and twopence**. Similar	*Extremely rare*
3160 **Two shillings**. Similar	*Extremely rare*
3161 **One shilling and ninepence**. Similar.	*Extremely rare*
3162 **One shilling and sixpence**. Similar	*Extremely rare*
3163 **One shilling and fourpence**. Similar.	*Extremely rare*

£

3164	**One shilling and threepence**. Similar	4000
3165	**Shilling**. As illustration	*Extremely rare*
3166	**Sixpence**. Similar	*Extremely rare*
3167	**Groat**. Similar	*Extremely rare*

Type II. Castle with two turrets, value punched below

3168	**Two shillings**. Two castles.	*Extremely rare*
3170	**One shilling and sixpence**. Single castle.	*Extremely rare*
3171	**One shilling and fourpence**. Similar	4000
3172	**One shilling and threepence**. Similar	*Extremely rare*
3173	**One shilling and twopence**. Similar	*Extremely rare*
3174	**One shilling and one penny**. Similar.	*Extremely rare*
3175	**Shilling**. Similar	4500
3176	**Elevenpence**. Similar.	*Extremely rare*
3177	**Tenpence**. Similar	*Extremely rare*
3178	**Ninepence**. Similar.	*Extremely rare*
3179	**Sevenpence**. Similar	*Extremely rare*
3180	**Sixpence**. Similar	*Extremely rare*

COPPER

For mintmarks see *English Copper, Tin and Bronze Coins in the British Museum, 1558–1958*, by C. Wilson Peck.

3185   3191   3194

		F	VF
		£	£
3181	**Royal farthing**. "Richmond" round, colon stops, 1a. CARO over IACO; *mm.* on *obv.*	6	18
3182	— — 1b. CARA; *mm.* on *obv.*	60	125
3183	— — 1c. CARO; *mm.* on *obv.*	4	12
3184	— apostrophe stops. 1d. Eagle-headed harp.	6	18
3185	— 1e. Beaded harp	5	15
3186	— 1f. Scroll-fronted harp, 5 jewels on circlet	10	30
3187	— 1g. — — 7 jewels on circlet	5	15
3188	Transitional issue, double-arched crowns	15	45
3189	"Maltravers" round, 3a; *mm.* on *obv. only*	8	20
3190	— 3b. *Mm.* both sides.	4	12
3191	— 3c. Different *mm.* either side.	5	16
3192	"Richmond" oval. 4a. CARO over IACO; *mm.* both sides	15	40
3193	— — — *mm.* on *obv.*	15	40
3194	— 4b. CARO, colon stops; *mm.* on *obv.*.	12	35
3195	— — — — *mm.* on *rev.*.	12	35
3196	— — — — *mm.* both sides	12	35

	F	VF
	£	£

3197 **Royal farthing.** — 4c. apostrophe stops; *mm.* rose on *obv.* 15 40
3198 — — — — *mm.* rose both sides 15 40
3199 — — — — *mm.* rose (*obv.*); scroll (*rev.*). 15 40
3200 "Maltravers" oval. 5. CAROLVS; *mm.* lis both sides 22 45

3201   3207

3201 **Rose farthing.** 1a. Double-arched crowns; double rose; sceptres within
inner circle, BRIT; *mm.* on *obv.* or *rev.* or both sides, or different each side 7 20
3202 — 1b. — — sceptres just break circle, BRIT; *mm.* on *obv.* or both sides or
no *mm.*. 6 18
3203 — 1c. — — sceptres almost to outer circle, BRIT; *mm.*s as 3201 . . . . . 4 15
3204 — 1d. — — — BRI; *mm.* on *obv.* or both sides, or different each side . . 4 15
3205 Transitional mules of types 1d/2, with double and single arched crowns;
mm. as 3204 . . . . 7 20
3206 — 2. Single-arched crowns; single rose; *mm.* as 3204. . . . . 3 9
3207 — 3. Sceptres below crown; *mm.* mullet. 10 30

COMMONWEALTH, 1649–60

The coins struck during the Commonwealth have inscriptions in English instead of Latin which was considered to savour too much of papacy. St. George's cross and the Irish harp take the place of the royal arms. The silver halfpenny was issued for the last time.

Coins with *mm.* anchor were struck during the protectorship of Richard Cromwell.

Mintmarks

1649–57 Sun   1658–60 Anchor

GOLD

3208   3213

		F £	VF £
3208	**Unite.** As illustration; *mm.* sun, 1649–57	375	750
3209	Similar, *mm.* anchor, 1658, 1660	1000	3000
3210	**Double-crown.** As illus., but X; *mm.* sun, 1649–57	350	625
3211	Similar, *mm.* anchor, 1660	1100	2500
3212	**Crown.** Similar, but V; *mm.* sun, 1649–57	250	450
3213	As illus., *mm.* anchor, 1658, 60	900	2000

SILVER

3214	**Crown.** Same type; *mm.* sun, 1649, 51–4, 56		200	400
3215	**Halfcrown.** Similar; *mm.* sun, 1649, 1651–6		110	225
3216	— *mm.* anchor, 1658–1660	*Fair* 125	350	750
3217	**Shilling.** Similar; *mm.* sun, 1649, 1651–7		60	125
3218	— *mm.* anchor, 1658–60	*Fair* 100	275	550
3219	**Sixpence.** Similar; *mm.* sun, 1649, 1651–7		50	120
3220	— *mm.* anchor, 1658–60	*Fair* 75	200	450

3221   3223

3221	**Halfgroat.** As illustration	20	45
3222	**Penny.** Similar, but I above shields	15	35
3223	**Halfpenny.** As illustration	15	35

Oliver Cromwell. All said to be only patterns, but some circulated, especially the 1656 halfcrown and the shillings. Half broads exist, but are not contemporary.

GOLD

3224   **Fifty shillings.** Head l. ℞. Shield, 1656. Inscribed edge . . . .   *Extremely rare*

An extremely fine specimen sold at auction in May 1989 for £15,250.

3225

	F	VF	EF
	£	£	£
3225 **Broad.** (= 20s.). Similar, but grained edge		1600	3750

SILVER

3227

		F	VF	EF
3226	**Crown.** Bust l. ℞. Shield, 1658. Inscribed edge	475	900	1650
3227	**Halfcrown.** Similar, 1656	*Extremely rare*		
3227A	— 1658	225	450	850
3228	**Shilling.** Similar, but grained edge, 1658	200	400	700
3229	**Sixpence.** Similar	*Extremely rare*		

COPPER

3230

		F	VF	EF
3230	**Farthing.** Dr. bust l. ℞. CHARITIE AND CHANGE, shield . .	1200	2250	—

There are also other reverses.

SEVENTEENTH-CENTURY TOKENS

As there was no authorized copper coinage under the Commonwealth, towns and traders took it into their own hands to issue small change. Between 1648 and 1672 there was an enormous and very varied issue of these tokens. They were mostly farthings and halfpennies, but there were also some pennies. No collection is truly representative unless it contains at least a few. Many collectors specialize in those of their own town or county.

	F
	£
Price of commoner pennies.	30
— — — heart shaped pennies	175
— — — round halfpennies.	8
— — — octagonal halfpennies.	20
— — — heart-shaped halfpennies.	110
— — — square or lozenge-shaped halfpennies.	125
— — — round farthings.	5
— — — square farthings.	75
— — — octagonal farthings.	30

For further details of seventeenth-century tokens, see *Trade Tokens issued in the Seventeenth Century* by G. C. Williamson, also Seaby's *British Tokens and their Values*, and *Seventeenth Century Tokens of the British Isles and their Values* by Michael Dickinson, 1986.

CHARLES II, 1660–85

For the first two years after the Restoration the same denominations, apart from the silver crown, were struck as were issued during the Commonwealth. In 1662 the hand hammering of coins was abandoned in favour of manufacture by the Roettiers improved mill and screw presses. As a prevention against clipping the larger coins were made with the edge inscribed DECVS ET TVTAMEN and the regnal year and the medium-sized coins were given a grained edge.

The new gold coins were current for 100s., 20s. and 10s., and they came to be called "guineas" as the gold from which some of them were made was imported from Guinea by the Africa Company (whose badge was the Elephant and Castle). It was not until some years later that the guinea increased in value to 21s. and more. The Africa Co. badge is also found on some silver, and so is the plume symbol indicating silver from the Welsh mines. The four smallest silver denominations, though known today as "Maundy Money", were actually issued for general circulation: at this period the silver penny was probably the only coin distributed at the royal Maundy ceremonies. The smaller "machine"-made coins were perhaps minted later than 1662.

A good regal copper coinage was issued for the first time in 1672, but later in the reign, farthings were struck in tin (with a copper plug) in order to help the Cornish tin industry.

For the emergency issues struck in the name of Charles II in 1648/9, see the siege pieces of Pontefract listed under Charles I, nos. 3150–1.

Mintmark: Crown.

GOLD

Hammered coinage, 1660–2

First issue. Without mark of value

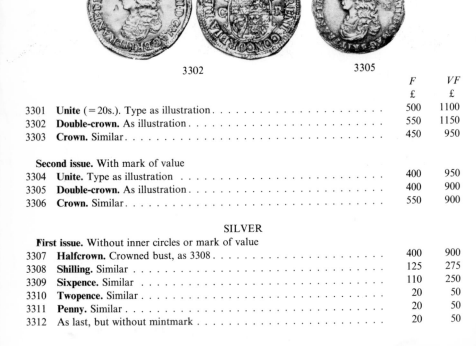

3302   3305

		F	VF
		£	£
3301	**Unite** (=20s.). Type as illustration.	500	1100
3302	**Double-crown.** As illustration.	550	1150
3303	**Crown.** Similar.	450	950
	Second issue. With mark of value		
3304	**Unite.** Type as illustration	400	950
3305	**Double-crown.** As illustration.	400	900
3306	**Crown.** Similar.	550	900

SILVER

First issue. Without inner circles or mark of value

3307	**Halfcrown.** Crowned bust, as 3308.	400	900
3308	**Shilling.** Similar	125	275
3309	**Sixpence.** Similar	110	250
3310	**Twopence.** Similar.	20	50
3311	**Penny.** Similar.	20	50
3312	As last, but without mintmark	20	50

3308	3313	3322

	F	VF
	£	£

Second issue. Without inner circles, but with mark of value

3313	Halfcrown. Crowned bust	550	1500
3314	Shilling. Similar	250	650
3315	Sixpence. Similar	500	1250
3316	Twopence. Similar, but *mm.* on *obv.* only	135	300
3317	Similar, but *mm.* both sides (machine made)	12	25
3318	Bust to edge of coin, legend starts at bottom l. (machine made, single arch crown)	12	25
3319	Penny. As 3317	15	30
3320	As 3318 (single arch crown)	12	25

3310	3317	3326

Third issue. With inner circles and mark of value

3321	Halfcrown. Crowned bust to i.c. (and rarely to edge of coin)	80	250
3322	Shilling. Similar	50	160
3323	Sixpence. Similar	50	150
3324	Fourpence. Similar	15	35
3325	Threepence. Similar	20	35
3326	Twopence. Similar	10	20
3327	Penny. Similar	25	45

GOLD

Milled coinage

3328　　　　　　　　　　　　　　　　3335

3328　Five guineas. First bust, pointed truncation

	F	VF	EF		F	VF	EF
	£	£	£		£	£	£
1668	700	1300	3600	1674	800	1400	3750
1669	750	1300	3600	1675	750	1250	3500
1670	700	1200	3400	1676	800	1400	3750
1671	800	1450	3750	1677	750	1300	3600
1672	700	1300	3600	1678	700	1300	3600
1673	700	1300	3600				

3329　— with elephant below bust

	F	VF	EF		F	VF	EF
1668	700	1200	3400	1675	950	1800	4500
1669	950	1800	4500	1677/5		*Extremely rare*	

3330　— with elephant and castle below

	F	VF	EF		F	VF	EF
1675		*Extremely rare*		1677	800	1400	3750
1676	750	1300	3600	1678	850	1500	4000

3331　Second bust, rounded truncation

	F	VF	EF		F	VF	EF
1678/7	850	1500	4000	1682	700	1200	3400
1679	700	1200	3400	1683	700	1300	3600
1680	750	1300	3600	1684	700	1200	3400
1681	700	1200	3400				

3332　— with elephant and castle below

	F	VF	EF		F	VF	EF
1680		*Extremely rare*					
1681	850	1500	4000	1683	850	1500	4000
1682	750	1300	3600	1684	700	1200	3400

3333　Two guineas. First bust, pointed truncation

	F	VF	EF		F	VF	EF
1664	350	800	3250	1669		*Extremely rare*	
1665		*Extremely rare*		1671	400	900	3500

3334　— with elephant below

	F	VF	EF
1664	275	650	2750

3335　Second bust, rounded truncation

	F	VF	EF		F	VF	EF
1675	375	800	3250	1680	400	900	3500
1676	300	650	2750	1681	250	650	2750
1677	250	650	2750	1682	250	650	2750
1678/7	250	600	2500	1683	250	600	2500
1679	300	650	2750	1684	375	750	3000

3336 — with elephant and castle below

	F	VF	EF		F	VF	EF
	£	£	£		£	£	£
1676	275	650	2750	1682	250	600	2500
1677		*Extremely rare*		1683	400	900	3500
1678	300	650	2750	1684	400	900	3500

3337 — with elephant only below, 1678 . . . .   *Extremely rare*

Overstruck dates are listed only if commoner than the normal date or if no normal date is known.

3343   3345

3338 **Guinea.** First bust, 1663   500   1450   3250
3339 — with elephant below, 1663   400   1150   3000
3340 Second bust, 1664   350   950   2500
3341 — with elephant below, 1664 . . . .   *Extremely rare*
3342 Third bust, normal portrait

1664	200	600	1750	1669	250	750	2000
1665	200	600	1750	1670	200	600	1750
1666	200	600	1750	1671	200	600	1750
1667	200	600	1750	1672	250	750	2000
1668	200	600	1750	1673	350	950	2250

3343 — with elephant below

1664	250	750	2000	1668		*Extremely rare*	
1665	250	750	2000				

3344 Fourth bust, rounded truncation

1672	175	500	1550	1679	150	450	1450
1673	175	500	1550	1680	150	450	1450
1674	250	750	2000	1681	175	500	1550
1675	200	600	1750	1682	175	500	1550
1676	150	450	1450	1683	150	450	1450
1677	150	450	1450	1684	175	500	1550
1678	150	450	1450				

3345 — with elephant and castle below

1674		*Extremely rare*		1680	400	1200	3000
1675	250	750	2000	1681	250	750	2000
1676	175	500	1550	1682	275	800	2000
1677	175	500	1550	1683	400	1200	3000
1678	350	950	2250	1684	275	800	2000
1679	250	750	2000				

		F £	VF £	EF £			F £	VF £	EF £

3346 Guinea. Fourth bust, with elephant below

1677			*Extremely rare*	1678			*Extremely rare*

3347 Half-guinea. First bust, pointed truncation

| 1669 . . . . | 175 | 500 | 1800 | 1671 . . . . | 225 | 650 | 2000 |
| 1670 . . . . | 150 | 350 | 1500 | 1672 . . . . | 200 | 650 | 2000 |

3348 Second bust, rounded truncation

1672	175	400	1600	1679	135	350	1500
1673	300	750	2250	1680	300	750	2250
1674	300	750	2250	1681	300	750	2250
1675		*Extremely rare*		1682	200	600	2000
1676	175	375	1500	1683	175	400	1600
1677	175	400	1600	1684	135	325	1500
1678	175	400	1600				

3349 — with elephant and castle below

1676	350	850	—	1682	300	800	2400
1677	300	800	2400	1683		*Extremely rare*	
1678/7	225	650	2000	1684	175	400	1600
1680		*Extremely rare*					

SILVER

3350

		F	VF	EF
3350	**Crown.** First bust, rose below, edge undated, 1662	35	175	950
3351	— — edge dated, 1662	45	225	1100
3352	— no rose, edge dated, 1662	50	275	1250
3353	— — edge not dated, 1662	45	225	1100
3354	— — new reverse, shields altered, 1663, regnal year on edge in Roman figures ANNO REGNI XV	40	200	1100

3355

	F	VF	EF		F	VF	EF
	£	£	£		£	£	£

3355 Second bust, regnal year on edge in Roman figures

1664	45	200	1100	1666	45	225	1100
1665	150	600	—				

3356 — — elephant below bust, 1666 130   450   —

3357 — regnal year on edge in words (e.g. 1667 = DECIMO NONO)

1667	35	165	1000	1670	45	200	1100
1668	35	165	1000	1671	35	165	1000
1669	100	400	—				

3358 Third bust

1671	35	165	1000	1676	35	165	1000
1672	35	165	1000	1677	35	165	1000
1673	35	165	1000	1678/7	100	400	—
1674		*Extremely rare*		1679	35	165	1000
1675/3	165	600	—	1680/79	50	200	1100

3359 Fourth bust

1679	35	165	1000	1682/1	45	200	1100
1680	35	165	1000	1683	110	450	—
1681	40	200	1100	1684	70	350	—

3360 — elephant and castle below bust, 1681 950   2250   —

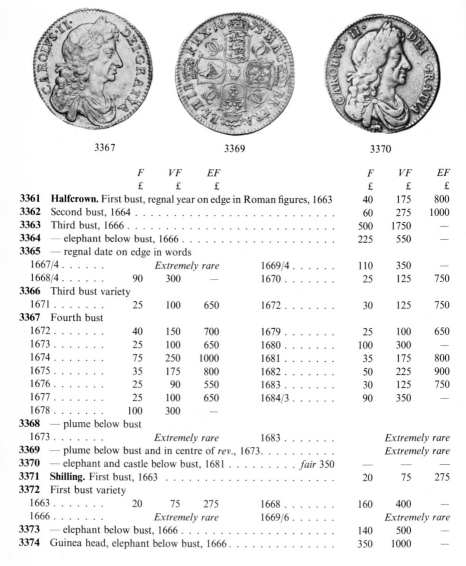

| | 3367 | | 3369 | | 3370 | |

		F	VF	EF		F	VF	EF
		£	£	£		£	£	£
3361	**Halfcrown.** First bust, regnal year on edge in Roman figures, 1663					40	175	800
3362	Second bust, 1664					60	275	1000
3363	Third bust, 1666					500	1750	—
3364	— elephant below bust, 1666					225	550	—
3365	— regnal date on edge in words							
	1667/4		*Extremely rare*		1669/4	110	350	—
	1668/4	90	300	—	1670	25	125	750
3366	Third bust variety							
	1671	25	100	650	1672	30	125	750
3367	Fourth bust							
	1672	40	150	700	1679	25	100	650
	1673	25	100	650	1680	100	300	—
	1674	75	250	1000	1681	35	175	800
	1675	35	175	800	1682	50	225	900
	1676	25	90	550	1683	30	125	750
	1677	25	100	650	1684/3	90	350	—
	1678	100	300	—				
3368	— plume below bust							
	1673		*Extremely rare*		1683		*Extremely rare*	
3369	— plume below bust and in centre of *rev.*, 1673						*Extremely rare*	
3370	— elephant and castle below bust, 1681 . . . . *fair* 350					—	—	—
3371	**Shilling.** First bust, 1663					20	75	275
3372	First bust variety							
	1663	20	75	275	1668	160	400	—
	1666		*Extremely rare*		1669/6		*Extremely rare*	
3373	— elephant below bust, 1666					140	500	—
3374	Guinea head, elephant below bust, 1666					350	1000	—

| 3371 | 3376 | 3380 |

	F £	VF £	EF £		F £	VF £	EF £
3375 Second bust							
1666		*Extremely rare*		1676	30	90	450
1668	20	60	275	1677	30	90	450
1669		*Extremely rare*		1678	45	175	650
1670	45	175	650	1679	30	100	450
1671	50	225	750	1680		*Extremely rare*	
1672	30	120	500	1681	50	225	750
1673	45	175	750	1682/1	225	500	—
1674	45	175	750	1683		*Extremely rare*	
1675	90	300	—				
3376 — plume below bust and in centre of *rev.*							
1671	80	350	—	1676	80	350	—
1673	80	400	—	1679	100	450	—
1674	80	350	—	1680	150	550	—
1675	80	400	—				
3377 — plume *rev.* only, 1674					125	450	—
3378 — plume *obv.* only							
1677	125	500	—	1679	90	400	—
3379 — elephant and castle below bust, 1681/0					750	—	—
3380 Third (large) bust							
1674	125	475	—	1675	75	275	1000
3381 Fourth (large) bust, older features							
1683	75	200	850	1684	60	175	750

3382

3382 **Sixpence**	F	VF	EF		F	VF	EF
1674	15	45	150	1680	25	90	300
1675	15	45	150	1681	15	45	150
1676	20	90	300	1682/1	18	65	200
1677	15	45	150	1683	15	45	150
1678/7	18	65	200	1684	15	50	180
1679	18	65	200				
3383 **Fourpence.** Undated. Crowned bust l. to edge of coin, value behind. ℞. Shield					7	15	30
3384 Dated. *O.* As illustration on p.226. ℞. Four C's							
1670	4	10	30	1678	4	9	27
1671	4	10	30	1679	3	9	27
1672/1	4	10	30	1680	3	9	27
1673	4	10	30	1681	3	9	27
1674	4	10	30	1682	4	9	27
1675	4	10	30	1683	3	9	27
1676	4	10	30	1684/3	3	9	27
1677	4	9	27				
3385 **Threepence.** Undated. As 3383					8	18	40

3384   3386   3388   3390

3386 Threepence. Dated. As illustration

	F	VF	EF		F	VF	EF
	£	£	£		£	£	£
1670	5	9	27	1678	5	8	25
1671	5	8	25	1679	4	7	25
1672/1	5	8	25	1680	5	9	27
1673	5	8	25	1681	5	9	27
1674	5	8	25	1682	5	9	27
1675	5	9	27	1683	5	9	27
1676	5	8	25	1684	5	9	27
1677	5	8	25				

3387 Twopence. Undated. As 3383 (double arch crown) 6 12 25

3388 Dated. As illustration

	F	VF	EF		F	VF	EF
1668	4	8	25	1677	4	8	25
1670	4	8	25	1678	4	8	25
1671	4	8	25	1679	4	8	25
1672/1	4	8	25	1680	4	8	25
1673	4	8	25	1681	4	8	25
1674	4	8	25	1682	4	8	25
1675	4	8	25	1683	4	8	25
1676	4	8	25	1684	4	8	25

3389 Penny. Undated. As 3383 (double arch crown) 8 17 40

3390 Dated. As illustration

	F	VF	EF		F	VF	EF
1670	7	16	35	1678	7	16	35
1671	7	16	35	1679	13	25	45
1672/1	7	16	35	1680	7	16	35
1673	7	16	35	1681	8	18	40
1674	7	16	35	1682	8	17	38
1675	7	16	35	1683	7	16	35
1676	8	17	38	1684	8	17	38
1677	7	16	35				

3391 Maundy Set. Undated. The four coins 45 100 150

3392 Dated. The four coins. Uniform dates

	F	VF	EF		F	VF	EF
1670	32	65	175	1678	35	70	180
1671	30	60	165	1679	32	65	175
1672	32	65	175	1680	30	60	165
1673	30	60	165	1681	35	70	180
1674	30	60	165	1682	32	65	175
1675	30	60	165	1683	30	60	165
1676	30	60	165	1684	32	65	175
1677	30	60	165				

COPPER AND TIN

3393   3394

3393 Copper **halfpenny**

	F	VF	EF		F	VF	EF
	£	£	£		£	£	£
1672	20	60	225	1675	20	60	225
1673	20	60	225				

3394 Copper **farthing**. As illustration

	F	VF	EF		F	VF	EF
1672	12	30	175	1675	18	40	175
1673	12	30	175	1679	20	50	225
1674	15	35	175				

3395

3395 Tin **farthing**. Somewhat similar, but with copper plug, edge inscribed NUMMORVM FAMVLVS, and date on edge only

	Fair	F	VF	EF
	£	£	£	£
1684	20	45	150	500
1685			*Extremely rare*	

JAMES II, 1685–8

Tin halfpence and farthings provided the only base metal coinage during this short reign. All genuine tin coins of this period have a copper plug.

GOLD

	F £	VF £	EF £		F £	VF £	EF £
3396 Five guineas. First bust l., sceptres misplaced, 1686	950	1600	3800				
3397 — sceptres normal.							
1687	900	1500	3600	1688	850	1450	3600
3397a Second bust							
1687	900	1500	3600	1688	850	1450	3600
3398 First bust. Elephant and castle below bust							
1687	1000	1650	4000	1688	1000	1650	4000
3399 Two guineas. Similar							
1687	450	1300	3000	1688/7	500	1400	3250

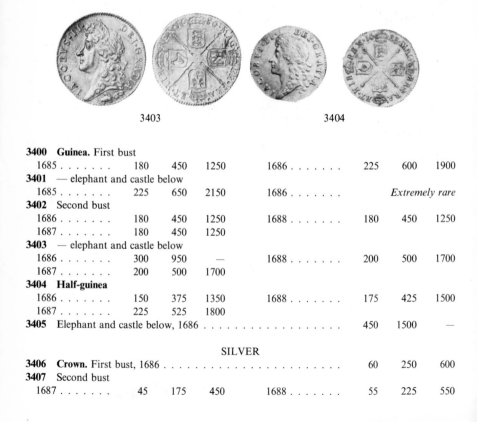

3403   3404

	F	VF	EF		F	VF	EF
3400 Guinea. First bust							
1685	180	450	1250	1686	225	600	1900
3401 — elephant and castle below							
1685	225	650	2150	1686		*Extremely rare*	
3402 Second bust							
1686	180	450	1250	1688	180	450	1250
1687	180	450	1250				
3403 — elephant and castle below							
1686	300	950	—	1688	200	500	1700
1687	200	500	1700				
3404 Half-guinea							
1686	150	375	1350	1688	175	425	1500
1687	225	525	1800				
3405 Elephant and castle below, 1686	450	1500	—

SILVER

	F	VF	EF		F	VF	EF
3406 Crown. First bust, 1686	60	250	600
3407 Second bust							
1687	45	175	450	1688	55	225	550

3406

3408   1st bust   2nd bust

	F £	VF £	EF £		F £	VF £	EF £
3408 Halfcrown. First bust							
1685	40	135	500	1687	40	135	500
1686	40	135	500				
3409 Second bust							
1687	50	200	600	1688	45	155	550
3410 Shilling							
1685	35	135	375	1687/6	40	155	450
1686	35	135	375	1688	40	155	450
3411 Plume in centre of *rev.*, 1685					*Extremely rare*		

3410   3412

3412 Sixpence. Early type shields							
1686	25	80	250	1687	30	90	275
3413 Late type shields							
1687	25	80	250	1688	30	90	275

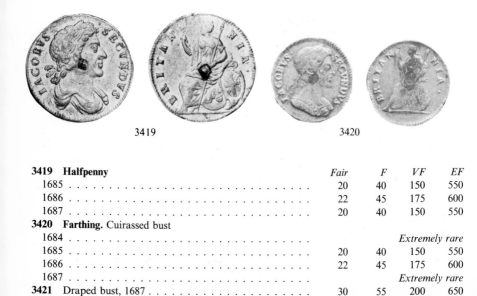

		F £	VF £	EF £			F £	VF £	EF £
3414	**Fourpence.** *O.* As illus. ℞. IIII crowned								
1686		6	14	30	1688		6	14	30
1687/6		6	13	28					
3415	**Threepence.** As illustration								
1685		6	13	27	1687/6		6	13	27
1686		6	13	27	1688		6	13	27
3416	**Twopence.** As illustration								
1686		6	13	25	1688		7	13	25
1687		6	13	25					
3417	**Penny.** As illustration								
1685		10	20	30	1687		10	20	30
1686		10	20	30	1688		10	20	30
3418	**Maundy Set.** As last four. Uniform dates								
1686		35	70	150	1688		35	70	150
1687		35	70	150					

TIN

		3419	3420		
		Fair	F	VF	EF
3419	**Halfpenny**				
1685		20	40	150	550
1686		22	45	175	600
1687		20	40	150	550
3420	**Farthing.** Cuirassed bust				
1684			*Extremely rare*		
1685		20	40	150	550
1686		22	45	175	600
1687			*Extremely rare*		
3421	Draped bust, 1687		30	55	200	650

WILLIAM AND MARY, 1688–94

Due to the poor state of the silver coinage, much of it worn hammered coin, the guinea, which was valued at 21s. 6d. at the beginning of the reign, circulated for as much as 30s. by 1694. The tin halfpennies and farthings were replaced by copper coins in 1694. The rampant lion of Orange is now placed as an inescutcheon on the centre of the royal arms.

GOLD

3422   Five guineas. Conjoined heads r.

	F	VF	EF			F	VF	EF
	£	£	£			£	£	£
1691	750	1600	3800		1693	750	1600	3800
1692	750	1600	3800		1694	800	1800	4000

3422

3423   — elephant and castle below

1691	850	1800	4500		1693	1100	2200	5000
1692	900	1800	4500		1694	1000	2100	4750

3424   Two guineas. Conjoined heads r.

1693	400	900	3000		1694/3	400	900	3000

3425   — elephant and castle below

1691		*Extremely rare*			1694/3	650	1400	4000
1693	650	1400	4000					

3427

3426   Guinea. Conjoined heads r.

1689	180	450	1250		1692	225	650	1700
1690	200	550	1450		1693	225	600	1450
1691	225	600	1450		1694	180	500	1350

3427   — elephant and castle below

1689	200	500	1350		1692	250	600	1450
1690	270	750	1950		1693		*Extremely rare*	
1691	225	550	1450		1694	250	600	1600

3428   — elephant only below

1692	270	750	1950		1693		*Extremely rare*	

Overstruck dates are listed only if commoner than the normal date or if no normal date is known.

3429   3430

	F £	VF £	EF £		F £	VF £	EF £
3429 **Half-guinea.** First heads, 1689					175	450	1300
3430 — Second head, normal portraits							
1690	180	450	1400	1693	*Extremely rare*		
1691	225	550	1600	1694	125	350	1100
1692	180	450	1400				
3431 — — elephant and castle below							
1691	155	450	1200	1692	125	350	1100
3432 — — elephant only below, 1692					*Extremely rare*		

SILVER

3433 **Crown.** Conjoined busts							
1691	120	300	950	1692	120	300	950

3433

3434   3435

3434 **Halfcrown.** First busts and first shields, 1689				25	70	300
3435 — and second shield						
1689	30	80	375	1690	35	120	450

	F £	VF £	EF £		F £	VF £	EF £
3436 Second busts. ℞. As illustration below							
1691	32	110	400	1693	30	90	375
1692	35	120	450				

3436   3438

	F £	VF £	EF £		F £	VF £	EF £
3437 Shilling. Similar							
1692	30	120	500	1693	25	110	450
3438 Sixpence. Similar							
1693	20	65	250	1694	40	140	400
3439 Fourpence. First busts, no tie to wreath							
1689	6	16	30	1691	8	19	40
1690	7	16	35	1694	8	17	38
3440 Second busts, tie to wreath							
1692	7	18	40	1694	10	21	45
1693	10	21	45				
3441 Threepence. First busts, no tie							
1689	6	14	28	1691	12	28	45
1690	7	14	30				
3442 Second busts, tie to wreath							
1691	7	19	40	1693	7	17	38
1692	7	19	40	1694	7	16	37
3443 Twopence							
1689	5	13	30	1693	7	14	35
1691	7	14	35	1694	8	15	38
1692	7	14	35				
3444 Penny. Legend continuous over heads, 1689					90	200	375
3445 Legend broken by heads							
1690	12	23	50	1693	12	23	50
1691	12	23	50	1694	12	23	50
1692	12	23	50				

3446

	F £	VF £	EF £		F £	VF £	EF £
3446 Maundy Set. As last pieces. Uniform dates							
1689	130	275	500	1693	60	120	210
1691	50	110	200	1694	50	110	200
1692	50	110	200				

TIN AND COPPER

3448

3451

	Fair £	F £	VF £	EF £
3447 Tin Halfpenny. Small draped busts, 1689	175	350	900	—
3448 Large cuirassed busts; date only on edge				
1690	20	40	115	450
3449 — date in exergue and on edge				
1691	20	40	115	450
1692	20	40	115	450
3450 Tin Farthing. Small draped busts				
1689	90	175	500	—
1689, edge 1690		*Extremely rare*		
3451 Large cuirassed busts				
1690, edge 1689		*Extremely rare*		
1690	20	50	120	475
1691	20	50	120	475
1692	22	55	125	525

3453

3452 Copper **Halfpenny**, 1694		15	35	300
3453 Copper **Farthing**, 1694		20	40	350

WILLIAM III, 1694–1702

In 1696 a great re-coinage was undertaken to replace the hammered silver that made up most of the coinage in circulation, much of it being clipped and badly worn. Branch mints were set up at Bristol, Chester, Exeter, Norwich and York to help with the re-coinage. For a short time before they were finally demonetized, unclipped hammered coins were allowed to circulate freely provided they were officially pierced in the centre. Silver coins with roses between the coats of arms were made from silver obtained from the West of England mines.

GOLD

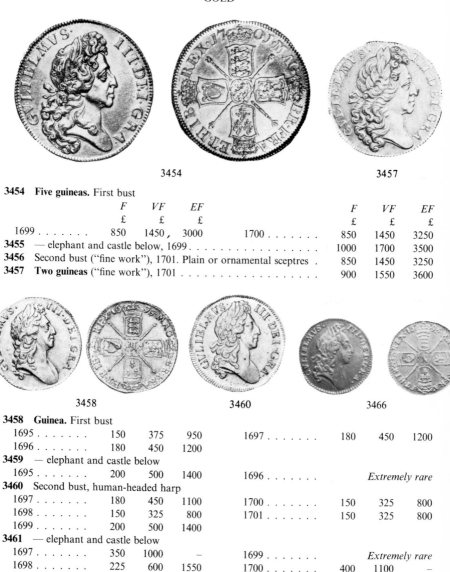

3454   3457

	F	VF	EF		F	VF	EF
	£	£	£		£	£	£
3454 Five guineas. First bust							
1699	850	1450,	3000	1700	850	1450	3250
3455 — elephant and castle below, 1699					1000	1700	3500
3456 Second bust ("fine work"), 1701. Plain or ornamental sceptres .					850	1450	3250
3457 Two guineas ("fine work"), 1701					900	1550	3600

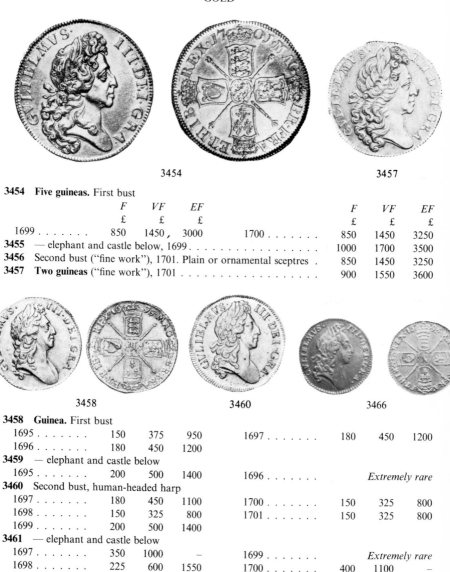

3458   3460   3466

	F	VF	EF		F	VF	EF
3458 Guinea. First bust							
1695	150	375	950	1697	180	450	1200
1696	180	450	1200				
3459 — elephant and castle below							
1695	200	500	1400	1696		Extremely rare	
3460 Second bust, human-headed harp							
1697	180	450	1100	1700	150	325	800
1698	150	325	800	1701	150	325	800
1699	200	500	1400				
3461 — elephant and castle below							
1697	350	1000	–	1699		Extremely rare	
1698	225	600	1550	1700	400	1100	–

	F	VF	EF
	£	£	£
3462 **Guinea.** — ℞. Large lettering and large date, 1698	150	375	950
3463 — ℞. Scrolled harp, 1701	150	375	950
3464 — — elephant and castle, 1701	*Extremely rare*		
3465 Third bust ("fine work"), 1701	300	700	2500
3466 **Half-guinea.** ℞. With early harp, 1695	100	250	700

3467 **Half-guinea.** Elephant and castle. ℞. With early harp

	F	VF	EF				
	£	£	£				
1695	225	550	1600	1696	115	300	900

3468 ℞. With late harp

1697	160	400	1200	1700	110	250	675
1698	110	250	675	1701	110	250	675
1699	*Extremely rare*						

3469 — elephant and castle, 1698	180	450	1400

SILVER

3470 **Crown.** First bust, first harp

1695	25	95	300	1696	25	95	275
3471 Second bust (hair across breast), 1696					*Unique*		
3472 Third bust, first harp, 1696				30	100	300	
3473 — second harp, 1697				250	800	—	
3474 Third bust variety, third harp, 1700				30	115	325	

3490

3475 **Halfcrown.** Small shields, 1696	15	50	175
3476 — B (*Bristol*) below bust, 1696	20	70	225
3477 — C (*Chester*) below bust, 1696	30	125	375
3478 — E (*Exeter*) below bust, 1696	45	175	500
3479 — N (*Norwich*) below bust, 1696	25	90	275
3480 — y (*York*) below bust, 1696	30	125	375
3481 Large shield, early harp, 1696	15	50	175
3482 — — B (*Bristol*) below bust, 1696	20	70	225
3483 — — C (*Chester*) below bust, 1696	25	90	275
3484 — — E (*Exeter*) below bust, 1696	30	125	375
3485 — — N (*Norwich*) below bust, 1696	45	175	500
3486 — — y (*York*) below bust, 1696	25	90	275

3487 Large shields, ordinary harp

1696	35	135	400	1697	15	50	175
3488 — — B (*Bristol*) below bust, 1697				20	80	250	

	F £	VF £	EF £		F £	VF £	EF £
3489 ——C(*Chester*) below bust							
1696	35	135	400	1697	20	70	225
3490 —— E (*Exeter*) below bust							
1696	35	135	400	1697	20	55	195
3491 —— N (*Norwich*) below bust							
1696	45	175	500	1697	20	70	225
3492 —— y (*York*) below bust, 1697.					20	55	195
3493 Second bust (hair across breast), 1696							*Unique*
3494 Halfcrown. Modified large shields							
1698	15	55	200	1700	20	60	225
1699	30	90	300	1701	25	65	250
3495 Elephant and castle below bust, 1701 . . . . *Fair* 250							
3496 Plumes in angles on *rev.*, 1701					30	100	300

1st bust   2nd bust   3rd bust   3507

3rd bust var.   4th bust   5th bust

3497 Shilling. First bust							
1695	18	50	150	1697	9	25	80
1696	9	25	80				
3498 — B (*Bristol*) below bust							
1696	18	45	135	1697	20	50	150
3499 — C (*Chester*) below bust							
1696	20	50	150	1697	20	50	150
3500 — E (*Exeter*) below bust							
1696	20	50	150	1697	20	50	150
3501 — N (*Norwich*) below bust							
1696	20	50	150	1697	20	50	150
3502 — y (*York*) below bust							
1696	20	50	150	1697	20	50	150
3503 — Y (*York*) below bust							
1696	22	60	175	1697	22	60	175

	F	VF	EF
	£	£	£

	F £	VF £	EF £
3504 Shilling. Second bust (hair across breast), 1696			*Unique*
3505 Third bust, 1697	9	25	80
3506 — B (*Bristol*) below bust, 1697	22	60	175
3507 — C (*Chester*) below bust			

	F £	VF £	EF £			F £	VF £	EF £
1696	45	150	450	1697		20	50	150

	F £	VF £	EF £
3508 — E (*Exeter*) below bust, 1697	22	60	175
3509 — N (*Norwich*) below bust, 1697	20	60	175
3510 — y (*York*) below bust			
1696 . . . . . . *Extremely rare* 1697	22	60	175
3511 Third bust variety			
1697 . . . . . . 9 25 85 1698	18	50	150
3512 — B (*Bristol*) below bust, 1697	22	60	175
3513 Third bust variety C (*Chester*) below bust, 1697	50	150	450
3514 — R. Plumes in angles, 1698	55	175	525
3515 Fourth bust ("flaming hair")			
1698 . . . . . . 30 70 250 1699	30	70	250
3516 Fifth bust (hair high)			
1699 . . . . . . 22 60 200 1701	22	60	200
1700 . . . . . . 15 35 100			
3517 — R. Plumes in angles			
1699 . . . . . . 40 115 350 1701	40	115	350
3518 — R. Roses in angles, 1699	55	150	450
3519 — plume below bust, 1700	750	—	—

3520   3542

	F £	VF £	EF £
3520 Sixpence. First bust, early harp			
1695 . . . . . . 20 60 175 1696	5	18	50
3521 — — B below bust, 1696	8	22	65
3522 — — C below bust, 1696	15	45	135
3523 — — E below bust, 1696	20	60	175
3524 — — N below bust, 1696	12	40	120
3525 — — y below bust, 1696	10	30	90
3526 — — Y below bust, 1696	20	60	175
3527 — later harp, large crowns, 1696	25	75	225
3528 — — — B below bust			
1696 . . . . . . 25 75 225 1697	20	60	175
3529 — — — C below bust, 1697	25	75	225
3530 — — — E below bust, 1697	22	70	225
3531 — — small crowns			
1696 . . . . . . 20 65 190 1697	8	22	65
3532 — — — B below bust			
1696 . . . . . . 18 55 160 1697	12	40	120

	F £	VF £	EF £		F £	VF £	EF £
3533 — — — C below bust							
1696	35	10	300	1697	12	40	120
3534 — — — E below bust, 1697					15	45	135
3535 — — — N below bust							
1696	30	90	275	1697	10	30	90
3536 — — — y below bust, 1697.					25	75	225
3537 Second bust							
1696	150	300	—	1697	35	120	350
3538 Third bust, large crowns							
1697	5	18	50	1700	8	22	65
1698	8	22	65	1701	11	35	90
1699	27	80	240				
3539 — — E below bust, 1697					15	45	135
3540 — — C below bust, 1697					25	70	200
3541 — — E below bust, 1697					30	90	275
3542 Third bust small crowns, 1697					10	30	90
3543 — — C below bust, 1697					22	65	180
3544 — — E below bust, 1697					16	50	150
3545 — — Y below bust, 1697					25	80	240
3546 — ℞. Plumes in angles							
1698	10	30	90	1699	14	40	120
3547 — ℞. Roses in angles, 1699					25	75	225
3548* — plume below bust, 1700					*Extremely rare*		

* An extremely fine specimen sold at auction in October 1985 for £3500.

3549   3550   3551   3552

3549 Fourpence. ℞. 4 crowned							
1697			*Unique*	1700	11	20	45
1698	12	22	50	1701	12	24	55
1699	11	22	50	1702	11	20	45
3550 Threepence. ℞. 3 crowned							
1698	11	20	45	1700	11	20	45
1699	12	22	48	1701	11	20	45
3551 Twopence. ℞. 2 crowned							
1698	11	19	38	1700	10	19	38
1699	10	18	36	1701	9	18	38
3552 Penny. ℞. 1 crowned							
1698	11	19	38	1700	12	20	40
1699	12	20	40	1701	11	19	38
3553 Maundy Set. As last four. Uniform dates							
1698	50	105	180	1700	60	115	190
1699	60	115	190	1701	50	105	180

COPPER

3554 Halfpenny. First issue. Britannia with r. hand raised

	F	VF	EF		F	VF	EF
	£	£	£		£	£	£
1695	8	30	175	1697	7	25	175
1696	7	25	175	1698	9	40	200

3554

3555 Second issue. ℞. Date in legend

1698	8	30	175	1699	7	25	175

3556 Third issue. ℞. Britannia with r. hand on knee

1699	7	25	175	1701	8	30	175
1700	7	25	175				

3557 3558

3557 Farthing. First issue

1695	10	35	225	1698	60	175	—
1696	9	30	200	1699	9	30	200
1697	9	30	200	1700	9	30	200

3558 Second issue. ℞. Date at end of legend

1698	25	75	400
1699	14	45	275

ANNE, 1702–14

The Act of Union of 1707, which effected the unification of the ancient kingdoms of England and Scotland into a single realm, resulted in a change in the royal arms—on the after-Union coinage the English lions and Scottish lion are emblazoned per pale on the top and bottom shields. After the Union the rose in the centre of the reverse of the gold coins is replaced by the Garter star.

Following a successful Anglo–Dutch expedition against Spain, bullion seized in Vigo Bay was sent to be minted into coin, and the coins made from this metal had the word VIGO placed below the queen's bust.

GOLD

Before Union with Scotland

3560 Five guineas

	F	VF	EF			F	VF	EF
	£	£	£			£	£	£
1705	1000	2250	6000	1706		950	2000	5500
3561 VIGO below bust, 1703						6000	15,000	43,000

3562   3564

3562 Guinea

	F	VF	EF			F	VF	EF
1702	175	550	1750	1706		275	700	2250
1705	275	675	2150	1707		325	800	2500
3563 VIGO below bust, 1703						3000	7000	—
3564 Half-guinea								
1702	225	550	1750	1705		225	550	1750
3565 VIGO below bust, 1703						2250	5000	—

After Union with Scotland. The shields on the reverse are changed

3566

		F	VF	EF
3566	**Five guineas.** Ordinary bust, 1706	850	1900	5000
3567	Narrower shields, tall narrow crowns, larger rev. letters, 1709 . .	950	2000	5500
3568	Broader shields			

1711	850	1900	5000	1714/3	850	1900	5000
1713	950	2000	5500				

	F £	VF £	EF £		F £	VF £	EF £
3569 Two guineas							
1709	400	950	2500	1713	400	950	2500
1711	400	950	2500	1714	450	1000	3000

3569   3574

	F £	VF £	EF £		F £	VF £	EF £
3570 Guinea. First bust							
1707	200	400	1100	1708		*Extremely rare*	
3571 — elephant and castle below, 1707					400	950	2500
3572 Second bust							
1707		*Extremely rare*		1709	200	425	1200
1708	180	375	1000				
3573 — elephant and castle below							
1708	350	900	2500	1709	325	800	2250
3574 Third bust							
1710	150	300	700	1713	150	275	650
1711	150	300	700	1714	150	275	650
1712	200	400	1100				
3575 Half-guinea							
1707	160	325	900	1711	135	260	700
1708	200	450	1200	1712	160	325	900
1709	135	275	750	1713	135	275	750
1710	120	260	700	1714	135	275	750

SILVER

Before Union with Scotland

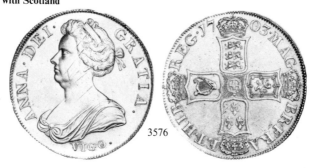

3576

	F	VF	EF		F	VF	EF
	£	£	£		£	£	£
3576	**Crown.** VIGO below bust, 1703				90	275	750
3577	R. Plumes in angles, 1705				150	450	1350
3578	R. Roses and plumes in angles						
	1706	70	225	600	1707	65	200	600
3579	**Halfcrown.** No marks below bust or on *rev.* (i.e. plain), 1703 . .				275	750	—
3580	VIGO below bust, 1703				25	80	275
3581	R. Plumes in angles						
	1704	45	150	400	1705	30	95	275
3582	R. Roses and plumes in angles						
	1706	25	80	250	1707	20	70	200

3583　　　　　　　　3589

3583	**Shilling.** First bust, 1702				30	90	225
3584	— R. Plumes in angles, 1702				30	100	275
3585	— VIGO below bust, 1702				30	100	275
3586	Second bust, VIGO below, 1703				20	60	150
3587	— plain						
	1704	165	400	—	1705	40	100	275
3588	— R. Plumes in angles						
	1704	40	120	300	1705	30	90	250
3589	— R. Roses and plumes in angles						
	1705	25	75	200	1707	30	85	225

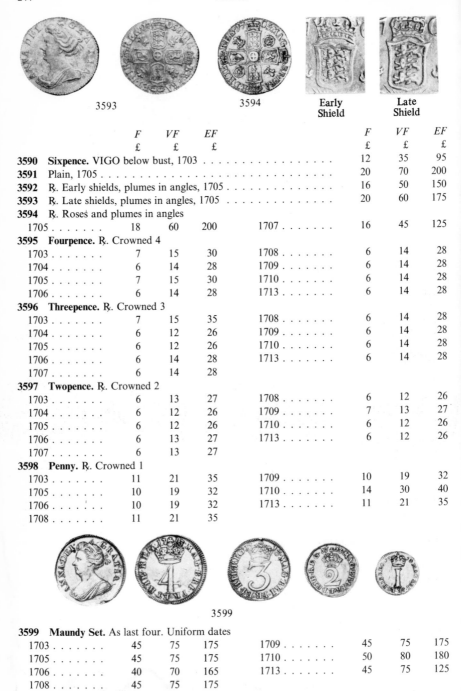

| | 3593 | | | 3594 | Early Shield | Late Shield |

		F £	VF £	EF £		F £	VF £	EF £
3590	Sixpence. VIGO below bust, 1703					12	35	95
3591	Plain, 1705					20	70	200
3592	℞. Early shields, plumes in angles, 1705					16	50	150
3593	℞. Late shields, plumes in angles, 1705					20	60	175
3594	℞. Roses and plumes in angles							
	1705	18	60	200	1707	16	45	125
3595	Fourpence. ℞. Crowned 4							
	1703	7	15	30	1708	6	14	28
	1704	6	14	28	1709	6	14	28
	1705	7	15	30	1710	6	14	28
	1706	6	14	28	1713	6	14	28
3596	Threepence. ℞. Crowned 3							
	1703	7	15	35	1708	6	14	28
	1704	6	12	26	1709	6	14	28
	1705	6	12	26	1710	6	14	28
	1706	6	14	28	1713	6	14	28
	1707	6	14	28				
3597	Twopence. ℞. Crowned 2							
	1703	6	13	27	1708	6	12	26
	1704	6	12	26	1709	7	13	27
	1705	6	12	26	1710	6	12	26
	1706	6	13	27	1713	6	12	26
	1707	6	13	27				
3598	Penny. ℞. Crowned 1							
	1703	11	21	35	1709	10	19	32
	1705	10	19	32	1710	14	30	40
	1706	10	19	32	1713	11	21	35
	1708	11	21	35				

3599

3599	Maundy Set. As last four. Uniform dates							
	1703	45	75	175	1709	45	75	175
	1705	45	75	175	1710	50	80	180
	1706	40	70	165	1713	45	75	125
	1708	45	75	175				

After Union with Scotland

The shields on reverse are changed. The Edinburgh coins have been included here as they are now coins of Great Britain.

3600

	F £	VF £	EF £		F £	VF £	EF £
3600 Crown. Second bust, E (Edinburgh) below							
1707	50	150	450	1708	50	165	500
3601 — plain							
1707	50	150	450	1708	50	150	450
3602 ℞. Plumes in angles, 1708					55	225	675
3603 Third bust. ℞. Roses and plumes, 1713					50	150	450

3604   3609

3604 Halfcrown. ℞. Plain							
1707	17	50	150	1709	18	55	165
1708	15	45	135	1713	20	60	180
3605 — E below bust							
1707	18	55	150	1709	65	225	675
1708	18	55	150				
3606 ℞. Plumes in angles, 1708					30	90	250
3607 ℞. Roses and plumes in angles							
1710	25	80	225	1713	25	80	225
1712	22	70	200	1714	22	70	200
3608 Shilling. Second bust, E below							
1707	18	50	150	1708	30	95	300
3609 — E* below							
1707	35	110	350	1708	20	60	175

Overstruck dates are listed only if commoner than normal date or if no normal date is known.

		F	VF	EF			F	VF	EF
		£	£	£			£	£	£

3610 Shilling. R̶. Third bust. Plain.

1707	12	35	90	1709	12	35	90
1708	8	25	75	1711	40	150	450

3611 — R̶. Plumes in angles

1707	22	60	175	1708	15	45	135

3612 — E below

1707	15	40	120	1708	25	80	250

3613 Second bust. R̶. Roses and plumes, 1708 . . . . 50 150 450

3614 Third bust. R̶. Roses and plumes

1708	25	70	200	1710	12	35	90

3615 — "Edinburgh" bust, E* below

1707		*Extremely rare*		1709	30	95	275
1708	25	80	250				

3616 — E below, 1709. . . . .   *Extremely rare*

3617 Fourth bust. R̶. Roses and plumes

1710	25	80	250	1713/2	15	50	150
1712	12	35	90	1714	12	35	90

3618 — plain, 1711 . . . . 8 20 60

3620

3623

3619 Sixpence. Normal bust. R̶. Plain

1707	9	22	65	1711	5	15	45
1708	10	30	90				

3620 — E below bust

1707	10	30	90	1708	12	40	120

3621 — E* below bust, 1708 . . . . 12 50 150

3622 "Edinburgh" bust, E* below, 1708. . . . . 15 55 165

3623 Normal bust. R̶. Plumes in angles

1707	11	35	95	1708	12	40	120

3624 — R̶. Roses and plumes in angles, 1710 . . . . 15 50 150

COPPER

3625

3625 Farthing, 1714 . . . . 75 150 350

GEORGE I, 1714–27

The coins of the first of the Hanoverian kings have the arms of the Duchy of Brunswick and Luneberg on one of the four shields, the object in the centre of the shield being the crown of Charlemagne. The king's German titles also appear, in abbreviated form, and name him "Duke of Brunswick and Luneberg. Arch-treasurer of the Holy Roman Empire, and Elector", and on the guinea of 1714, "Prince Elector". A quarter-guinea was struck for the first time in 1718, but it was an inconvenient size and the issue was discontinued.

Silver coined from bullion supplied to the mint by the South Sea Company in 1723 shows the company's initials S.S.C.; similarly Welsh Copper Company bullion has the letters W.C.C. below the king's bust and plumes and an interlinked CC on the reverse. Roses and plumes together on the reverse indicate silver supplied by the Company for Smelting Pit Coale and Sea Coale.

GOLD

3626 Five guineas

	F £	VF £	EF £		F £	VF £	EF £
1716	1000	2250	4750	1720	1250	2550	5000
1717	1250	2550	5000	1726	1000	2500	4750

3626

3627 Two guineas

1717	575	1000	3000	1726	475	950	2800
1720	575	1000	3000				

3627

3628

3628 Guinea. First head. ℞. Legend ends ET PR . EL (Prince Elector),
1714. . . . . 300 750 2000
3629 Second head, tie with two ends, 1715 . . . . 175 375 900
3630 Third head, no hair below truncation
1715 . . . . . . 150 300 850   1716 . . . . 200 450 1000

3633   3638

	F	VF	EF		F	VF	EF
	£	£	£		£	£	£

3631 Guinea. Fourth head, tie with loop at one end

1716	150	300	850	1720	150	300	850
1717	175	350	1000	1721	175	400	1000
1718		*Extremely rare*		1722	150	300	850
1719	150	300	850	1723	175	400	1000

3632 — elephant and castle below

| 1721 | | *Extremely rare* | | 1722 | | *Extremely rare* | |

3633 Fifth (older) head, tie with two ends

1723	200	400	1000	1726	150	350	800
1724	200	400	1000	1727	225	500	1350
1725	200	400	1000				

3634 — elephant and castle below, 1726 . . . . 500 1200 —

3635 Half-guinea. First head

1715	150	300	700	1721		*Extremely rare*	
1717	125	300	700	1722	125	300	700
1718	100	250	650	1723		*Extremely rare*	
1719	100	250	650	1724	175	400	775
1720	175	450	850				

3636 — elephant and castle below, 1721 . . . . *Extremely rare*

3637 Second (older) bust

| 1725 | 90 | 225 | 600 | 1727 | 100 | 300 | 700 |
| 1726 | 100 | 300 | 700 | | | | |

3638 Quarter-guinea, 1718 . . . . 35 85 165

SILVER

3639 Crown. ℞. Roses and plumes in angles

| 1716 | 115 | 250 | 850 | 1720/18 | 175 | 350 | 1100 |
| 1718/6 | 175 | 350 | 1100 | 1726 | 125 | 300 | 950 |

3639

	F	VF	EF		F	VF	EF
	£	£	£		£	£	£
3640 R̥. SSC (South Sea Company) in angles, 1723.					125	300	950
3641 Halfcrown. Plain (proof only), 1715 *FDC* £4000							
3642 R̥. Roses and plumes in angles							
1715	45	150	500	1720/17	45	150	500
1717	45	150	500				

3643

	F	VF	EF		F	VF	EF
3643 R̥. SSC in angles, 1723					45	140	450
3644 R̥. Small roses and plumes, 1726					600	1400	—
3645 Shilling. First bust. R̥. Roses and plumes							
1715	15	45	140	1720	15	45	140
1716	30	120	325	1721/0	18	55	175
1717	15	45	140	1722	15	45	140
1718	15	40	135	1723	15	45	140
1719	30	120	325				
3646 — plain (i.e. no marks either side)							
1720	15	45	140	1721	55	200	500
3647 R̥. SSC in angles, 1723					9	25	75
3648 Second bust, bow to tie. R̥. Similar, 1723					15	45	135

3647 3650

	F	VF	EF		F	VF	EF
3649 — R̥. Roses and plumes							
1723	18	50	150	1726	110	350	1100
1724	18	50	150	1727	90	300	850
1725	18	50	150				
3650 — W.C.C. (Welsh Copper Company) below							
1723	90	300	850	1725	90	325	90J
1724	90	325	900	1726	90	325	900
3651 Sixpence. R̥. Roses and plumes in angles							
1717	25	75	175	1720/17	25	75	175
3652 R̥. SSC in angles, 1723					5	20	65
3653 R̥. Small roses and plumes, 1726					20	50	150

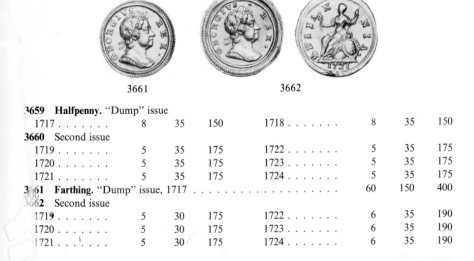

3654   3655   3656   3657

	F £	VF £	EF £		F £	VF £	EF £
3654 Fourpence							
1717	8	18	36	1723	9	18	36
1721	8	18	36	1727	10	19	38
3655 Threepence							
1717	8	19	33	1723	10	20	35
1721	9	20	35	1727	10	20	35
3656 Twopence							
1717	5	10	22	1726	5	9	20
1721	5	9	20	1727	5	10	22
1723	6	10	22				
3657 Penny							
1716	3	7	16	1725	3	6	15
1718	3	7	16	1726	5	10	20
1720	3	7	16	1727	5	10	20
1723	5	7	16				
3658 Maundy Set. As last four. Uniform dates							
1723	40	95	175	1727	40	95	175

COPPER

3661   3662

	F	VF	EF		F	VF	EF
3659 Halfpenny. "Dump" issue							
1717	8	35	150	1718	8	35	150
3660 Second issue							
1719	5	35	175	1722	5	35	175
1720	5	35	175	1723	5	35	175
1721	5	35	175	1724	5	35	175
3661 Farthing. "Dump" issue, 1717	60	150	400				
3662 Second issue							
1719	5	30	175	1722	6	35	190
1720	5	30	175	1723	6	35	190
1721	5	30	175	1724	6	35	190

GEORGE II, 1727–60

Silver was coined only spasmodically by the Mint during this reign and no copper was struck after 1754. Gold coins made from bullion supplied by the East India Company bear the company's initials; some of the treasure seized by Admiral Anson during his circumnavigation of the globe, 1740–4, and by other privateers, was made into coin which had the word LIMA below the king's bust to celebrate the expedition's successful harassment of the Spanish colonies in the New World. Hammered gold was finally demonetized in 1733.

GOLD

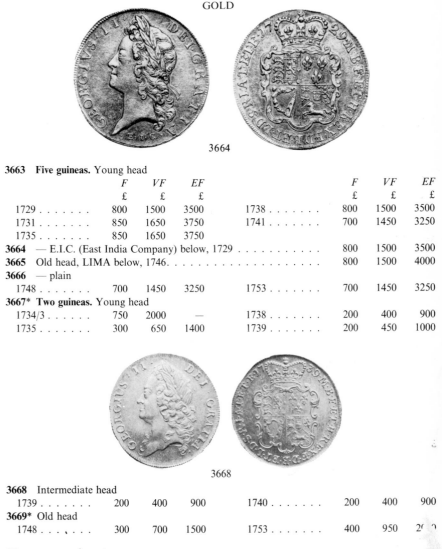

3664

3663 Five guineas. Young head

	F	VF	EF		F	VF	EF
	£	£	£		£	£	£
1729	800	1500	3500	1738	800	1500	3500
1731	850	1650	3750	1741	700	1450	3250
1735	850	1650	3750				

3664 — E.I.C. (East India Company) below, 1729	800	1500	3500
3665 Old head, LIMA below, 1746.	800	1500	4000

3666 — plain

	F	VF	EF		F	VF	EF
1748	700	1450	3250	1753	700	1450	3250

3667* **Two guineas.** Young head

	F	VF	EF		F	VF	EF
1734/3	750	2000	—	1738	200	400	900
1735	300	650	1400	1739	200	450	1000

3668

3668 Intermediate head

	F	VF	EF		F	VF	EF
1739	200	400	900	1740	200	400	900

3669* Old head

	F	VF	EF		F	VF	EF
1748 . . . . , . . .	300	700	1500	1753	400	950	2⁰ ⁰

*Beware recent forgeries.

Overstruck dates are listed only if commoner than normal date or if no normal date is known.

		3671			3674		
	F	**VF**	**EF**		**F**	**VF**	**EF**
	£	**£**	**£**		**£**	**£**	**£**
3670 Guinea. First young head, small lettering, 1727	350	1000	2200				
3671 — larger lettering, smaller shield							
1727	250	650	1500	1728	300	700	1650
3672 Second (narrower) young head							
1729 *proof only FDC* £3600				1731	160	400	1250
1730	200	400	1500	1732	200	500	1500
3673 — E.I.C. below							
1729	350	900	2500	1732	250	600	1650
1731	250	600	1650				
3674 — larger lettering on *obv.*							
1732	225	500	1450	1736	180	450	1250
1733	150	375	950	1737	200	500	1450
1734	150	375	950	1738	180	450	1250
1735	160	350	1100				
3675 — — E.I.C. below, 1732	300	700	1750				
3676 Intermediate head							
1739	150	375	900	1741/39	*Extremely rare*		
1740	160	450	1250	1743*	*Extremely rare*		
3677 — E.I.C. below, 1739	300	700	1750				
3678 — larger lettering on *obv.*							
1745	225	500	1450	1746	200	450	1000
3679 — LIMA below, 1745	275	500	1300				
3680 Old head							
1747	150	350	800	1753	125	300	700
1748	125	300	700	1755	175	375	850
1749	125	300	700	1756	125	275	650
1750	150	350	700	1758	115	250	600
1751	125	300	650	1759	115	250	600
1752	125	300	650	1760	120	275	650

3681   3679   3685

A very fine specimen sold at auction in March 1990 for £3300 plus 10% buyer's premium.

	F £	VF £	EF £		F £	VF £	EF £

3681 Half-guinea. Young head

1728	150	375	900	1734	120	350	800
1729	120	400	1000	1735			*? exists*
1730		*Extremely rare*		1736	120	400	1000
1731	200	600	1500	1737		*Extremely rare*	
1732	150	425	1100	1738	110	325	800
1733			*? exists*	1739	110	325	800

3682 — E.I.C. below

1729	250	500	1500	1732		*Extremely rare*	
1730	300	1000	—	1739		*Extremely rare*	
1731		*Extremely rare*					

3683 Intermediate head

1740	200	600	1500	1745	200	600	1500
1743			*? Unique*	1746	120	350	750

3684 — LIMA below, 1745. .... 350 | 900 | 1850

3685 Old head

1747	160	500	1200	1753	100	250	500
1748	130	300	625	1755	100	250	450
1749		*Extremely rare*		1756	90	225	450
1750	110	275	550	1758	90	225	450
1751	120	325	700	1759	80	175	400
1752	120	325	700	1760	80	175	400

SILVER

3686 Crown. Young bust. R̸. Roses and plumes in angles

1732	80	200	500	1735	80	200	500
1734	110	275	650	1736	90	225	550

3686

3687 — R̸. Roses in angles

1739	80	200	500	1741	80	200	500

3688 Old head. R̸. Roses in angles, 1743. .... 80 | 200 | 500

3689 — LIMA below, 1746. .... 80 | 200 | 500

3690 — Plain (i.e. no marks either side)
1746 *proof only FDC* £1750

1750	100	275	650	1751	135	325	750

3692

	F £	VF £	EF £		F £	VF £	EF £
3691 Halfcrown. Young bust Ŗ. plain (proof only), 1731 *FDC* £1800							
3692 — Ŗ. Roses and plumes							
1731	25	80	275	1735	30	90	325
1732	25	80	275	1736	35	125	400
1734	30	90	325				
3693 — Ŗ. Roses							
1739	22	70	225	1741	22	75	300
3694 Old bust. Ŗ. Roses							
1743	20	65	200	1745	20	65	200
3695 — LIMA below							
1745	18	45	135	1746	18	45	135
3696 — Ŗ. Plain							
1746 *proof only FDC* £700							
1750	35	130	350	1751	50	175	500
3697 Shilling. Young bust. Ŗ. Plumes							
1727	35	100	300	1731	50	175	450
3698 — Ŗ. Roses and plumes							
1727	20	50	135	1731	20	50	135
1728	30	75	175	1732	30	75	175
1729	30	75	175				
3699 — larger lettering. Ŗ. Roses and plumes							
1734	12	35	110	1736	12	35	110
1735	12	35	110	1737	12	35	110
3700 — Ŗ. plain, 1728.					40	150	400
3701 — Ŗ. Roses							
1739	10	35	85	1741	12	35	95
3702 Old bust. Ŗ. Roses							
1743	10	30	75	1747	12	35	100
1745	20	55	150				

3701　　　　　　　　　　　　　　3702

	F £	VF £	EF £		F £	VF £	EF £
3703 — LIMA below							
1745	10	30	75	1746	30	90	250
3704 — R̟. plain							
1746 *proof only* FDC £450				1751	30	90	200
1750	20	55	125	1758	4	12	35

3708   3710

	F	VF	EF		F	VF	EF
3705 Sixpence. Young bust. R̟. Plain, 1728					30	90	250
3706 — R̟. Plumes, 1728					25	70	175
3707 — R̟. Roses and plumes							
1728	12	32	90	1734	25	50	135
1731	12	32	90	1735	25	50	135
1732	12	32	90	1736	20	45	125
3708 — R̟. Roses							
1739	12	32	90	1741	12	32	90
3709 Old bust. R̟. Roses							
1743	12	32	90	1745	15	35	100
3710 — LIMA below							
1745	10	30	75	1746	7	20	50
3711 — plain							
1746 *proof only* FDC £325							
1750	20	50	145	1757	3	8	22
1751	25	75	200	1758	3	8	22
3712 Fourpence. Young head. R̟. Crowned 4							
1729	4	10	17	1739	4	10	17
1731	4	10	17	1740	4	10	17
1732	4	10	17	1743	4	10	17
1735	4	10	17	1746	4	10	17
1737	4	10	17	1760	4	10	17
3713 Threepence. Young head. R̟. Crowned 3							
1729	5	11	18	1739	5	11	18
1731	5	11	18	1740	5	11	18
1732	5	11	18	1743	5	11	18
1735	5	11	18	1746	5	11	18
1737	5	11	18	1760	5	11	18
3714 Twopence. Young head. R̟. Crowned 2							
1729	3	7	14	1740	4	9	16
1731	3	7	14	1743	3	7	14
1732	3	7	14	1746	3	7	14
1735	3	7	14	1756	3	7	14
1737	3	7	14	1759	3	7	14
1739	4	8	15	1760	3	7	14

3715 Penny. Young head. ℞. Crowned 1

	F £	VF £	EF £		F £	VF £	EF £
1729	3	5	10	1752	3	5	10
1731	3	5	10	1753	3	5	10
1732	3	5	10	1754	3	5	10
1735	3	5	10	1755	3	5	10
1737	3	5	10	1756	3	5	10
1739	3	5	10	1757	3	5	10
1740	3	5	10	1758	3	5	10
1743	3	5	10	1759	3	5	10
1746	3	5	10	1760	3	5	10
1750	3	5	10				

3716

3716 Maundy Set. As last four. Uniform dates

	F	VF	EF		F	VF	EF
1729	30	60	120	1739	28	55	100
1731	30	60	120	1740	28	55	110
1732	28	55	110	1743	28	55	110
1735	28	55	110	1746	28	55	110
1737	28	55	110	1760	30	60	120

COPPER

3717

3717 Halfpenny. Young bust

	F	VF	EF		F	VF	EF
1729	5	25	95	1735	5	25	95
1730	5	25	95	1736	5	25	95
1731	5	25	95	1737	5	25	95
1732	5	25	95	1738	4	22	85
1733	5	25	95	1739	5	25	95
1734	5	25	95				

	F £	VF £	EF £		F £	VF £	EF £
3718 Old bust, GEORGIUS							
1740	4	20	80	1744	4	18	70
1742	4	20	80	1745	4	18	70
1743	4	18	70				
3719 — GEORGIVS							
1746	4	20	80	1751	4	18	70
1747	4	20	80	1752	4	18	70
1748	4	18	70	1753	4	18	70
1749	4	18	70	1754	4	18	70
1750	4	18	70				

3720

3722

	F £	VF £	EF £		F £	VF £	EF £
3720 **Farthing.** Young bust							
1730	5	25	85	1735	4	20	75
1731	5	25	85	1736	5	25	85
1732	6	30	90	1737	4	20	75
1733	5	25	85	1739	4	20	75
1734	6	30	90				
3721 Old bust. GEORGIUS							
1741	5	30	100	1744	5	30	100
3722 — GEORGIVS							
1746	4	18	65	1750	5	25	85
1749	5	22	70	1754	1	10	35

GEORGE III, 1760–1820

During the second half of the 18th century very little silver or copper was minted. In 1797 Matthew Boulton's "cartwheels", the first copper pennies and twopences, demonstrated the improvement from the application of steam power to the coining press.

During the Napoleonic Wars bank notes came into general use when the issue of guineas was stopped between 1797 and 1813, but gold 7s. pieces were minted to relieve the shortage of smaller money. As an emergency measure Spanish "dollars" were put into circulation for a short period after being countermarked, and in 1804 Spanish dollars were overstruck and issued as Bank of England dollars.

The transition to a "token" silver coinage began in 1811 when the Bank of England had 3s. and 1s. 6d. tokens made for general circulation. Private issues of token money in the years 1788–95 and 1811–15 helped to alleviate the shortage of regal coinage. A change over to a gold standard and a regular "token" silver coinage came in 1816 when the Mint, which was moved from its old quarters in the Tower of London to a new site on Tower Hill, began a complete re-coinage. The guinea was replaced by a 20s. sovereign, and silver coins were made which had an intrinsic value lower than their face value. The St. George design used on the sovereign and crown was the work of Benedetto Pistrucci.

Early coinages

GOLD

3724

3723	**Five guineas.** Pattern only			
	1770 *FDC* £62,000		1777 *FDC* £62,000	
	1773 *FDC* £62,000			
3724	**Two guineas.** Pattern only			
	1768 *FDC* £22,000		1777 *FDC* £22,000	
	1773 *FDC* £22,000			

There are different bust varieties for 3723 and 3724, for further details see Douglas-Morris, November 1974, lots 127–132.

		F	VF	EF
		£	£	£
3725	**Guinea.** First head, 1761 (also with three leaves at top of wreath).	375	850	2500

| 3725 | | | 3726 | | | 3727 | | |

| 3726 | Second head | | | | | | | |
| | 1763 . . . . . . | 250 | 650 | 1250 | 1764 . . . . . . | 200 | 550 | 1000 |

	F £	VF £	EF £			F £	VF £	EF £
3727 Third head								
1765	110	225	450	1770		120	250	475
1766	85	175	325	1771		100	200	425
1767	125	250	525	1772		85	175	325
1768	100	200	400	1773		85	175	325
1769	100	200	400					
3728 Fourth head								
1774	75	150	300	1781		85	175	350
1775	75	150	300	1782		85	175	350
1776	75	150	300	1783		85	175	350
1777	75	150	300	1784		85	175	350
1778	95	190	375	1785		75	150	300
1779	85	175	350	1786		75	150	300

3728

3729

3729 Fifth head. R. "Spade"-shaped shield

	F £	VF £	EF £			F £	VF £	EF £
1787	75	130	250	1794		75	130	250
1788	75	130	250	1795		100	175	400
1789	75	135	275	1796		100	175	400
1790	75	130	250	1797		80	140	275
1791	75	130	250	1798*		75	130	250
1792	75	135	250	1799		90	150	350
1793	75	130	250	*Beware counterfeits*				

3730 Sixth head. R. Shield in Garter, known as the Military guinea, 1813 . . .   350   600

3730

3731 Half-guinea. First head

	F £	VF £	EF £			F £	VF £	EF £
1762	150	400	1200	1763		200	600	1350
3732 Second head								
1764	90	225	475	1772		*Extremely rare*		
1765/4	250	600	—	1773		110	275	575
1766	100	250	500	1774		175	400	1200
1768	110	275	575	1775		175	400	1200
1769	100	250	500					

3733   3734   3737

	F £	VF £	EF £		F £	VF £	EF £
3733 Half-guinea Third head (less fine style)							
1774		*Extremely rare*		1775	175	450	1250
3734 Fourth head							
1775	70	135	275	1781	80	140	300
1776	70	135	275	1783	300	800	—
1777	65	120	250	1784	70	135	275
1778	80	140	300	1785	65	120	250
1779	95	200	500	1786	65	120	250
3735 Fifth head. ℞. "Spade" type							
1787	60	115	225	1794	60	125	250
1788	60	115	225	1795	80	175	300
1789	65	125	250	1796	65	125	250
1790	60	115	225	1797	60	115	225
1791	65	125	250	1798	60	115	225
1792	350	850	—	1800	125	350	—
1793	60	115	225				
3736 Sixth head. ℞. Shield in Garter							
1801	45	60	125	1803	45	65	135
1802	45	65	135				
3737 Seventh head. Hd. with short hair. ℞. As last							
1804	45	60	125	1809	45	65	135
1805		*Extremely rare*		1810	45	65	135
1806	45	65	135	1811	75	150	350
1808	45	65	135	1813	65	135	275

3738   3740   3741

	F	VF	EF		F	VF	EF
3738 Third-guinea. I. First head							
1797	30	50	115	1799	35	70	175
1798	30	50	115	1800	30	50	115
3739 II. Similar but date not in legend							
1801	30	50	120	1803	30	50	120
1802	30	50	120				

	F	VF	EF		F	VF	EF
	£	£	£		£	£	£

3740 III. Second head with short hair

1804	30	50	120	1810	30	50	120
1806	30	50	120	1811	125	300	650
1808	30	50	120	1813	75	150	300
1809	30	50	120				

3741 **Quarter-guinea,** 1762 35   75   150

For gold of the "new coinage", 1817–20, see page 268.

SILVER

3742

3742 **Shilling.** Young bust, known as the "Northumberland" shilling,
1763.   100   175   350

3743 Older bust, no semée of hearts in the Hanoverian shield, 1787. .   3   6   30

3744 — — no stop over head, 1787   5   10   40

3745 — — no stops at date, 1787   5   10   45

3745A — — no stops on *obv.,* 1787   30   100   250

3746   no hearts   with hearts

3746 — with semée of hearts, 1787.   3   6   30

3747 — no stop over head, 1798: known as the "Dorrien and Magens" shilling   *UNC*   £3250

3748 **Sixpence.** Without hearts, 1787.   2   5   20

3749 — with hearts, 1787   2   5   22

3750 **Fourpence.** Young bust

1763	3	8	16	1776	4	8	16
1765	100	250	650	1780	4	8	16
1766	5	9	17	1784	5	9	17
1770	5	9	17	1786	5	9	17
1772	5	9	17				

3751 Older bust. R̝. Thin 4 ("Wire Money"), 1792   7   15   3(

3752 — R̝. Normal 4

1795	3	7	15	1800	3	7	15

3750   3751   3755

3753   Threepence. Young bust

	F	VF	EF		F	VF	EF
	£	£	£		£	£	£
1762	2	5	9	1772	3	6	14
1763	2	5	9	1780	3	6	14
1765	100	250	500	1784	3	7	15
1766	3	6	14	1786	3	6	14
1770	3	6	14				

3754   Older bust. ℞. Thin 3 ("Wire Money"), 1792   7   15   30

3755   — ℞. Normal 3

1795	3	7	14	1800	3	7	14

3756   Twopence. Young bust

1763	2	5	11	1776	2	5	11
1765	75	175	450	1780	2	5	11
1766	2	5	11	1784	2	5	11
1772	2	5	11	1786	2	5	11

3757   Older bust. ℞. Thin 2 ("Wire Money"), 1792   5   12   25

3758   — ℞. Normal 2

1795	2	4	7	1800	2	4	7

3759   Penny. Young bust

1763	2	5	11	1779	2	5	10
1766	2	5	10	1780	2	5	11
1770	2	5	10	1781	2	5	10
1772	2	5	10	1784	2	5	10
1776	2	5	11	1786	2	5	10

3760   Older bust. ℞. Thin 1 ("Wire Money"), 1792   2   5   8

3761   — ℞. Normal 1

1795	1	2	6	1800	1	2	6

3762   Maundy Set. Uniform dates

1763	26	45	115	1780	26	45	115
1766	26	45	115	1784	26	45	115
1772	26	45	115	1786	26	45	115

3763   — Older bust. ℞. Thin numerals ("Wire Money"), 1792   50   80   175

3764   — ℞. Normal numerals. Uniform dates

1795	20	35	80	1800	20	35	75

Emergency issue

3765   Dollar (current for 4s. 9d.). Spanish American 8 *reales* countermarked with head of George III in oval   50   125   250

3766   — octagonal countermark   75   150   350

3767   Half-dollar with similar oval countermark   60   135   300

| 3765 | 3767 | 3766 |

Bank of England issue

3768

	F	*VF*	*EF*
	£	£	£

3768 Dollar (current for 5s.). Laureate bust of king. ℞. Britannia seated
l., 1804   35   70   175

*These dollars were re-struck from Spanish–American 8 reales until at least 1811. Dollars that show
dates of original coin are worth rather more.*

3769

3769 Three shillings. Draped bust in armour. ℞. BANK / TOKEN / 3 SHILL / date (in oak
wreath)

	F	*VF*	*EF*				
	£	£	£				
1811	8	15	45	1812	9	16	50

	F	VF	EF			F	VF	EF
	£	£	£			£	£	£

3770 Three shillings. Laureate head r. ℞. As before but wreath of oak and laurel

	F	VF	EF			F	VF	EF
1812	8	15	45	1815		8	15	45
1813	8	15	45	1816		90	175	450
1814	8	15	45					

3771   3772

3771 Eighteen pence. Draped bust in armour

	F	VF	EF			F	VF	EF
1811	5	12	35	1812		5	12	35

3772 — Laureate head

	F	VF	EF			F	VF	EF
1812	4	11	30	1815		4	11	30
1813	4	11	30	1816		4	11	30
1814	4	11	30					

3773 Ninepence. Similar, 1812 (pattern only)   *FDC*   £900

For the last or "new coinage", 1816–20, see page 268.

COPPER

First issue—London

3774

3774 Halfpenny. Cuirassed bust r. ℞. Britannia

	F	VF	EF			F	VF	EF
1770	3	12	60	1773		2	10	55
1771	2	10	55	1774		3	12	60
1772	2	10	55	1775		3	15	65

3775

3775 Farthing

	F	VF	EF			F	VF	EF
1771	15	35	110	1774		3	12	65
1773	2	8	50	1775		4	15	70

Second issue—Soho mint. "Cartwheel" coinage

3776

	F	VF	EF
	£	£	£
3776 Twopence. Legends incuse on raised rim, 1797	7	18	90
3777 Penny, 1797. Similar.	6	15	55

Halfpence and farthings of this issue are patterns.

Third issue—Soho mint

3778

3778 Halfpenny. Draped bust r., 1799	3	30
3779 Farthing, 1799	3	30

Fourth issue—Soho mint

3780   3782

3780 Penny. Different bust							
1806	1	4	50	1807	1	6	55
3781 Halfpenny							
1806		2	30	1807		3	40
3782 Farthing							
1806		2	30	1807		3	40

EIGHTEENTH-CENTURY TOKENS

In 1787 the regal copper coinage was very scanty, and so pennies and halfpennies were struck by the Anglesey Copper Mining Company and a fresh token epoch began. They present an immense variety of types, persons, buildings, coats of arms, local legends, political events, etc., all drawn upon for subjects of design. They were struck by many firms in most cities and towns in the country and are to be found in good condition. Circulated specimens are so common that they have little value.

For further details of 18th-century tokens see *The Provincial Token-Coinage of the Eighteenth Century*, by Dalton and Hamer, and Seaby's *British Tokens and Their Values*.

	VF	EF
	£	£
Price of commoner pennies	5	14
— — — halfpennies	4	11
— — — farthings.	3	9

Bury St. Edmunds penny

Coventry halfpenny

Isaac Newton farthing

NINETEENTH-CENTURY TOKENS

With the issue of the copper coinage of 1797 tokens were made illegal, but the dearth of silver currency was still felt. During the Napoleonic wars, a small wave of prosperity in the industrial districts brought the inevitable need for small change, so in 1811 tokens again made their appearance. On this occasion silver ones were made as well as copper. These, with two exceptions, were suppressed before the last coinage of George III.

For further details of 19th-century silver tokens see *The Nineteenth Century Token Coinage* by W. J. Davis and *Silver Token-Coinage 1811–1812*, by R. Dalton, also Seaby's *British Tokens and Their Values*.

	VF	EF
	£	£
Price of the commoner five shillings	350	700
— — — four shillings	125	250
— — — three shillings	135	275
— — — halfcrowns	60	120
— — — two shillings	55	110
— — — eighteen pence	20	40
— — — shillings	11	22
— — — sixpences	10	20

Newcastle Shilling   Charing Cross Sixpence

	VF	EF
	£	£
Price of the commoner threepences	25	125
— — — twopences	12	50
— — — pennies	3	13
— — — halfpennies	2	8
— — — farthings	2	9

Withymoor Scythe Works Penny, 1813

GEORGE III

Last or new coinage, 1816–20

The year 1816 is a landmark in the history of our coinage. For some years at the beginning of the 19th century, Mint production was virtually confined to small gold denominations, regular full production being resumed only after the Mint had been moved from the Tower of London to a new site on Tower Hill. Steam-powered minting machinery made by Boulton and Watt replaced the old hand-operated presses and these produced coins which were technically much superior to the older milled coins.

In 1816 for the first time British silver coins were produced with an intrinsic value substantially below their face value, the first official token coinage.

Our present "silver" coins are made to the same weight standard and are still legal tender back to 1816 with the exception of the halfcrown. The old guinea was replaced by a sovereign of twenty shillings in 1817, the standard of 22 carat (.916) fineness still being retained.

Engraver's and/or designer's initials:
B.P. (Benedetto Pistrucci)

GOLD

3783

3783* **Five pounds,** 1820 (Pattern only)   *FDC..... Extremely rare*
A Brilliant mint-state specimen sold at auction in November 1989 for £47,500 plus 10% buyer's premium.

3784 **Two pounds,** 1820 (Pattern only)   *FDC.....* £12,000

3785 **Sovereign.** Coarse hair, legend type A (Descending colon after BRITANNIAR, no space between REX and F:D:). ℞. St. George

	F	VF	EF		F	VF	EF
	£	£	£		£	£	£
1817	75	125	375	1819	*Extremely rare*		
1818	85	150	450				

3785A — legend type B (Ascending colon after BRITANNIAR, space between REX and F:D:)
1818   85   150   450

3785B Wiry curls, legend type A.
1818 . . . .   *Extremely Rare*

3785C — legend type B.
1818 . . . .   *Extremely Rare*   1820   75   125   375

3785   3785A   3786

* Beware counterfeits.

	F £	VF £	EF £		F £	VF £	EF £
3786 Half-sovereign. ℞. Crowned shield							
1817	50	85	175	1820	55	90	200
1818	55	90	200				

SILVER

3787

3787 Crown. Laureate head r. ℞. Pistrucci's St. George and dragon within Garter

	F £	VF £	EF £
1818, edge LVIII	9	25	115
— — LIX	10	30	120
1819 — LIX	9	25	115
— — LX	10	30	120
1820 — LX	9	25	115

3788

3788 Halfcrown. Large or "bull" head

1816	6	18	80	1817	6	18	80

3789

	F £	VF £	EF £		F £	VF £	EF £
3789 Halfcrown. Small head							
1817	6	18	80	1819	7	20	90
1818	7	20	90	1820	9	28	130

3790   3791

	F £	VF £	EF £		F £	VF £	EF £
3790 Shilling. R. Shield in Garter							
1816	2	6	25				
1817	3	7	30	1819	3	7	30
1818	7	20	85	1820	3	7	30
3791 Sixpence. R. Shield in Garter							
1816	2	5	22	1819	3	7	30
1817	2	6	25	1820	3	7	30
1818	3	7	30				

3792

3792 Maundy Set (4d., 3d., 2d. and 1d.)	EF £	FDC £		EF £	FDC £
1817	80	150	1820	80	150
1818	80	150			
3793 — **fourpence,** 1817, 1818, 1820 . . . . *from*				14	30
3794 — **threepence,** 1817, 1818, 1820. *from*				14	30
3795 — **twopence,** 1817, 1818, 1820 . . . . *from*				8	13
3796 — **penny,** 1817, 1818, 1820 . . . . *from*				7	11

GEORGE IV, 1820–30

The Mint resumed the coinage of copper farthings in 1821, and pennies and halfpennies in 1825. A gold two pound piece was first issued for general circulation in 1823.

Engraver's and/or designer's initials:
B. P. (Benedetto Pistrucci)
J. B. M. (Jean Baptiste Merlen)

GOLD

3797

3797 **Five pounds,** 1826 (proof only). R. Shield . . . . *FDC* £8000

3798

	VF £	EF £
3798 **Two pounds,** 1823. Large bare head. R. St. George	275	550
3799 1826. Type as 3797 (proof only)	*FDC*	£2750

3800

3800 **Sovereign.** Laureate head. R. St. George

	F £	VF £	EF £		F £	VF £	EF £
1821	75	140	375	1824	75	140	400
1822*	75	140	400	1825	100	275	1000
1823	110	300	1100				

* *Beware counterfeits.*

3801

	F £	VF £	EF £		F £	VF £	EF £

3801 Sovereign. Bare head. ℞. Crowned shield

1825	75	135	350	1828*	500	1500	2750
1826	75	135	350	1829	85	140	375
— Proof *FDC* £1500				1830	85	140	375
1827*	85	140	375				

3802   3803   3804

3802 Half-sovereign. Laureate head. ℞. Ornately garnished shield.

| 1821 | 175 | 375 | 1000 |

3803 — ℞. Plain shield

| 1823 | 65 | 125 | 350 | 1825 | 60 | 110 | 300 |
| 1824 | 60 | 120 | 325 | | | | |

3804 — Bare head. ℞. Garnished shield

| 1826 | 60 | 110 | 300 | 1827 | 60 | 110 | 300 |
| — Proof *FDC* £875 | | | | 1828 | 55 | 100 | 250 |

Beware counterfeits

SILVER

3805

3805 Crown. Laureate head. ℞. St. George

1821, edge SECUNDO	12	40	250
1822 — SECUNDO	15	50	325
— — TERTIO	14	45	275

3806

3806 Crown. Bare head. R. Shield with crest (proof only), 1826   *FDC*   £2250

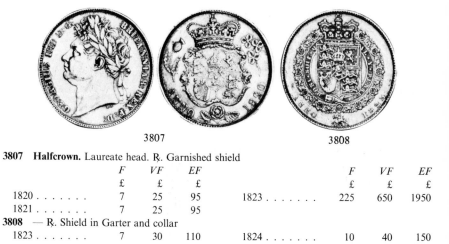

3807   3808

3807 Halfcrown. Laureate head. R. Garnished shield

	F	VF	EF		F	VF	EF
	£	£	£		£	£	£
1820	7	25	95	1823	225	650	1950
1821	7	25	95				

3808 — R. Shield in Garter and collar

1823	7	30	110	1824	10	40	150

3809

3809 Bare head. R. Shield with crest

1824		*Extremely rare*		1826 Proof *FDC* £400			
1825	7	25	85	1828	12	40	175
1826	6	22	80	1829	10	35	150

	3810	3811	3812

	F £	VF £	EF £		F £	VF £	EF £
3810 Shilling. Laureate head. ℞. Garnished shield							
1821	5	15	60				
3811 — ℞. Shield in Garter							
1823	12	40	150	1825	5	18	75
1824	5	18	75				
3812 Bare head. ℞. Lion on crown							
1825	3	9	40	1827	8	30	110
1826	3	8	35	1829	6	20	80
— Proof *FDC* £200							

	3813	3814	3815

	F £	VF £	EF £		F £	VF £	EF £
3813 Sixpence. Laureate head. ℞. Garnished shield							
1821	3	10	45				
3814 — ℞. Shield in Garter							
1824	3	10	45	1826	15	40	140
1825	3	10	45				
3815 Bare head. ℞. Lion on crown							
1826	3	8	30	1828	4	15	60
— Proof *FDC* £110				1829	3	10	45
1827	8	30	100				

3816

3816 Maundy Set (4d., 3d., 2d. and 1d.)	EF £	FDC £		EF £	FDC £
1822	65	125	1827	55	105
1823	55	105	1828	55	105
1824	60	115	1829	55	105
1825	55	105	1830	55	105
1826	55	105			

			EF	FDC
			£	£
3817	**Maundy fourpence,** 1822–30. *from*	11	18
3818	— **threepence,** small head, 1822.		20	35
3819	— — normal head, 1823–30 . . . . *from*	10	17
3820	— **twopence,** 1822–30 . . . . *from*	8	10
3821	— **penny,** 1822–30 . . . . *from*	5	8

COPPER

First issue, 1821–6

3822

		F	VF	EF			F	VF	EF
		£	£	£			£	£	£
3822	**Farthing.** Laureate bust, draped								
	1821		4	20		1825		4	18
	1822		4	18		1826	1	6	30
	1823		4	22					

Second issue, 1825–30

3826

3823   3827

3823	**Penny.** Laureate head. R. Britannia								
	1825	4	12	50	1826 Proof *FDC* £200				
	1826	4	10	40	1827	25	80	900
3824	**Halfpenny.** Similar								
	1825	9	25	90	1826 Proof *FDC* £100				
	1826		5	24	1827	3	8	40
3825	**Farthing.** Similar								
	1826		3	15	1828		4	20
	— Proof *FDC* £100				1829		6	35
	1827		5	25	1830		4	20
3826	**Half-farthing** (for use in Ceylon). Similar								
	1828	4	12	45	1830	4	12	45
3827	**Third-farthing** (for use in Malta). Similar								
	1827		3	15					

WILLIAM IV, 1830–7

In order to prevent confusion between the sixpence and half-sovereign the size of the latter was reduced in 1834, but the smaller gold piece was not acceptable to the public and in the following year it was made to the normal size. In 1836 the silver groat was again issued for general circulation: it is the only British silver coin which has a seated Britannia as the type. Crowns were not struck during this reign for general circulation; but proofs or patterns of this denomination were made and are greatly sought after. Silver threepences and three-halfpence were minted for use in the Colonies.

Engraver's and/or designer's initials:
W. W. (William Wyon)   GOLD

3828

3828 Two pounds, 1831 (proof only) . . . .   *FDC*   £5000

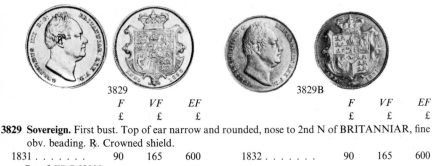

3829   3829B

	F £	VF £	EF £			F £	VF £	EF £

3829 Sovereign. First bust. Top of ear narrow and rounded, nose to 2nd N of BRITANNIAR, fine obv. beading. R. Crowned shield.

1831	90	165	600		1832	90	165	600

— Proof *FDC* £2000

3829A — — W W without stops
1831 . . . .   *Extremely rare*

3829B Second bust. Top of ear broad and flat, nose to 2nd I in BRITANNIAR, coarser obv. beading.

1832	85	150	425		1836	85	150	425
1833	85	150	425		1837	85	150	500
1835	85	150	450					

3830   3831

3830 Half-sovereign. Small size

1831 Proof *FDC* £1250					1834	90	150	400

3831 Large size

1835	75	150	400		1837	90	165	450
1836	100	225	500					

3832 *Obv.* struck from 6d. die, 1836   500   950   2000

SILVER

3833

3833 **Crown.** ℞. Shield on mantle, 1831 (proof only) . . . . *FDC* £3500

3834

	F £	VF £	EF £		F £	VF £	EF £
3834 **Halfcrown.** ℞. Shield on mantle							
1831 Proof *FDC* £400				1836	9	30	125
1834	8	25	95	1837	12	50	200
1835	12	50	175				

3835   3836

3835 **Shilling.** ℞. Value in wreath
1831 Proof *FDC* £225				1836	5	18	80
1834	5	18	80	1837	7	30	125
1835	6	22	95				
3836 **Sixpence.** ℞. Value in wreath							
1831	3	9	40	1835	3	9	40
— Proof *FDC* £150				1836	6	20	90
1834	3	10	40	1837	4	18	80

3837

	F	VF	EF		F	VF	EF
	£	£	£		£	£	£

3837 Groat. ℞. Britannia seated

1836		3	16	1837		3	16

3838 Threepence (for use in the West Indies). As Maundy threepence but with a dull surface

1834	1	6	30	1836	1	5	28
1835	1	5	28	1837	2	7	36

3838

3839

3839 Three-halfpence (for Colonial use). ℞. Value

1834		3	16	1836		4	20
1835		3	18	1837	5	20	75

3840

3840 Maundy Set (4d., 3d., 2d. and 1d.).

	EF	FDC		EF	FDC
	£	£		£	£
1831	80	150	1834	75	140
— Proof *FDC* £250			1835	75	140
1832	75	140	1836	75	140
1833	75	140	1837	75	140
3841 — **fourpence,** 1831–7 . . . . *from*				11	20
3842 — **threepence,** 1831–7 . . . . *from*				20	30
3843 — **twopence,** 1831–7 . . . . *from*				7	13
3844 — **penny,** 1831–7 . . . . *from*				7	12

COPPER

3845

	F £	VF £	EF £		F £	VF £	EF £
3845 Penny. No initials on truncation							
1831	6	25	90	1834	7	30	100
— Proof *FDC* £225				1837	9	40	150
3846 WW on truncation, 1831					8	35	125
3847 Halfpenny. As penny							
1831	2	7	30	1834	2	7	35
— Proof *FDC* £125				1837	1	6	25
3848 Farthing. Similar							
1831		3	16	1835		3	16
— Proof *FDC* £120				1836		4	20
1834		3	16	1837		3	16

3847   3848

		F	VF	EF
3849 Half-farthing (for use in Ceylon). Similar				
1837		12	40	175
3850 Third-farthing (for use in Malta). Similar				
1835			3	15

3849   3850

VICTORIA, 1837–1901

In 1849, as a first step towards decimalization, a silver florin ($\frac{1}{10}$th pound) was introduced, but the coins of 1849 omitted the usual *Dei Gratia* and these so-called "Godless" florins were replaced in 1851 by the "Gothic" issue. The halfcrown was temporarily discontinued but was minted again from 1874 onwards. Between 1863 and 1880 reverse dies of the gold and silver coins were numbered in the course of Mint experiments into the wear of dies. The exception was the florin where the die number is on the obverse below the bust.

The gold and silver coins were redesigned for the Queen's Golden Jubilee in 1887. The double-florin which was then issued was abandoned after only four years; the Jubilee sixpence of 1887, known as the "withdrawn" type, was changed to avoid confusion with the half-sovereign. Gold and silver were again redesigned in 1893 with an older portrait of the Queen, but the "old head" was not used on the bronze coinage until 1895. The heavy copper penny had been replaced by the lighter bronze "bun" penny in 1860. In 1874–6 and 1881–2 some of the bronze was made by Heaton in Birmingham, and these have a letter H below the date. From 1897 farthings were issued with a dark surface.

Early sovereigns had a shield-type reverse, but Pistrucci's St. George design was used again from 1871. In order to increase the output of gold coinage, branches of the Royal Mint were set up in Australia at Sydney and Melbourne and, later, at Perth for coining gold of imperial type.

Engraver's and/or designer's initials:
W. W. (William Wyon)
L. C. W. (Leonard Charles Wyon)

J. E. B. (Joseph Boehm)
T. B. (Thomas Brock)

GOLD

Young head coinage, 1838–87

3851

3851 Five pounds. 1839. ℞. "Una and the lion" (proof only) . . . . . .   *FDC* £18,500

3852		3852C	3852D

	F	VF	EF		VF	EF
	£	£	£		£	£

3852 Sovereign. Type I, first (small) young head. R. First shield. London mint

1838	70	90	300	1844	60	140
1839	120	250	800	1845	60	150
— Proof *FDC* £2500				1846	60	150
1841	400	800	2500	1847	60	140
1842		60	140	1848	*Extremely rare*	
1843		60	140			

3852A* — narrower shield. Considerably modified floral emblems

1843	*Extremely rare*

3852B Type I, second (large) head. W W still in relief. R. Shield with repositioned legend

1848	60	140	1853	60	120
1849	60	140	1854	60	130
1850	60	160	1855	60	120
1851	60	130	1872	60	120
1852	60	120			

3852C — — W W incuse

1853	60	120	1858	60	160
— Proof *FDC* £4500			1859	60	130
1854	60	130	1860	60	120
1855	60	120	1861	60	120
1856	60	130	1862	60	120
1857	60	130	1863	60	120

3852D — — As 3852C "Ansell" ribbon. Additional raised line on the lower part of the ribbon

1859	150	350	1100

3852E — — As 3852C with 827 on truncation

1863	*Extremely rare*

3852B   3853

3853 — — As 3852C die number below wreath

1863	60	120	1868	60	120
1864	60	110	1869	60	110
1865	60	130	1870	70	160
1866	60	110			

3853A — — As 3853 with 827 on truncation (Always die no 22)

1863	*Extremely rare*

3853B — — W W in relief die number below wreath

1870	60	120	1873	60	120
1871	60	110	1874	1100	—
1872	60	110			

*A brilliant mint state specimen sold at auction in November 1989 for £3200 plus 10% buyers premium.

3854   3855

	VF £	EF £		VF £	EF £

3854 — — As 3853B but with M below wreath for Melbourne

1872 M	65	160	1882 M	65	160
1873 M	*Extremely rare*		1883 M	200	600
1874 M	65	160	1884 M	65	160
1879 M	*Extremely rare*		1885 M	65	160
1880 M	900	2750	1886 M	1600	3750
1881 M	70	225	1887 M	900	2500

3854A — — As 3853 W W incuse but with S below wreath for Sydney

| 1871 S . . . . . . | 60 | 90 | 200 |

3855 — — As 3854 but with S below wreath for Sydney

1871 S	60	160	1881 S	60	140
1872 S	60	160	1882 S	60	140
1873 S	60	160	1883 S	60	140
1875 S	60	140	1884 S	60	140
1877 S	60	140	1885 S	60	160
1878 S	60	140	1886 S	60	160
1879 S	60	140	1887 S	60	180
1880 S	60	140			

3856A

3856 Sovereign, type II, first young head. W W buried in narrow truncation.
℞. St. George. London mint. Horse with short tail. Large BP

| 1871. . . . . | 110 | | |

3856A — — As 3856 ℞. Horse with long tail. Small BP

1871.	90	1876.	90
1872.	90	1878.	100
1873.	100	1879. 150	500
1874.	110	1880.	90

3856B — — As 3856 but with small BP

| 1880. . . . . | 90 | 1885. . . . . | 110 |
| 1884. . . . . | 100 | | |

3856C — — As 3856 but no BP

| 1880. . . . . | 90 | | |

	VF	EF		VF	EF
	£	£		£	£

3856D — — Second head. W W on broad truncation. ℞. Horse with long tail, small BP
1880.   110
3856E — — As 3856D but horse with short tail. No BP
1880.   90
3856F — — As 3856E but small BP
1884.   100   1885.   110

3857   3858

3857 — — First head. W W buried in truncation, M below head for Melbourne mint. ℞. Horse with long tail, small BP

	VF	EF		VF	EF
1872 M	90	270	1877 M		95
1873 M		160	1878 M		95
1874 M		160	1879 M		115
1875 M		115	1880 M		95
1876 M		115	1881 M		95

3857A — — As 3857 but horse with short tail, no BP
| 1881 M . . . . | | 95 | 1882 M . . . . | | 95 |

3857B — — As 3857A but with small BP
| 1882 M . . . . | | 95 | 1884 M . . . . | | 95 |
| 1883 M . . . . | | 95 | 1885 M . . . . | | 95 |

3857C — — Second head. W W on broad truncation. ℞. Horse with short tail, small BP
1882 M		95	1885 M		95
1883 M		95	1886 M		95
1884 M		95	1887 M		95

3858 — — First head. W W buried in narrow truncation, S below head for Sydney mint. ℞. Horse with short tail, large BP
| 1871 S . . . . | 90 | 200 | | | |

3858A — — As 3858 but horse with long tail, small BP
1871 S	80	180	1876 S		90
1872 S	60	160	1877 S		*Extremely rare*
1873 S		140	1879 S	60	160
1874 S		90	1880 S		95
1875 S		90			

3858B — — As 3858 but with no BP
| 1880 S . . . . | | 95 | 1881 S . . . . | | 95 |

	EF			*EF*
	£			£

3858C **Sovereign.** Second head. W W on broad truncation. R̶. Horse with long tail, small BP

| 1880 S. . . . . | 110 | | |

3858D — — As 3858C but horse with short tail, no BP

| 1881 S. . . . . | 95 | 1882 S. . . . . | 95 |

3858E — — As 3858D but small BP

1882 S.	95	1885 S.	95
1883 S.	95	1886 S.	95
1884 S.	95	1887 S.	95

3859   3860

3859 **Half-sovereign.** R̶. Shield. London mint

	VF	*EF*		*VF*	*EF*
	£	£		£	£
1838	75	200	1852	80	175
1839 Proof only *FDC* £1000			1853	60	135
1841	90	250	— Proof *FDC* £2750		
1842	60	135	1854	*Extremely rare*	
1843	90	250	1855	65	140
1844	70	200	1856	65	140
1845	250	800	1857	80	175
1846	75	200	1858	60	140
1847	75	200	1859	60	140
1848	75	200	1860	60	135
1849	65	175	1861	60	150
1850	200	500	1862	750	—
1851	65	150	1863	65	135

	VF £	EF £		VF £	EF £
3860 — — die number below shield					
1863	80	200	1873	55	150
1864	60	135	1874	65	150
1865	60	135	1875	55	135
1866	60	135	1876	55	130
1867	60	135	1877	55	130
1869	60	135	1878	55	130
1870	70	135	1879	75	250
1871	60	135	1880	55	130
1872	60	135			
3861 — — As 3859 (no die number) but head in slightly lower relief					
1880	60	135	1884	55	115
1883	55	115	1885	55	115

3862		3863	

	VF	EF		VF	EF
3862 — — S below shield for Sydney mint					
1871 S	85	475	1881 S	150	650
1872 S	95	500	1882 S	175	1250
1875 S	90	400	1883 S	95	350
1879 S	95	450	1886 S	95	450
1880 S	95	475	1887 S	95	450
3863 — — M below shield for Melbourne mint					
1873 M	100	450	1884 M	200	1000
1877 M	125	500	1885 M	300	1500
1881 M	200	700	1886 M	125	550
1882 M	125	500	1887 M	250	1250

Jubilee coinage, 1887–93

3864

3864 Five pounds. ℞. St. George

1887	450	650

— Proof *FDC* £2100

	VF £	*EF* £		*VF* £	*EF* £
3865 Two pounds. Similar					
1887.	160	350			
— Proof *FDC* £850					
3866 Sovereign. R̸. St. George. London mint					
1887.		80	1890.		80
— Proof *FDC* £500			1891.		80
1888.		80	1892.		80
1889.		80			

3866   3867   3869

3867 — Sovereign. M on ground for Melbourne mint					
1887 M		80	1891 M		80
1888 M		80	1892 M		80
1889 M		80	1893 M		80
1890 M		80			
3868 — — S on ground for Sydney mint					
1887 S	125	325	1891 S		80
1888 S	110		1892 S		85
1889 S		80	1893 S		85
1890 S		80			
3869 Half-sovereign. R̸. Shield. London mint					
1887.		70	1891.		80
— Proof *FDC* £350			1892.		75
1890.		70	1893.		80
3870 — — M below shield for Melbourne mint					
1887 M	95	275	1893 M	110	350
3871 — — S below shield for Sydney mint					
1887 S	90	250	1891 S	90	250
1889 S	110	350			

Old head coinage, 1893–1901
3872   Five pounds. R̸. St. George
1893   500   950
— Proof   *FDC*   £2500

3873

	VF £	EF £

3873 Two pounds. Similar

1893.   250   450

— Proof *FDC* £1100

3874 Sovereign. ℞. St. George, London mint

1893.	BV	1898.	BV
— Proof *FDC* £650		1899.	BV
1894.	BV	1900.	BV
1895.	BV	1901.	BV
1896.	BV		

3876   3877

3875 — ℞. St. George. M on ground for Melbourne mint

1893 M	BV	1898 M	BV
1894 M	BV	1899 M	BV
1895 M	BV	1900 M	BV
1896 M	BV	1901 M	BV
1897 M	BV		

3876 — — P on ground for Perth mint

1899 P.	95	1901 P.	BV
1900 P.	BV		

3877 — — S on ground for Sydney mint

1893 S.	BV	1898 S.	BV
1894 S.	BV	1899 S.	BV
1895 S.	BV	1900 S.	BV
1896 S.	BV	1901 S.	BV
1897 S.	BV		

3878

	F £	VF £	EF £		F £	VF £	EF £
3878 **Half-sovereign.** R. St. George. London mint							
1893.			60	1897.			60
— Proof *FDC* £400				1898.			60
1894.			60	1899.			60
1895.			60	1900.			60
1896.			60	1901.			60
3879 — — M on ground for Melbourne mint							
1893 M		*Extremely rare*		1899 M		75	200
1896 M		75	200	1900 M		75	200
3880 — — P on ground for Perth mint							
1899 P.		Proof *unique*		1900 P.		90	300
3881 — — S on ground for Sydney mint							
1893 S.		70	200	1900 S.		60	150
1897 S.		70	200				

SILVER

Young head coinage

3882

3882 **Crown.** Young head. R. Crowned shield

	F	VF	EF
1839 Proof only *FDC* £2500			
1844	16	55	400
1845	16	45	375
1847	18	60	500

	VF £	EF £	FDC £
3883* "Gothic" type, as illustration; inscribed edge,			
mdcccxlvii = 1847	275	450	850
— Proof, Plain edge *FDC* £950			

* *Beware of recent forgeries.*

3884 — — mdcccliii = 1853. Proof *FDC* £3000

3883

3888

	F	VF	EF		F	VF	EF
	£	£	£		£	£	£

3885 **Halfcrown.** Type A¹. Young head with one ornate and one plain
fillet binding hair. WW in relief on truncation, 1839 . . . . 250 600 2000

3886 — Proof *FDC* £650

3887 Type A³. Two plain fillets. WW incuse

	F	VF	EF		F	VF	EF
1839	250	600	2000	1840	12	40	175

3888 Type A⁴. Similar but no initials on truncation

1841	30	100	400	1846	9	35	130
1842	10	35	150	1848/6	30	100	500
1843	18	60	275	1849	15	60	225
1844	9	35	130	1850	12	45	200
1845	9	35	130	1853 Proof *FDC* £1000			

3889 Type A⁵. As last but inferior workmanship

1874	7	18	75	1881	7	18	75
1875	7	22	80	1882	7	22	80
1876	7	22	85	1883	7	18	75
1877	7	22	80	1884	7	18	75
1878	7	22	80	1885	7	18	75
1879	8	30	110	1886	7	18	75
1880	7	22	80	1887	7	18	80

3890   3892

	F	VF	EF		F	VF	EF
	£	£	£		£	£	£

3890   **Florin,** "Godless" type (i.e. without D.G.), 1849   5   20   65

3891   "Gothic" type B[1], reads brit:, WW below bust, date at end of obverse legend in gothic numerals (1851 to 1863)

mdcccli		*? Proof only*		mdccclvii	6	25	100
mdccclii	5	20	85	mdccclviii	6	25	100
mdcccliii.	5	22	95	mdccclix	6	25	100
— Proof *FDC* £1100				mdccclx	7	30	135
mdcccliv.	200	500	1750	mdccclxii	20	100	300
mdccclv	6	25	100	mdccclxiii	50	175	650
mdccclvi.	6	27	120				

3892   — type B[2]; as last but die number below bust (1864 to 1867)

mdccclxiv	6	25	100	mdccclxvi	7	30	130
mdccclxv	6	27	110	mdccclxvii. . . .	14	60	175

3893   — type B[3], reads britt:, die number (1868 to 1879)

mdccclxviii . . .	6	27	120	mdccclxxiv . . .	6	25	100
mdccclxix	6	25	100	mdccclxxv. . . .	6	25	100
mdccclxx	6	25	100	mdccclxxvi . . .	6	25	110
mdccclxxi	6	25	100	mdccclxxvii . . .	6	25	110
mdccclxxii. . . .	5	20	80	mdccclxxix . . .		*Extremely rare*	
mdccclxxiii . . .	5	20	80				

3894   — type B[4]. As last but with border of 48 arcs and no WW
1877   mdccclxxvii . . . .   *Extremely rare*

3895   — type B[5]. Similar but 42 arcs (1867, 1877 and 1878)

mdccclxvii. . . .		*Extremely rare*		mdccclxxviii. . .	6	25	100
mdccclxxvii . . .	6	25	110				

3896   — type B[5/6]. As last but no die number (1877, 1879)

mdccclxxvii . . .		*Extremely rare*		mdccclxxix . . .	*Extremely rare*

3897   — type B[6], reads britt:, WW; 48 arcs (1879)
mdccclxxix . . .   6   25   100

3898   — type B[7]. As last but no WW, 38 arcs (1879)
mdccclxxix . . .   6   25   100

3899   — type B[3/8]. As next but younger portrait (1880)
mdccclxxx . . . .   *Extremely rare*

3900   — type B[8]. Similar but 34 arcs (1880 to 1887)

mdccclxxx. . . .	6	25	100	mdccclxxxv . . .	5	20	90
mdccclxxxi . . .	5	20	90	mdccclxxxvi. . .	5	22	95
mdccclxxxiii. . .	5	20	90	mdccclxxxvii . .		*? exists*	
mdccclxxxiv. . .	5	20	90				

| | F | VF | EF | | F | VF | EF |
| | £ | £ | £ | | £ | £ | £ |

3901 — type B⁹. Similar but 46 arcs
1887 mdccclxxxvii. 8 30 140

3906

3902 Shilling. Type A¹. First head, WW on truncation

| 1838 | 4 | 15 | 60 | 1839 | 5 | 15 | 65 |

3903 Type A². Second head, WW (proof only), 1839 *FDC* £225
3904 Type A³. Second head, no initials on truncation

1839	4	13	50	1853	4	14	50
1840	8	30	130	— Proof *FDC* £400			
1841	8	30	130	1854	30	110	400
1842	7	15	55	1855	4	13	50
1843	4	20	85	1856	4	13	50
1844	6	14	55	1857	4	13	50
1845	4	15	65	1858	4	13	50
1846	4	15	55	1859	4	13	50
1848 over 6	24	70	350	1860	6	22	80
1849	4	20	70	1861	6	22	80
1850	90	300	800	1862	10	35	110
1851	20	60	200	1863	10	55	175
1852	4	14	55				

3905 Type A⁴. As before but die number above date

| 1864 | 4 | 13 | 50 | 1866 | 4 | 13 | 50 |
| 1865 | 4 | 13 | 50 | 1867 | 4 | 14 | 55 |

3906 Type A⁶. Third head, die number above date

1867	20	65	225	1874	3	9	35
1868	4	13	50	1875	3	9	35
1869	4	16	70	1876	3	13	55
1870	4	16	70	1877	3	9	35
1871	3	9	35	1878	3	9	35
1872	3	9	35	1879	7	30	150
1873	3	9	35				

3907 Type A⁷. Fourth head; no die number

1879	4	14	50	1884	3	8	27
1880	3	8	27	1885	2	5	20
1881	3	8	27	1886	2	5	20
1882	7	28	80	1887	5	15	60
1883	3	8	27				

	F	VF	EF			F	VF	EF
	£	£	£			£	£	£

3908 Sixpence. Type A[1]. First head

| 1838 | 2 | 9 | 35 |
| 1839 | 2 | 9 | 35 |
| — Proof *FDC* £150 |
1840	3	10	40
1841	4	15	50
1842	3	10	40
1843	3	11	40
1844	2	9	35
1845	3	10	40
1846	2	9	35
1848	20	65	250
1850	3	10	40
1851	3	10	40

| 1852 | 3 | 10 | 40 |
| 1853 | 2 | 9 | 35 |
| — Proof *FDC* £250 |
1854	30	100	350
1855	2	9	35
1856	3	10	40
1857	3	10	40
1858	3	10	40
1859	2	9	35
1860	3	10	40
1862	15	60	250
1863	8	35	150
1866		*Extremely rare*	

3909   3912

3909 Type A[2]. First head; die number above date

| 1864 | 3 | 8 | 40 |
| 1865 | 4 | 12 | 50 |

| 1866 | 3 | 8 | 40 |

3910 Type A[3]. Second head; die number above date

1867	4	14	55
1868	4	14	55
1869	4	20	80
1870	4	20	80
1871	3	8	40
1872	3	8	40
1873	2	7	35

1874	2	7	35
1875	2	7	35
1876	4	14	60
1877	2	7	35
1878	2	7	35
1879	4	16	60

3911 Type A[4]. Second head; no die number

| 1871 | 4 | 12 | 50 |
| 1877 | 3 | 8 | 40 |

| 1879 | 3 | 8 | 40 |
| 1880 | 4 | 12 | 50 |

3912 Type A[5]. Third head

1880	1	5	22
1881	1	5	20
1882	4	16	60
1883	1	5	20

1884	1	5	20
1885	1	5	20
1886	1	5	20
1887	1	4	18

3913 Groat (4d.). R. Britannia

| 1838 | | 4 | 20 |
| 1839 | | 5 | 25 |
| — Proof *FDC* £110 |
1840		5	22
1841		6	32
1842		5	30
1843		5	30
1844		5	30
1845		5	30
1846		5	30

1847/6 (or 8)	12	40	135
1848		4	22
1849		4	22
1851	15	50	150
1852	22	75	225
1853	30	90	275
— Proof *FDC* £275
1854		4	22
1855		4	22

3913   3914   3915

3914 Threepence. R. Crowned 3; as Maundy threepence but with a less prooflike surface

	VF £	EF £		VF £	EF £
1838*	4	30	1864	4	30
1839*	6	40	1865	6	45
— Proof (see Maundy)			1866	4	30
1840*	6	45	1867	4	35
1841*	6	50	1868	4	25
1842*	6	50	1869*	6	55
1843*	4	30	1870	4	22
1844*	6	45	1871	4	30
1845	4	22	1872	4	25
1846	7	60	1873	3	18
1849	6	45	1874	3	18
1850	4	25	1875	3	18
1851	4	35	1876	3	18
1853	6	60	1877	3	18
1854	6	35	1878	3	18
1855	6	50	1879	3	18
1856	6	45	1880	4	20
1857	6	45	1881	4	20
1858	4	35	1882	4	35
1859	4	20	1883	3	15
1860	4	30	1884	3	15
1861	4	25	1885	3	12
1862	4	35	1886	3	12
1863	6	45	1887	3	15

* Issued for Colonial use only.

3915 Three-halfpence (for Colonial use). R. Value, etc.

1838	3	18	1842	3	25
1839	3	16	1843	2	14
1840	4	35	1860	4	40
1841	3	16	1862	4	35

3916

Overstruck dates are listed only if commoner than the normal date or if no normal date is known.

3916 Maundy Set (4d., 3d., 2d. and 1.)

	EF £	FDC £		EF £	FDC £
1838	35	60	1862	35	55
1839	35	60	1863	35	55
— Proof *FDC* £200			1864	35	55
1840	35	60	1865	35	55
1841	40	60	1866	35	55
1842	35	60	1867	35	55
1843	35	60	1868	35	55
1844	35	60	1869	35	55
1845	35	60	1870	35	55
1846	35	60	1871	35	55
1847	35	60	1872	35	55
1848	35	60	1873	35	55
1849	40	70	1874	35	55
1850	35	60	1875	35	55
1851	35	60	1876	35	55
1852	35	60	1877	35	55
1853	35	60	1878	35	55
— Proof *FDC* £300			1879	35	55
1854	35	60	1880	35	55
1855	40	70	1881	35	55
1856	35	60	1882	35	55
1857	35	60	1883	35	55
1858	35	60	1884	35	55
1859	35	60	1885	35	55
1860	35	60	1886	35	55
1861	35	60	1887	35	55

		EF	FDC
3917	— **fourpence,** 1838–87 .... *from*	6	10
3918	— **threepence,** 1838–87 .... *from*	12	20
3919	— **twopence,** 1838–87 .... *from*	4	7
3920	— **penny,** 1838–87 .... *from*	3	6

Maundy Sets in the original dated cases are worth approximately £5 more than the prices quoted.

Jubilee Coinage

3921

3921 Crown. R. St. George

	F	VF	EF		F	VF	EF
	£	£	£		£	£	£
1887	6	15	30	1890	8	22	55
— Proof *FDC* £375				1891	8	24	65
1888	9	22	50	1892	10	25	80
1889	6	15	30				

3922

3922 Double-florin (4s.). R. Cruciform shields. Roman I in date

	F	VF	EF
1887	5	8	25

3923 Similar but Arabic 1 in date

	F	VF	EF		F	VF	EF
1887	5	8	25	1889	6	10	30
— Proof *FDC* £175				1890	6	12	35
1888	6	12	35				

3924   3925

3924 Halfcrown. R. Shield in collar

	F	VF	EF		F	VF	EF
1887	3	4	16	1890	3	12	45
— Proof *FDC* £115				1891	3	12	45
1888	3	7	30	1892	3	12	45
1889	3	7	30				

3925 Florin. R. Cruciform shields

	F	VF	EF		F	VF	EF
1887	3	3	14				
— Proof *FDC* £75				1890	5	20	60
1888	3	5	20	1891	8	35	125
1889	3	6	24	1892	8	30	110

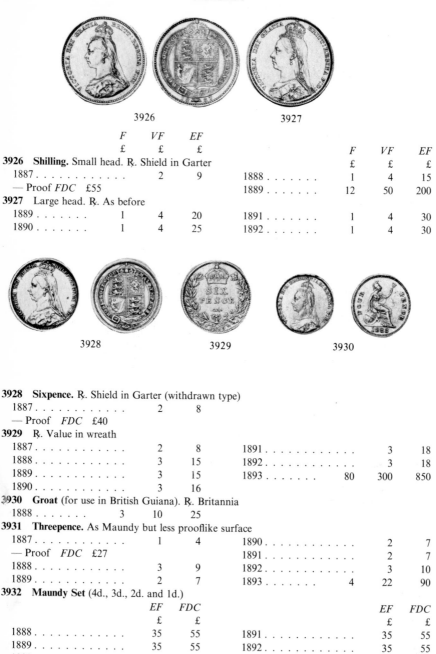

3926   3927

	F £	VF £	EF £			F £	VF £	EF £
3926 Shilling. Small head. Ṛ. Shield in Garter								
1887		2	9	1888		1	4	15
— Proof *FDC* £55				1889		12	50	200
3927 Large head. Ṛ. As before								
1889	1	4	20	1891		1	4	30
1890	1	4	25	1892		1	4	30

3928   3929   3930

3928 Sixpence. Ṛ. Shield in Garter (withdrawn type)

1887		2	8				

— Proof *FDC* £40

3929 Ṛ. Value in wreath

1887		2	8	1891		3	18
1888		3	15	1892		3	18
1889		3	15	1893	80	300	850
1890		3	16				

3930 Groat (for use in British Guiana). Ṛ. Britannia

1888	3	10	25

3931 Threepence. As Maundy but less prooflike surface

1887		1	4	1890		2	7
— Proof *FDC* £27				1891		2	7
1888		3	9	1892		3	10
1889		2	7	1893	4	22	90

3932 Maundy Set (4d., 3d., 2d. and 1d.)

	EF £	FDC £		EF £	FDC £
1888	35	55	1891	35	55
1889	35	55	1892	35	55
1890	35	55			

Maundy Sets in the original dated cases are worth approximately £5 more than the prices quoted.

3932

			EF	FDC
			£	£
3933	— fourpence, 1888–92 . . . *from*	9	13
3934	— threepence, 1888–92 . . . *from*	11	21
3935	— twopence, 1888–92 . . . *from*	5	10
3936	— penny, 1888–92 . . . *from*	5	10

Old head coinage

3937

	F	VF	EF
	£	£	£
3937 Crown. R. St. George. Regnal date on edge			
1893 — LVI.	6	20	95
— — Proof *FDC* £375			
— — LVII	12	35	150
1894 — LVII	6	25	110
— — LVIII	6	25	110
1895 — LVIII.	6	22	100
— — LIX.	6	22	100
1896 — LIX.	9	30	135
— — LX .	6	22	100
1897 — LX .	6	22	100
— — LXI.	6	20	95
1898 — LXI.	12	35	150
— — LXII .	6	25	110
1899 — LXII .	6	25	110
— — LXIII.	6	25	110
1900 — LXIII.	6	20	95
— — LXIV.	6	20	95

3938

	F	VF	EF
	£	£	£
3938 Halfcrown. ℞. Shield in collar			
1893	3	6	25
— Proof *FDC* £125			
1894	3	8	45
1895	3	6	30
1896	3	6	30
3939 Florin. ℞. Three shields within Garter			
1893	3	5	25
— Proof *FDC* £80			
1894	3	8	40
1895	3	6	35
1896	3	5	30

	F	VF	EF
	£	£	£
1897	3	6	25
1898	3	6	30
1899	3	6	30
1900	3	6	25
1901	3	6	25
1897	3	5	25
1898	3	5	30
1899	3	5	25
1900	3	5	25
1901	3	5	25

3939   3940

3940 Shilling. ℞. Three shields within Garter		
1893	3	12
— Proof *FDC* £60		
1894	4	18
1895	3	14
1896	3	12
3941 Sixpence. ℞. Value in wreath		
1893	3	10
— Proof *FDC* £40		
1894	4	16
1895	3	12
1896	3	12

1897	3	12
1898	3	12
1899	3	14
1900	3	12
1901	3	12
1897	3	12
1898	3	12
1899	3	12
1900	3	10
1901	3	10

3941   3942

	EF £		EF £
3942 Threepence. R. Crowned 3. As Maundy but less prooflike surface			
1893.	3	1897.	4
— Proof *FDC* £30		1898.	4
1894.	6	1899.	3
1895.	6	1900.	3
1896.	4	1901.	3

3943

3943 Maundy Set (4d., 3d., 2d. and 1d.)

	EF £	FDC £		EF £	FDC £
1893.	30	45	1898.	30	45
1894.	30	45	1899.	30	45
1895.	30	45	1900.	30	45
1896.	30	45	1901.	30	45
1897.	30	45			
3944 — **fourpence, 1893–1901** . . . .*from*				5	8
3945 — **threepence, 1893–1901** . . . .*from*				10	17
3946 — **twopence, 1893–1901**. . . . .*from*				5	6
3947 — **penny, 1893–1901**. . . . .*from*				5	6

Maundy Sets in the original dated cases are worth approximately £5 more than the prices quoted.

COPPER AND BRONZE
Young head copper coinage, 1838–60

3948

	F £	VF £	EF £
3948 Penny. R. Britannia			
1839 Bronzed proof *FDC* £225			
1841		4	25
1843	20	75	300
1844	2	5	35
1845	3	12	60
1846	2	8	45
1847	2	6	35
1848/7	2	6	30
1849	20	75	300
1851	2	8	45

	F £	VF £	EF £
1853		3	16
— Proof *FDC* £225			
1854		3	16
1855		3	16
1856	5	20	90
1857		3	20
1858		3	18
1859		4	22
1860*		225	400

3949

3949 Halfpenny. R. Britannia

	F	VF	EF
1838		2	16
1839 Bronzed proof *FDC* £90			
1841		2	14
1843	1	8	40
1844		3	20
1845	15	45	150
1846		4	25
1847		4	25
1848		5	30
1851		3	22

	F	VF	EF
1852		3	24
1853		2	9
— Proof *FDC* £125			
1854		2	9
1855		2	9
1856		3	22
1857		3	14
1858		2	16
1859		3	18
1860*			2750

Overstruck dates are listed only if commoner than normal date, or if no normal date is known.

Copper

3950

	F £	VF £	EF £		F £	VF £	EF £
3950 Farthing. ℞. Britannia				1849	7	30	110
1838		4	20	1850		4	22
1839		3	18	1851	3	10	45
— Bronzed proof *FDC* £110				1852	3	11	45
1840		3	18	1853		3	22
1841		3	18	— Proof *FDC* £250			
1842		7	45	1854		4	22
1843		3	18	1855		5	25
1844	15	40	150	1856	2	7	40
1845		4	22	1857		3	22
1846		7	35	1858		3	22
1847		4	22	1859	5	15	45
1848		4	22	1860*	—	—	3000

* These 1860 large copper pieces not to be confused with the smaller and commoner bronze issue with date on reverse (nos. 3954, 3956 and 3958).

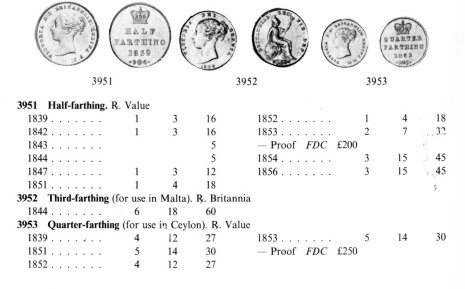

3951   3952   3953

3951 Half-farthing. ℞. Value							
1839	1	3	16	1852	1	4	18
1842	1	3	16	1853	2	7	32
1843			5	— Proof *FDC* £200			
1844			5	1854	3	15	45
1847	1	3	12	1856	3	15	45
1851	1	4	18				

3952 Third-farthing (for use in Malta). ℞. Britannia

1844	6	18	60

3953 Quarter-farthing (for use in Ceylon). ℞. Value

1839	4	12	27	1853	5	14	30
1851	5	14	30	— Proof *FDC* £250			
1852	4	12	27				

Bronze coinage, "bun head" issue, 1860–95

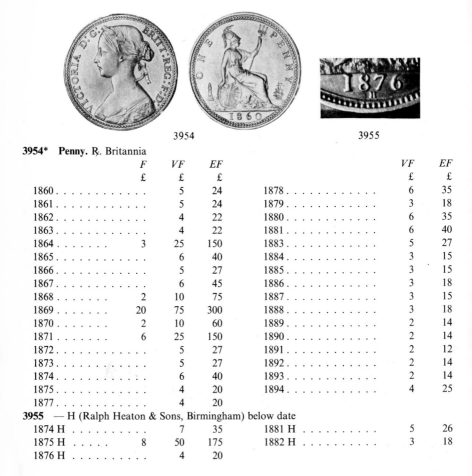

3954   3955

3954*   Penny. R. Britannia

	F	VF	EF		VF	EF
	£	£	£		£	£
1860		5	24	1878	6	35
1861		5	24	1879	3	18
1862		4	22	1880	6	35
1863		4	22	1881	6	40
1864	3	25	150	1883	5	27
1865		6	40	1884	3	15
1866		5	27	1885	3	15
1867		6	45	1886	3	18
1868	2	10	75	1887	3	15
1869	20	75	300	1888	3	18
1870	2	10	60	1889	2	14
1871	6	25	150	1890	2	14
1872		5	27	1891	2	12
1873		5	27	1892	2	14
1874		6	40	1893	2	14
1875		4	20	1894	4	25
1877		4	20			

3955   — H (Ralph Heaton & Sons, Birmingham) below date

		VF	EF			VF	EF
1874 H		7	35	1881 H		5	26
1875 H	8	50	175	1882 H		3	18
1876 H		4	20				

*1882 without 'H' was sold in auction condition extremely fine for £1700, March 1988.

3956

3956 Halfpenny. R. Britannia

	F	VF	EF		F	VF	EF
	£	£	£		£	£	£
1860		3	15	1878	2	6	40
1861		3	15	1879		3	15
1862		3	13	1880		4	25
1863		5	25	1881		4	25
1864		5	30	1883		3	22
1865	2	6	40	1884		2	12
1866		5	30	1885		2	12
1867	2	6	40	1886		2	12
1868		5	32	1887		2	10
1869	3	25	90	1888		2	12
1870		5	26	1889		2	12
1871	6	30	100	1890		2	10
1872		4	24	1891		2	10
1873		5	30	1892		2	20
1874	2	8	60	1893		2	12
1875		3	20	1894		3	22
1877		3	20				

3957 — H below date

	F	VF	EF		F	VF	EF
1874 H		3	22	1881 H		2	20
1875 H		5	28	1882 H		2	20
1876 H		2	20				

3958   3960

3958 Farthing. R. Britannia

	F	VF	EF		F	VF	EF
1860		2	10	1880		2	14
1861		2	12	1881		1	8
1862		2	12	1883		4	20
1863	10	30	90	1884			5
1864		2	18	1885			5
1865		2	12	1886			5
1866		2	10	1887			8
1867		3	16	1888			7
1868		3	16	1890			7
1869		5	22	1891			5
1872		2	12	1892	2	6	20
1873		1	9	1893			5
1875	4	10	35	1894			7
1878			7	1895	3	8	30
1879			7				

3959 Farthing ℞. Britannia. H below date

	F	VF	EF		VF	EF
	£	£	£		£	£
1874 H			14	1881 H		12
1875 H			6	1882 H		12
1876 H		4	10	30		

3960 Third-farthing (for use in Malta). ℞. Value

1866	8	1881		10
1868	9	1884		9
1876	10	1885		9
1878	9			

Old head issue, 1895–1901

3961

3961 Penny. ℞. Britannia

1895	6	1899	5
1896	5	1900	3
1897	5	1901	2
1898	10		

3961   "High tide"   3961A   "Low tide"

3961A As last but "Low tide", 1895   18   75

3962

3962 Halfpenny. Type as Penny. ℞. Britannia

1895	6	1899	4
1896	5	1900	3
1897	5	1901	2
1898	5		

3963 Farthing. ℞. Britannia. Bright finish

1895	4	1897	5
1896	4		

3964

3964 — Dark finish	*EF* £		*EF* £
1897.	4	1900.	3
1898.	4	1901.	2
1899.	4		

EDWARD VII, 1901–10

Five pound pieces, two pound pieces and crowns were only issued in 1902. A branch of the Royal Mint was opened at Ottawa and coined sovereigns of imperial type from 1908.

Unlike the coins in most other proof sets, the proofs issued for the Coronation in 1902 have a matt surface in place of the more usual brilliant finish.

Designer's initials:
De S. (G. W. de Saulles)

GOLD

3965

		VF	EF	UNC.
		£	£	£
3965	**Five pounds.** 1902. R. St. George	450	650	800
3966	— Proof. 1902. *Matt surface FDC* £750			
3967	**Two pounds.** 1902. Similar.	200	350	500
3968	— Proof. 1902. *Matt surface FDC* £425			

3967

3969

	EF	UNC.		EF	UNC.
	£	£		£	£
3969 Sovereign. R. St. George. London mint					
1902 Matt proof *FDC* £140			1906		BV
1902		BV	1907		BV
1903		BV	1908		BV
1904		BV	1909		BV
1905		BV	1910		BV
3970 — C on ground for Ottawa mint					
1908 C (Satin proof only) *FDC* £2750			1910 C	200	300
1909 C	200	300			

3971 — M on ground for Melbourne mint

	VF	EF	UNC.		VF	EF	UNC.
	£	£	£		£	£	£
1902 M			BV	1907 M			BV
1903 M			BV	1908 M			BV
1904 M			BV	1909 M			BV
1905 M			BV	1910 M			BV
1906 M			BV				

3972 — P on ground for Perth mint

	VF	EF	UNC.		VF	EF	UNC.
1902 P			BV	1907 P			BV
1903 P			BV	1908 P			BV
1904 P			BV	1909 P			BV
1905 P			BV	1910 P			BV
1906 P			BV				

3973 — S on ground for Sydney mint

	VF	EF	UNC.		VF	EF	UNC.
1902 S			BV	1907 S			BV
1903 S			BV	1908 S			BV
1904 S			BV	1909 S			BV
1905 S			BV	1910 S			BV
1906 S			BV				

3974

3974 Half-sovereign. R. St. George. London mint

		VF	EF			VF	EF
1902 Matt proof	*FDC*	£100		1906		45	50
1902		45	50	1907		45	50
1903		45	50	1908		45	50
1904		45	50	1909		45	50
1905		45	50	1910		45	50

3975 — M on ground for Melbourne mint

	VF	EF	UNC		VF	EF	UNC
1906 M	55	80	175	1908 M	55	80	200
1907 M	55	80	175	1909 M	55	80	175

3976 — P on ground for Perth mint

	VF	EF	UNC		VF	EF	UNC
1904 P	175	550	—	1909 P	140	400	—
1908 P	175	600	—				

3977 — S on ground for Sydney mint

	VF	EF	UNC		VF	EF	UNC
1902 S	60	125	250	1908 S	55	110	175
1903 S	55	110	175	1910 S	55	110	175
1906 S	55	110	175				

SILVER

3978

	F	VF	EF	UNC.
	£	£	£	£
3978 Crown. ℞. St. George				
1902	20	35	70	130

3979 — but *matt proof FDC* £100

3980

	F	VF	EF	UNC.		F	VF	EF	UNC.
	£	£	£	£		£	£	£	£
3980 Halfcrown. ℞. Shield in Garter									
1902	3	8	30	55	1906	4	10	70	110
— Matt proof *FDC* £55					1907	4	12	75	120
1903	25	90	350	550	1908	5	14	100	150
1904	15	55	250	400	1909	4	12	80	130
1905*	70	250	750	975	1910	4	10	55	90
3981 Florin. ℞. Britannia standing									
1902	2	6	30	50	1906	3	9	50	75
— Matt proof *FDC* £40					1907	4	12	60	90
1903	3	9	50	75	1908	4	14	80	120
1904	4	12	60	90	1909	4	13	75	110
1905*	10	30	175	300	1910	2	7	40	65

*Beware of recent forgeries.

| 3981 | 3982 | 3983 |

	F	VF	EF	UNC.		F	VF	EF	UNC.
	£	£	£	£		£	£	£	£

3982 Shilling. ℞. Lion on crown

	F	VF	EF	UNC.		F	VF	EF	UNC.
1902		2	15	25	1906		2	20	35
— Matt proof *FDC* £25					1907		4	25	40
1903	1	5	50	90	1908	1	6	60	90
1904	1	5	40	65	1909	1	5	50	85
1905*	25	85	300	475	1910		2	15	25

* Beware of recent forgeries.

3983 Sixpence. ℞. Value in wreath

	F	VF	EF	UNC.		F	VF	EF	UNC.
1902		1	15	25	1906		2	20	35
— Matt proof *FDC* £20					1907		2	25	40
1903		2	20	35	1908		3	30	50
1904	1	4	35	55	1909		2	25	40
1905		2	25	40	1910		1	15	25

3984 Threepence. As Maundy but dull finish

			EF	UNC.				EF	UNC.
1902			3	5	1907			8	14
1903			8	14	1908			8	14
1904			30	45	1909			8	14
1905			20	35	1910			6	10
1906			20	35					

3985

3985 Maundy Set (4d., 3d., 2d. and 1d.)

	EF	FDC		EF	FDC
	£	£		£	£
1902	25	40	1906	25	40
— Matt proof *FDC* £40			1907	25	40
1903	25	40	1908	25	40
1904	25	40	1909	30	50
1905	25	40	1910	35	55

	EF	FDC
	£	£
3986 — **fourpence,** 1902–10 . . . . *from*	5	9
3987 — **threepence,** 1902–10 . . . . . . *from*	5	11
3988 — **twopence,** 1902–10 . . . . *from*	5	8
3989 — **penny,** 1902–10 . . . . *from*	5	8

Maundy sets in the original dated cases are worth approximately £5 more than the prices quoted.

BRONZE

3990

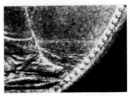

3990   "High tide"   3990A   "Low tide"

3990 Penny. ℞. Britannia	EF	UNC.		VF	EF	UNC.
	£	£		£	£	£
1902	4	8				
1903	8	20	1907		8	20
1904	12	25	1908		8	20
1905	10	22	1909		8	20
1906	8	20	1910		7	14
3990A As last but "Low tide", 1902.				3	20	40

3991

	EF £	UNC. £		VF £	EF £	UNC. £
3991 Halfpenny. R. Britannia						
1902	4	8	1907		5	12
1903	6	14	1908		5	12
1904	8	20	1909		8	20
1905	8	20	1910		7	15
1906	7	15				
3991A As last but "Low tide", 1902				10	25	45

3992   3993

	EF £	UNC. £		EF £	UNC. £
3992 Farthing. Britannia. Dark finish					
1902	3	6	1907	5	10
1903	5	10	1908	5	10
1904	7	14	1909	5	10
1905	5	10	1910	7	14
1906	5	10			

3993 Third-farthing (for use in Malta)

1902 R. Value	3	6

No proofs of the bronze coins were issued in 1902.

GEORGE V, 1910–36

Paper money issued by the Treasury during the First World War replaced gold for internal use after 1915 but the branch mints in Australia and South Africa (the main Commonwealth gold producing countries) continued striking sovereigns until 1930–2. Owing to the steep rise in the price of silver in 1919/20 the issue of standard (.925) silver was discontinued and coins of .500 silver were minted.

In 1912, 1918 and 1919 some pennies were made under contract by private mints in Birmingham. In 1918, as half-sovereigns were no longer being minted, farthings were again issued with the ordinary bright bronze finish. Crown pieces had not been issued for general circulation but they were struck in small numbers about Christmas time for people to give as presents in the years 1927–36, and in 1935 a special commemorative crown was issued in celebration of the Silver Jubilee.

As George V died in January, it is likely that all coins dated 1936 were struck during the reign of Edward VIII.

Designer's initials:
B. M. (Bertram Mackennal)
P. M. (Percy Metcalfe)
K. G. (Kruger Gray)

GOLD

3994

		FDC
		£
3994	**Five pounds.*** R. St. George, 1911 (Proof only).	1300
3995	**Two pounds.*** R. St. George, 1911 (Proof only).	625

Forgeries exist.

3996

	UNC.		VF	EF	UNC.
	£		£	£	£
3996 Sovereign. R. St. George. London mint					
1911.	BV	1915			BV
— Proof *FDC* £275		1916			90
1912.	BV	1917*	2250	4500	—
1913.	BV	1925			BV
1914.	BV				

* *Forgeries exist of these and of most other dates and mints.*

	VF	EF	UNC.		VF	EF	UNC.
	£	£	£		£	£	£

3997 — C on ground for the Ottawa mint

	VF £	EF £	UNC. £		VF £	EF £	UNC. £
1911 C		95	110	1917 C		95	110
1913 C	225	450	—	1918 C		95	110
1914 C	125	250	—	1919 C		95	110
1916 C		7500					

| 3997 | 3998 | 4004 |

3998 — I on ground for India (Bombay) mint, 1918   100

3999 — M on ground for Melbourne mint

	VF	EF	UNC.		VF	EF	UNC.
1911 M			BV	1920 M	450	950	1400
1912 M			BV	1921 M		4000	5000
1913 M			BV	1922 M	1200	3500	4750
1914 M			BV	1923 M			BV
1915 M			BV	1924 M			BV
1916 M			BV	1925 M			BV
1917 M			BV	1926 M			BV
1918 M			BV	1928 M	300	950	1400
1919 M			100				

4000 — small head

	VF	EF	UNC.		VF	EF	UNC.
1929 M	250	950	—	1931 M	90	250	—
1930 M	135	175					

| 4001 | 4002 |

4001 — P on ground for Perth mint

	VF	EF	UNC.		VF	EF	UNC.
1911 P			BV	1920 P			BV
1912 P			BV	1921 P			BV
1913 P			BV	1922 P			BV
1914 P			BV	1923 P			BV
1915 P			BV	1924 P			BV
1916 P			BV	1925 P			BV
1917 P			BV	1926 P			BV
1918 P			BV	1927 P			BV
1919 P			BV	1928 P			BV

	VF £	EF £	UNC. £		VF £	EF £	UNC. £
4002 Sovereign. — — small head							
1929 P			BV	1931 P			BV
1930 P			BV				
4003 — S on ground for Sydney mint							
1911 S			BV	1919 S			BV
1912 S			BV	1920 S		*Extremely rare*	
1913 S			BV	1921 S	350	700	1200
1914 S			BV	1922 S	775	2000	4750
1915 S			BV	1923 S	775	2000	4750
1916 S			BV	1924 S	300	600	1000
1917 S			BV	1925 S			BV
1918 S			BV	1926 S	800	2350	5000
4004 — SA on ground for Pretoria mint							
1923 SA		1500	3000	1926 SA			BV
1923 SA Proof *FDC* £750				1927 SA			BV
1924 SA		2650	—	1928 SA			BV
1925 SA			BV				
4005 — — small head							
1929 SA			BV	1931 SA			BV
1930 SA			BV	1932 SA			100

4006

4006 Half-sovereign. ℞. St. George. London mint

	VF	EF	UNC.		VF	EF	UNC.
1911		45	50	1913		45	50
— Proof *FDC* £200				1914		45	50
1912		45	50	1915		45	50
4007 — M on ground for Melbourne mint							
1915 M					55	80	125
4008 — P on ground for Perth mint							
1911 P	55	70	80	1918 P	200	350	500
1915 P	55	70	80	1919 P, 1920 P (*Not circulated*)			
4009 — S on ground for Sydney mint							
1911 S	50	70	90	1915 S	45	50	60
1912 S	50	70	90	1916 S	45	50	60
1914 S	50	60	75				
4010 — SA on ground for Pretoria mint							
1923 SA Proof *FDC* £475				1926 SA		45	50
1925 SA		45	50				

SILVER

First coinage. Sterling silver (.925 fine)

4011

	EF £	UNC £		EF £	UNC £
4011 Halfcrown. R. Crowned shield in Garter					
1911............	25	50	1915............	12	25
— Proof *FDC* £70			1916............	12	25
1912............	30	55	1917............	18	35
1913............	35	70	1918............	12	25
1914............	12	30	1919............	18	35

4012

	EF	UNC		EF	UNC
4012 Florin. R. Cruciform shields					
1911............	20	40	1915............	12	25
— Proof *FDC* £50			1916............	12	25
1912............	25	45	1917............	18	35
1913............	35	65	1918............	12	25
1914............	12	25	1919............	18	35
4013 Shilling. R. Lion on crown, inner circles					
1911............	8	18	1915............	8	18
— Proof *FDC* £35			1916............	8	18
1912............	18	35	1917............	10	20
1913............	25	50	1918............	8	18
1914............	8	18	1919............	12	25

4013   4014

4014   Sixpence. R̫. Similar

	EF	UNC		EF	UNC
	£	£		£	£
1911	8	15			
— Proof *FDC* £30			1916	8	18
1912	12	25	1917	14	40
1913	16	30	1918	8	18
1914	8	18	1919	10	20
1915	8	18	1920	12	25

4015   Threepences. As Maundy but dull finish

	EF	UNC		EF	UNC
1911	3	5	1916	3	5
1912	3	5	1917	3	5
1913	3	5	1918	3	5
1914	3	5	1919	3	5
1915	3	5	1920	4	6

4016

4016   Maundy Set (4d., 3d., 2d. and 1d.)

	EF	FDC		EF	FDC
	£	£		£	£
1911	25	45	1916	25	40
— Proof *FDC* £60			1917	25	40
1912	25	40	1918	25	40
1913	25	40	1919	25	40
1914	25	40	1920	25	40
1915	25	40			

				EF	FDC
4017 — **fourpence**, 1911–20 .... *from*				5	8
4018 — **threepence**, 1911–20 .... *from*				8	12
4019 — **twopence**, 1911–20 .... *from*				5	8
4020 — **penny**, 1911–20 .... *from*				7	10

Second coinage. Debased silver (.500 fine). Types as before.

	EF £	UNC £		VF £	EF £	UNC £
4021 Halfcrown						
1920	20	40	1924		30	50
1921	25	50	1925	15	100	175
1922	20	40	1926		30	55
1923	12	20				
4022 Florin						
1920	20	35	1924		30	50
1921	20	35	1925	8	75	135
1922	16	30	1926		30	50
1923	14	25				
4023 Shilling						
1920	16	30	1924		20	35
1921	20	50	1925		35	55
1922	16	30	1926		12	27
1923	14	25				
4024 Sixpence						
1920	10	18	1923		16	30
1921	10	18	1924		10	18
1922	11	20	1925		12	20

4025　　　　　4026

	EF £	UNC £			EF £	UNC £
4025 — new beading and broader rim						
1925	10	18	1926		12	20
4026 Threepence						
1920	3	5	1925		10	20
1921	3	5	1926		10	20
1922	4	6				

4027 Maundy Set (4d., 3d., 2d. and 1d.)

	EF £	FDC £			EF £	FDC £
1921	25	40	1925		25	40
1922	25	40	1926		25	40
1923	25	40	1927		25	40
1924	25	40				

		EF	FDC
4028 — fourpence, 1921–7	from	6	9
4029 — threepence, 1921–7	from	8	12
4030 — twopence, 1921–7	from	6	10
4031 — penny, 1921–7	from	7	11

2nd coinage   3rd coinage

Third coinage. As before but **modified effigy**, with details of head more clearly defined. The BM on truncation is nearer to the back of the neck and without stops; beading is more pronounced.

	VF	EF	UNC.		VF	EF	UNC.
	£	£	£		£	£	£
4032 Halfcrown							
1926	4	30	50	1927		18	30
4033 Shilling							
1926		12	20	1927		18	30
4034 Sixpence							
1926		6	14	1927		10	18
4035 Threepence							
1926						3	5

Fourth coinage. New types, 1927–35

4036

4036 Crown. R. Crown in wreath

1927 Proof only	FDC	£110			1932	65	140	200
1928	35	80	135		1933	40	95	150
1929	40	95	150		1934	400	600	950
1930	40	95	150		1936	65	140	200
1931	45	110	175					

4037

4038

4037 Halfcrown. ℞. Shield

	VF £	EF £	UNC £		VF £	EF £	UNC £
1927 Proof only FDC £30				1932		10	30
1928		8	14	1933		9	16
1829		8	14	1934		25	40
1930	10	75	130	1935		6	12
1931		9	16	1936		5	10

4038 Florin. ℞. Cruciform sceptres, shield in each angle

	VF £	EF £	UNC £		VF £	EF £	UNC £
1927 Proof only FDC £35				1932	9	70	125
1928		7	12	1933		9	16
1929		7	12	1935		7	12
1930		11	18	1936		6	10
1931		8	18				

4039

4040

4039 Shilling. ℞. Lion on crown, no inner circles

	EF	UNC		EF	UNC
1927	12	20			
— Proof FDC £20			1932	8	14
1928	7	12	1933	7	12
1929	7	12	1934	14	25
1930	18	30	1935	7	12
1931	8	14	1936	6	10

4040 Sixpence. ℞. Three oak sprigs with six acorns

	EF	UNC		EF	UNC
1927 Proof only FDC £18			1929	3	6
1928	3	6	1930	4	6

4041 — closer milling

	EF	UNC		EF	UNC
1931	7	14	1934	8	16
1932	12	20	1935	5	10
1933	6	12	1936	3	6

4042

4042 **Threepence.** ℞. Three oak sprigs with three acorns

	EF	UNC.		EF	UNC.
	£	£		£	£
1927 Proof only *FDC* £30			1933	1	2
1928	10	18	1934	1	2
1930	8	14	1935	1	2
1931	1	2	1936	1	2
1932	1	2			

4043 **Maundy Set.** As earlier sets

	EF	FDC		EF	FDC
	£	£		£	£
1928	30	45	1933	30	45
1929	30	45	1934	30	45
1930	30	45	1935	30	45
1931	30	45	1936	35	50
1932	30	45			

			EF	FDC
4044 — **fourpence,** 1928–36	*from*	6	10
4045 — **threepence,** 1928–36	*from*	7	12
4046 — **twopence,** 1928–36	*from*	6	9
4047 — **penny,** 1928–36	*from*	8	13

Silver Jubilee Commemorative issue

4048

	VF	EF	UNC.
	£	£	£
4048 **Crown,** 1935. ℞. St. George, incuse lettering on edge	3	8	15
4049 — Specimen striking issued in box			£30
4050 — raised lettering on edge. Proof (.925 Æ) *FDC* £200			

BRONZE

4051

	F £	VF £	EF £	UNC £		F £	VF £	EF £	UNC £
4051 Penny. ℞. Britannia									
1911.			4	10	1918.			4	10
1912.			4	10	1919.			3	8
1913.			4	10	1920.			3	8
1914.			5	14	1921.			3	8
1915.			5	14	1922.			12	25
1916.			4	10	1926.			15	35
1917.			3	8					
4052 — H (The Mint, Birmingham, Ltd.) to l. of date									
1912 H		1	20	45	1919 H		7	65	125
1918 H		8	75	135					
4053 — KN (King's Norton Metal Co.) to l. of date									
1918 KN . . .	2	10	90	175	1919 KN . . .	2	12	110	200
4054 — modified effigy									
1926.	3	25	250	450	1927.			3	5
4055 — small head									
1928.			3	5	1933*		*Extremely rare*		
1929.			3	5	1934.			10	18
1930.			4	6	1935.			2	4
1931.			5	9	1936.			1	2
1932.			12	20					
4056 Halfpenny. ℞. Britannia									
1911.			4	9	1919.			4	9
1912.			4	9	1920.			4	9
1913.			4	9	1921.			4	9
1914.			4	9	1922.			7	15
1915.			4	9	1923.			5	11
1916.			4	9	1924.			4	9
1917.			4	9	1925.			5	11
1918.			4	9					
4057 — modified effigy									
1925.			7	15	1927.			4	9
1926.			6	14					

* *An extremely fine specimen sold at auction for £15,000 in November 1985.*

4056   4058

	EF £	UNC. £		EF £	UNC. £
4058 — small head					
1928	2	5	1933	2	5
1929	2	5	1934	4	9
1930	2	5	1935	2	5
1931	2	5	1936	1	2
1932	2	5			

4059   4062

4059 Farthing. ℞. Britannia. Dark finish

1911	3	6	1915	4	8
1912	2	4	1916	2	4
1913	2	4	1917	1	2
1914	2	4	1918	9	18

4060 — Bright finish, 1918–25 1   2

4061 — Modified effigy

1926	1	2	1932	0.50p	1
1927	1	2	1933	1	2
1928	1	2	1934	2	4
1929	1	2	1935	2	4
1930	1	2	1936	0.75p	2
1931	1	2			

4062 Third-farthing (for use in Malta). ℞. Value

1913 3   5

EDWARD VIII, Jan.–Dec. 1936

Abdicated 10 December. Created Duke of Windsor (1936–72)

No coins of Edward VIII were issued for currency within the United Kingdom bearing his name and portrait. The mint had commenced work on a new coinage prior to the Abdication, and various patterns were made. No proof sets were issued for sale and only a small number of sets were struck.

Coins bearing Edward's name, but not his portrait, were issued for the colonial territories of British East Africa, British West Africa, Fiji and New Guinea. The projected U.K. coins were to include a shilling of essentially 'Scottish' type and a nickel brass threepence with twelve sides which might supplement and possibly supersede the inconveniently small silver threepence.

Designer's initials:
 H. P. (T. Humphrey Paget)
 K. G. (Kruger Gray)

4063

4063* Proof Set
 Gold, £5, £2 and £1, 1937. . . . . *not issued*

Silver Crown, Halfcrown, Florin, Scottish shilling, sixpence and three-pence, 1937. . . . . *not issued*

The following coins were sold at auction in December 1984 and October 1985.

	£
Sovereign, brilliant, with some hair lines in field	40,000
Halfcrown, brilliant mint state	16,000
Shilling, brilliant mint state	12,000
Sixpence, brilliant mint state	9,500

Nickel brass. Threepence, 1937.	*not issued*
Bronze. Penny. Halfpenny and Farthing, 1937	*not issued*

Pattern

4064   Nickel brass dodecagonal threepence, 1937. ℞. Thrift plant of more   *Extremely rare*
naturalistic style than the modified proof coin. A small number of these
coins were produced for experimental purposes and a few did get into
circulation . . . .

Colonial issues

4068   4071

UNC.
£

4065	**British East Africa.** Bronze 10 cents, 1936.	4
4066	— — 5 cents, 1936	3
4067	**British West Africa.** Cupro-nickel penny, 1936	2
4068	— — Halfpenny, 1936	2
4069	— — One-tenth penny, 1936	1
4070	**Fiji.** Cupro-nickel penny, 1936	4
4071	**New Guinea.** Bronze penny, 1936.	3

The coins of East Africa and West Africa occur without mm. (London) and with H (Heaton) Birmingham and KN (King's Norton) Birmingham. The prices quoted are for the commonest of each type, regardless of mm.

GEORGE VI, 1936–52

Though they were at first issued concurrently, the twelve-sided nickel-brass threepence superseded the small silver threepence in 1942. Those dated 1943–4 were not issued for circulation in the U.K. In addition to the usual English "lion" shilling, a shilling, of Scottish type was issued concurrently. This depicts the Scottish lion and crown flanked by the shield of St. Andrew and a thistle. In 1947, as silver was needed to repay the bullion lent by the U.S.A. during the war, silver coins were replaced by coins of the same type and weight made of cupro-nickel. In 1949, after India had attained independence, the title *Indiae Imperator* was dropped from the coinage. Commemorative crown pieces were issued for the Coronation and the 1951 Festival of Britain.

Designer's initials:
  K. G. (Kruger Gray)
  H. P. (T. Humphrey Paget)
  W. P. (Wilson Parker)

GOLD

4074

			FDC
			£
4074	**Five pounds.** ℞. St. George, 1937. Proof		650
4075	**Two pounds.** Similar, 1937. Proof		375
4076	**Sovereign.** Similar, 1937. Proof		350
4077	**Half-sovereign.** Similar, 1937. Proof		125

SILVER

First coinage. Silver, .500 fine, with title IND:IMP

4078

		VF	EF	UNC.
		£	£	£
4078	**Crown.** Coronation commemorative, 1937. ℞. Arms and supporters	4	10	18
4079	— — Proof *FDC* £35			

4080   4081

4080 Halfcrown. ℞. Shield

	EF	UNC.		UNC.
	£	£		£
1937.		6	1942.	5
— Proof *FDC* £10			1943.	6
1938.	3	16	1944.	4
1939.		6	1945.	4
1940.		6	1946.	4
1941.		6		

4081 Florin. ℞. Crowned rose, etc.

1937.		6	1942.	4
— Proof *FDC* £8			1943.	4
1938.	3	15	1944.	4
1939.		5	1945.	4
1940.		5	1946.	4
1941.		4		

4082   4083

4082 Shilling. "English". ℞. Lion on large crown

1937.		5	1942.	4
— Proof *FDC* £6			1943.	4
1938.	2	15	1944.	4
1939.		5	1945.	3
1940.		5	1946.	3
1941.		5		

	EF	UNC.		VF	EF	UNC.
	£	£		£	£	£

4083 Shilling. "Scottish". R. Lion seated facing on crown, etc.

1937		5	1942		5
— Proof *FDC* £7			1943		5
1938	2	15	1944		5
1939		5	1945		3
1940		6	1946		3
1941		6			

4084   4085

4084 Sixpence. R. GRI crowned

1937		3	1942		2
— Proof *FDC* £4			1943		2
1938	1	6	1944		2
1939		4	1945		2
1940		4	1946		2
1941		4			

4085 Threepence. R. Shield on rose

				VF	EF	UNC.
1937		2	1941		1	3
— Proof *FDC* £4			1942*	1	5	12
1938		2	1943*	2	8	15
1939	3	8	1944*	3	12	25
1940		3				

* For colonial use only.

4086

4086 Maundy Set. Silver, .500 fine. Uniform dates

	FDC		FDC
	£		£
1937	45	1942	45
— Proof *FDC* £50		1943	45
1938	45	1944	45
1939	45	1945	45
1940	45	1946	45
1941	45		

		FDC £			*FDC* £

4087 — **fourpence,** 1937–46. . . . . *from* 9
4088 — **threepence,** 1937–46 . . . . *from* 9
4089 — **twopence,** 1937–46 . . . . *from* 9
4090 — **penny,** 1937–46. . . . . *from* 12

Second coinage. Silver, .925 fine, with title IND.IMP (Maundy only)
4091 Maundy Set (4d., 3d., 2d. and 1d.). Uniform dates

1947.	45	1948.		45

4092 — **fourpence,** 1947–8 9
4093 — **threepence,** 1947–8. 10
4094 — **twopence,** 1947–8. 9
4095 — **penny,** 1947–8 12

Third coinage. Silver, .925 fine, but omitting IND.IMP. (Maundy only)
4096 Maundy Set (4d., 3d., 2d. and 1d.). Uniform dates

1949.	45	1951.		45
1950.	45	1952.		45

The 1952 Maundy was distributed by Queen Elizabeth II.

4097 — **fourpence,** 1949–52. . . . . *from* 9
4098 — **threepence,** 1949–52 . . . . *from* 9
4099 — **twopence,** 1949–52 . . . . *from* 9
4100 — **penny,** 1949–52. . . . . *from* 12

CUPRO-NICKEL

Second coinage. Types as first (silver) coinage, IND.IMP.
4101 Halfcrown. R̠. Shield

	UNC. £			*UNC.* £
1947.	4	1948.		4

4102 Florin. R̠. Crowned rose

1947.	4	1948.		3

4103 Shilling. "English" type

1947.	5	1948.		3

4104 "Scottish" type

1947.	4	1948.		3

4105 Sixpence. GRI crowned

1947.	3	1948.		2

Third coinage. Types as before but title IND.IMP. omitted

4106   4110

	UNC. £		UNC. £
4106 Halfcrown			
1949.	5	— Proof *FDC* £9	
1950.	6	1951.	7
— Proof *FDC* £9		1952 . . . . *Extremely rare*	
4107 Florin			
1949.	7	1951.	7
1950.	7	— Proof *FDC* £8	
— Proof *FDC* £8			
4108 Shilling. "English" type			
1949.	6	1951.	6
1950.	6	— Proof *FDC* £6	
— Proof *FDC* £6			
4109 "Scottish" type			
1949.	8	1951.	7
1950.	7	— Proof *FDC* £6	
— Proof *FDC* £6			

Cupro-nickel
4110 Sixpence. As illustration

	VF £	EF £		VF £	EF £	
1949.	4		1951.			4
1950.	4		— Proof *FDC* £4			
— Proof *FDC* £4			1952.	1	10	30

Festival of Britain issue

4111

	EF	UNC.
	£	£
4111 **Crown.** R̵. St. George, 1951. *Proof-like*	2	5

NICKEL BRASS

4112   4113

First issue, with title IND.IMP.

4112 Threepence (dodecagonal). R̵. Thrift

	VF	EF	UNC.		VF	EF	UNC.
	£	£	£		£	£	£
1937.			2	1942.			2
— Proof *FDC* £4				1943.			2
1938.		2	6	1944.			3
1939.		3	15	1945.			5
1940.			5	1946.	3	30	110
1941.			3	1948.		3	15

Second issue, omitting IND.IMP.

4113 — —

	VF	EF	UNC.			EF	UNC.
1949.	4	35	120	1951.		8	30
1950.		8	25	— Proof *FDC* £25			
— Proof *FDC* £25				1952.			3

BRONZE

First issue, with title IND.IMP.

4114

	UNC. £		*UNC.* £
4114 Penny. ℞. Britannia			
1937	2	1944	7
— Proof *FDC* £6		1945	5
1938	2	1946	2
1939	5	1947	2
1940	6	1948	2

4115 Halfpenny. ℞. Ship

4115   4116

1937	2	1943	2
— Proof *FDC* £4		1944	2
1938	3	1945	3
1939	4	1946	6
1940	6	1947	3
1941	5	1948	2
1942	2		
4116 Farthing. ℞. Wren			
1937	1	1943	0.65p
— Proof *FDC* £4		1944	0.65p
1938	2	1945	0.65p
1939	0.65p	1946	0.65p
1940	1	1947	0.65p
1941	0.75p	1948	0.75p
1942	0.75p		

Bronze
Second issue, without IND.IMP. Types as before
4117 Penny

	VF	EF	UNC.		VF	EF	UNC.
	£	£	£		£	£	£
1949			2	1951	6	12	18
1950	4	10	20	— Proof *FDC* £16			
— Proof *FDC* £16							

4118   4119

4118 Halfpenny

1949.	5	1951.	5
1950.	4	— Proof *FDC* £4	
— Proof *FDC* £4		1952.	3

4119 Farthing

1949.	1	1951.	0.70p
1950.	0.70p	— Proof *FDC* £3	
— Proof *FDC* £4		1952.	0.80p

The coins dated 1952 were issued during the reign of Elizabeth II.

ELIZABETH II, acc. 1952

The earliest coins of this reign have the title BRITT·OMN, but in 1954 this was omitted from the Queen's titles owing to the changing status of so many Commonwealth territories. The minting of "English" and "Scottish" shillings was continued. A Coronation commemorative crown was issued in 1953, another crown was struck on the occasion of the 1960 British Exhibition in New York and a third was issued in honour of Sir Winston Churchill in 1965. A very small number of proof gold coins were struck in 1953 for the national museum collections, but between 1957 and 1968 gold sovereigns were minted again in quantity for sale in the international bullion market and to counteract the activities of counterfeiters.

Owing to inflation the farthing had now become practically valueless; production of these coins ceased after 1956 and the coins were demonetized at the end of 1960. In 1965 it was decided to change to a decimal system of coinage in the year 1971. As part of the transition to decimal coinage the halfpenny was demonetized in August 1969 and the halfcrown in January 1970. (See also introduction to Decimal Coinage on p. 340.)

Designer's initials:

G. L. (Gilbert Ledward)	Other designers whose initials
W. P. (Wilson Parker)	do not appear on the coins:
M. G. (Mary Gillick)	Christopher Ironside
W. G. (William Gardner)	Arnold Machin
E. F. (Edgar Fuller)	David Wynne
C. T. (Cecil Thomas)	Professor Richard Guyatt
P. N. (Philip Nathan)	Eric Sewell
R. D. M. (Raphael David Maklouf)	Leslie Durbin
N. S. (Norman Sillman)	Derek Gorringe

PRE-DECIMAL ISSUES

GOLD

First coinage, with title BRITT·OMN, 1953. *Proof only*

4120	**Five pounds.** R̟. St. George	*None issued for collectors*
4121	**Two pounds.** Similar	*None issued for collectors*
4122*	**Sovereign.** Similar.	*None issued for collectors*

* *A brilliant mint state specimen sold at auction for £24,000 in June 1985.*

4123	**Half-sovereign.** Similar	*None issued for collectors*

Second issue, BRITT·OMN omitted

4125

4124 Sovereign. R̟. St. George
1957 . . . . BV

4125 Similar, but coarser graining on edge

1958	BV	1965	BV
1959	BV	1966	BV
1962	BV	1967	BV
1963	BV	1968	BV
1964	BV		

SILVER

The Queen's Maundy are now the only coins struck regularly in silver.
The location of the Maundy ceremony is given for each year.

First issue, with title BRITT·OMN.

FDC
£

4126	**Maundy Set** (4d., 3d., 2d. and 1d.), 1953. *St Paul's.*	225
4127	— **fourpence**, 1953.	40
4128	— **threepence**, 1953.	40
4129	— **twopence**, 1953.	40
4130	— **penny**, 1953.	50

Second issue, with BRITT·OMN omitted

4131

4131 **Maundy Set** (4d., 3d., 2d. and 1d.). Uniform dates

	FDC		*FDC*
	£		£
1954 *Westminster.*	50	1963 *Chelmsford*	50
1955 *Southwark*	50	1964 *Westminster.*	50
1956 *Westminster.*	50	1965 *Canterbury*	50
1957 *St. Albans.*	50	1966 *Westminster.*	50
1958 *Westminster.*	50	1967 *Durham.*	50
1959 *Windsor.*	50	1968 *Westminster.*	50
1960 *Westminster.*	50	1969 *Selby*	50
1961 *Rochester*	50	1970 *Westminster.*	50
1962 *Westminster.*	50	*See also p. 343.*	

4132	— **fourpence**, 1954–70.	*from*	10
4133	— **threepence**, 1954–70.	*from*	10
4134	— **twopence**, 1954–70.	*from*	10
4135	— **penny**, 1954–70.	*from*	11

CUPRO-NICKEL

First issue, 1953, with title BRITT·OMN.

4136

		EF	*UNC.*	*Proof FDC*
		£	£	£
4136	**Crown.** Queen on horseback. ℞. Crown in centre of cross, shield in each angle, 1953	1	3	25

4137   4138

4137	**Halfcrown,** with title BRITT·OMN. ℞. Arms, 1953	3	8
4138	**Florin.** ℞. Double rose, 1953	3	6

4139   4140   4141

4139	**Shilling.** "English". ℞. Three lions, 1953	1	4
4140	"Scottish". ℞. Lion rampant in shield, 1953	1	4
4141	**Sixpence.** ℞. Interlaced rose, thistle, shamrock and leek, 1953	0.70p	3
4142	Set of 9 uncirculated cu-ni, ni-br and Æ coins (2/6 to ¼d.) in Royal Mint plastic envelope		8

Cupro-nickel
Second issue, similar types but omitting BRITT·OMN.

4143   4144

		EF	UNC.
		£	£
4143	**Crown,** 1960. Bust r. ℞. As 4136	2	5
—	— Similar, from polished dies (New York Exhibition issue)	4	18
4144	Churchill commemorative, 1965. As illustration. ℞. Bust of Winston		
	Churchill r.		0.75p
—	— Similar, satin-finish. *Specimen*		250
4145	**Halfcrown.** ℞. As 4137		

	EF	UNC.			
	£	£			
1954	2	15	1961		1
1955		4	1962		1
1956		5	1963		1
1957		2	1964		3
1958	2	12	1965		1
1959	2	15	1966		0.60p
1960		3	1967		0.60p

4146

4146 Florin. ℞. As 4138

1954	3	30	1961		2
1955		3	1962		1
1956		3	1963		0.75p
1957	2	20	1964		0.60p
1958	1	10	1965		0.50p
1959	2	25	1966		0.45p
1960		2	1967		0.40p

4147 Shilling. "English" type. ℞. As 4139

	EF	UNC.		UNC.
	£	£		£
1954		2	1961	0.75p
1955		2	1962	0.50p
1956		7	1963	0.25p
1957		1	1964	0.30p
1958	2	15	1965	0.30p
1959		1	1966	0.30p
1960		1		

4148 "Scottish" type. ℞. As 4140

	EF	UNC.		UNC.
1954		2	1961	5
1955		3	1962	1
1956		7	1963	0.25p
1957	2	15	1964	0.50p
1958		1	1965	0.50p
1959	2	15	1966	0.30p
1960		1		

4149 Sixpence. ℞. As 4141

	UNC.		UNC.
1954	3	1961	3
1955	1	1962	0.30p
1956	1	1963	0.25p
1957	0.65p	1964	0.20p
1958	4	1965	0.15p
1959	0.35p	1966	0.15p
1960	4	1967	0.15p

NICKEL BRASS

4152   4153

First issue, with title BRITT.OMN.

4152 Threepence (dodecagonal). ℞. Crowned portcullis, 1953 1
— Proof *FDC* £4

Second issue (omitting BRIT.OMN)

4153 Similar type

	UNC.		UNC.
1954	4	1961	0.35p
1955	5	1962	0.30p
1956	5	1963	0.20p
1957	3	1964	0.20p
1958	6	1965	0.20p
1959	3	1966	0.15p
1960	3	1967	0.15p

BRONZE

First issue, with title BRITT.OMN.

4154 4158

	VF £	EF £	UNC. £	Proof FDC £
4154 Penny. R. Britannia (only issued with Royal Mint set in plastic envelope), 1953	0.60p	2	5	6
4155 Halfpenny. R. Ship, 1953			2	4
4156 Farthing. R. Wren, 1953			0.75p	3

Second issue, omitting BRITT.OMN.

	UNC. £		UNC. £
4157 Penny. R. Britannia (1954–60 *not issued*)			
1954	*Extremely rare*	1964	0.10p
1961	0.50p	1965	0.10p
1962	0.15p	1966	0.10p
1963	0.15p	1967	0.10p
4158 Halfpenny. R. Ship (1961 *not issued*)			
1954	4	1962	0.10p
1955	4	1963	0.10p
1956	4	1964	0.10p
1957	0.60p	1965	0.10p
1958	0.35p	1966	0.10p
1959	0.20p	1967	0.10p
1960	0.10p		

4156 4159

		EF £	UNC. £
4159 Farthing. R. Wren			
1954	0.80p	1956	0.55p 2
1955	0.75p		

DECIMAL COINAGE

In December 1967 a decision to build a new mint at Llantrisant in South Wales was announced. The first phase was completed by December 1968 when H.M. The Queen struck the first coins at the official opening. The second phase was completed during late 1975 at which time all coin production at Tower Hill ceased.

Though the official change-over to a decimal currency did not take place until 15th February 1971, three decimal denominations were circulated prior to this date. The 10 and 5 *new pence*, equivalent to the former florin and shilling, were introduced in 1968 and the seven-sided 50 *new pence* (equal to 10 shillings) was issued during October 1969. The old halfpenny was demonetized on 1st August 1969, and the halfcrown was withdrawn on 1st January 1970.

In 1968 bronze 2, 1 and ½ *new pence* dated 1971 were issued, together with the 1968 10 and 5 *new pence*, as specimens of the new coinage, but these bronze coins were not legalized for current use until 1971.

Britain's accession to the E.E.C. was commemorated by a special 50 pence piece in 1973. A crown-sized 25 pence has been issued to celebrate the Silver Wedding of H.M. The Queen and Prince Philip in 1972, the Queen's Silver Jubilee in 1977, the 80th birthday of Queen Elizabeth, the Queen Mother and for the Royal Wedding in 1981.

A further crown-sized coin was issued in 1990 for the 90th birthday of Queen Elizabeth, the Queen Mother, with a face value of £5. The face value of a cupro-nickel crown had been five shillings or 25 pence since 1951 although the equivalent of 5/- in 1951 was £3.27 in 1990. Thus it is hoped that this new £5 face value will stand for many years.

In 1979 the first proof sovereign since 1937 was issued and 1980 saw a proof five pound, two pound and half-sovereign.

Britain's first 20 pence piece appeared in 1982 and 1983 saw the first circulating non-precious metal £1 coin. In 1986 the Royal Mint introduced a nickel-brass £2 piece specially struck in honour of the XIII Commonwealth Games held in Scotland (see illus. 4279). The word "NEW" was omitted from the 1982 cupro-nickel coins which now bear the denomination in words and figures. The ½ pence was demonetized in December 1984.

1990 saw the first of a number of changes to the coinage. In addition to the increase in the face value of a crown-sized coin from 25p to £5, a smaller 5p was introduced thus bringing to an end a specification for the 5p and its 1/- equivalent first introduced in 1816. A smaller size 10p is planned for 1992, and proposals are being considered to replace the 1p and 2p bronze coins with pieces made of copper plated steel.

All pre-decimal 1/- coins plus the same size 5p coins ceased to be legal tender on 31st December 1990.

Some base metal coins, from 50p downwards, only appear in Royal Mint Proof and/or Specimen sets. These are indicated in the texts by asterisks following the dates.

All silver (-AR) coins are minted in .925 sterling silver unless otherwise stated.

GOLD

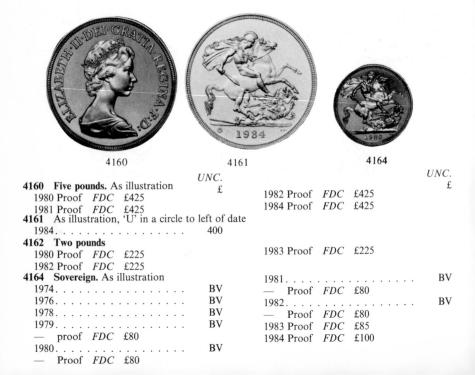

4160   4161   4164

		UNC. £					UNC. £
4160 Five pounds. As illustration			1982 Proof	*FDC*	£425		
1980 Proof *FDC* £425			1984 Proof	*FDC*	£425		
1981 Proof *FDC* £425							
4161 As illustration, 'U' in a circle to left of date							
1984.		400					
4162 Two pounds							
1980 Proof *FDC* £225			1983 Proof	*FDC*	£225		
1982 Proof *FDC* £225							
4164 Sovereign. As illustration			1981.				BV
1974.		BV	— Proof *FDC* £80				
1976.		BV	1982.				BV
1978.		BV	— Proof *FDC* £80				
1979.		BV	1983 Proof *FDC* £85				
— proof *FDC* £80			1984 Proof *FDC* £100				
1980.		BV					
— Proof *FDC* £80							

UNC.

4166 Half-sovereign £
1980 Proof *FDC* £50
1982. 45
— Proof *FDC* £50

1983 Proof *FDC* £50
1984 Proof *FDC* £55

(For proof sets which include some or all of the above coins, see the list on pages 354–5.)

SILVER

	FDC £		FDC £
4170 Maundy Set (4p, 3p, 2p and 1p). Uniform dates. Types as 4131			
1971 *Tewkesbury Abbey*	55	1988 *Lichfield Cathedral*	75
1972 *York Minster*	55	1989 *Birmingham Cathedral*	75
1973 *Westminster Abbey*	55	1990 *Newcastle Cathedral*	75
1974 *Salisbury Cathedral*	55	1991 *Westminster Abbey*	75
1975 *Peterborough Cathedral*	55		
1976 *Hereford Cathedral*	55		
1977 *Westminster Abbey*	65		
1978 *Carlisle Cathedral*	55		
1979 *Winchester Cathedral*	55		
1980 *Worcester Cathedral*	55		
1981 *Westminster Abbey*	55		
1982 *St. David's Cathedral*	55		
1983 *Exeter Cathedral*	55		
1984 *Southwell Minster*	55		
1985 *Ripon Cathedral*	55		
1986 *Chichester Cathedral*	55		
1987 *Ely Cathedral*	75		

4180 — **fourpence,** 1971–90 . . . . *from* 13
4181 — **threepence,** 1971–90 . . . . *from* 13
4182 — **twopence,** 1971–90 . . . . *from* 13
4183 — **penny,** 1971–90 . . . . *from* 15

The Queen's Maundy are now the only coins struck regularly in .925 silver. The place of distribution is shown after each date.

NICKEL-BRASS

4185   4186

UNC.
£

4185 One pound (U.K. type). Edge DECUS ET TUTAMEN
1983 2
— Specimen in presentation folder 3
— Proof in *Æ* 27
— Proof piedfort in *Æ* 110

UNC.
£

4186 One pound (Scottish type). Edge NEMO ME IMPUNE LACESSIT

1984 2

— Specimen in presentation folder 5

— Proof in *Æ* *FDC* £21

— Proof piedfort in *Æ* *FDC* £60

CUPRO-NICKEL

4190

4191

		UNC. £				UNC. £

4190 Fifty new pence (seven-sided). ℞. Britannia r.

1969.	2	1978.	2
1970.	4	1979.	2
1976.	2	1980.	2
1977.	2	1981.	2

4191 Fifty (50) pence. "New" omitted. As illustration

1982.	2	1984*	
1983.	2		

4195 Accession to European Economic Community. ℞. Clasped hands, 1973 . . . . . . 1.50

— — (Proof in case) *FDC* £2

4195

4200

4200 **Twenty-five pence** (crown). Silver Wedding Commemorative, 1972 . . . . 0.75p
— (*AR* proof in case) *FDC* £20
— (Cu.-ni. proof.) Issued in 1972/Mint set. See PS22 4

4201

4201 Silver Jubilee Commemorative, 1977 . . . . 0.60p
— (*AR* proof in case) *FDC* £12
— (Cu.-ni. proof.) Only issued in 1977/Mint set. See PS27 . . . . — 4
— (Cu.-ni. Specimen striking.) Issued in Royal Mint folder . . . . — 2

4202

4202 Queen Mother 80th Birthday Commemorative, 1980. . . . . 0.60p
— (*AR* proof in case) *FDC* £35
— (Cu.-ni. Specimen striking.) Issued in Royal Mint folder 1

UNC.
£

4203

4203 Twenty-five pence. Royal Wedding Commemorative, 1981 . . . . 0.45p
— (Ѧ proof in case) *FDC* £30
— (Cu.-ni. Specimen striking.) Issued in Royal Mint folder 1

4208

4208 Twenty (20) pence. As illustration

| 1982 . . . . 0.40p | 1983 . . . . 0.40p |
| — (Ѧ Proof piedfort) *FDC* £45 | 1984 . . . . 0.40p |

4210   4211

4210 Ten new pence. Ṛ. Lion passant guardant.

UNC.
£

1968 . . . . 0.30p	1975 . . . . 0.50p
1969 . . . . 0.30p	1976 . . . . 0.50p
1970 . . . . 0.30p	1977 . . . . 0.75p
1971 . . . . 0.40p	1979 . . . . 0.50p
1973 . . . . 0.40p	1980 . . . . 0.75p
1974 . . . . 0.40p	1981 . . . . 0.75p

4211 Ten (10) pence. As illustration

| 1982* . . . . | 1984* . . . . |
| 1983* . . . . | |

4220 4221

4220 Five new pence. R. Crowned thistle

	UNC £		UNC £
1968.	0.20p	1977.	0.20p
1969.	0.30p	1978.	0.20p
1970.	0.30p	1979.	0.20p
1971.	0.20p	1980.	0.20p
1975.	0.20p		

4221 Five (5) pence. As illustration

1982*			
1983*		1984*	

BRONZE

4230 4231

4230 Two new pence. R. Plumes

	UNC		UNC
1971.	0.10p	1978.	0.30p
1975.	0.20p	1979.	0.15p
1976.	0.20p	1980.	0.15p
1977.	0.10p	1981.	0.15p

4231 Two (2) pence. As illustration

1982*			
1983*		1984*	

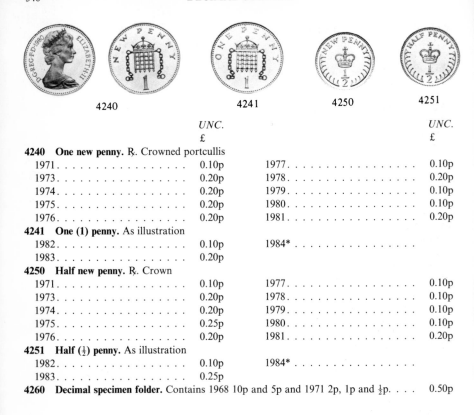

| 4240 | 4241 | 4250 | 4251 |

	UNC. £		UNC. £
4240 One new penny. ℞. Crowned portcullis			
1971.	0.10p	1977.	0.10p
1973.	0.20p	1978.	0.20p
1974.	0.20p	1979.	0.10p
1975.	0.20p	1980.	0.10p
1976.	0.20p	1981.	0.20p
4241 One (1) penny. As illustration			
1982.	0.10p	1984*	
1983.	0.20p		
4250 Half new penny. ℞. Crown			
1971.	0.10p	1977.	0.10p
1973.	0.20p	1978.	0.10p
1974.	0.20p	1979.	0.10p
1975.	0.25p	1980.	0.10p
1976.	0.20p	1981.	0.20p
4251 Half (½) penny. As illustration			
1982.	0.10p	1984*	
1983.	0.25p		

4260 Decimal specimen folder. Contains 1968 10p and 5p and 1971 2p, 1p and ½p. . . . 0.50p

NEW PORTRAIT

The new effigy is designed by Raphael David Maklouf, FRSA. It is only the third portrait of the Queen to be used on U.K. coinage, the previous change of portrait being in 1968 with the introduction of decimal coins. The designer's initials R.D.M. appear on the truncation. There is no portrait change on the Maundy coins.

GOLD

| 4261 | 4263 | 4276 |

UNC.
£

4261 Five pounds. ℞. St. George
1985 Proof *FDC* £450   1991 Proof *FDC* £450
1990 Proof *FDC* £450

4262 ℞. St. George, "U" in a circle to left of date
1985   400
1986   400

4263 Uncouped portrait of Queen Elizabeth II. As illustration. ℞. St. George, 'U' in a circle to left
of date.
1987   450
1988   450
1990   450
1991   450

4264 500th Anniversary of Sovereign
1989   460
1989 Proof *FDC* £470

4266 Two pounds. ℞. St. George
1985 Proof *FDC* £225   1990 Proof *FDC* £300
1987 Proof *FDC* £225   1991 Proof *FDC* £300
1988 Proof *FDC* £300

4267 ℞. St. Andrew's cross surmounted by a thistle of Scotland. Edge XIII COMMONWEALTH GAMES
SCOTLAND 1986 (*See illus. 4279*)
1986 Proof *FDC* £300

4268 500th Anniversary of Sovereign
1989 Proof *FDC* £300

4271 Sovereign. ℞. St. George
1985 Proof *FDC* £90   1988 Proof *FDC* £150
1986 Proof *FDC* £100   1990 Proof *FDC* £150
1987 Proof *FDC* £100   1991 Proof *FDC* £150

4272 Sovereign. 500th Anniversary
1989 Proof *FDC* £150

4276 Half-sovereign. ℞. St. George
1985 Proof *FDC* £55   1988 Proof *FDC* £80
1986 Proof *FDC* £60   1990 Proof *FDC* £80
1987 Proof *FDC* £60   1991 Proof *FDC* £80

4276A

4276A 500th Anniversary of Sovereign
1989 Proof *FDC* £80

4277

UNC.
£

4277 Britannia. One hundred pounds. (1oz of fine gold).

R̨. Britannia standing.

1987	275
— Proof *FDC* £450	
1988	275
— Proof *FDC* £450	
1989	275
— Proof *FDC* £450	
1990 . . . . . . :	275
— Proof *FDC* £450	
1991	275
— Proof *FDC* £450	

4278

4278 Britannia. Fifty pounds. (½oz of fine gold).

R̨. Britannia standing.

1987	140
— Proof *FDC* £250	
1988	140
— Proof *FDC* £250	
1989	140
— Proof *FDC* £250	
1990	140
— Proof *FDC* £250	
1991	140
— Proof *FDC* £250	

4278A

4278A Britannia. Twenty five pounds. (¼oz of fine gold).

R̨. Britannia standing.

1987	75
— Proof *FDC* £130	

UNC.
£

1988 75
— Proof *FDC* £130
1989 75
— Proof *FDC* £130
1990 75
— Proof *FDC* £130
1991 75
— Proof *FDC* £130

4278B

4278B **Britannia. Ten pounds.** ($\frac{1}{10}$oz of fine gold).

Ɽ. Britannia standing.

1987 35
— Proof *FDC* £65
1988 35
— Proof *FDC* £65
1989 35
— Proof *FDC* £65
1990 35
— Proof *FDC* £65
1991 35
— Proof *FDC* £65

NICKEL-BRASS

4279

4279 Two pounds. ℞. St. Andrew's cross surmounted by a thistle of Scotland. Edge XIII
COMMONWEALTH GAMES SCOTLAND 1986

1986   3
— Struck in ·500 silver.   12
— Proof in Æ   *FDC*   £20
— Specimen in presentation folder   5

4280   4280A

4280   300th Anniversary of Bill of Rights. Cypher of William and Mary, House of Commons mace
and St. Edward's crown.

1989   3
— Specimen in presentation folder   5
— Proof Æ   *FDC*   £23
— Proof piedfort in Æ   *FDC*   £40

4280A   300th Anniversary of Claim of Right (Scotland). ℞. As 4280, but with
crown of Scotland.

—1989   4
— Specimen in presentation folder   6
— Proof in Æ   *FDC*   £23
— Proof piedfort in Æ   *FDC*   £40

4281

UNC.

4281 One pound (Welsh type). Edge PLEIDIOL WYF I'M GWLAD   £

1985   2

— Specimen in presentation folder   3

— Proof in Æ   *FDC* £21

— Proof piedfort in Æ   *FDC* £55

1990   2

— Proof in Æ   *FDC* £21

4282	4283	4284

4282 (Northern Ireland). Edge DECUS ET TUTAMEN

1986   2

— Specimen in presentation folder   3

— Proof in Æ   *FDC* £21

— Proof piedfort in Æ   *FDC* £45

1991   2

— Proof in Æ   *FDC* £20

4283 (English type). Edge DECUS ET TUTAMEN

1987   2

— Specimen in presentation folder   3

— Proof in Æ   *FDC* £21

— Proof piedfort in Æ   *FDC* £45

4284 (Royal arms). Edge DECUS ET TUTAMEN

1988   2

— Specimen in presentation folder   3

— Proof in Æ   *FDC* £21

— Proof piedfort Æ   *FDC* £45

4285 (Scottish type). Edge NEMO ME IMPUNE LACESSIT (Illus. as 4186)

1989   2

— Proof in Æ   *FDC* £21

— Proof piedfort in Æ   *FDC* £50

CUPRO-NICKEL

4285A

UNC.

4285A   Five pounds (crown). Queen Mother 90th birthday commemorative.   £
—1990   7
Specimen in presentation folder   9
— Proof in Æ in case   *FDC* £28.75
— Proof in Æ in case   *FDC* £750

4286

4286   Fifty pence. ℞. Britannia r.
1985   2
1986* . . . .
1987* . . . .
1988* . . . .
1989* . . . .
1990* . . . .
1991

4291

4291   Twenty pence. ℞. Crowned double rose
1985 . . . .
1986* . . . .
1987 . . . .
1988 . . . .
1989 . . . .
1990 . . . .
1991 . . . .

4301

4301 Ten pence. R. Lion passant guardant

1985* ....
1986* ....
1987* ....
1988* ....
1989* ....
1990* ....
1991 ....

4306

4306 Five pence. R. Crowned thistle

1985* ....
1986* ....
1987 ....
1988 ....
1989 ....
1990* ....
— Proof in AR *FDC* £18

4307

4307 Five pence. R. Crowned thistle: diam 18mm

1990 ....
— Proof in AR *FDC* £18
— Proof piedfort in AR *FDC* £25
1991 ....

BRONZE

4311

4311 Two pence. ℞. Plumes

1985 . . . .
1986 . . . .
1987 . . . .
1988 . . . .
1989 . . . .
1990 . . . .
1991 . . . .

4316

4316 One penny. ℞. Portcullis with chains

1985 . . . .
1986 . . . .
1987 . . . .
1988 . . . .
1989 . . . .
1990 . . . .
1991 . . . .

PROOF or SPECIMEN SETS

Issued by the Royal Mint in official case from 1887 onwards, but earlier sets were issued privately by the engraver.

All pieces have a finish superior to that of the current coins.

		No. of coins	FDC £
PS1	**George IV.** New issue, **1826.** Five pounds to farthing	(11)	18,000
PS2	**William IV.** Coronation, **1831.** Two pounds to farthing	(14)	16,000
PS3	**Victoria,** young head, **1839.** "Una and the Lion" five pounds, and sovereign to farthing	(15)	27,500
PS4	— **1853.** Sovereign to quarter-farthing, including Gothic type crown . . .	(16)	18,000
PS5	Jubilee head. Golden Jubilee, **1887.** Five pounds to threepence	(11)	4,750
PS6	— — Crown to threepence	(7)	850
PS7	Old head, **1893.** Five pounds to threepence	(10)	5,750
PS8	— — Crown to threepence	(6)	900
PS9	**Edward VII.** Coronation, **1902.** Five pounds to Maundy penny. Matt surface	(13)	1,450
PS10	— — Sovereign to Maundy penny. Matt surface	(11)	375
PS11	**George V.** Coronation, **1911.** Five pounds to Maundy penny	(12)	2,450
PS12	— — Sovereign to Maundy penny	(10)	650
PS13	— — Halfcrown to Maundy penny	(8)	300
PS14	New types, **1927.** Crown to threepence	(6)	200
PS15	**George VI.** Coronation, **1937.** Gold. Five pounds to half-sovereign. . . .	(4)	1,450
PS16	— — — Silver, etc. Crown to farthing, including Maundy	(15)	110
PS17	Mid-Century, **1950.** Halfcrown to farthing	(10)	35
PS18	Festival of Britain, **1951.** Crown to farthing.	(10)	50
PS19	**Elizabeth II.** Coronation, **1953.** Crown to farthing	(10)	35
PS20	"Last Sterling" set, **1970.** Halfpenny to halfpenny plus medallion	(8)	10
PS21	Decimal coinage set, **1971.** 50 new pence ("Britannia") to ½ penny, plus medallion.	(6)	6
PS22	— **1972.** As last, but includes the cu.-ni. Silver Wedding crown	(7)	8
PS23	— **1973.** As PS21 but "EEC" 50p	(6)	5
PS24	— **1974.** As PS21	(6)	5
PS25	— **1975.** As last	(6)	5
PS26	— **1976.** As last	(6)	5
PS27	— **1977.** As PS21 but including the proof Silver Jubilee crown struck in cupro-nickel	(7)	8
PS28	— **1978.** As PS21	(6)	8
PS29	— **1979.** As last	(6)	10
PS30	— **1980.** As last	(6)	6
PS31	— — Five pounds to half-sovereign	(4)	750
PS32	— **1981.** U.K. Proof coin Commemorative collection. (Consists of £5, £1, Royal Wedding crown (25p) in Æ, plus base metal proofs as PS21.) .	(9)	500
PS33	— — As PS21	(6)	6
PS34	**Elizabeth II, 1982.** U.K. Uncirculated (specimen) set in Royal Mint folder. New reverse types, including 20 pence	(7)	3
PS35	— — As last but proofs in Royal Mint sealed plastic case, plus medallion.	(7)	10
PS36	— Æ Five pounds to half-sovereign	(4)	850
PS37	— **1983.** As PS34, includes "U.K." £1	(8)	8
PS38	— — As PS35, includes "U.K." £1	(8)	12

PS39	— — N £2, £1, £$\frac{1}{2}$ in case.	(3)	325
PS40	— **1984.** As PS37 but with "Scottish" £1	(8)	5
PS41	— — As PS38 but with "Scottish" £1	(8)	10
PS42	— — N £5, £1, £$\frac{1}{2}$ in case.	(3)	600
PS43	— **1985.** As PS37 but with new portrait, also includes "Welsh" £1. The set does not contain the now discontinued halfpenny	(7)	5
PS44	— — As last but proofs in Royal Mint sealed plastic case, plus medallion	(7)	10
PS45	— — As last but within a deluxe red leather case.	(7)	15
PS46	— — N £5, £2, £1, £$\frac{1}{2}$ in case.	(4)	850
PS47	— **1986.** As PS37 but with new two pounds and the "Northern Ireland" £1.	(8)	8
PS48	— — As PS44 but with two pounds and "Northern Ireland" £1	(8)	15
PS49	— — As last but within a deluxe red leather case.	(8)	18
PS50	— — N £2 (as 4267), £1, £$\frac{1}{2}$ in a deluxe red leather case.	(3)	350
PS51	— **1987.** As PS43 but with "English" £1	(7)	5
PS52	— — As last but proofs in Royal Mint sealed plastic case, plus medallion	(7)	18
PS53	— — As last but within a deluxe red leather case.	(7)	23
PS54	— — N £2 (as 4266), £1, £$\frac{1}{2}$ in a deluxe red leather case.	(3)	400
PS55	— — **Britannia** N proofs. £100, £50, £25, £10 in a deluxe case	(4)	900
PS56	— — As last but only containing the £25, £10 in a deluxe case	(2)	215
PS57	— **1988.** As PS43 but with "Royal Arms" £1.	(7)	6
PS58	— — As last but proofs in Royal Mint sealed plastic case, plus medallion	(7)	21
PS59	— — As last but within a deluxe leather case.	(7)	27
PS60	— — N £2 (as 4266), £1, £$\frac{1}{2}$ in a deluxe case	(3)	500
PS61	— — **Britannia** proofs. As PS55	(4)	900
PS62	— — As PS56.	(2)	215
PS63	— **1989.** As PS43 but with "Scotland" £1.	(7)	7
PS64	— — As last but proofs and with 2 × £2.	(9)	23
PS65	— — As last but within red leather case.	(9)	30
PS66	— — Sovereign Anniversary N £5, £2, £1, £$\frac{1}{2}$	(4)	1250
PS67	— — As last but only containing £2, £1, £$\frac{1}{2}$.	(3)	500
PS68	— — 2 × £2 in Royal Mint folder	(2)	8
PS69	— — As last but silver piedfort proofs	(2)	95
PS70	— — As last but silver proofs	(2)	42
PS71	— — **Britannia** proofs. As PS55	(4)	1000
PS72	— — As PS56.	(2)	215
PS73	— **1990.** As PS43 but with "Welsh" £1 and new 5p	(8)	6.25p
PS74	— — As last but proofs.	(8)	22
PS75	— — As last but within red leather case.	(8)	29
PS76	— — N £5, £2, £1, £$\frac{1}{2}$ in case	(4)	1100
PS77	— — N £2, £1, £$\frac{1}{2}$ in case	(3)	500
PS78	— — 2 × 5p R proofs (as 4306 & 4307).	(2)	35
PS79	— — **Britannia** proofs. As PS55	(4)	1000
PS80	— **1991.** As PS43 but with "Northern Ireland" £1	(7)	6.95
PS81	— — As last but proofs.	(7)	23
PS82	— — As last but within red leather case	(7)	30
PS83	— — N £5, £2, £1, £$\frac{1}{2}$ in case	(4)	1150
PS84	— — N £2, £1, £$\frac{1}{2}$ in case	(3)	500
PS85	— — Britannia proofs. As PS55	(4)	1000

The prices given are for absolutely perfect sets with uncleaned, brilliant or matt surfaces. Sets are often seen with one or more coins showing imperfections such as scratches, bumps on the edge, etc. Any flaws will substantially affect the value of a set.

APPENDIX I

A SELECT NUMISMATIC BIBLIOGRAPHY

Listed below is a selection of general books on British numismatics and other works that the specialist collector will need to consult.

General Books:

NORTH, J. J. *English Hammered Coins*, Vol. I, *c. 650–1272*; Vol. II, *1272–1662*.
BROOKE, G. C. *English Coins*. (3rd Ed., 1951).
SUTHERLAND, C. H. V. *English Coinage, 600–1900*.
KENYON, R. LL. *Gold Coins of England*.
GRUEBER, H. A. *Handbook of the Coins of Great Britain and Ireland*.

Specialist Works:

MACK, R. P. *The Coinage of Ancient Britain*.
ALLEN, D. *The Origins of Coinage in Britain: A Reappraisal*.
VAN ARSDELL, R. *Celtic Coinage of Britain*.
DOLLEY, R. H. M. (ED.). *Anglo-Saxon Coins; studies presented to Sir Frank Stenton*.
KEARY, C. and GREUBER, H. *English Coins in the British Museum: Anglo-Saxon Series*.
BROOKE, G. C. *English Coins in the British Museum: The Norman Kings*.
ALLEN, D. F. *English Coins in the British Museum: The Cross-and-Crosslets ("Tealby") type of Henry II*.
LAWRENCE, L. A. *The Coinage of Edward III from 1351*.
WHITTON, C. A. *The Heavy Coinage of Henry VI*.
BLUNT, C. E. and WHITTON, C. A. *The Coinages of Edward IV and of Henry VI (Restored)*.
MORRIESON, LT.-COL. H. W. *The Coinages of Thomas Bushell, 1636–1648*.
NORTH, J. J. and PRESTON-MORLEY, P. J. *The John G. Brooker Collection: Coins of Charles I*.
SEABY, H. A. and RAYNER, P. A. *The English Silver Coinage from 1649*. 5th ed. due 1991.
MARSH, M. A. *The Gold Sovereign* and *The Gold Half Sovereign*.
SPINK & SON, LTD. *The Milled Coinage of England, 1662–1946*.
PECK, C. W. *English Copper, Tin and Bronze Coins in the British Museum, 1558–1958*.
LINECAR, H. W. A. *British Coin Designs and Designers*.

and other authoritative papers published in the *Numismatic Chronicle* and *British Numismatic Journal*.

APPENDIX II

FOREIGN LEGENDS ON ENGLISH COINS

A DOMINO FACTUM EST ISTUD ET EST MIRABILE IN OCULIS NOSTRIS. (This is the Lord's doing and it is marvellous in our eyes: *Psalm* 118, 23.) First used on "fine" sovereign of Mary.

AMOR POPULI PRAESIDIUM REGIS. (The love of the people is the King's protection.) Reverse legend on angels of Charles I.

ANNO REGNI PRIMO, etc. (In the first year of the reign, etc.) Used around the edge of many of the larger milled denominations.

CHRISTO AUSPICE REGNO. (I reign under the auspice of Christ.) Used extensively in the reign of Charles I.

CIVIUM INDUSTRIA FLORET CIVITAS. (By the industry of its people the State flourishes.) On the 1951 Festival crown of George VI.

CULTORES SUI DEUS PROTEGIT. (God protects His worshippers.) On gold double crowns and crowns of Charles I.

DECUS ET TUTAMEN. (An ornament and a safeguard.) This inscription on the edge of all early large milled silver was suggested by Evelyn, he having seen it on the vignette in Card. Richelieu's Greek Testament, and of course refers to the device as a means to prevent clipping. (Virgil, *Aen* v.262.) This legend also appears on the edge of U.K. and Northern Ireland one pound coins.

DIRIGE DEUS GRESSUS MEOS. (May the Lord direct my steps.) On the "Una" 5 pounds of Queen Victoria.

DOMINE NE IN FURORE TUO ARGUAS ME. (O Lord, rebuke me not in Thine anger: *Psalm* 6, 1.). First used on the half-florin of Edward III and then on all half-nobles.

DomiNus DeuS Omnipotens REX. (Lord God, Almighty King.) (Viking coins.)

DUM SPIRO SPERO. (Whilst I live, I hope.) On the coins struck at Pontefract Castle during the Civil War after Charles I had been imprisoned.

EXALTABITUR IN GLORIA. (He shall be exalted in glory.) On all quarter-nobles.

EXURGAT DEUS ET DISSIPENTUR INIMICI EIUS. (Let God arise and let His enemies be scattered: *Psalm* 68, 1.) On the Scottish ducat and early English coins of James I (VI) and was chosen by the King himself.

FACIAM EOS IN GENTEM UNAM. (I will make them one nation: *Ezek.* 37, 22.) On unites and laurels of James I.

FLORENT CONCORDIA REGNA. (Through concord kingdoms flourish.) On gold unite of Charles I and broad of Charles II.

HANC DEUS DEDIT. (God has given this, *i.e. crown.*) On siege-pieces of Pontefract struck in the name of Charles II.

HAS NISI PERITURUS MIHI ADIMAT NEMO. (Let no one remove these [letters] from me under penalty of death.) On the edge of crowns and half-crowns of Cromwell.

HENRICUS ROSAS REGNA JACOBUS. (Henry *united* the roses, James the kingdoms.) On English and Scottish gold coins of James I (VI).

INIMICOS EJUS INDUAM CONFUSIONE. (As for his enemies I shall clothe them with shame: *Psalm* 132, 18.) On shillings of Edward VI struck at Durham House, Strand.

JESUS AUTEM TRANSIENS PER MEDIUM ILLORUM IBAT. (But Jesus, passing through the midst of them, went His va   iv. 30.) The usual reverse legend on English nobles, ryals and hammered sovereign   nes I; also on the very rare Scottish noble of David II of Scotland and the unique /   noble of Edward the Black Prince.

JUSTITIA THR   T. (Justice strengthens the throne.) On Charles I half-groats and pennies and Scotti   penny pieces.

LUCERNA PEDI   VERBUM EST. (Thy word is a lamp unto my feet: *Psalm* 119, 105.) Obverse legend on a   f-sovereign of Edward VI struck at Durham House, Strand.

MIRABILIA FECI   nade marvellously.) On the Viking coins of (?) York.

NEMO ME IMPUNE LACESSIT. (No-one provokes me with impunity.) On the 1984 Scottish one pound.

NUMMORUM FAMULUS. (The servant of the coinage.) The legend on the edge of the English tin coinage at the end of the seventeenth century.

O CRUX AVE SPES UNICA. (Hail! O Cross, our only hope.) On the reverse of all half-angels.

PAX MISSA PER ORBEM. (Peace sent throughout the world.) The reverse legend of a pattern farthing of Anne.

PAX QUÆRITUR BELLO. (Peace is sought by war.) The reverse legend of the Cromwell broad.

PER CRUCEM TUAM SALVA NOS CHRISTE REDEMPTOR. (By Thy cross, save us, O Christ, our Redeemer.) The normal reverse of English angels.

PLEIDIOL WYF I·M GWLAD. (True am I to my country.) Taken from the Welsh National Anthem. Used on the 1985 Welsh one pound.

POST MORTEM PATRIS PRO FILIO. (For the son after the death of the father.) On siege-pieces struck at Pontefract in 1648 (old style) after the execution of Charles I.

POSUI DEUM ADJUTOREM MEUM. (I have made God my Helper: *comp. Psalm* 54, 4.) Used on many English and Irish silver coins from Edward III until 1603. Altered to POSUIMUS and NOSTRUM on the coins of Philip and Mary.

PROTECTOR LITERIS LITERÆ NUMMIS CORONA ET SALUS. (A protection to the letters [on the face of the coin], the letters [on the edge] are a garland and a safeguard to the coinage.) On the edge of the rare fifty-shilling piece of Cromwell.

QUÆ DEUS CONJUNXIT NEMO SEPARET. (What God hath joined together let no man put asunder: *Matt.* 19, 6.) On the larger silver English and Scottish coins of James I after he succeeded to the English throne.

REDDE CUIQUE QUOD SUUM EST. (Render to each that which is his own.) On a Henry VIII type groat of Edward VI struck by Sir Martin Bowes at Durham House, Strand.

RELIGIO PROTESTANTIVM LEGES ANGLIÆ LIBERTAS PARLIAMENTI. (The religion of the Protestants, the laws of England, the liberty of the Parliament.) This is known as the "Declaration" and refers to Charles I's declaration to the Privy Council at Wellington, 19th Sept., 1642; it is found on many of his coins struck at the provincial mints during the Civil War. Usually abbreviated to REL : PROT : LEG : ANG : LIB : PAR :

ROSA SINE SPINA. (A rose without a thorn.) Found on some gold and small coins of Henry VIII and later reigns.

RUTILANS ROSA SINE SPINA. (A dazzling rose without a thorn.) As last but on small gold only.

SCUTUM FIDEI PROTEGET EUM *or* EAM. (The shield of faith shall protect him *or* her.) On much of the gold of Edward VI and Elizabeth.

TALI DICATA SIGNO MENS FLUCTUARI NEQUIT. (Consecrated by such a sign the mind cannot waver: from a hymn by Prudentius written in the fourth century, entitled "Hymnus ante Somnum".) Only on the gold "George noble" of Henry VIII.

TIMOR DOMINI FONS VITÆ. (The fear of the Lord is a fountain of life: *Prov.* 14, 27.) On many shillings of Edward VI.

TUEATUR UNITA DEUS. (May God guard these united, i.e. kingdoms.) On many English Scottish and Irish coins of James I.

VERITAS TEMPORIS FILIA. (Truth, the daughter of Time.) On English and Irish coins of Mary Tudor.

ICH DIEN. (I serve.) Aberystwyth Furnace 2d, and Decimal 2p.

Some Royal Titles:

REX ANGLO*rum*—King of the English.

Rex saxonum occidentalium—King of the West Saxons.

DEI GRA*tia* ANGL*iae* ET FRANC*iae* DOMI*Nus* HYB*erniae* ET AQVIT*aniae*—By the Grace of God, King of England and France, Lord of Ireland and Aquitaine.

D*ei* G*ratia* M*agnae* B*ritanniae*, FR*anciae* ET H*iberniae* REX F*idei* D*efensor* BRU....T L*uneburgensis* D*ux*, S*acri* R*omani* I*mperii* A*rchi*-TH*esaurarius* ET EL*ector* = By the Grace of God, King of Great Britain, France and Ireland, Defender of the Faith, Duke of Brunswick Luneburg, High Treasurer and Elector of the Holy Roman Empire.

BRITANNIARUM REX—King of the Britains (i.e. Britain and British territories overseas).

BRITT:OMN :REX :FID :DEF :IND :IMP—King of all the Britains, Defender of the Faith, Emperor of India.

Although not *Latin* legends, the following Norman-French mottoes might usefully be added here:

DIEU ET MON DROIT. (God and my right.) On halfcrowns of George IV and later monarchs.

HONI SOIT QUI MAL Y PENSE. (Evil to him who evil thinks.) The Motto of the Order of the Garter, first used on the Hereford (?) halfcrowns of Charles I. It also occurs on the Garter Star in the centre of the reverse of the silver coins of Charles II, but being so small it is usually illegible; it is more prominent on the coinage of George III.

Seaby's Coin and Medal Bulletin
This is a magazine published for all interested in numismatics. It contains articles and notes on coins and medals; details of numismatic society meetings; answers to questions; letters to the Editor; cuttings from the press, etc., etc.; also many pages of coins and medals of all kinds offered for sale. These are well catalogued and act as a good guide to help collectors to catalogue and classify their own coins. Please send for a specimen copy and current subscription rates to B.A. Seaby Ltd, 7 Davies Street, London W1Y 1LL. Bound Bulletins for some previous years are available (prices upon request).

Numismatic Clubs and Societies
There are well over one hundred numismatic societies and clubs in the British Isles, a number of which form part of the social and cultural activities of scholastic institutions or commercial industrial concerns.

The two principal learned societies are the Royal Numismatic Society and the British Numismatic Society, both of which publish an annual journal.

Many local clubs and societies are affiliated to the British Association of Numismatic Societies (the B.A.N.S., which holds an annual conference). Details of your nearest local club may be obtained from: The Hon. Sec., B.A.N.S., K. F. Sugden, Dept. of Numismatics, Manchester Museum, the University, Oxford Road, Manchester.

APPENDIX III

MINTMARKS AND OTHER SYMBOLS ON ENGLISH COINS

A MINTMARK (*mm.*), a term borrowed from Roman and Greek numismatics where it showed the place of mintage, was generally used on English coins to show where the legend began (a religious age preferred a cross for the purpose). Later, this mark, since the dating of coins was not usual, had a periodic significance, changing from time to time. Hence it was of a secret or "privy" nature; other privy marks on a coin might be the code-mark of a particular workshop or workman. Thus a privy mark (including the *mm.*) might show when a coin was made, or who made it. In the use of precious metals this knowledge was necessary to guard against fraud and counterfeiting.

Mintmarks are sometimes termed "initial marks" as they are normally placed at the commencement of the inscription. Some of the symbols chosen were personal badges of the ruling monarch, such as the rose and sun of York, the boar's head of Richard III, the dragon of Henry Tudor or the thistle of James I; others are heraldic symbols or may allude to the mint master responsible for the coinage, e.g. the *mm.* bow used on the Durham House coins struck under John Bowes and the ws mark of William Sharrington of Bristol.

A table of mintmarks is given on the next page. Where mintmarks appear in the catalogue they are sometimes referred to only by the reference number, in order to save space, i.e. *mm.* 28 (=mintmark Sun), *mm.* 28/74 (=*mm.* Sun on obverse, *mm.* Coronet on reverse), *mm.* 28/- (=*mm.* Sun on obverse only).

APPENDIX III

MINTMARKS AND OTHER SYMBOLS

1 Edward III, Cross 1 (Class B + C).
2 Edward III, broken Cross 1 (Class D).
3 Edward III, Cross 2 (Class E).
4 Edward III, Cross 3 (Class G).
5 Cross Potent (Edw. III Treaty).
6 Cross Pattée (Edw. III Post Treaty)
   Rich. III).
7 (a) Plain of Greek Cross.
   (b) Cross Moline.
8 Cross Patonce.
9 Cross Fleurée.
10 Cross Calvary (Cross on steps).
11 Long Cross Fitchée.
12 Short Cross Fitchée.
13 Restoration Cross (Hen. VI).
14 Latin Cross.
15 Voided Cross (Henry VI).
16 Saltire Cross.
17 Cross and 4 pellets.
18 Pierced Cross.
19 Pierced Cross & pellet.
20 Pierced Cross & central pellet.
21 Cross Crosslet.
22 Curved Star (rayant).
23 Star.
24 Spur Rowel.
25 Mullet.
26 Pierced Mullet.
27 Eglantine.
28 Sun (Edw. IV).
29 Mullet (Henry V).
30 Pansy.
31 Heraldic Cinquefoil (Edw. IV).
32 Heraldic Cinquefoil (James I).
33 Rose (Edw. IV).
34 Rosette (Edw. IV).
35 Rose (Chas. I).
36 Catherine Wheel.
37 Cross in circle.
38 Halved Sun (6 rays) & Rose.
39 Halved Sun (4 rays) & Rose.
40 Lis-upon-Half-Rose.
41 Lis-upon-Sun & Rose.
42 Lis-Rose dimidiated.
43 Lis-issuant-from-Rose.
44 Trefoil.
45 Slipped Trefoil, James I (1).
46 Slipped Trefoil, James I (2).
47 Quatrefoil.
48 Saltire.
49 Pinecone.
50 Leaf (-mascle, Hen. VI).
51 Leaf (-trefoil, Hen. VI).
52 Arrow.
53 Pheon.
54 A.
55 Annulet.
56 Annulet-with-pellet.
57 Anchor.
58 Anchor & B.
59 Flower & B.
60 Bell.
61 Book.
62 Boar's Head (early Richard III).
63 Boar's Head later Richard III).
64 Boar's Head Charles I.
65 Acorn (a) Hen. VIII (b) Elizabeth.
66 Bow.
67 Br. (Bristol, Chas. I).

68 Cardinal's Hat.
69 Castle (Henry VIII).
70 Castle with H.
71 Castle (Chas. I).
72 Crescent (a) Henry VIII (b) Elizabeth.
73 Pomegranate. (Mary; Henry VIII's is broader).
74 Coronet.
75 Crown.
76 Crozier (a) Edw. III (b) Hen. VIII.
77 Ermine.
78 Escallop (Hen. VII).
79 Escallop (James I).
80 Eye (in legend Edw. IV).
81 Eye (Parliament).
82 Radiate Eye (Hen. VII).
83 Gerb.
84 Grapes.
85 Greyhound's Head.
86 Hand.
87 Harp.
88 Heart.
89 Helmet.
90 Key.
91 Leopard's Head.
91A Crowned Leopard's Head with
    collar (Edw. VII).
92 Lion.
93 Lion rampant.
94 Martlet.
95 Mascle.
96 Negro's Head.
97 Ostrich's Head.
98 P in brackets.
99 Pall.
100 Pear.
101 Plume.
102 Plume. Aberystwyth and Bristol.
103 Plume. Oxford.
104 Plume. Shrewsbury.
105 Lis.
106 Lis.
107 Portcullis.
108 Portcullis. Crowned.
109 Sceptre.
110 Sunburst.
111 Swan.
112 R in brackets.
113 Sword.
114 T (Henry VIII).
115 TC monogram.
116 WS monogram.
117 y or Y.
118 Dragon (Henry VII).
119 (a) Triangle (b) Triangle in Circle.
120 Sun (Parliament).
121 Uncertain mark.
122 Grapple.
123 Tun.
124 Woolpack.
125 Thistle.
126 Figure 6 (Edw. VI).
127 Floriated cross.
128 Lozenge.
129 Billet.
130 Plume. Lundy Is.
131 Two lions.
132 Clasped book.
133 Cross pomee.
134 Bugle.

The reign after a mintmark indicates that from which the drawing is taken. A similar mm. may have been used in another reign and will be found in the chronological list at the beginning of each reign.

MINTMARKS AND OTHER SYMBOLS

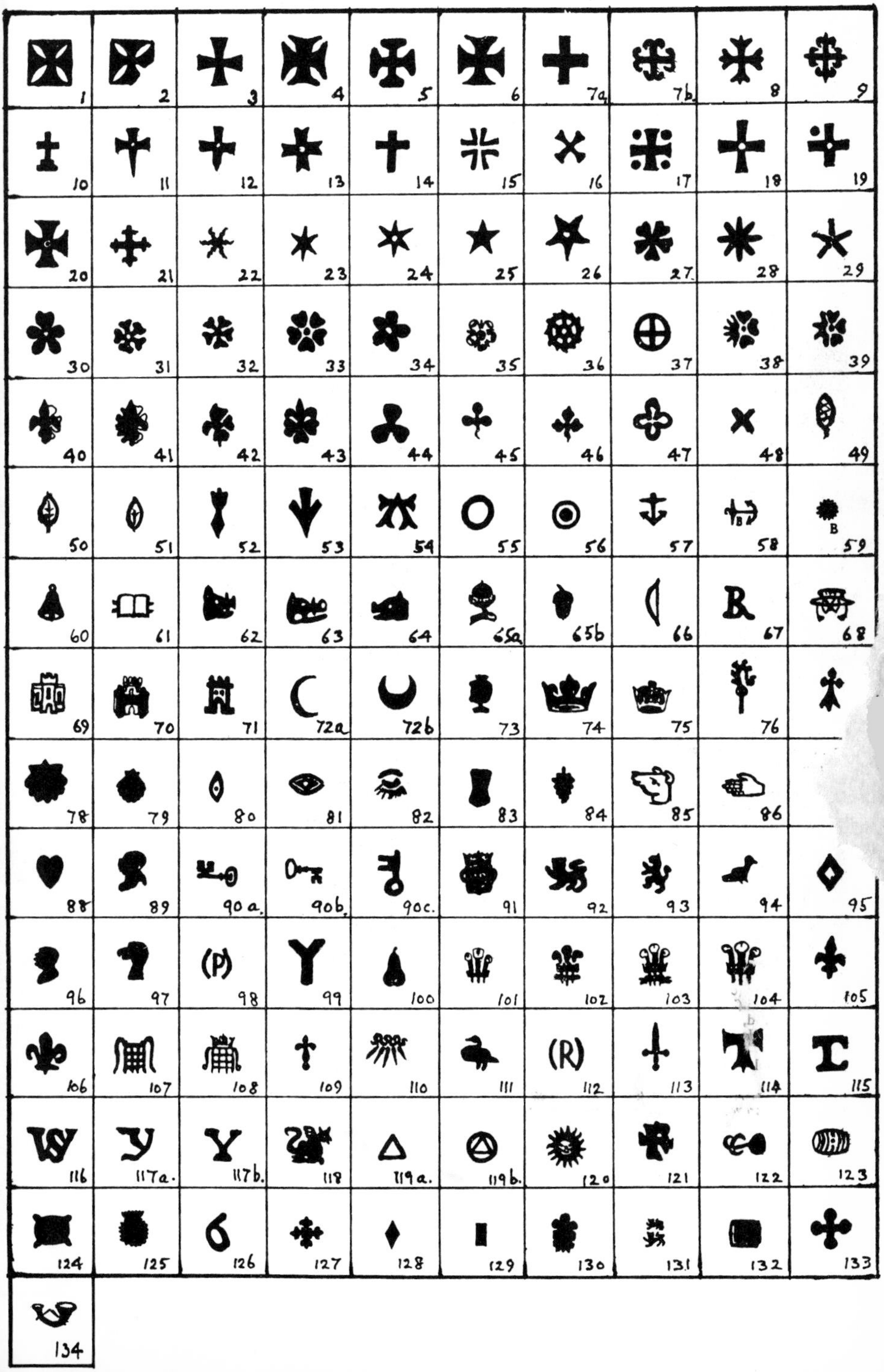

NOTES

NOTES

NOTES